By the same author:

A QUESTION OF MADNESS (*with Zhores A. Medvedev*)

LET HISTORY JUDGE

ON SOCIALIST
DEMOCRACY

Roy A. Medvedev

TRANSLATED FROM THE RUSSIAN AND
EDITED BY ELLEN de KADT

ON SOCIALIST
DEMOCRACY

The Norton Library

W·W·NORTON & COMPANY·INC·

NEW YORK

Books That Live
The Norton imprint on a book means that in the publisher's
estimation it is a book not for a single season but for the years.
W. W. Norton & Company, Inc.

Library of Congress Cataloging in Publication Data
Medvedev, Roĭ Aleksandrovich.
    On socialist democracy.
    (Norton Library)
    Translation of Kniga o sotsialisticheskoĭ demokratii.
    Includes bibliographical references and index.
    1. Communist state. 2. Russia—Politics and govern-
ment—1953-   I. Title.
JN6515 1972.M413   1977   320.9'47'085   76-39907
ISBN 0-393-00850-9

1 2 3 4 5 6 7 8 9 0

Contents

Translator's Foreword

This book was not originally written for a Western audience. Nor was it written with any hope of converting the most senior present-day Soviet leaders. Its purpose was to stimulate discussion among the educated public in the Soviet Union, both within and outside the party, and in particular to influence opinion among that progressive element in the lower echelons of the leadership which Roy Medvedev is convinced does exist.

It may sound paradoxical to speak of influencing opinion, since there was never any chance of publishing *On Socialist Democracy* in the USSR; yet the book circulates and is read and argued about. For *samizdat* reaches an ever-growing number of people, and in the last decade has transformed both the Soviet intellectual and the Soviet moral climate beyond recognition. Foreign radio stations play an important role: works published in the West by Soviet authors or by members of the new emigration are broadcast back to the Soviet Union. Thus we are now witnessing an extraordinary new debate about the future of Russia, with Medvedev, Sakharov, Solzhenitsyn, Chalidze, Maximov, Litvinov, Shragin, Turchin, and many others taking part—some living in Moscow, others in various Western cities. And no censor has a chance to intervene. Even ten years ago, this would have been unimaginable.

Within the past few years an enormous change has occurred within the sphere of Soviet dissent. Formerly the entire dissident intelligentsia community was a kind of brotherhood united by certain very basic common convictions (such as the desirability of freedom of speech). But this is no longer the case. As in earlier eras, there is now a spectrum of different views and attitudes, and the result is an ongoing debate, sometimes acrimonious, which inevitably tends to break down the solidarity that once existed. In a sense, this is a natural development which must be regarded as part of the painful process of finding new paths for a country in which for decades no meaningful discussion of alternatives was possible.

Roy Medvedev was born in Tbilisi, Georgia, on November 14, 1925. His father was a philosopher and professor of history at the Tolmachev Military-Political Academy; arrested in 1938 during the purges, he died in a far east camp in 1941. Roy later studied philosophy at Leningrad University, taught history at a school in the Urals, became the director of a secondary school in Leningrad, and went on to receive an advanced degree in education. Between 1961 and 1968 he was a Head of Department at the Moscow Vocational Training Research Institute and published two books and many articles in this field. After Khrushchev's denunciation of Stalin at the Twentieth Party Congress in 1956, Medvedev joined the party and began an intensive study of Soviet history. But by the time his book on Stalin (*Let History Judge*) was completed in 1968, the political climate was already very different from what it had been in 1956 and for some years after, and there was no longer any possibility of publication. In 1969 Roy Medvedev was expelled from the party when his letter to the editor of *Kommunist,* protesting against the appearance in that journal of an article defending Stalin, found its way abroad and was published in Germany. A further encounter with the authorities came in the spring of 1970, when his twin brother Zhores, author of a study exposing Lysenko, was whisked off to a mental hospital—a more "convenient" way of dealing with dissent than an open trial. But Roy was successful in rousing a massive protest among the Soviet intelligentsia, telegrams poured in from scientists abroad, and within 2½ weeks Zhores was released. (He now lives in London.) The brothers' joint account of the whole episode was published in England and America under the title *A Question of Madness* (Macmillan/Knopf 1971). In 1971, not long before the publication of *Let History Judge* in the West, Roy Medvedev was dismissed from his job. At present he works as a free-lance historian and sociologist. Various essays by him on current political themes have been published in the West, and a new book by him, dealing with certain aspects of the Russian Civil War, will appear shortly.

On Socialist Democracy is certainly one of the most controversial *samizdat* works to come out of the USSR, because it is a critique written from *inside* the system by an author who remains a Marxist: while uncompromising in his condemnation of Stalinism and the ways in which it still survives, Medvedev believes that the only possibility for change lies within the framework of the existing structure.

His theoretical views are, of course, very different from the barren rigidities of official ideology. Marxism, he insists, cannot be regarded as a finished system and was never intended as such by its creators. And if Lenin developed the doctrine in accordance with the needs of his time and situation, how absurd, half a century later, to speak of Leninism in terms of universal applicability. Thus, what passes for theory in the Soviet Union is for Medvedev much more like theology; although the basic methodology is still valid, Marxism-Leninism must be modified and developed to correspond with contemporary conditions.

As for socialism, there can, in Medvedev's view, be no *genuine* socialism where democracy is absent. And by democracy he means those traditional rights and freedoms which after centuries of struggle came to prevail in Western countries, i.e., the very "bourgeois democratic" rights so often the object of derision in official Soviet theory. Socialism, he believes, must be an *extension* of democracy, and Marx and Lenin are quoted in support of this view.

It must be said, however, that *On Socialist Democracy* is not primarily an ideological work; the basic approach is empirical and pragmatic. The reader is presented with a very rich and detailed (and occasionally comic) picture of how Soviet institutions actually function. The tone is always sober, reasoned; analysis is consistently supported by factual evidence. And what ultimately emerges is a powerful practical argument: the present rigid bureaucratic structure has become an impediment to progress in almost every area of economic, social, and political life, and the only way out is democratization. Most compelling, of course, is the economic issue, and this is a central theme of the book—at the present stage of Soviet development there is a crucial relationship between democracy and modernization, and for this reason the pressure for change will in time become irresistible. To put the matter in Marxist terms: a basic contradiction now exists.

Medvedev puts forward concrete proposals for the introduction and strengthening of democratic freedoms in every sphere of life: in government (including the opportunity to create opposition parties), within the party, in industry, in the machinery of justice, in the treatment of national groups, and—most vital of all—in the press and the world of ideas. But the transformation which such reforms would entail will hardly take place automatically. Medvedev envisages a gradual and evolutionary process of change which will come about only in the wake of a long drawn-out political struggle. Well aware of the dangers of anarchy, he urges that the methods of struggle must be nonviolent and strictly constitutional.

Given Soviet conditions, Medvedev believes that change will have to come through the party and the eventual conversion of its leadership in response to various pressures. The population at large is likely to remain politically passive for the time being. But the democratic movement, which is at present limited to small groups within the intelligentsia, must expand and gradually wrest democratic concessions from above by means of political struggle. Medvedev is hopeful that a new generation will be interested in applying the advances of science and technology to concrete social problems. But it will find it impossible to do so without objective scholarship in the social sciences. The West can exercise influence, up to a point. There is also the question of technological innovation, now an irreversible process; to give one example particularly relevant to Medvedev's argument, it will soon be difficult to control the use of Xerox machines as an aid to *samizdat*.

Roy Medvedev has been called utopian, unrealistic, an

unwitting supporter of the status quo—particularly by those who feel that Stalin's legacy goes too deep, that the structure he created remains basically unchanged and cannot possibly be transformed either from below or from above. One of Medvedev's friends, after reading the present work in manuscript, wrote him: "Your ideas are harmful, because they create illusions about the ease with which reform can be realized." Medvedev is certainly well aware of the difficulties of the struggle he is proposing, and also that there could well be a regression to the ways of the past; but he continues, nonetheless, to believe that there is a very real possibility of an alliance between the best part of the intelligentsia and the most forward-looking among the governing *apparat*. He quotes in this respect the anonymous author of a *samizdat* document entitled *Words Are Also Deeds:* "Because the language of the party-democrats' program is loyal and will not shock, it can and should rely on 'consumers' among party and state cadres. Particularly in view of the growing emphasis on science and technology in the higher reaches of government, our words can become their deeds." It is in this context that *On Socialist Democracy* can be regarded as a political act, as a part of the struggle that is already under way.

In recent essays Medvedev has extended and made more explicit certain themes suggested in *On Socialist Democracy*. In "Problems of Democratization and Détente"* he discusses the tendency toward international economic integration and the greater contacts that now exist between the Soviet Union and the West. He feels that these will *ultimately* have a beneficial effect on internal Soviet developments, in spite of the fact that one of the short-term effects of détente has been an intensification of repression against dissidents. In an article called "What Lies Ahead"† (in part a commentary on Solzhenitsyn's "Letter to Soviet Leaders"), he advocates a fresh step forward: the creation of a new socialist party. Such a party would represent a loyal and legal opposition to the present leadership and at the same time would have the effect of promoting reform within the Communist Party. The approach of the new party would not be dogmatic: its theory would embrace those tenets of Marx, Engels, and Lenin

---

* *New Left Review*, Jan./Feb. 1974, and *Die Zeit*, Nov. 16 and 23, 1973.
† *Der Spiegel*, September 9, 1974.

which have stood the test of time. Free from responsibility for the crimes of the past, it would be able to evaluate recent history more objectively and be better able to work out a socialist and democratic alternative.

About this translation: The original of the present work represents a revised and expanded version of Medvedev's *Kniga o sotsialisticheskoi demokratii,* published in Russian by the Herzen Foundation, Amsterdam, 1972, and translated into French (*De la démocratie socialiste,* Grasset & Fasquelle, 1972) and German (*Sowjet-Bürger in Opposition,* Classen Verlag, 1973). I have tried to be as faithful to the author's manuscript as possible, making only a few cuts where the material was clearly repetitious. Some readers may feel that even more editing would have been advisable, but I thought it was important for a Western audience to see in full elaboration the kind of arguments that need to be marshalled in the context of the debate now going on inside the Soviet Union.

I would particularly like to call the reader's attention to the author's long notes which appear at the back of the book and are indicated by numerals in the text; they contain much fascinating additional material and should not be skipped.

Most of the quotations from Lenin are from the fifth edition of his works, the *Polnoe sobranie sochinenii,* and are cited as *PSS* followed by the volume number. References from other editions are designated accordingly. Citations from Marx and Engels are from the second Russian edition (*Sochinenia*) unless otherwise specified, and have been translated from the Russian.

One of the most valuable features of Medvedev's book lies in the many lengthy quotations from *samizdat* texts circulating in Moscow or put at the disposal of the author. Sometimes, of course, these texts are anonymous or signed with a pseudonym; but, however frustrating it may be for the scholar, this practice is simply one of the facts of contemporary Soviet intellectual life. Where no place and date are given, therefore, it means that the work cited is unpublished. However, in cases where *samizdat* texts have been published in the West in Russian or in English, I have supplied the references.

I am extremely grateful to Peter Wiles for reading the material on economics and for making a number of helpful suggestions, to Max Hayward who has been an enormous source of moral support and practical help throughout, and to Zhores Medvedev for being always available in time of need.

Ellen de Kadt
London, October 1974

Introduction to the English-language Edition

The first version of this book was written between September 1970 and April 1971.* During the following year my friends read the manuscript and made a number of criticisms and suggestions. I also had the chance to study many important new documents as well as various articles on democracy published in the Soviet press over the last years. As a result I have made substantial changes, and the present work is a new, revised edition.

I have tried to give a general picture of the ideas and trends that emerged and developed during the ten years after the Twenty-second Party Congress. Although there have been many differences in approach, general agreement has existed about one thing—the demand for democracy: freedom of speech and of the press, freedom for science, scholarship, and the arts. Real democracy cannot exist (and socialist democracy is no exception) unless the rights of both majority and minority are guaranteed, unless there is a place for dissent and opposition and the possibility of forming independent social and political associations. There must also be freedom of conscience, freedom of movement, free elections

* R. Medvedev, *Kniga o sotsialisticheskoi demokratii*, Alexander Herzen Foundation, Amsterdam, 1972.—Trans.

by secret ballot, and absolute equality before the law. In
Soviet conditions, socialist democracy should provide greater
rights for the Union Republics. There is a need to reduce
irrational centralization in all areas of economic, political,
and cultural life and to ensure effective popular control over
all activities of government—with a separation of power between the legislative, executive, and judicial branches.

It is incorrect to view the present Soviet system as a form
of state capitalism. But there can be no question of "mature"
or "developed" socialism while basic democratic rights and
freedoms are absent. Not only is our socialism undeveloped, it
has also been corrupted by various forms of pseudo socialism.

Marx and Engels wrote that under socialism, society
would be ordered in such a way that the free development of
each serves the free development of all. We are still far from
this ideal—real guarantees for the free development of each
individual do not exist.

Of course, freedom can never be absolute or uncondi-
tional. Considerations of state security, the rights of other
citizens, public morals and public order—all these necessitate
restrictions. But if such restrictions do not remain within
reasonable limits, freedom becomes illusory and constitutional guarantees are an empty formality.

Unfortunately, in the last two to three years there has
been no observable progress toward the democratization of
Soviet society. On the contrary, different forms of ideological
and political pressure on the intelligentsia have grown more
intense. Substantial success in foreign policy and progress
toward détente have not put a stop to the offensive against
dissidents that began in 1968. Fresh directions in social
thought were given no chance to develop, and newly emerging political trends were stifled. Many people with much to
contribute were at least temporarily reduced to silence, unwilling to risk their own freedom, such as it was, or the well-
being of their families.

Intimidation from above included outright judicial repression as well as detention in psychiatric hospitals. But for
the majority of ordinary dissidents, it was enough simply to
intensify administrative pressures. As everyone knows, in the
Soviet Union the state is not just the principal but for all
practical purposes the *only* employer; this creates an ex-

tremely simple and enormously effective means of putting pressure on individuals who may be totally competent professionally but insufficiently "loyal" in the view of some powerful functionary or other. An attempt was made to influence scientists and scholars by depriving them of well-deserved titles and degrees.

The various democratic trends were also affected by the easing of restrictions on emigration to Israel. In this new situation and under the pressure of growing discrimination, many Jews who had been active participants in the general struggle for civil rights, with no intention of leaving the country, now began to emigrate. And in the last two years individuals of other nationalities, particularly courageous and uncompromising members of the democratic movement, were either encouraged to depart voluntarily or were virtually expelled from the Soviet Union.

Yet all the same, the discussion continues—in *samizdat* and in the Western press. Protests against violations of democratic rights have by no means come to an end; in certain respects they have even intensified, assuming new and more resolute forms. Certain individuals are playing a much more active role than was possible several years ago. They publish scholarly and literary works abroad, give interviews, and make public statements that are widely reported by foreign newspapers and radio stations. Much more than in the past, these actions have a resounding influence and have become an important element in our political life. Many of the new emigrants continue to be preoccupied with Soviet problems and they too provide enormous support for the democratic movement. All this makes it possible to hope that the present decline in the movement is only temporary and that in the next years it will find new strength and new advocates.

Our official ideology boasts of the monolithic unanimity presumed to exist in Soviet society and the Communist Party, but it is, in fact, completely artificial and nothing to be proud of. In the democratic countries of the West, with their relative freedom of speech and of the press and the existence of so many organizations from the extreme right to the extreme left, the links between society and the state apparatus are indirect and highly complex. In many respects the social infrastructure is independent of the state. Moreover, private ownership of a large part of the means of production, of the media and the service sector is not just a means of exploitation leading to the anarchy of production and abuse of public interest; private production does in fact satisfy definite social requirements and to a certain degree creates a self-regulating economy. It takes many burdens away from the state and also restricts the state's influence in public affairs. (It is also true that private companies use the state for their own ends while remaining largely independent of its control.)

The social structure of the Soviet Union is far less complicated. Of course here too opinions vary and there are conflicts of interest between different groups and strata, but expression of these conflicts is almost nonexistent. The one-party system, the absence of genuine worker control, the lack of independent newspapers or publishers, etc., mean that virtually the entire economic and social life of our vast country is run from a single center. The smallest organization, even a club of dog lovers or cactus growers, is supervised by an appropriate body of the CPSU. Needless to say, all published materials are subject to particularly stringent control.

Party and state bodies are responsible for the work of huge enterprises and small repair shops, large restaurants and tiny snack bars, the construction of new towns and residential districts but also the elevators and plumbing in each individual apartment house. Every aspect of a Soviet citizen's life is dependent on the actions of state and party bureaucrats who lose no opportunity to press this point home.

There can be no question that this enormous, clumsy governmental structure, unchecked by any countervailing social force, obstructs the economic, intellectual, and moral development of Soviet society. Bureaucracy thrives in party and state. And inefficiency or incompetence on one level of leadership has an extremely unhealthy effect on the whole social organism. Extremely destructive conflicts flare up from time to time between different departments or between individual leaders, unrestrained by public control; more often than not there is no question of principle involved, merely departmental or personal rivalry. Centralized state planning and leadership undoubtedly provide great advantages; but this should not blind us to the tremendous weaknesses created by excessive centralization and a monopoly of economic and political power. The loss to society is possibly just as great as that caused by the anarchy of production and the trend toward monopoly under capitalism.

Our present system can also prove to be extremely vulnerable in the face of serious internal or external crises, as can be seen from the experience of Hungary, Poland, and Czechoslovakia. Yet the inflexible, in some sense even fragile, structure is at the same time immensely powerful. A social infrastructure has evolved that provides the leadership with unprecedented means of manipulation and control. Given such a system, it is difficult to imagine any rapid or radical changes taking place (although the possibility should not be discounted altogether). The most realistic hope is that of slow and gradual evolutionary transformation. In spite of increasing pressure from above, the democratic opposition of all shades should strive for greater freedom of speech and organization and for the extension of public control (i.e., the creation of indispensable democratic checks and balances). Any initiative in this direction merits close attention—not even the slightest chance must be lost.

Clearly most party leaders and ideologists fear democratization more as a threat to their own positions than to the existence of Marxism and socialism. Even if the maximum demands of the democratic movement were put into practice (for example, the creation of newspapers and organizations independent of party control), it would not mean the end of Marxism or of the leading role of the CPSU. On the contrary, it would promote a more normal situation in party life, bringing new vitality into the leadership and curtailing bureaucracy in the *apparat;* in the final analysis it would bring about the enrichment and development of Marxism in conformity with twentieth-century conditions. The real danger for the USSR and for the general socialist cause lies elsewhere: in the fact that violations of democratic principles continue and are even increasing.

An enormous contradiction now exists in our society: rapid scientific, technical, and economic progress is being blocked by an excessively centralized bureaucratic system. The structure is too unwieldy even to formulate the right questions at the right time, leaving extremely important problems with no solution. The demands of development conflict

with the behavior of the bureaucratic oligarchic caste governing the country. This is what has created an objective need
for reform, an objective need for the democratization of social
life. I have tried to show the desirability of such reform and
also to suggest certain directions it might take.

I am a Marxist, and the questions discussed in this book
have been approached from a Marxist position. But Marxism,
in my view, is not some kind of dogma but a science that
should be developed and enriched by new ideas and theories,
while propositions that prove to be obsolete, one-sided, or
even wrong must be discarded. It is absolutely not true that
Marxism and socialism are incompatible with democracy. Yet
we must acknowledge that the works of neither Marx and
Engels nor Lenin adequately deal with the complex problems
involved. Thus there is a real gap in our theory which should
be filled as rapidly as possible.

It is my hope that this book will help foreign readers to
understand our internal problems better. Not only is the
democratization of Soviet society vital for the Soviet people, it
is indispensable for the whole of mankind. And the support
that our democratic movement receives from abroad is particularly valuable—we hope that it will continue to grow in
strength. Only when all nations pursue peaceful foreign policies backed up by genuine democratization at home can there
be a real reduction of international tension and a durable
peace throughout the world.

Roy Medvedev
May 1974

Glossary

APPARAT	Apparatus, staff; party and state officials
ARTEL	Traditional form of small workers' cooperative
CC	Central Committee (of the Communist Party)
CENTNER	100 kilograms (220.46 pounds)
COMINTERN	Communist International (1919–43)
COUNCIL OF MINISTERS (USSR)	Highest executive and administrative body of government
CPSU	Communist Party of the Soviet Union
DRUZHINNIKI	Voluntary militia
GLAVLIT	The censorship
HECTARE	Unit of land area = 2.471 acres
KGB	Committee of State Security
KOMSOMOL	Young Communist League (the party's youth organization for the age group 14–27)
MVD	Ministry of Internal Affairs
NOMENKLATURA	Refers to a system of appointment lists, controlled directly or indirectly by the party, covering virtually all responsible posts in the country.

OCTOBER PLENUM	References to this Plenum allude to the fall of Khrushchev in 1964.
PASSPORT	Usually refers to internal identity card.
POLITBURO	Supreme body of the CPSU (called Presidium between 1952 and 1966)
RSDLP	Russian Social Democratic Labor Party. The Bolshevik faction changed its name to Communist Party in 1918.
RSFSR	Russian Soviet Federated Socialist Republic
SAMIZDAT	Self-publication—acronym modeled on *Gosizdat* (State Publishing House). Uncensored works that circulate in typed manuscript form.
SOVNARKHOZ	Regional economic council, established in 1957
SOVNARKOM	Council of People's Commissars, renamed Council of Ministers in 1946
SPETSKHRAN	Special depository—rooms where "forbidden" literature is stored in Soviet libraries with access only by special permission
SRs	Socialist Revolutionaries

ON SOCIALIST
DEMOCRACY

I

The Soviet Union During the 1960's

The 1960's were an enormously important period in the history of the Soviet Union. This first chapter is intended to be a general account of the extremely contradictory developments that took place during the decade and does not attempt to be strictly systematic or exhaustive.

Above all, it was a time of considerable industrial expansion. Overall industrial production increased by 230 per cent. The production of consumer goods doubled, while the production of the means of production increased approximately two and a half times. Capital investment in industry more than doubled. Tens of thousands of new industrial enterprises were built, and the majority of old plants and factories were modernized. There was a major development of the industrial potential of Siberia and the Far East.[1]

Thousands of kilometers of new railway lines and highways were built, as well as hundreds of bridges. Hundreds of new sanatoriums and rest homes were set up, also thousands of new schools, hospitals, and kindergartens. All kinds of consumer services were expanded and improved, including almost every aspect of the health service.

The productivity of labor in industry rose during the decade by 66 per cent, and the basic capital available to industry increased by 2½ times. Overall industrial production reached 75 per cent of the level of production in the United States.

There were further improvements in the country's defense capacity. The Soviet army and navy were equipped with many new types of modern weapons: missiles, antimissile-missiles, atom and hydrogen bombs, cruisers, submarines and aircraft carriers, artillery, tanks, and airplanes.

From the middle of the decade, economic reform resulted in better management and planning of the economy, which to a large extent began to rely more on economic criteria as well as on material incentives. Industrial and building enterprises were allowed greater independence, and increasing emphasis was placed on profit and economic self-sufficiency. Sales figures became the chief indicator for output, and the result was an improvement in the quality of many products. An increase in both collective and individual incentives made for gains in efficiency, thus strengthening the economy and leading, through the harnessing of latent resources, to a growth in productivity.

With a population growth of 30 million, the average total of persons gainfully employed increased by nearly 25 million (from 66 to 90 million). There was also an appreciable rise in the average wages of most categories of workers.

But in spite of all these evident achievements, progress was neither as rapid nor as impressive as might have been hoped at the beginning of the decade. For both the Seven-Year Plan of 1959–65 and the eighth Five-Year Plan of 1966–70 many important indices of economic development were not met, even though the plans were successful in terms of "gross output."[2]

As we know, in all the leading capitalist countries the general rate of industrial development had already begun increasing sharply at the end of the forties. In 1948–57, the average yearly rate of growth increased in the United States to 4.4 per cent, in France to 6.5 per cent, in Italy to 9.1 per cent, in West Germany to 15.3 per cent, and in Japan to 18.2 per cent.[3] In the course of the next twelve years these figures noticeably declined in a number of countries. For example, in West Germany in 1958–69, the average yearly growth was 6 per cent; in Italy, 8 per cent; in Japan, 13.8 per cent. But in other capitalist countries, including the United States, the rate of growth continued to rise—thus the capitalist world as a whole maintained its previous rates of growth during the sixties (5.8 per cent in 1958–69 as against 5.9 per cent in 1948–57).

Unfortunately, in the Soviet Union the average rate of increase of the gross national product and of industrial production was lower in the sixties than in the fifties. For example, during all the years of the 1951–60 period, the growth in industrial production was higher than 10 per cent, and the average for the decade was about 12 per cent per year. In the 1960's only once—in 1967—did industrial production increase by 10 per cent, and the average yearly growth rate for the decade was only 8.5 per cent. As a result the Soviet Union was unable to achieve the prime task set out in the party programme : that of catching up and overtaking all the capitalist countries by the end of the sixties.[4] The USSR's share in the world's industrial production did not rise in the sixties—it remained stationary at about 20 per cent. And even today the Soviet Union continues to lag substantially behind the major capitalist countries with respect to the basic indicators of economic efficiency, including that most important one, the productivity of labor.

The Soviet Union surpassed the United States in coal and iron ore production, in the manufacture of cement, diesel locomotives, tractors and combines, in the supply of timber to industry, and also in the production of leather footwear, cotton fabrics, and various other types of goods. We caught up with the United States, or almost so, in the smelting of steel and pig iron, in the production of mineral fertilizer, in the use of transport for freight, and in the volume of capital investment. Thus one could say that the Soviet Union caught up with and even surpassed the United States in many of the older and more traditional branches of industrial production, which progressed at a slower rate in almost all industrially developed countries during the sixties.

However, electric power and the production of electricity in the United States are still more than twice that of the USSR. The United States produces *within its own borders* almost one and a half times as much oil and three times as much natural gas as the Soviet Union. At the end of the sixties, the Soviet Union manufactured a quarter of the number of trucks produced in the United States or Japan. We produced far fewer passenger cars than countries like Italy, France, Japan, and West Germany; the United States manufactured almost twenty times as many as we. We make half as many television sets as the United States or Japan, half as many radios as the United States, and one quarter as many as Japan. As to refrigerators, we are about on the level of the United States in 1950. In the production of synthetic resins and plastics we remain behind almost all the European countries including Italy; the United States produces six times as much as we do. In 1970 Japan manufactured five times and the United States ten times as much synthetic fiber as we did.

The level of our cellulose and paper industry is today the most backward of all the developed countries. The United States produces seven times and Canada one and a half times our output of paper and cardboard. Moreover it must be noted that in the sixties our wood-processing and cellulose-paper industry developed at a much slower rate than industry as a whole.

The total extent of the railway network in the United States, despite a much smaller land area involved, is two and one half times as great as the USSR's. Furthermore, during the decade our track was extended by only 12,000 kilometers (from 209,000 to 221,000). The total length of hard-surfaced roads was one-tenth that of the United States, where roads are also wider and of better quality. Airlines transport two and one half times as many passengers in the United States as in the USSR.

The Soviet Union is exceedingly backward compared to Western countries in the means of communication, particularly in the development and quality of its telephone system. The total number of telephones in use is lower than in any of the major European countries, each of which has a considerably smaller population. The U.S. has fifteen times as many and is ten times as fast in the installation of new telephone equipment, in the development of electronic automatic telephone exchanges, in the extension of the automatic dialing system, in the volume of overall telephone traffic, in the development of cable television, etc.

In a similar way we are behind the countries of Western Europe, Japan, and particularly the United States in the

production and use of electronic computers and fully automated machine tools. Yet the computerization of industrial
production and management is the essence of the scientific
and technological revolution.

Because of the inadequate training of personnel, shortcomings in the redeployment of labor, excessive strains on
the budget, and also the conservatism of many administrative
and party authorities, the economic reform of 1965–70 was
carried through too slowly and unevenly. At many levels of
economic management, purely administrative methods continue to predominate over economic criteria. Consequently
most economic indicators for the working of industry have
improved too slowly, and the quality of many major types of
industrial production still lags behind world standards. Our
industry continues to produce unsalable goods on a large
scale, yet there is still a very great shortage of various products that could easily be manufactured from the resources
and materials thus going to waste.

In the developed capitalist countries, up to 70–80 per
cent of the increase of the GNP is provided by intensive
factors, such as the growth of the efficiency and productivity
of labor, improvement in the quality of goods, etc., while in
the development of Soviet industry, until very recently, the
main emphasis has in fact been on extensive factors—i.e., on
an increase in the number of workers, the construction of
new factories and plants, and the exploitation of new mineral
deposits. But when a scientific-technological revolution is un-
derway, intensive methods of production—that is, the ability
to achieve the best results with limited resources—assume
prime importance. It is significant that the rate of technical
progress (for which the indicator is the increase of new equipment effectively brought into productive use) decreased during the sixties compared with the years 1956–60.[5] At present
the productivity of labor in the United States is approximately
two to two and a half times as high as in Soviet industry and
in the major capitalist countries of Western Europe and
Japan it is one and a half to two times as high.[6] Yet Lenin
himself, at the very beginning of the Soviet era, pointed out
that the productivity of labor would in the final analysis be
the most important, the major factor in the victory of the new
social order. "Capitalism," wrote Lenin, "can and will be fi-

nally defeated by the achievement of a very much higher productivity of labor under socialism."[7]

We still have far too many ancillary workers, occupied
with loading, unloading, and repairing equipment. According
to the calculation of Soviet economists, we employ more
workers to repair tractors than to make them. Approximately
one-third of the metal-cutting equipment of the country is
concentrated in repair shops and in the repair departments of
factories.

Soviet economists have noted that in the sixties there
was an appreciable slowing down in the turnover of current
assets in industry. Industrial stocks in enterprises are still
enormous—the reserves of raw materials, half-finished products and equipment. Also quite excessive is the percentage of
output left uncompleted. For many kinds of industrial goods,
the increase of industrial reserves outstrips even the growth
of manufacture as a whole.

The number of difficult problems plaguing capital construction is particularly large. During the whole of the sixties
attention was constantly being drawn to the volume of un-
finished building work, the dissipation of resources, the failure to meet schedules, and the overrunning of estimated
costs. Our major enterprises are designed and built much
more slowly than those in the United States or Western
Europe.

If the Soviet Union has caught up with and even over-
taken the United States in the production of many kinds of
raw materials, we are still far behind in the efficient use of
these resources in industrial production. For example, in the
USSR more fuel is consumed in the production of one kilo-
watt hour of electricity. We use more pig iron to produce one
ton of steel and more steel to make one ton of rolled steel.
Our machine tools and equipment are as a rule heavier than
those in the United States and are generally used at a much
lower level of efficiency. There is an enormous amount of
uninstalled or unused equipment in our industrial system.

The cost of production of many kinds of industrial products and raw materials also remains very high. All this makes
it extremely difficult for our industry to compete on the world
market, which in turn explains the completely unsatisfactory
pattern of the USSR's foreign trade. No country in the world

is richer in natural resources than the USSR, but our foreign exports, including those to socialist countries, still consist largely of raw materials rather than manufactured goods: oil, gas, ores, timber—not to mention gold, furs, rare kinds of fish, crab, black and red caviar, and other foodstuffs. Machines and equipment account for only a little more than 20 per cent of our exports, and manufactured consumer goods for only 3 per cent. The foreign trade turnover of the USSR is less than a third that of the United States.

Finally there is that most important test of the efficiency of heavy machine production, capital intensiveness—the ratio between the cost of the machinery in use and the value of the output. Obviously if, in the production of a unit, an ever-decreasing amount of capital and equipment is spent— i.e., if the capital intensiveness of production is reduced— then, other things being equal, there is growth in the efficiency of production. Statistics show that during the sixties in the United States and in the other developed capitalist countries, the capital intensiveness of production went down, while in the Soviet Union during the same period there was a steady upward trend. This is one of the most ominous symptoms in considering the outlook for future economic competition between socialism and capitalism.

The development of Soviet agriculture during the 1960's was also marked by great contradictions. Between 1953 and 1958, as a result of measures taken by the party and the government, there was a substantial rise in agricultural production, and the situation in the countryside gradually improved. But by the end of the fifties the position again began to deteriorate. There were many serious blunders in agricultural policy due to incompetence and "voluntarism"* in the leadership, including the indiscriminate planting of maize in all regions of the country, a ban on the system of letting land lie fallow, disregard for regular crop rotation, neglect of fodder-grass cultivation, and the plowing up of many meadows and pastures without justification. The utilization of virgin land was not accompanied by a rational system of farming, and this soon led to a decrease in crop yield in all the virgin lands and to the loss of millions of hectares of plowed

---

* A term used in the Soviet press, particularly after the fall of Khrushchev in 1964, to describe erratic measures of leadership.—Trans.

fields. Afforestation was neglected in the southern regions, which led to heavy losses because of dust storms. The reorganization of the machine tractor stations* was carried out with extreme haste, which often had ruinous results for many collective farms; it caused chaos in the whole system of servicing and repair of agricultural machinery, a fall in the production and supply of agricultural equipment, and deterioration in the qualitative indicators for agriculture. There was a failure, moreover, to correct many errors in the system of procurement and purchase prices, particularly in the area of animal husbandry. As a result of a number of ill-advised campaigns at the very end of the fifties, there was a mass slaughter of cattle, along with a compulsory limitation of cattle on private plots. For no good reasons, many collective farms were turned into state farms, and there were frequent arbitrary and precipitate changes in the system of management of agriculture. All these and many other serious errors in agricultural production led to prolonged stagnation, which in fact continued from 1959 to 1965. Not only was there no increase in the yield of principal agricultural crops during this period, in many cases there was even a decrease, while the cost of production of agricultural products went up. Many other economic indicators also showed deterioration. For a long time there was no rise in the standard of living of agricultural workers, and they were given less and less material incentive to play their part in the increase of agricultural output. Needless to say, the Seven-Year Plan for the development of agriculture came nowhere near to being met.

It was only after the October Plenum of the Central Committee (1964)† and the March Plenum (1965) that there was some improvement in agricultural policy. Purchase and procurement prices for most agricultural produce were raised. Particular attention was paid to boosting agricultural production in the non-black-soil regions.‡ There were changes

---

* Between 1932 and 1958, most agricultural machinery (tractors, combines, etc.) was concentrated in the machine tractor stations, separate state enterprises that carried out specific agricultural operations on the collective farms for a fixed fee paid in kind. They also had a general supervisory role.—Trans.

† Khrushchev was removed from power at the October Plenum.—Trans.

‡ The black-soil regions are the richest farming areas of the Soviet Union, particularly in the Ukraine.—Trans.

in the former system of state procurements, which had created uncertainty in the work of collective and state farms and prevented them from planning their production on a sound basis. There was substantial improvement in the system of financing collective and state farm production and in the procedure for taxing collective farms. Measures were taken to develop animal husbandry on the private plots. Crucial decisions were made to promote mechanization and the use of chemicals in agriculture, the development of land improvement and irrigation. Material incentives for agricultural specialists were increased and a guaranteed wage for collective farmers established. In these same years important measures were carried out to improve methods of cultivation: there was a return to the policy of letting land lie fallow with regular crop rotation, soil erosion was prevented, and the sowing of maize was cut down. Capital investment in agriculture was substantially increased. As a result, between 1966 and 1970 production improved on collective and state farms and the income of collective farms and farmers, workers on state farms, and all agricultural specialists rose appreciably.[8]

While it is important to take this progress into account, one cannot ignore the fact that it was extremely slow and uneven. Most of the indicators for agricultural development envisaged in both the Seven-Year Plan (1959–65) and the last Five-Year Plan were not reached. Agricultural output went up by only 10–11 per cent in 1961–65 and by only 20–21 per cent in 1966–70—or, to take the figure for the whole decade, by about 35 per cent all together. Yet the party programme had called for an increase of 250 per cent during the ten-year period 1961–70! The increase in meat production was supposed to be 300 per cent, whereas in fact it was only about 40 per cent. This means that not only have we been unable to create necessary reserve stocks of foodstuffs, but that even in a good year we are unable to meet the normal needs of the country for food and industrial raw materials. Grain, meat, and many other agricultural products have been turned into export items, but in years of poor harvest (which occurred three times during the decade) we had to spend many hundreds of millions of rubles worth of gold and foreign currency to buy grain and other produce abroad.

The reduction of the rural population during the decade was only from 108.8 million to 104.7 million—very far behind what was envisaged in the party programme—and implies an extremely slow rise in the productivity of labor in agriculture. And indeed, the productivity of agricultural labor in the United States is five or six times that in the Soviet Union and three or four times that in most West European countries. If one includes in the calculation not only the state and collective farms but also the working time spent on private plots, then the productivity of labor in the countryside is on the same level as in the United States in 1920.

The Soviet Union is very much behind Western countries in mechanization and in the use of chemicals in agriculture. The number of tractors in use is approximately a third that in the United States and they are used less efficiently. Given that tractors have a life of five to six years, the supply to collective and state farms barely keeps pace with the number that have to be replaced, namely, about 300,000 per annum.[9] Moreover, the annual yield per tractor on collective farms in the sixties, far from rising, actually went down—in the period 1960–7, by 17 per cent. At the same time, the cost per hectare of standardized plowing rose by 25 per cent.[10] All this indicates a decline in the use of machinery on collective and state farms. Despite our country's enormous size, only a third as many trucks are used in agriculture as in the United States. Many vital types of machinery and equipment, long in use on farms in the United States and Western Europe, are simply not available.

At the present time, an agricultural worker in the United States is in effect as well equipped with the means of production as an industrial worker and in some respects is even ahead of him. In 1960, each American agricultural worker had 39 horsepower at his disposal, compared with a mere 5.4 for his Soviet opposite number. By 1967 the supply of power to an agricultural worker in the United States had increased to 78 hp—it had exactly doubled. The equivalent figure in the USSR for the same period was only 8.8 hp, an increase of about 65 per cent.[11] While agriculture in the United States is by now largely electrified, this process in the Soviet Union is only barely under way. Out of all the electrical energy produced in our country, only 5 per cent serves both the production and consumer needs of the rural population.

There is still an acute shortage of agronomists in the

countryside, as well as a general lack of all kinds of trained personnel. To this day, 50 per cent of those employed in agriculture are completely unskilled. The level of capital investment remains insignificant and, understandably therefore, the creation of progressive forms of large-scale farming and the introduction of complex mechanization proceeds at an extremely slow pace. The use of chemicals is still quite primitive—the USSR is far behind most developed countries in the amount of fertilizer applied to a hectare of crops.[12]

During the sixties as a whole, the average annual increase in agricultural production was 3.4 per cent—substantially lower than in 1954–60.

Animal husbandry continues to be the most economically backward sector of agriculture. Both the numbers of cattle and poultry and the yield from them grew very slowly during the sixties, and the cost of raising livestock in 1966–70 was even higher than in 1961–65, when it was already high. As a result, in many parts of the country the breeding of livestock remains an unprofitable branch of farming. Although the supply of machinery and equipment for the mechanization of animal husbandry has been stepped up during the last five or six years, it proved impossible to substitute mechanization for manual labor because machinery delivered to the farms was usually unreliable—there was almost always some part missing—and the rate of depreciation rose. Moreover in recent years the plans for the construction of buildings for livestock as well as for the supply of machinery and equipment essential to the application of new technology in animal husbandry were not met. The plans for the production of mixed feed for livestock farms were also not fulfilled. On the overwhelming majority of collective and state farms, the techniques for maintaining and feeding cattle differ very little from the practice of decades ago. This is why the average number of cattle tended by one worker remained almost the same at the end of the sixties as it had been at the end of the thirties. For twenty years—from 1951 to 1970— the productivity of labor in the basic branches of livestock raising increased by approximately 30 per cent. For the same period in the United States it went up by no less than 300 per cent and in certain countries of Western Europe by as much as 500–600 per cent. At the moment, the feeding of cattle on

Soviet farms is less than 15 per cent mechanized, the removal of dung about 30 per cent and only milking is 56 per cent mechanized. Mechanized feeding on pig farms has reached a level of about 30 per cent, and the cleaning of the sties 40 per cent. Of all the 560,000 livestock and poultry farms throughout the country, there is complete mechanization on only 25,000, or less than 5 per cent. Yet only mechanization can produce tangible economic results.

The orders from collective and state farms for machinery and equipment were 82 per cent fulfilled in 1965, 64 per cent in 1967, and only 40 per cent in 1969. Moreover, the equipment produced today for livestock is of poor quality, has a short life, and is extremely expensive. Unfortunately most of our machinery is greatly inferior to the best foreign models. The buildings in which our livestock is housed are also quite inferior to what is found abroad. We are enormously behind in the production of cheap and varied animal fodders, with the result that there are constant breakdowns in supplies to the farms. Indeed, the production of certain basic fodders even decreased in the second half of the sixties. There is a shortage of the most essential machines needed for the harvesting and processing of fodder crops, the yield of which has scarcely increased at all in recent years. There is no developed mixed-feed industry, and existing enterprises in this field work badly and produce a great deal of inferior fodder. The result has been that in the last years there has again been a decrease in the number of livestock cattle on the private plots; they did not receive enough fodder for their needs.

One could go on for many more pages, extending the list of shortcomings in agriculture. The figures show that with our present rate of growth, the Soviet Union will still be far behind the capitalist countries even a few decades from now, and that at any event the gap will not have significantly narrowed by 1980.

Looking at the state of our economy as a whole, we are bound to note that the sixties did not see the end of a number of distortions, and in some cases they even grew worse, seriously holding up the country's development. Thus, for example, toward the end of the sixties an acute shortage of electricity and fuel, including petroleum and gas, suddenly emerged. The economy was also drastically affected by a shortage of a number of important commodities needed for both industrial and nonindustrial purposes—e.g., pressed steel, forging and dye-casting machines, cement, refrigerators, shrinkproof and non-crease fabrics, knitwear, meat, high-quality fish products, etc.

Because of the low productivity of labor in the basic raw material sectors, the amount of labor and investment resources needed to obtain primary mineral and agricultural raw materials is still far too high. Thus, for example, toward the end of the 1960's, about 35 million people were employed in agriculture, the extractive industries, and timber cutting—approximately 25 per cent of the whole working population. When labor and material resources are used in this way, the cost of production is high and the possibility for developing a processing industry and service sector limited.

More than 30 million persons now work in agricultural production, but according to the data of the 1966 input-output table, only 2.1 per cent of the products of industry were utilized in agriculture, while industry consumed 43.9 per cent of the products of agriculture.[13]

During the last decade a serious imbalance between the production of consumer goods and of the means of production (plus military technology) continued, and even grew worse. The proportion of consumer goods in the total volume of output declined from 27.5 per cent in 1960 to 26.6 per cent in 1970.[14] Our heavy industry on the whole continues to be self-serving. Up to 75–80 per cent of the means and tools of production are manufactured for use in heavy industry and not for the development of sectors working on the production of consumer goods. In contrast, one may point out that in the United States heavy industry absorbs only about one-third of all industrial production while consumer goods industries account for approximately two-thirds.

Until very recently, an excessive proportion of the national income of the USSR was being spent either directly or indirectly on the needs of the military and thus played no part in the growth of the economy. According to the calculations of Western specialists, the strategic weaponry of the United States was increased at least tenfold in the sixties.[15] This had to be matched by the USSR. However, having a smaller GNP than the United States, the Soviet Union must spend a much

larger proportion of its national income on defense than the
United States does, not to mention the West European countries and Japan. All this means that our economy is over-
strained, and it limits our capacity to compete economically.
And in the course of the next few decades this may impair
our ability to provide for the defense of ourselves and our
allies.

Because of the disproportions described above, the aggregate wage fund of the country, including all monetary payments to workers, collective farmers, employees, and all other
categories of Soviet citizens, increased much more rapidly
during the last decade than the volume of consumer goods.
This naturally gave rise to inflationary tendencies which grew
stronger in the course of the sixties. Toward the end of the
decade, the average price level for many hundreds of different types of goods rose substantially. There was a heavy
increase in prices at collective farm markets,* and the cost of
many kinds of services went up, including all private services.[16] As a result there was a reduction in the real purchasing power of the ruble. During the decade the amount of
money in circulation constantly increased and the supply of
consumer goods could therefore not keep pace with effective
demand for them. The sum total of savings bank deposits
(postponed demand) grew four to five times, hardly a sign of
healthy economic development. The ruble continues to be
extremely unreliable, and other countries have little confidence in it.

Of course not only more money but also more goods and
services were in fact available in 1970 than in 1960, which
means that, on the whole, there was an appreciable rise in
the standard of living. But effective demand grew even faster.
There was also a rapid growth in the number of new types of
consumer items that almost every Soviet family began to
regard as essential to a minimum standard of living. Yet in
1970 only 32 families out of 100 had refrigerators, 51 out of
100 had television sets, and 52 out of 100 had washing
machines. Not more than 2 per cent of Soviet families pos-

---

* Markets at which collective farmers are allowed to sell part of their
  produce direct to the consumer. Prices are generally higher than
  at state shops and reflect market conditions.—Trans.

sessed automobiles.[17] Moreover, improvement in the standard of living was most uneven. There was least improvement for people on rigidly fixed salaries, particularly among the intelligentsia—teachers, doctors, engineers and technicians, scientists in the lower and middle categories, etc. Salaries in these groups did rise during the decade, but the increase did not always keep pace with the rise in the price of goods and services. Inflationary tendencies and the inadequacy of consumer-goods production meant that living standards on the whole rose much more slowly during the decade than was foreseen in the party programme. We were not able to double real income. Even today there are tens of millions of people who are experiencing serious material hardship, working for pay that is substantially below the minimum standard. The housing problem has still not been solved, although it was supposed to have been completely eliminated in the course of the sixties. At present millions of people live in uncomfortable quarters, in overcrowded rooms, in basements, waiting their turn to get apartments. The whole system of social and medical services as well as social security has developed at a much slower pace than planned. The thirty-five-hour work week (and a thirty-hour week for work underground), as outlined in the programme, has not been put into practice. Thus the Soviet Union has not yet become the country with the shortest working day, any more than it is the country where workers produce the most for the highest pay. The total amount of goods and services a skilled worker or white-collar worker can command for his monthly salary continues to be less than in the developed capitalist countries, and particularly less than in the United States, even taking into consideration the various free benefits that Soviet citizens receive (free medical care and partly subsidized holidays, etc.). In its average living standard the Soviet Union remains between the twentieth and thirtieth among countries of the world.[18]

The need for unskilled and heavy physical labor has not been eliminated as predicted by the programme. Even now, at least 20 million persons in industry, agriculture, and transport are engaged in mainly heavy and unskilled manual labor. The process of eliminating social, economic, and cultural differences between city and country and between urban centers and the provinces has been very slow. The gap between high and comparatively low income is being narrowed only very gradually. Public catering is still less widespread than cooking at home, and the establishment of preschool kindergartens as well as homes for the aged and invalids has lagged far behind expectations.

It is thus all too obvious that the overall economic situation in our country is far from satisfactory; the outlook for economic competition between the Soviet Union and the major capitalist countries must remain extremely problematical for at least the next ten to twenty years.

Although on the whole pollution of the environment is still not a problem on the same scale as in the United States and other industrially developed countries, the virtual neglect of the question throughout the sixties has led to a very alarming situation with regard to the protection and preservation of nature. Our lakes and rivers have become increasingly dirty, and the number of fish in most reservoirs is steadily going down. Lake Baikal and the Azov, Caspian, and Aral seas are all suffering enormous damage, while the Balkhash and Issyk-Kul lakes are threatened. Soil erosion proceeded on a colossal scale during the sixties, and many millions of hectares of valuable land were lost to agriculture. As a result, damage from soil erosion alone amounted to several billions of rubles per year.[19] Because of inadequate and slipshod soil-improvement techniques in overhumid regions, hundreds of thousands of hectares of peat were practically destroyed and turned into barren soil. Tens of thousands of hectares of sand have formed on the light soil of Belorussia and are blown about by the slightest wind. A large number of small rivers have dried up and scores of middle-sized and large lakes in the western and northwestern regions of the country have become very shallow. All this was the result of an intensive and rapacious felling of trees in regions of fluctuating rainfall—for example, in the middle and upper Volga regions. During the decade the level of subsoil waters fell noticeably in these regions, making rivers shallower and increasing the frequency of drought. The building of hydroelectric stations on a huge scale in the Volga, Dnieper, and Don basins, in Siberia and Central Asia, led to grave and unforeseen consequences. Enormous tracts of agricultural and forest land were flooded to make reservoirs, and an even larger area was indirectly affected: there has been a formation of salt in the soil, a destruction of river banks, the creation of bogs, erosion, etc. All the processes that cause the deterioration of land adjacent to the new reservoirs went on unchecked. The construction of these enormous reservoirs in the basins of the major rivers of the country has reduced the overall water flow, and the reduction has in turn greatly weakened the capacity of many rivers to purify themselves from the ever-increasing accumulation of industrial and domestic waste. Because of this there has been an acute deterioration of the water supply in many industrial areas. The destruction of the natural waterway system, the deltas and estuaries, has wreaked huge damage on the fisheries of almost all the inland waterways of the country. Because of inadequate methods of irrigation applied in the arid regions of the country, not only did huge areas of irrigated land decline in fertility, but also many hundreds of thousands of hectares of land have been lost outright to agriculture. In most of the more accessible sparsely wooded and moderately wooded regions of the country, the felling of timber is careless and greedy. This has resulted in a further decline in the area of land under forest in the most developed regions, and the quality of timber has also deteriorated. The exploitation of the forests has been carried out in an extremely irrational manner. There have been huge losses because of improper methods of timber floating. Logs sink in the rivers and are carried out to sea. In many regions the wildlife of the forest has suffered considerably. At the same time the important work of afforestation, designed to protect agricultural land, has come almost to a standstill; measures to prevent the formation of ravines or to create new ponds and reservoirs in the forest-steppe and steppe zones have been totally inadequate. Thus we see that socialism in itself is no protection against a predatory approach to the natural wealth of our country, when for the sake of solving problems of the moment, enormous and to some extent irretrievable damage is inflicted on the country's resources.[20]

All over the world the sixties were marked by a rapid development of science and education, and the Soviet Union was no exception. The number of people with completed higher education increased from 3.8 million on January 15, 1959 to 8.3 million on January 15, 1970, while the corresponding figures for partial higher education went up from 1.7 to 2.6 million, and for completed secondary education (specialized and general) from 17.8 to 46.8 million. In 1970 47.3 million people received partial secondary education, as against 35.4 in 1959. There were 4.6 million students in the USSR in 1970 with 257,000 graduating in engineering, a much greater number than in the United States (about 50,000 per year). There was a substantial increase in graduates from secondary schools and vocational-technical training colleges. In many educational institutions, new curricula with improved teaching methods were introduced.

The number of scientific institutions in the USSR expanded during the decade from 4,200 to 5,000, while the numbers of scientists and scholars grew from 350,000 to 930,000, doctors of science from 11,000 to 24,000, and candidates of science from 98,000 to 224,500 persons. There was a substantial growth of scientific research. Soviet scholars made important contributions in many fields—in mathematics and the natural and social sciences. One ought to mention particularly the return to normal in biology and agronomy, after the fraudulent Lysenko clique lost its monopoly.* Cybernetics, artificially blocked during the fifties, is now being rapidly developed. There were advances in the technical and other applied sciences. The Soviet Union can be justifiably proud of its achievement in space research. At the beginning of the sixties a Soviet citizen was the first person in history to orbit the earth in a space ship. And at the end of the decade, a Soviet automatic space laboratory, *Lunakhod,* was landed on the moon.

Yet achievements in education and science turned out to be substantially below expectation and clearly did not meet the needs of a modern economy. While the United States experienced an explosive development of science and technology during the sixties, the Soviet Union is still at the very preliminary stages of the same process, and in many respects stands only at the threshold.

* Trofim Lysenko believed that acquired characteristics could be inherited. He dominated Soviet genetics and biology for more than twenty-five years.—Trans.

Compulsory secondary school education is still not universal. Only about 60 per cent of our young people have a complete secondary education, while 10–15 per cent do not have even eight full years of primary school. Although the American population is smaller, we have fewer children in senior classes and fewer students in universities. We are also behind Japan and a number of other capitalist countries in the development of secondary and higher education. In terms of numbers of secondary school and university graduates per ten thousand of the population, the Soviet Union is considerably behind the United States and Japan. In the overall educational level of the population, i.e., both in absolute numbers and in the proportion of people with secondary and higher education, the Soviet Union is fifteen to twenty years behind the United States. A larger proportion of the American working class has received secondary education than its Soviet counterpart, and the discrepancy in education of the two rural populations is even wider. Aggregate expenditure on all types of education in the USSR is just a little more than one half that of the United States and is increasing at a slower rate. During the past decade, the total outlay on education approximately tripled in the United States but only doubled in the USSR.

Teachers' salaries in the Soviet Union are still very low judged by contemporary standards. Although the party programme promised a substantial rise, it was never carried out, and many categories of teachers receive pay checks that fail to provide a living wage. At the same time their workload is enormous and exceeds that of many white-collar workers and members of the intelligentsia. This is why a great number of capable young people do not enter the teaching profession, and there are very few male teachers. The provision for raising teachers' qualifications is very inadequate. On the whole, the profession does not get the respect and support it deserves in a socialist society.

Ordinary Soviet schools changed very little during the decade. Their external appearance, teaching methods, equipment, and general effectiveness all remained much the same, although in some respects there was deterioration, particularly in the area of vocational training. Secondary school education was shortened by one year, with no compensatory

increase in efficiency. Because the whole direction of education was inadequate, with clumsy planning and a tendency
toward "harebrained schemes,"* the enormous efforts devoted
to improving vocational training during the first half of the
sixties were not very successful, and whatever gains were
accomplished were in any case lost in the second half of the
decade. Our secondary schools are again out of step with the
requirements of the real world. Most of the vocational schools
are vocational in name only; both psychologically and practically, they do very little to prepare our young people for
actual jobs. Vocational and technical training has developed
very slowly and satisfied only a small part of our economy's
need for skilled workers. There are also serious weaknesses
in our specialized secondary and higher education.

In science, too, the situation is highly inadequate. Only
in certain fields did the advantages of centralized direction
and planning enable our scientists to lead the world. In most
areas of research, including the most rapidly advancing ones,
Soviet science is behind capitalist and particularly American
science. The equipment in institutes and laboratories is inferior
to that in the United States, labor productivity is less efficient
(the numbers of scientists in both countries are approximately
the same), there are fewer scientific discoveries and not as
many scientific publications. In other words, the Soviet Union
today lags well behind the United States in the production and
utilization of scientific-technical information and even has
lost its once indisputable position as leader in many aspects
of space research—the first men on the moon, after all, were
Americans. The gap is particularly large in biological research, as well as in applied mathematics, chemistry, and in
a number of technological fields.

Although pretending to be a state guided by scientific
principles, the Soviet Union also lags behind capitalist countries in the development of many of the applied social sciences, including empirical sociological investigation, theories
of industrial and agricultural management, and educational
research. The vast field of political science is almost entirely
neglected. We are also backward in certain important aspects
of applied economics, and in the field of law.

* Another epithet applied to Khrushchev in the official denunciation
   after his removal.—Trans.

*   *   *

Political developments during the sixties were extremely confused and often contradictory. The sixties of course began under the aegis of the Twenty-second Party Congress, in some ways an even more important event than the Twentieth Congress from the point of view of domestic policy. Decisions of the Twentieth Congress were reaffirmed and significantly extended; there was not only an open, but a much more categorical denunciation of many of the worst crimes and abuses of power under Stalin. A beginning was made in the task of overcoming the grievous aftereffects of his rule. Many of his henchmen and accomplices were also specifically denounced on this occasion. And various symbols of the Stalin cult, so alien to socialism, were eliminated: the sarcophagus containing the usurper's body was removed from the Lenin Mausoleum, and many cities, streets, squares, and institutions were renamed.

Following the Twenty-second Congress, there was a noticeable growth of political activity throughout Soviet society and particularly among the creative intelligentsia. Within three years, hundreds of books and thousands of articles were published, taking up the official line of the Congress on the need for a truthful account of the history of the Soviet Union and its Communist Party. Certain themes received extensive treatment in literature and art—the cult of personality and arbitrary rule, what life was really like in Stalin's prisons and camps; there had been nothing quite like this after the Twentieth Congress. As a result, not only many of the social sciences but also art and literature made comparatively rapid strides in the first half of the sixties. The public was able to read several important works of literature that provided a penetrating analysis of life in Soviet society. The atmosphere created by repression and terror gradually began to fade, and socialist legality was made more effective. Socialist principles and socialist relations, largely in abeyance during the Stalin dictatorship, were given new impetus.

All these salutory political processes were, however, not absolutely consistent or reliable. For example, as early as 1963–64 several strident campaigns were organized against certain writers and artists, causing a deterioration in relations between the party leadership and the creative intelligentsia. Ill-qualified people were again allowed to interfere in literature and the arts and also to meddle in many complicated scientific and technological matters. The ambiguous political situation continued and got even worse after the October Plenum.

Khrushchev's regime of personal power came to an end and was condemned. There was outspoken denunciation of his crude and arbitrary behavior, his "voluntarism," "subjectivism," and "hare-brained scheming," which had increasingly become characteristic of his style. In order to forestall any attempt to create a new cult of personality, the Plenum decided to forbid any future concentration of excessive power in the hands of one man. This was certainly a very positive step which also encouraged a more profound reappraisal, a critical attempt to understand and evaluate recent history and the contemporary situation.

But unfortunately progress has been very slow in many important areas, and there has been a certain regression, particularly noticeable in the last four or five years. Various kinds of press censorship have been intensified. Literature and art have been subject to increasingly vicious abuse by conservative and reactionary forces and many important new works of literature have been prevented from reaching the public, so that in turn there has been a general decline in creative activity. Promising research in the social sciences has been blocked. The event most symbolic of the whole trend was the purging of the editorial board of *Novy Mir,* which had been responsible for the most striking contributions to Soviet literature during the sixties. Considering the enormous potential of our artistic and scientific intelligentsia, the Soviet people do not receive even a small proportion of the spiritual sustenance that could be available.

In the last years, violations of socialist legality have been increasing—individuals are subjected to administrative and judicial persecution because of their convictions. Starting in 1966, there were more than a score of political trials which were severely and rightly condemned by Soviet public opinion, and which caused widespread concern both among the Soviet intelligentsia and in progressive circles abroad. Cases of healthy people being committed to psychiatric hospitals for

political reasons became more frequent. Persistent attempts
to rehabilitate Stalin encountered no appropriate rebuff from
the ideological leadership of the party; instead there was
sometimes even encouragement from that quarter. There is a
new, very complex nationality problem, with an intensification of both nationalism and great-power chauvinism. The
overwhelming majority of the working people do not participate as they should in the political life of the country and are
not involved in solving crucial political and economic problems. They continue to be politically passive.

Another characteristic of the sixties that cannot be ignored was the almost continuous growth of alcoholism and
crime, not least among young people.[21] Drug addiction, for a
long time a problem only in capitalist countries, began to
appear on the scene in the Soviet Union as well. Far from
being eliminated, bribery and corruption increased, particularly in the work of many economic and trade organizations,
in institutions of higher education, in various state organizations and enterprises, and even within the party.

The position of the USSR in international affairs and the
evolution of the world communist movement were also confused and inconsistent in the course of the sixties.

The last decade saw a number of important measures
intended to strengthen world peace and security and to enhance the international position of the Soviet Union, notably
the signing of the nuclear test ban treaty and also the treaty
on nonproliferation of nuclear weapons. Compared to the end
of the fifties, there were improved relations between the
Soviet Union and other countries such as France, Italy, West
Germany, and Japan. Economic cooperation between Comecon countries improved, and there was a considerable
growth in mutually advantageous trade between the Soviet
Union and capitalist countries. Our links were strengthened
with many underdeveloped countries of Asia, Africa, and
Latin America. There were, however, a number of opposite
developments which directly contradict the positive trends
just described and which, on the whole, caused a deterioration in the international position of the Soviet Union, while
the threat of a new world war became greater than ever.

The most serious development to change the balance of forces in the world was the split in the socialist camp. Nationalism, adventurism, and dogmatism triumphed in Chinese foreign and domestic policy, reaching a climax in the so-called cultural revolution, with the destruction of the Chinese Communist Party as such and the establishment of a regime that can be described only as a military despotism. As a result, the friendship between China and the Soviet Union, which had been a particular source of strength for the socialist camp, turned into estrangement, mutual hostility, and, by the end of the sixties, even to open military confrontation, diverting a vast part of the military resources of both countries. This in turn produced rifts in other parties—in India, Ceylon, and elsewhere.

Fewer countries in the socialist camp remain under Soviet leadership; by the end of the sixties they included some 300 million people, or one-tenth of the world's population. And for a number of reasons recent years have witnessed an almost continuous growth of centrifugal tendencies even in that part of the socialist camp still within the Soviet bloc. The decade saw a deterioration of relations with Cuba and also with Rumania, whose membership in the Warsaw Pact became increasingly nominal. The bitter crisis of 1968 between the USSR and Czechoslovakia ended in military intervention by five Warsaw Pact countries and to the stationing of a sizable contingent of Soviet forces on Czech soil.

Economic integration within Comecon has proceeded slowly and inconsistently, and is very much behind that of Western Europe.

The accumulation of troubles within the socialist camp were compounded in the sixties by a worsening in relations between the Soviet Union and the United States. Continuing military rivalry between them led to an intensification of the arms race. Toward the end of the sixties, the invention of a new type of intercontinental ballistic missile, along with a system of antimissile defense, meant the beginning of a new round in the race for strategic weapons, very damaging to the American economy but even worse for the Soviet one.

During the sixties there was a growing number of increasingly serious local armed conflicts, with the United States and the USSR either directly or indirectly drawn in.

American aggression in Vietnam led to a protracted bloody war which absorbed enormous resources from both the United States and the socialist countries, and created a constant threat to peace, not only in Southeast Asia but throughout the world. There has been a great increase of tension in recent years in the Middle East, where in 1967 our Arab allies suffered a heavy military defeat and lost a substantial amount of territory. The unfortunate developments in this part of the world have forced the Soviet Union to expend an enormous amount of energy and funds in order to restore Arab military and economic potential, but the Arab position, even today, remains precarious.

Relations deteriorated with many countries of the "third world." In Indonesia, Ghana, Cambodia, and to some extent in Mali and Algeria, regimes friendly to the USSR were overthrown by military coups. The growing arms race and the country's military posture vis-à-vis China and the United States make it impossible for the Soviet Union to increase its economic and cultural aid to the underdeveloped countries of Asia, Africa, and Latin America; our position in these countries is hardly strengthened thereby.

One also cannot ignore the fact that along with a weaker military and economic position, there has also been a decline in the moral and political status of the Soviet Union. The number of our active and sincere friends throughout the world has noticeably dwindled and there has been a growing anti-Soviet mood almost everywhere due to a variety of factors. At first it was a case of attitudes being deliberately encouraged by the ruling circles in a number of countries, including the United States, China, and certain nations of Western Europe. But anti-Soviet feelings are also a response to various negative aspects of Soviet foreign policy and domestic politics. We must now face the bitter truth that there has been a distinct growth of anti-Soviet sentiments even among the masses of the socialist countries of Europe. Anti-Soviet attitudes are also very common in the Arab countries, in spite of vast amounts of military and economic aid, substantially greater than that given to our European socialist allies. Progressive intellectuals have grown increasingly critical of the USSR, as have young people in Western Europe and the United States. Thus the Soviet Union has lost much of the position it occupied toward the end of the fifties. Once more we find ourselves isolated, with serious consequences for our economic situation.

The sixties also witnessed a conspicuous decline in the international communist movement, which was shaken by a number of severe crises. Most serious of all was the damage inflicted by the divisive activities of the Chinese Party leadership. In the wake of a counterrevolutionary military coup, the Communist Party of Indonesia, once an important segment of the world communist movement, was destroyed. Serious internal dissension weakened the communist parties in many other Asian countries. In a number of Arab countries, communist parties were brutally persecuted and suffered heavy losses. A long and bitter quarrel continued to dominate relations between the Communist Party of Japan and the CPSU. Serious differences arose between the Cuban Communist Party and the CPSU, and also between the Cuban Communist Party and those of many Latin-American countries. In the sixties there was little improvement of relations between the CPSU and the League of Yugoslav Communists. The intervention in Czechoslovakia caused an extremely serious crisis in the international communist movement; the majority of West European communist parties categorically condemned our action.[22]

Communist party membership in capitalist countries did not increase during the sixties, and in many countries it even went down. Nor was there a growth in party membership in the Third World. Only at the end of the sixties, after protracted and difficult negotiations, was it possible to convene a new international communist conference, but almost one-third of the parties that had been present at the International Conference of Communist and Workers' Parties in 1960 were not represented. And some of the parties taking part in the later conference either refused to sign the final resolution or signed with many reservations and after substantial criticism.[23]

This, in the most general outline, was our situation as we embarked on the eighth decade of the twentieth century. Inevitably we have to ask ourselves: How will the international situation develop in this decade? Will it change for the better, or will present dangerous trends prevail as tension continues to mount? Of course many things are beyond our control. But nevertheless, a great deal does depend very much on us, the Soviet Union, the Soviet government, and the Soviet people. And not only on our foreign, but perhaps to an even greater extent on our domestic policies. The chief problem underlying everything else is the extremely complicated one of how to bring about a far-reaching democratization of our social and political life.

II

The Development of Socialist Democracy

The triumph of Soviet power after the October Revolution meant the appearance of a new proletarian socialist democracy. The proletariat, in alliance with the poorest peasants, not only seized state power from the former ruling classes, but also expropriated all the basic means of production, ending the exploitation of man by man. Bourgeois and gentry privileges were abolished and the creation of a new socialist society had begun.

Lenin never excluded the possibility of the proletariat coming to power peacefully by taking maximum advantage of the democratic institutions the bourgeois-democratic revolution had established. However, he believed that, with all its extraordinary opportunities, this path was only rarely possible and was therefore hardly likely to be so in the world's first victorious proletarian revolution.

And indeed, in the upshot, the victory of Soviet power was the result of armed insurrection and forcible overthrow of the bourgeois Provisional Government. Soon afterward the intervention of international imperialism along with internal counterrevolution resulted in a cruel and prolonged civil war which demanded not only maximum mobilization of all the economic and human resources of the young Soviet republic, but also substantial limitations on political and civil freedom. "The dictatorship of a class," wrote Lenin, "must mean the abolition (or the most substantial restriction, which is in fact a type of abolition) of democracy for that class over whom or against whom the dictatorship is being exercised."[1] As Lenin pointed out in the first manifesto he wrote for the Comintern, "to demand from the proletariat that in the final life-and-death struggle with capital they piously observe the rules of political democracy . . . is the same as asking a man defending his life against a group of thugs that he observe the artificial and conventional rules of wrestling established but not observed by his enemies."[2]

But although Lenin was categorical in his defense of the need for limitations on political democracy as something inevitable and justified at critical revolutionary periods, he clearly understood that all these restrictions were to be temporary and transitional; they were inevitable under conditions of an open, armed struggle of the proletariat against its enemies, but afterwards it was both possible and desirable for the victorious proletariat gradually to lift such restrictions. When the opponents of proletarian dictatorship renounce their attempts to overthrow the dictatorship by force, then the proletarian state can also refrain from the use of various forms of revolutionary violence. For revolutionary violence, as Lenin pointed out, is "an indispensable and legitimate method of revolution *only at certain points of its development, only in certain special conditions,* but the much more crucial feature of revolution and a condition of its victory is and always will be the organization of the proletarian masses, the organization of the workers."[3] Lenin frequently made the point that if during the transitional period from capitalism to socialism there are still some restrictions on democracy (and the extent of these restrictions must be gradually reduced), nonetheless with the full victory of socialism all restrictions on political democracy fall away. *"The victory of socialism is impossible without the realization of democracy."*[4]

The word "democracy" originates, as is well known, from the Greek words *demos,* meaning "the people," and *kratos,* meaning "power." Thus democracy, in its original sense, means the power of the people. The concept of democracy arose in ancient times in slave-owning republics, where in contrast to monarchies, tyrannies, and oligarchies, all citizens possessed of full rights could either directly or through freely chosen representatives take part in the discussion of the most important issues affecting the fate of the republic and help to decide them.

Democracy again became a common theme during the bourgeois-democratic revolution, when the majority of the people, led by bourgeois and petty-bourgeois groups and parties, rose up against king and aristocracy and demanded liberty, equality, and popular power. After a long-drawn-out and complicated struggle, the majority of European and North American countries, differing from each other in form and structure, had become the so-called bourgeois democracies.

We have become accustomed to speak about bourgeois democracy with disdain as something incomplete, illusory, false, designed for effect, etc. But this approach is tendentious and wrong. Bourgeois democracy is, of course, an extremely limited form of democracy and is therefore open to criticism. It is easy to demonstrate that opportunities are not equal for worker and capitalist, for the poor and the rich. The fundamental principle of bourgeois democracy is the formal equality of all citizens before the law, and there is little concern for the social rights and freedoms of working people or for material guarantees to support the rights and freedoms that have been proclaimed. This is why the programmes of communist parties in all capitalist countries, including those with the most highly developed system of bourgeois democracy, continue to put forward general democratic demands— while at the same time calling on people to struggle for socialism.

But with all these reservations, it is important to stress that the sum total of various political and social institutions which taken together form the system of bourgeois democracy is not simply a fiction, in spite of the assertions to this effect by many left-wing groups, past and present. On the contrary, all of these institutions and mechanisms are the product of decades, sometimes centuries, of stubborn struggle by the people for their rights. The democratic order of many Western countries constitutes their most important tradition, their most precious political heritage. It is democracy of this kind that makes it possible for workers in capitalist countries not only to fight for an extension of their rights or for a higher standard of living under capitalism, but also to strive for the abolition of capitalism and its replacement by socialism. Communist parties exist legally in Italy, France, and many other capitalist countries; they hold open meetings, publish newspapers, magazines, and books, organize trade unions, strikes, and political campaigns—and all this is no fiction, but a very real achievement of the working class. The temporary victory of fascism in Germany and other countries demonstrated rather clearly not only the shortcomings of bourgeois democracy but also its virtues, which must not be underestimated. Furthermore, history has shown how the democratic forms established in several Western countries in the nineteenth century, besides helping the workers of these countries in the struggle to extend their own rights, also gave support to the struggle of working people all over the world. It was not without significance that Marx and Engels decided to spend a large part of their adult lives in relatively democratic England and that the headquarters of the First International were also set up there. All of Russia's revolutionary parties, including the Bolsheviks, established centers beyond the Russian frontier in Switzerland, France, Belgium, and England. Even today, political organizations struggling to overthrow fascist dictatorships in Spain, Portugal, and Greece are based in France and Italy.

While contrasting bourgeois with socialist democracy, one should never lose sight of the definite continuity between them, which is twofold in nature. First of all, bourgeois-democratic freedoms help the working class and its party to gather strength, to prepare their struggle for socialism. Secondly, many democratic forms and institutions, created before the socialist revolution, may and ought to be retained even after it, as long as they are given new content. In 1916 Lenin wrote:

. . . it is impossible for the proletariat to accomplish the socialist revolution if it has not been prepared for it by the struggle for democracy. . . . The struggle against opportunism in the guise of a refusal to utilize the democratic institutions of a given capitalist society because they have been perverted by the bourgeoisie that created them, is in fact a complete capitulation to opportunism.[5]

Just as a socialist society makes use of the forces of production created before the socialist revolution, so socialist culture profits by the achievements of all preceding cultures, and in the political sphere, a socialist society must adopt many democratic norms and institutions established in the course of centuries of human development. Today we can see very well that the less experience a people has had of bourgeois democracy, the more difficult it will be for them to create the institutions of genuine socialist democracy. It is not a question of rejecting the mechanisms of bourgeois democracy, but of transforming them. Empty rhetoric becomes effective law, illusory rights are made real, and many formal democratic institutions are given new content and meaning. For socialist democracy embodies not just the power of the people, but the power of the working people, or more precisely still, rule by all people who work led by the working class, which in a developed capitalist society is the majority and takes power in order to carry out a transformation in the interests of all the workers in order to build a socialist and communist society.

In the past, democracy was in the first instance associated with certain concepts of the state, the nature of political power, and the procedure for making political decisions and implementing them. In our time, the increasing complexity of social life has altered and extended the meaning of democracy so that aside from the social and political spheres, almost all aspects of life in contemporary society tend to be included: work, leisure, culture, and science. Yet even today one could list a certain number of the most essential civil rights the presence or absence of which make it possible to judge the degree of democracy in a given society.

Very recently a most valuable attempt was made to list the basic rights and institutions obligatory for any democratic society, whether it calls itself socialist or simply democratic. The result was the two Covenants adopted by the General Assembly of the United Nations in December 1966: "On Economic, Social and Cultural Rights" and "On Civil and Political Rights." Significantly, delegates from both capitalist and socialist countries took part in the work on these documents. It was a long drawn-out process which took nearly twenty years. The Soviet delegation to the UN voted in favor of the two Covenants. It was stated in the Soviet press that the Soviet Union had participated very actively in their elaboration and that thanks to the constructive work of our delegation, many important provisions were included. Unfortunately the Soviet Union still has not yet ratified either Covenant,* although according to *Izvestia* on December 9, 1966, "all the provisions contained in the UN Covenants have long been a normal feature of life for the Soviet people." They have never appeared in Soviet newspapers or journals, or even in specialized legal publications. Only typed versions have circulated among a small circle of people. Yet familiarity with the texts would make it easier to understand the problems of both bourgeois and socialist democracy.

How democratic is contemporary Soviet society? There are two diametrically opposed views on the subject. On one hand, it is frequently asserted that Soviet citizens have all democratic rights without exception, that our society is the most democratic in the world, etc. On the other extreme, one often hears that there is no democracy whatsoever in our country, that Soviet citizens lack all, or at least the most important, democratic rights. Both opinions are equally mistaken. If one examines the UN documents on the rights of man with an unbiased eye, it is clear that Soviet society has come a long way in terms of economic, social, and cultural rights in the fifty-three years since the October Revolution. They include the right to work and to receive vocational training, the right to organize trade unions, the right to education, social security, family and maternity benefits, medical aid, the protection of minors, the right to participate in cultural life and to benefit from the results of scientific progress. Immediately after the Revolution, the eight-hour working day was introduced, and afterwards, the seven-hour day. The right to leisure was guaranteed; child labor in industry was first restricted and then abolished. Soviet women were the first in the world to receive equal rights, and an enormous effort was made to secure their emancipation. There has been substantial progress in the drive to overcome the immense inequality between physical and mental work, and between country and town. As all socialists have traditionally demanded, every able-bodied Soviet citizen is engaged in useful labor, and it is no longer possible for the idle rich to exist by exploiting the labor of others. Both national and

* The two Covenants were ratified by the Soviet Union in September 1973.—Trans.

racial discrimination have been abolished, and much has been done to overcome the economic and cultural backwardness of the minority peoples who lived in the borderlands of tsarist Russia. During the Soviet period, the lives of working people have been enriched both materially and culturally.

It is certainly a record of remarkable social and economic achievement and could be extended. In view of the widespread misery and poverty of tsarist Russia, and the economic backwardness that made degrading dependence on the Western capitalist countries inevitable, it is easy to understand why not only the leadership but also the majority of ordinary participants in the October Revolution were concerned in the first instance with assuring social, economic, and cultural rights for workers.

Of course in the most developed capitalist countries recent decades have witnessed some progress in the development of economic and cultural rights. There is a higher standard of living and a shorter working day; educational opportunities for working-class children have improved. Women and young people have been given the right to vote almost everywhere, social security benefits for the elderly have been increased, and there is better protection of children, etc. However, even bourgeois social scientists usually admit that all these democratic achievements were not simply given to the workers, but were the result of a persistent struggle, with the Soviet example as an enormous source of encouragement.

However, although it is right to be proud of Soviet achievements with respect to social, economic, and cultural rights, it must also be recognized that Soviet society is today still very backward when it comes to the whole complex of civil and political rights.[6] Of course there has been considerable progress, if one compares the present situation with that of tsarist Russia or with the more recent Stalinist autocracy. A great deal has been done to correct and eliminate the consequences of Stalinism. But it is not good enough to compare the present with the past. Considering the potential and the needs of a socialist society, clearly whatever advance has been made in the realm of political and civil rights is still completely inadequate.

Many of the most terrible Stalinist practices are now

altogether a thing of the past. But even today the shadow remains and a great deal is left to be put right. The present political regime in our country is still not that of a socialist democracy. Elitist methods continue to prevail in the running of the country and of the party, and this hardly reflects the principles of democracy. There are still very strong elements of bureaucracy and a caste system in the highest organs of power, and public control over their work is minimal or nonexistent. Elections for all Soviet institutions are a formality—there is no element of contest, although contest is in fact completely compatible with a socialist society. Elections to leading party bodies are also a formality, starting with the district party committee. As a result, the elected party leadership does not feel itself compelled to answer for its actions either to the party or to the people. Even now there are no normal democratic procedures for regularly replacing the country's political leadership. Changes have always taken place during crises—and have therefore inevitably been unhealthy, confronting the nation with sudden *faits accomplis* of an ominous kind.

The fact that the social sciences play an extremely insignificant role in the formation of policy and the methods of governing is a denial of the principles and ideals of scientific communism. Censorship grows even more restrictive, putting enormous limitations on the exchange of information and ideas and on intellectual freedom. It was recently stated in a widely circulated *samizdat* document, that

there is open distrust of all imaginative, critical, and active individuals. In this situation, conditions are created whereby advancement in one's career is not furthered by professional excellence or adherence to principle; promotion is for those who mouth words of devotion to the party cause while in fact they pursue only their narrow personal interests or passively carry out orders. Limitations on freedom of information not only make control of the leadership more difficult and undermine the initiative of the people, they also mean that authorities at intermediate levels are deprived of knowledge and are thus transformed into bureaucratic functionaries, lacking any kind of independence. At the highest level, information is incomplete and predigested, which makes it impossible for the leadership to make effective use of its authority.

For the great majority of workers, collective farmers, and intelligentsia, political participation hardly exists. This is largely because the structure of government and the way it operates reduce to a minimum any possibility for workers or intellectuals to influence the formation of economic, political, or other important policies. On almost all levels of government, the role of the individual remains a subservient one. Industrial and office workers and collective farmers to a very large extent are alienated from production and hardly participate at all in the real running of their enterprises and institutions.

We still do not possess the freedoms our socialist society deserves: freedom of speech, opinion, of the press and of thought. There is still no freedom for artistic creativity and scientific research, particularly in the social sciences. Nor is there freedom of the individual or inviolability of the person. We still do not possess freedom of movement and choice of residence. There is no freedom to travel abroad, nor is there the right to leave one's country, as laid down in the International Covenant on Civil and Political Rights. We still do not have freedom of association and organization or the right to hold peaceful meetings and demonstrations, as befits a socialist society.

Of course it is obvious that freedom in society cannot be absolute and unlimited—it must be subject to reasonable restrictions. I am far from advocating unlimited freedom for every individual, since this would inevitably entail encroachments on the freedom of others, as was clearly understood by the authors of the Covenant on Civil and Political Rights. In many of the articles of the Covenant they stipulated that "the above-mentioned rights shall not be subject to any restrictions, except those which are provided for by law, are necessary to protect national security, public order, public health or morals, or the rights and freedoms of others."

We must, however, protest in no uncertain terms against the restrictions on human and social rights mentioned above, restrictions that reduce these rights to zero, turning them into empty declarations, paper formalities designed to deceive the people. It is absolutely not true that there is a contradiction between democratic freedom and public order, although this view is often expressed by Soviet writers and sometimes by certain foreign Marxists.[7]

The party program envisages the development of socialist democracy as the main trend in the next stage of the development of the Soviet state:

An all-round extension and perfection of socialist democracy, the active participation of all citizens in the administration of the state, in the management of economic and cultural development, an improvement in the functioning of the government apparatus and increased public control over its activity—constitute the main direction in which the socialist state develops in the period of building communism.[8]

Certainly all groups in society would benefit from a rapid development of socialist democracy—industrial and office workers, collective farmers, and the intelligentsia. Only an insignificant minority—it is largely a question of bureaucratic elements in the governing apparatus—is still unyielding in its opposition and tries to frighten and deceive the ill-informed about the possible consequences of democratization. The threat to bureaucracy is claimed to be a threat to the whole of society.

Socialist democracy is simultaneously a goal and a means. Democracy is essential as a value in itself. To be able to express one's thoughts and convictions freely without fear of persecution or repression is a vital aspect of a free socialist way of life. Without freedom to receive and impart information, without freedom of movement and residence, without freedom of creativity in science and the arts, and without many other democratic freedoms, a true socialist society is impossible. Democracy—with all government activity open to public scrutiny as its most important element—is also necessary as a means of ridding our society of bureaucracy and corruption. It offers firm protection against a relapse into arbitrary lawlessness. As we read in the document referred to on p. 37, it is only democratization that

can restore dynamism and creativity to our ideological life (the social sciences, art, and propaganda) by putting an end to the bureaucratic, ritualistic, dogmatic, hypocritical and vapid style at present so widespread. A policy of democratization will eliminate the gap between the party-state apparatus and the intelligentsia, and mutual misunderstanding will give way to close cooperation. Democratization will evoke a surge of enthusiasm comparable to that of the twenties. The best intellectual abilities of the country will be mobilized to solve its economic and social problems.

Thus a consistent policy of genuine socialist democratization will not only enrich Soviet society both materially and spiritually, it will also speed the process of eliminating various shortcomings and evils still present in our social, political, and economic institutions.

Without genuine democracy it will be impossible to instill authentic communist morality, to educate Soviet citizens to be independent, responsible, and politically active. It is very clear today that the important advantage of socialism is not merely the maximal satisfaction of material needs. The latest achievements of the scientific-technological revolution mean that for an overwhelming majority of the population capitalism will be able to provide relatively adequate satisfaction of most basic requirements. Therefore the problem of education takes on special significance in a socialist society— how to raise integrated, fully developed, humane, and moral human beings. The development of production hardly provides an answer.

What is needed for the upbringing of this new kind of man is a huge release of the country's spiritual potential, possible only in conditions of genuine freedom and democracy. Some people believe that the Soviet Union has reached this stage, that it is already a developed socialist society which has not only achieved an unprecedented level of material production but also an equally high degree of intellectual and spiritual freedom. The Soviet people, it is argued, has access to a profusion of spiritual resources. But such a view is wishful thinking. It would be more accurate to say that the Soviet people has *only just embarked* on the creation of a *developed* socialist society but has still not advanced very far along that path. It is also an illusion to think that "spiritual nourishment" can be artificially prepared in advance and doled out as required. Procedures appropriate for devising a school or university program cannot be relied on to guide the spiritual life of society. The Soviet people must have the widest choice, they must have a real opportunity to judge for themselves and make decisions about all questions related to the formation of their mental world.

Of course there was a period (this does not refer to the

distortions of Stalinism) when certain reasonable limitations on socialist democracy were necessary, not to speak of democracy in general. Many serious restrictions on inner-party democracy were also inevitable. But that was a long time ago. Today limitations on socialist democracy do not make the state stronger—quite the contrary; socialism is undermined, and cultural and economic advance are inhibited both in the Soviet Union and in all socialist countries. The obstacles are becoming increasingly obvious.

The acceleration of technological progress makes it imperative for people to be as well educated and informed as possible and to develop their mental capacities, their whole potential to the utmost. But again, this can be achieved only against a background of freedom and democracy. Contemporary technology frees the worker from the mechanical repetition of identical movements and demands more creativity at work and the ability to make nonstandardized decisions. It is also essential that those in the highest leadership positions as well as senior administrators display a creative approach to their jobs. Therefore the fully developed individual has become the most important condition for an all-round material advance.[9]

The fact that many theoretical problems have not yet been adequately studied is also a serious obstacle to the development of socialist democracy. There is a tendency to accept as generally valid many propositions that were appropriate for only one period of our history. Similarly we apply to all socialist countries and even to the world communist movement as a whole ideas that were valid only in one particular socialist country. Relative truths, which need to be clarified and interpreted, are frequently held up as unquestioned dogma.

For example, democracy is usually defined as the rule of the majority over the minority, and this is fundamentally correct. As a result of the socialist revolution, the exploiting minority was overthrown, and political power was consolidated in the hands of representatives of the working people, who constituted the overwhelming majority of society.[10]

Only a socialist revolution is able to achieve in actual practice the democratic principle of majority rule. In the first years after the revolution it basically means that the working people, as the majority, make decisions, and the former exploiters—the landowners and capitalists and their political representatives—submit. But even after the victory of socialism and the establishment of a socialist society, when it would seem that the notion of exploitation would have become obsolete, the majority principle still retains its validity as the most important feature of socialism. In the party, a majority decides, and the minority bows to its decision. In all collective bodies, during elections and referendums, at party meetings, everywhere, decisions are taken by a majority of votes. This has become a truism that appears over and over again in all works on socialist democracy. "Democracy," writes Yu. Shabanov,

means the subordination of the minority to the majority in all areas of political life. . . . The term *democracy* is also used in another context to indicate the submission of the minority to the will of the majority in any public body. This is what is meant when we speak of inner-party, trade union, *Komsomol,* or collective farm democracy.[11]

But with so much concentration on implementing this fundamental democratic principle—and a socialist democracy meant the first real opportunity to do so—there has been a tendency to neglect another no less important element of democracy: the right of the minority to formulate and defend its point of view. A society cannot be genuinely democratic if the majority is not secure in its right to govern, if it cannot make decisions and carry them out. But real democracy cannot survive if there is no protection for the expression of minority opinion. The minority must comply with majority decisions—but only up to a point, in the sense that there must be no question of its voluntary or enforced liquidation, or of its being made to espouse majority beliefs.[12] In other words, within the framework of democracy the minority must be able to maintain and advocate its separate point of view. And this is important not only for the minority, but for the majority as well, for the whole of society. As we know, the judgment of the majority does not always prove to be correct.

It is often the case that the majority is wrong; what is a minority view today may be supported by the majority tomorrow. There was a time when only an insignificant minority within the working class was convinced of the validity of Marxism-Leninism. But later it was to become the ideology of the majority of workers and indeed of the nation as a whole.

Communists are still only an insignificant minority in many countries today and are making an enormous effort to convert others to their views. Naturally they demand that the governments of their countries should respect the rights of political minorities such as themselves. Unfortunately we do not encounter a similar attitude toward the rights of minorities in countries where communists have come to power.

Thomas Jefferson, one of the most eminent exponents (both in theory and practice) of bourgeois democracy and the author of the U.S. Declaration of Independence, declared that the right of the minority to express its point of view is the essence of democracy, and that the denial of this right leads to the "tyranny of the majority." Robespierre said something similar in one of his speeches:

The minority everywhere has one eternal right—the right to proclaim the truth, or what it considers to be the truth.

These propositions are true not only for a bourgeois but also for a socialist society.

Lenin, of course, believed that in the future it would be possible to solve the problem of political rights for the dispossessed bourgeoisie in another way. In different conditions, without civil war and foreign intervention, the defeated bourgeoisie, once stripped of power, could be allowed to retain certain political rights. But in our country, even after the civil war, it was necessary to continue restrictions on the political rights of those who opposed Soviet power and the dictatorship of the proletariat. They did not have the right to organize and were deprived of freedom of expression and of the press. However, these restrictions on democracy were justifiable only during a state of emergency, when the Soviet Union was the only socialist country in existence and was preparing for inevitable conflict with the capitalist world. To insist that this approach is universally applicable—valid at all times for all socialist countries—implies a lack of faith in the strength of revolutionary ideology and the power of Marxism-Leninism.

But the problem of political minorities in a socialist

country is not so much a question of the former exploiting classes and their political representatives as of different trends and attitudes within the working class itself, among the masses. Stalin had a simple solution: he accused any dissident minority of exerting a hostile bourgeois influence on the working class and the communist movement—it was acting either as a voluntary or an unconscious agent of the enemy. His view of reality was obviously very crude.

Any country in the process of building socialism will experience an enormous number of immensely difficult problems, and sound solutions are seldom found immediately. It is also the case that conceptions of socialism and communism differ. Even within the framework of a united socialist programme, there can be various views about method, about the means of achieving the goal. Disagreements can arise about matters that may seem minor in the perspective of history but are enormously important at the time, perhaps even crucial. Since great disparities still exist among working people of socialist countries—in educational level, in standard of living, in social and political experience—one event will often evoke a number of different responses among the workers themselves. The point is that disagreements may arise for any number of perfectly natural reasons such as differences in age and the degree to which people are informed about this, that, or the other. The crucial thing, in the interest of truth, is to protect not only the rights of the majority, but the rights of the minority as well.

If the rights of the minority include being able not only to formulate but also to defend a point of view on any issue, this in fact means opposition. Should political opposition be allowed in a socialist democracy?[13]

The "conservatives" answer no, as we see in the following pronouncement by one of them:

Freedom for "opposition" is a very different matter. The question is, Should the revolution grant freedom for counterrevolutionaries? . . . demagogic clamor about denial of "freedom of expression" must not be allowed to confuse the main issue—to *whom* is it being denied and for saying *what*? It is a particular feature of socialist democracy and communist humanism, that their adherents are able to say loudly and clearly, without hypocrisy or pharisaism, without taking refuge in rhetoric about "universal democracy," that in the name of happiness for millions, the dictatorship of the proletariat has the right, conferred on it by world history, to abolish freedom for counterrevolution.[14]

The famous slogan of the Czech students in the spring of 1968—"Only he fears opposition who is uncertain of the truth of his own opinion"—was subsequently judged to be antisocialist and counterrevolutionary. For instance, in the resolutions of the Fifth Congress of the Polish Workers Party it was stated that there is no place for opposition in the political structure of socialist countries.

The free play of political forces and a competitive struggle between different parties would lead to their becoming a focus for antisocialist opposition. There would be a development of unrestrained demagogy, a deflection of society from its tasks, and anarchism in political and economic life.

In a socialist society, according to the Bulgarian writer, Ya. Radev, there cannot be political opposition. Because:

. . . in capitalist society opposition to the exploiters expresses the will of the majority. But in a socialist society, opposition to the dictatorship of the working class is the antisocialist position of a reactionary minority. Therefore restrictions on the activity of this minority further the interests of democracy and are necessary to protect the freedom of the working classes.[15]

These statements are riddled with logical and political absurdities. In the first place, there is the *a priori* identification of "opposition" with "counterrevolution," "antisocialist forces," and "anarchy." But in fact opposition can exist within the framework of a socialist or communist ideology common to both majority and minority. Although there is no disagreement about ends, the opposition may be in favor of alternative means, supporting a different approach to the solution of certain practical or theoretical problems.

Of course none of the authors quoted above rejects the need for discussion of the various problems that will arise in the course of building socialism. But they usually stress that such discussion is permissible only before a decision is made. After a question is decided, discussion must come to an end, and the minority not only must submit to the will of the majority but also must relinquish the right to advocate its own point of view, i.e., refrain from opposition. It must accept the majority opinion unreservedly and help to put it into practice. But this is to misunderstand the basic principles of socialist democracy.

Majority decisions must be put into effect once they have been adopted. But this should certainly not mean an end to all discussion. Political decisions are not the same as military orders. It often happens that the disadvantages of a certain decision are revealed only in practice. Sometimes it is not until this stage that it becomes obvious whether or not the decision was correct. Therefore the minority ought to have the right and opportunity to defend its point of view not only before but also after a decision is reached, and this means the right to opposition. The minority cannot refuse to implement a majority decision. But it should not renounce its own views on controversial matters.

Between 1954 and 1963, how many extremely important political and economic policies were decided by an overwhelming majority or even unanimously! In practice, however, some proved to be right, some only partially so, and others were completely misguided. Nevertheless, almost no discussion or open criticism was allowed until the October Plenum in 1964. Although there had been a great deal of discontent and disagreement, none of it could be voiced, with the result that errors were compounded even further, bringing the country and the party to the verge of political and economic disaster. After the October Plenum, comparatively free discussion became possible, and many of the errors of the preceding decade were brought into the open. But this freedom of discussion and criticism did not extend to decisions taken after October 1964. Will this not bring the country to the brink of crisis once again after some years have elapsed?

But if genuine socialist democracy allows opposition within the framework of socialist or communist doctrine (which under socialism will always be the ideology of the overwhelming majority), it should also allow the expression of nonsocialist views and opinions and even the creation of corresponding political platforms and trends. Obviously it is a question of opposition in the realm of views and convictions —there must be adherence to democratic forms of political struggle, including observance of existing laws and a basic respect for the political authority of the majority.

It is completely wrong to think that the right of opposition to the government in power is a feature of bourgeois democracy alone. In fact it is a most important aspect of any democracy.[16] Only in very exceptional situations, during some kind of emergency or at a time of war, may a democratic society forbid or impose limitations on opposition. And it must be temporary. Even in England, where the presence of "her Majesty's Opposition" is considered to be almost the most important feature of the English political system, there was a coalition government during the Second World War. So too in the Soviet state during the terrible conditions of civil war and in the first years afterward, the organization of political opposition outside the party was prohibited, and there were restrictions on opposition within the party as well. But it is unjustifiable to project a state of emergency situation onto the whole period of building socialism and communism in the Soviet Union. Nor may one assume that a peculiar set of historical conditions will be duplicated in other socialist countries. It is ridiculous to transform solutions adopted in the heat of a savage class struggle into irrefutable dogmas and then apply them where antagonistic classes no longer exist. For it may well be the case that under different conditions, what was once accepted as being in the interests of the majority becomes a means of defending the interests and privileges of a tiny bureaucratic minority. Therefore it is crucial to create both within the party and in the country at large some kind of mechanism for normal dialogue between majority and minority, dialogue with dissidents and among the dissidents themselves. This is now a very real problem in that various political trends already do exist both within the party and outside it—trends that can no longer be prohibited or ignored.[17]

III

Trends Within the Party and the Question of Party Unity

Stalin's dictatorship in the thirties, based as it was on ideological conditioning and mass terror, led most communists to become politically passive and apathetic. In party organizations at all levels, unquestioning and blind obedience became the rule. Unity was thus achieved, since all machinery allowing a democratic discussion of party politics ceased to exist. Dissidents were systematically removed and physically destroyed.

The Twentieth and Twenty-second congresses of the CPSU denounced the Stalin cult and the lawlessness and abuse of power associated with it. The resolutions of these congresses marked the beginning of a new stage in the life of our party, a turning point in party and government policies and in the lives of Soviet citizens. They led to the growth of political activity among communists, a revitalization within the party. The October Plenum's condemnation of Khrushchev's "subjectivism" and "voluntarism" and his numerous economic and political errors made even more necessary, in the eyes of party members, a fundamental reconsideration of many aspects of party history along with a review of its present organizational principles and policies.

One cannot fail to see, of course, that, deprived of various beliefs and illusions, a section of the party has embraced a peculiar kind of political pragmatism. Many communists take a comparatively short-term view, giving little thought to basic problems or the crucial questions facing the communist movement in its present crisis. And even worse, the economic and political difficulties of the last decade have led a large number of rank-and-file party members as well as various categories of workers to idealize the Stalinist past. People see that prices are continually rising and talk about the way that "Stalin lowered them." Seeing the split in the socialist camp and disagreement in the communist movement, they recall the time when such things were inconceivable. But few stop to think how "order" in the communist movement was maintained under Stalin, or what those "price reductions" really cost us. A considerable part of our industrial and office workers, never having received an adequate education, find it difficult to adjust to the conditions of contemporary scientific and technological progress. Their lives have been difficult, their hopes disappointed, and it is hardly surprising that ignorance leads them to seek refuge in the past.[1] But apart from these nostalgic sentiments, we find other widespread attitudes among the masses. Within a large section of the party and particularly the party intelligentsia, as well as among progressively minded members of the working class, there is a great desire to move forward, to revitalize and develop Marxism, to return to lost ideals and create a new system of political and moral values rooted in Marxism.

This has been the basis for the growth within our party in recent years of certain trends and groups that have generated a number of new political and ideological platforms. Party members no longer react uniformly to events, whether inside the country or abroad. Of course there have always been differences of opinion within the party, but now they are more concrete and better defined, embracing an even wider range of social problems. Is this to be regarded as a good thing, or not? The fact is that at the present stage of our party's development it is inevitable. In the last forty to forty-five years, the deviations from Marxism and Leninism have been so extensive that without penetrating scholarly and political study, without the free play of different points of view, the party will never be able to get back to the right road. Without struggle between trends and platforms, neither our party nor the whole communist movement will be able to fulfill its historical mission. And the more active and uninhibited our discussion, the more rapid will be the return to health.

Unfortunately political discussion in a real sense is still out of the question. There is only a very limited confrontation of views and ideas in the popular press or even in scholarly publications. The most important discussions and exchanges of opinion still occur unofficially—in the privacy of people's homes, in speeches at meetings, and through the widespread circulation of typescript materials (*samizdat*). This state of affairs puts great obstacles in the way of political and literary debate and makes it hard to differentiate between the various groups. The overwhelming majority of party members are unaware of existing disagreements and have no opportunity to compare the various points of view and then express their own opinion. The effect of this is that many party members who would be capable of political activity play virtually no role in political life. The resultant intellectual stagnation is particularly noticeable in the provinces.

Among the many trends and groups that have formed in the party, or, rather, that have come to the surface since the October Plenum, the most active in recent years have been the neo-Stalinists. As Valentin Turchin correctly points out, this faction is actually not even conservative, but reactionary and would like to push our society in a reverse direction. They may be still powerless themselves, ". . . but their pernicious influence comes from the fact that they infect those around them with prejudices, and prejudice, alas, has a tendency to spread. They try to arouse distrust and hostility toward the intelligentsia among the working class and in the party, and are not too squeamish to use such an old and tried obscurantist weapon as anti-Semitism. . . . They accuse the intelligentsia of cunning and deceit, of using democratization as a cover while really intending to undermine the party. . . . Everything not to their personal liking is immediately labeled 'anti-Soviet,' a word like a poison dart. Words of this kind can

never be purely abstract—they always have emotional over-
tones and past associations. . . . Because during the Stalin
years, hundreds of thousands of completely innocent people
were arrested and killed on the basis of this charge, when an
ordinary person hears 'anti-Soviet' he feels weak at the knees
and his wits desert him. Anyone threatening an honest Soviet
citizen in this way is no better than a thug with a knife up his
sleeve."

Neo-Stalinists to all intents and purposes would like to
revise the decisions of the Twentieth and Twenty-second
congresses and are in favor of the political rehabilitation of
Stalin. Using their positions in the party and state apparatus
and in the mass media, in recent years they have been able to
publish articles and works of literature in which Stalin is
portrayed not as a criminal who destroyed millions of totally
innocent people, not as a despot who established a regime of
unlimited personal dictatorship, not as a perverter of Marxism-Leninism, but as a "wise statesman," "an outstanding
military leader," a "good boss," the "greatest theoretician of
Marxism," and even as a man who "treated Soviet laws with
respect." Unfortunately this whole propaganda campaign has
had partial success among certain backward strata of the
population, ordinary party members, and even some young
people.[2]

But what matters most in the neo-Stalinist political platform is not their attitude toward Stalin, but rather the fact
that they wish to restore "firm" leadership and a "strong"
regime—essentially to bring back Stalin's administrative and
terrorist methods, excluding only some of the extreme forms.
Far from wishing to see any development of socialist democracy, the neo-Stalinists stand for further restrictions—a
tightening of censorship and the restoration of "order" in the
social sciences, literature, and art, with greater bureaucratic
centralization in all spheres of public life. They oppose economic reform and would actually like to put an end to it.[3]
They are also against greater rights for the constituent republics of the Soviet Union; they advocate a rapprochement
with Maoist China and a tougher policy toward the European
socialist countries and communist parties. It was in fact neo-
Stalinists who most actively supported armed intervention in
Czechoslovakia in 1968. They presented a very distorted

picture of the situation there, putting extraordinary pressure on the leadership of the party, with the most extreme members of the faction also demanding intervention in Rumania and Yugoslavia. They want to cut down contacts of every kind with the capitalist countries and would like in effect to resume the "cold war," which in practice would mean greater Soviet isolation in international affairs. Almost all that is new in the policies of Western communist parties is denounced as "opportunism," "revisionism," or "right-wing deviation," and they are particularly hostile toward the Italian Communist Party. Great-power arrogance is a very important element of neo-Stalinism, not only as a practical tool for instilling patriotism in young people, but also as an essential feature of the ideology itself. It is the neo-Stalinists who most insistently argue that at the present time we must intensify ideological confrontation—this is, in effect, only a new version of Stalin's theory on the need to intensify class warfare as the building of socialism proceeded. In its present-day form, this notion plays the same reactionary role and is very close to the ideological arguments behind the "cultural revolution" in China. Neo-Stalinism springs essentially from a conviction that socialism is so weak that it cannot defend itself except by totally suppressing all forces supposedly antagonistic to it. Neo-Stalinists are capable of defending their own socialist ideology against criticism only by administrative methods and persecution. And they believe that Marxism-Leninism and Stalinism are identical.

The reactionary policies of neo-Stalinism, if they were able to prevail in the party, could lead only to the most disastrous consequences. Domestically it would mean inevitable stagnation and decline of the economy, of science and culture, of all areas of social and political life. There would certainly be mass persecution among all sections of the population, which would particularly affect the creative intelligentsia.

As is by now well known, the basic feature of Stalinism was the politically irrational use of terror and administrative methods. They were used not because they were needed but because they were available. In most countries the need to resort to terror is a function of weakness and is accompanied by complete disregard for the enormous expense and harmful consequences involved. When the state feels secure in its strength and stability, it prefers a more liberal policy and does not rely on coercion. But under Stalin, the stronger the state became, the more it took advantage of its increasing capacity to employ terror. A Stalinist seeks to crush and destroy dissidents simply because they are dissidents, and the more power he has, the keener he is to use it to eliminate all who incur his disfavor. This barbarous feature of Stalinist psychology is characteristic of the majority of neo-Stalinists. On the international scene, the victory of neo-Stalinism could lead not only to a sharp increase of tension but even to a new world war. And this danger is very real. There is no point in exaggerating the strength of neo-Stalinism, but it also must not be underestimated. It still is the prevailing ideology in a large section of the party and state apparatus, particularly at the middle level—in the regional and city party committees and among functionaries concerned with ideology.[4] There are also neo-Stalinist tendencies in the leadership of the party, as well as in the top ranks of the army, trade unions, and youth organizations; they are a powerful influence in literature, art, and the social sciences. It was they who were the first to create their own faction after the October Plenum. Their contributions at ideological meetings, their publications in journals like *Oktyabr, Ogonyok, Moskva, Zhurnalist,* and even in *Kommunist* have a very pronounced factional ring.[5] The neo-Stalinist political platform was set forth in its most comprehensive form in Kochetov's novel *What Do You Want?* (1969).[6] In recent years they have been exerting increasingly effective pressure on the higher leadership of the party, as they strive to gain control over the main levers of power in party and state. They have already achieved a great deal, and the only thing that can stop them is further progress toward socialist democracy.

A second trend may provisionally be called moderate-conservative. This intermediate "centrist" trend is the one that is evidently most strongly represented in the present party and state leadership. It is a very complex amalgam that on closer analysis can be seen to divide into groups very different from each other—some of them fairly close to the neo-Stalinists and others, to judge from their speeches and behavior, more progressive in character. As is typical of

middle-of-the-road groups, the moderate-conservatives tend to
oscillate violently between two extremes—either resorting to
"drastic" measures that put the clock back, or, on the contrary, finding themselves compelled to take agonizing decisions that advance us somewhat in a progressive direction.
Their eclecticism and lack of a positive programme, unlike
the neo-Stalinists who at least have a negative one, make it
extremely difficult to say what the members of this group
stand for, particularly since on most questions they have no
specific line. What chiefly distinguishes them is simply a
desire to preserve the present regime and to prevent any kind
of appreciable shift either to the left or to the right. Turning a
blind eye to the many acute political and economic problems
facing the country, they oppose the modernization of our
social system, deny the need for a comprehensive review of
all our past and present policies, and obstruct the application
of new and more progressive principles to domestic and foreign affairs. At the same time, however, they are unwilling to
countenance a complete rehabilitation of Stalin,[7] the winding
up of economic reform, the resumption of widespread persecution of dissidents, or a complete return to an aggressive
foreign policy. They believe, or at least they say, that "Leninist norms" have already been restored in the party. But
politically, culturally, and on the question of Stalin, these
moderate-conservatives have in fact already retreated from
many of the positions adopted by the party after the Twentieth and Twenty-second congresses. This retreat is, however,
partial and comparatively slow, and is accompanied by much
uncertainty and many reservations, provoking intense dissatisfaction in the neo-Stalinist faction. As for economics,
here the moderate-conservatives have carried out a number of
progressive although limited measures, which are likely to
continue since without them there can be no rapid advance of
the economy.

The moderate-conservative grouping is basically made
up of people with a bureaucratic mentality, i.e., badly informed and accustomed to rely on their *apparat*. Therefore
their decisions are frequently shaped not by actual needs but
by the desires of diehard officials who are out of touch with
real life. Subjected to pressure from all sides, most moderate-
conservative leaders will sooner give way to pressure from the

right—the neo-Stalinists—than to pressure from the left—
the various progressive trends. And one must admit that the
leadership of the party has until now also been more suscep-
tible to influence from the right, as witness the 1968 decision
to send Warsaw Pact armies into Czechoslovakia. At the time
many people believed that this decision meant a radical shift
to the right which would be followed by a wave of persecution
inside the USSR. But, as it turned out, our action in Czechoslovakia with all its unfortunate consequences did not in fact
signify any radical change in foreign or domestic policy—it
was a limited move falling short of what the neo-Stalinists
would have liked. Similarly, one cannot regard the regrettable
political trials of 1966–68 or the politically motivated repressive measures against certain individuals reported in the
*Chronicle of Current Events** as a decisive victory of the neo-
Stalinists. All such things are the result of the interaction of a
great many forces and influences. And although people subjected to administrative or judicial persecution because of
their political opinions will inevitably take a pessimistic view,
I cannot agree with those who declare that "all is lost," that
"by now nothing can help," that "the Stalinists have already
won," etc.

To some extent the moderate-conservative group has in
recent years tried to bring pressure to bear on the neo-Stalinists, and some of the most fanatical reactionaries were removed from the *apparat;* there were changes in the editorial
boards of *Kommunist* and *Molodaya Gvardia*, and some blatantly Stalinist works came under attack. However on the
whole, the "moderates" usually displayed a strange indecisive-
ness, an indulgence toward even the most brazen forays of
the neo-Stalinists. It was under pressure from the right that
the editorial board of *Novy Mir* was virtually broken up. A
most important determining factor in the activity of the
moderate-conservatives of all shades is the desire to avoid any

---

* A *samizdat* journal of the Soviet human rights movement containing
  information about political trials, extrajudicial persecution, political prisoners in jails and labor camps, and also about other
  samizdat works. Twenty-seven issues appeared regularly in Moscow between April 1968 and October 1972, when publication was
  suspended under KGB pressure. Publication was resumed in May
  1974, and five further issues reached the West during 1974.—
  Trans.

kind of crisis or open conflict and as far as possible to maintain or in any case to prolong the none-too-stable equilibrium which now exists in the top ranks of the party. They are therefore in no hurry to find now long overdue solutions for many economic and political problems, and some very crucial ones they simply try to ignore or hush up.

A third trend consists of what for convenience' sake may be called the "party-democrats." This is a left-wing group within the party which proceeds from a communist, Marxist-Leninist position. They too are very mixed in composition, subdividing into many different groups. Some are rather more moderate, focusing attention on only a limited number of contemporary problems. Others come forward with more radical proposals, sometimes using unnecessarily sharp and exaggerated language. The party-democrats as a whole are in favor not only of restoring but also of further developing Leninist norms in state and party life; they call for an unqualified condemnation of the Stalin cult and all its deplorable consequences. Marxism-Leninism, they argue, should still be the basis of our ideology and social science, but it must be developed in accordance with a changing social reality as well as achievements in science and technology. One of the fundamental demands of this trend is the need for a more extensive and consistent democratization of our party and public life. There must be greater freedom of speech, freedom of the press, freedom of assembly and organization; and freedom for science, scholarship, and the arts must be assured. Both within and outside the party, normal mechanisms must be created for the exchange of opinions, for discussion, for dialogue with dissidents. It is necessary to wage a determined struggle against bureaucracy in the party and state apparatus, purging them of functionaries who prove to be incapable of change. Wherever possible, central control should be relaxed and local initiative encouraged. There must be a vigorous campaign against corruption and abuses of various kinds. A law on the press should be passed, with provisions for minimal and only absolutely necessary restrictions, and censorship should be replaced by a more flexible form of party supervision over the printed word. In economics, they are in favor of a more consistent application of the principles of reform with a substantial increase in the production of consumer goods and an extension of the service sector. It is necessary, they argue, to develop the different forms of economic democracy, including workers' self-management, to extend the rights and responsibilities of the trade unions, and to put the principles of self-management into practice on the collective farms. There must be a change in the procedure for elections to the Soviets, by introducing an element of contest. Deputies should be made more responsible to their electors in order to strengthen the ties between the people and their representatives. The rights and responsibilities of the Union Republics ought to be increased to make democratic principles effective for the national minorities both large and small; there must be respect for their legitimate rights and avoidance of any kind of coercion. In particular it is necessary to solve the problem of the Soviet Germans, the Crimean Tatars, and also to put an end to political and other forms of discrimination against Soviet citizens of Jewish nationality. In foreign policy what is needed in their view is not only active opposition to imperialism and the threat of war, but also firmer adherence to the basic principles of peaceful coexistence. Support must be given to all progressive socialist and democratic movements as well as to the national-liberation struggle; more should be done, however, to counter extremist nationalist and chauvinist elements which often spring up within them. I consider myself to be a representative of this third trend and in what follows shall give a more detailed account of its platform as I understand it.

It must be said straightaway that at the moment it is evidently the weakest trend both within and outside the party. But all the same it is my firm belief that only this trend is capable of suggesting solutions to the urgent problems and difficulties that confront us in a form acceptable to the majority. I believe that it has been the most active in recent years in elaborating *positive* political and economic ideas, thereby voicing the interests of the majority of the Soviet intelligentsia and the most politically conscious and educated section of the working class.

The party-democrats are at present almost completely unrepresented in the highest organs of the party. However, it is likely that even on that level there are some who understand contemporary problems better than others and who in different circumstances and in another environment would be an important source of support. There are a good many sympathizers among officials of the party and state apparatus at all levels—particularly those relatively young ones who came into the *apparat* after the Twentieth and Twenty-second congresses.[8] At present the party-democrats can also count on considerable support from the scholarly community—philosophers, sociologists, historians, etc.—as well as from a section of the scientific and technical intelligentsia, some writers, and other people engaged in cultural activities. There are also certain groups belonging to this trend among the Old Bolsheviks, particularly those who returned from prison and exile after the death of Stalin. In the future it may well become very popular among students and young people.

One is bound to note a striking resemblance between this trend in our party and certain currents in the world communist movement—for example, in the Italian, Spanish, Australian, and certain other parties.

Looking ahead to the future potential of the party-democrats, one may dare to predict that in the course of the seventies they will gain very widespread support. It is not impossible that what today exists only as the sentiments of a minority will in the near future be transformed into a mass social movement. But will this movement be chaotic, disorganized, without a definite platform, and therefore extremely open to conservative-dogmatist criticism, as was the case in Czechoslovakia in 1968? Or will it in fact be coherent, well defined, sure of means and ends, and thus invulnerable? This to a large extent depends on the preparatory theoretical work going on at present.

Insofar as several different trends already exist within the party, a certain amount of inner-party conflict has become inevitable. Substantial disagreement about so many issues makes it impossible to avoid a clash. The neo-Stalinists are completely unreconciled to the decisions of the Twentieth and Twenty-second congresses, while, on the other hand, a large section of the party intelligentsia is striving to take them even further, determined at all costs to prevent a return to the procedures and dogmas of the Stalin period, which they believe would be disastrous for our party and for the whole communist movement. Clearly it is not a question of secondary problems but of the most basic aspects of ideology and policy. In effect this inner-party struggle is already under way and growing more intense, assuming a variety of different forms.

But the question arises, Is inner-party conflict permissible? How can it be reconciled with the need to preserve party unity?

Of course only incorrigible dogmatists can see some kind of incompatibility here. For any genuine Marxist, it is an elementary proposition that party unity can never be made into an absolute that excludes all discussion or conflict. When it is a question of fundamentals, of disagreements about the most important problems of party policy, conflict is necessary, and it is the basic way of overcoming obstacles to the party's development and of achieving a new, more durable unity.[9] Party unity is not an end in itself; what is important is unity of outlook, since the party is first and foremost an organization of like-minded persons. However, this unanimity cannot be attained by directives issued from above, but only through the interplay and clash of opposing points of view. It must be based on principle, whereas the neo-Stalinists advocate blind discipline and unquestioning submission to the leadership, which contradicts the essence of the Leninist interpretation of party unity. Lenin was never in favor of unity and discipline in the party at any price, regardless of the underlying principles involved. He himself was always passionately opposed to unity with opportunists, constantly urging the importance of fighting them and insisting on the need to disassociate oneself from them both on the ideological plane and, if need be, organizationally. When it came to those who perverted Marxism, Lenin called for a decisive struggle, whether or not they constituted the majority or minority in the leadership of the party. But no brand of opportunism or pseudo-Marxism has ever done so much harm to the world socialist and communist movement as Stalinism. And now neo-Stalinism is also inflicting enormous damage on our movement throughout the world.

It is no secret that Leninist views on unity and discipline in the party were misrepresented in the Stalin era. During our party's first years of existence, Lenin proposed that safeguards should be provided by putting procedures for debate within the party in the party rules. "The need for such a reform emerges clearly," wrote Lenin, "from all our experience of struggle after party congresses. What is called for is a provision in the party rules to protect the rights of any minority, in order thereby to do away with the perennial sources of contention, dissatisfaction, and irritation typical of the old underground revolutionary circles with their love of scandal and petty-minded squabbles; it must provide instead a channel for a dignified and proper debate about matters of conviction."[10] Lenin himself proposed at that time that there be the broadest guarantees "with respect to the publication of party literature, criticizing the work of central party institutions."[11] During the Prague Conference of the RSDLP, it was again Lenin who rejected in no uncertain terms a resolution condemning struggles between various groups and trends within the party. "It is impossible to condemn inner-party conflict as such," Lenin declared. "We must only oppose unprincipled struggle. For to condemn struggle as such between groups would mean to condemn the struggle of the Bolsheviks against the Liquidators."*[12]

In his writings Lenin very precisely defined the permissible boundaries for struggle in a revolutionary party. They should include the sphere of ideas and convictions and there could be argument about the most expedient ways and means of revolutionary and political activity; but struggle must not serve as an obstacle to united action by the party. In other words, the minority in the party, given its own opinion on some problem or other, must submit to the decision of the majority when it comes to practical work. Of course, as Lenin pointed out, not all views can be tolerated within a communist party. Every member must accept its programme and rules. However, within the limits determined by the party programme, there must be wide freedom for party members to criticize and discuss any matter, including the activities of the highest party organs. "The principle of democratic centralism and of autonomy of local organizations," wrote Lenin, "means nothing less than full freedom of criticism at all

* *Liquidators* was the pejorative name applied to a trend within social democracy that advocated the creation of a mass party through work in the State Duma, trade unions, workers' educational associations, etc. and the abandonment of illegal activity.—Trans.

levels, provided the unity needed to achieve a certain aim is not thereby disrupted; any criticism that undermines or impedes unity in a course of action decided on by the party is inadmissible."[13] Defining the idea of discipline in a truly revolutionary party, Lenin said: *"Unity of action, freedom of discussion and criticism*—this is our definition. This is the only discipline worthy of a democratic party of the leading class."[14] "Without freedom of discussion and criticism, the proletariat does not accept unity of action."[15]

In their opposition to legitimate forms of struggle against neo-Stalinism, dogmatists today still go on quoting the resolution of the Tenth Party Congress on party unity. But this resolution was adopted as a *temporary* measure during the emergency situation of 1921.

A quick glance through the first two volumes of the collected *Resolutions and Decrees of Congresses, Conferences, and Plenary Sessions of the CPSU* is enough to show how many very remarkable decrees and resolutions on the development of inner-party democracy were adopted at the beginning of the twenties, only to be completely forgotten today. But *these* resolutions were intended not as temporary measures but as a long-term basis for party life. Yet it is the resolution of the Tenth Congress on unity in the party, regarded by the congress as an emergency measure, as a temporary violation of certain important principles of inner-party democracy, that continues to be regarded as valid although the conditions that gave rise to it have long since disappeared.

In itself, the fact of adoption by the Tenth Party Congress of a special resolution on unity in the party temporarily forbidding the creation of factions and groups based on different political platforms, shows that up until the Tenth Congress factions and groups were not formally prohibited in our communist party. And indeed, we know that such factions as the Left Communists, Democratic Centralists, Workers' Opposition, and others had a completely legal existence within our party. Although Lenin condemned certain irregular methods used by the Left Communists in their protest against the Brest peace, he did not question the right of this faction to exist and agreed to elections being held for the Seventh Party Congress on the basis of different platforms.

Moreover, even the elections of delegates to the Tenth Congress were held on the basis of different political platforms, as decided by a majority vote of the Central Committee on the proposal of Lenin.[16]

Although constantly citing the resolution of the Tenth Congress, our dogmatists never refer to the full text or to Lenin's commentaries on it. Yet in the resolution it is pointed out that while firmly "rejecting unbusinesslike and factional criticism, the party will experiment with new methods and use all means at its disposal to continue its tireless struggle against bureaucracy and to extend democracy and spontaneity." In the resolution on unity there is the extremely important Point 4, in which it is stated: "It is necessary for every party organization to keep a strict watch to ensure that the absolutely necessary criticism of the party's failings, all analyses of its general line, reports on its practical activity, all checks on the execution of its decisions and methods of correcting errors, etc.—should be referred for discussion not to groups formed on some platform or other, but to all party members. To this end the Congress orders the regular publication of a *Discussion Bulletin* as well as special collections of materials on these subjects. Any person coming forward with criticism must bear in mind that the party is surrounded by enemies, but at the same time through his direct contribution to Soviet and party work, he must strive to correct the party's mistakes in practice." Explaining to delegates of the Tenth Congress the necessity for forbidding all factions and platforms in the party, Lenin stressed insistently that it was only a temporary measure, dictated by the particularly difficult position of the party after the civil war. "The banning of opposition in the party," said Lenin, "results from the political logic of the *present* moment. . . . *Right now* we can do without an opposition, comrades, *it's not the time for it!* . . . This is demanded by the objective moment, it is no use complaining. . . . The *present* moment is one at which the non-party mass is subject to the kind of petty-bourgeois wavering which in the *present* economic position of Russia is inevitable. We must remember that the internal danger is in certain respects greater than that which was threatened by Denikin and Yudenich,* and we must show unity not only of a

---

* White (anti-Bolshevik) generals during the civil war.—Trans.

nominal but of a deep, far-reaching kind. To create such unity we cannot do without a resolution like this."[17]

Lenin made a point of saying that the resolution adopted by the congress should not be given a broader validity, that it could not even be binding on the party during the elections for the next congress. When Ryazanov* suggested that elections to party congresses according to political platforms be banned altogether, Lenin absolutely rejected this proposal. "I believe," he declared, "that Comrade Ryazanov's proposal is, however unfortunate that may be, unrealizable. . . . *The present Congress cannot make binding decisions that would in any way affect elections to the next congress.* If circumstances provoke fundamental disagreements, how can one forbid their submission to the judgment of the party as a whole? We cannot!"[18]

Lenin did not deny that the resolution on party unity, adopted by the Tenth Congress, restricted certain elementary norms of party democracy, but it was necessary in view of the emergency situation. Thus, for example, there is a point in the resolution giving the Central Committee the right, by means of a two-thirds vote of the members of its plenum, to transfer a member of the Central Committee to candidate membership or even to exclude him from the CC and from the party. Clarifying this point of the resolution, Lenin said: "That the Central Committee, elected by the Congress, could have the right to expel its own members has nothing whatsoever to do with democracy or centralism. . . . The Congress elects the Central Committee, and by this it expresses the highest trust, bestowing the leadership on it. But that the Central Committee could have such a right in relation to its members is something our party has never ever tolerated. It is an extreme measure, specially adopted in consciousness of the dangers of our situation."[19]

It is important to note also that, while making the proposal at the congress that factions and groups be banned, Lenin in no way demanded that their leaders and members be compelled to renounce their views or the right to defend them

---

* Marxist theorist who later founded the Marx-Engels Institute and headed it until 1930. Implicated in the Menshevik trial, he was expelled from the party in 1931 and disappeared during the purges.—Trans.

in the press. He found it necessary even in conditions of an emergency to retain specific mechanisms in the party for dialogue with dissidents. It was still impossible, according to Lenin, to publish opposition views in pamphlets printed in a quarter of a million copies. But it was quite a different matter to do so in special publications—collections of materials for limited circulation among party members—and he urged that this be done.[20]

It is important to note that as early as 1923, when discussion again arose about a number of important questions of principle, it became obvious that no serious discussion was possible without the creation of some sort of temporary groups. Therefore even then the resolution of the Tenth Congress, although not revoked, was applied only in a very limited way. Thus, for example, on December 14, 1923, *Pravda* published an article by the prominent figure in party and government N. Krylenko, entitled "The Permissible Limits for Groups within the Party." In this article Krylenko wrote: "To reduce the whole of democracy inside the party only to the right of separate speeches by individual, isolated comrades means to abolish workers' democracy as such in the party. For even within a united party one cannot conceive of real democracy where there is no opportunity for joint action by individual comrades in defense of their opinions. Once people have really been given the right to stand up for their views, they cannot be forbidden to agree beforehand to speak on any given platform at any given place and at any given time. . . . The right to unite according to platforms is an inalienable right of inner-party democracy, without which democracy itself is turned into an empty shell. . . . The limits must be drawn at the point when an individual group, united on some particular platform, begins to set itself up in opposition to the party as a whole and imposes its own group discipline, different from that binding on the party, and lays down beforehand how its members must behave in deciding questions at general party meetings. This is inadmissible, and must be ruthlessly countered and eradicated in the party. We may call this stage that of 'inadmissible groupings.' "

In the further development of inner-party discussions in the twenties, it became apparent that on the whole no serious discussion was possible without the creation of groupings, albeit temporary ones, based on some political platform or other. Of course a party must close ranks at critical moments, shelving all disagreements for a time, as happened in 1921. During the bitter political crisis that followed the civil war, there was hunger and devastation, a discontented peasantry and an evident weakening and even numerical decrease of the proletariat in the most important industrial centers of the country. The very existence of the dictatorship of the proletariat and the primacy of the party as the leading force were threatened.

However, in normal political circumstances where there is no danger of a violent overthrow of the dictatorship of the proletariat, our party, like any healthy political organism, cannot exist without reasonably free discussion, without inner-party conflict, carried on within prescribed limits and, consequently, without the emergence of various inner-party tendencies and groupings.

From what has been said it is perfectly clear that the resolution of the Tenth Party Congress cannot be a basis for life within the party today. For our party now operates in an entirely different social environment from that of 1921. Open conflict between trends within the party may threaten one leader or another, or even a group in the leadership, but not the party as a whole or the future of socialism in our country. Moreover, such a struggle is entirely necessary for the revitalization of the party, in order to cleanse it of alien elements. Such an enormous burden of error has accumulated in the work of the party leadership since the death of Lenin that no analysis or cure is possible without open political discussion. Disagreement on many fundamental questions of principle is today more intense than at the time of Brest-Litovsk, and it would be illusory to believe we can dispense with the formation of various different trends and political platforms. Such trends already exist, and the platforms embodying them are in the process of taking shape. Conflict is inevitable, and our only concern should be that it take place in full view and with the participation of the whole party, without abuses of power by those in authority.

IV

Political Trends Outside the Party. Nationalist Trends and Groups

The terrible crimes of the Stalin period were accompanied by a considerable degeneration of the party *apparat* and the development, on one hand, of the most extreme forms of bureaucratic centralism, and on the other, of political passivity in the party and among the people. The most important tenets of Marxism-Leninism were distorted and transformed into empty dogma with the result that theory, cut off from real life, stagnated. The process of liquidating the grievous consequences of the Stalin cult and restoring health to the party had been extremely slow and inconsistent; there have been dangerous symptoms of a revival of certain elements of Stalinism along with persistent attempts at his rehabilitation which meet no serious resistance from the party leadership and are actively supported in various middle layers of the *apparat*. The party has no leaders who are genuinely popular and close to the masses, nor has it any theoreticians capable of giving a new impulse to Marxism-Leninism. All these and many other factors have in the past ten to fifteen years led to a decline in the ideological influence and authority both of Marxism-Leninism and of the party.

Our party grows numerically; however, its influence in society and particularly on the minds of young people and the intelligentsia is decreasing. Yet the young are the future of our country and society, while the intelligentsia is the most rapidly growing social group, both in numbers and in status.

Present-day party propaganda is based on a stultified, dogmatic, distorted and highly oversimplified version of Marxism-Leninism. In this form, the ideology of our party can hardly provide an answer to the many complex problems of contemporary life, and so for most thinking people it cannot serve as a guide to action. Of course our propaganda still exerts considerable influence on the ill-informed. But even this is continually diminishing. The enormous and costly party propaganda machine increasingly works in a vacuum, often leaving no trace in the minds of Soviet citizens.[1]

The various attempts to suppress dissent, more and more frequent in recent years, have even further reduced the ideological influence of the party, lowered the prestige of the present leadership, exacerbated disagreement within it, and ultimately undermined the party's capacity to play a leading role in the government of the country. It was inevitable that we should witness the growth of widespread sentiments running directly counter to the aims of party propaganda. These attitudes reflect disappointment with the specific forms of present-day Soviet socialism and distrust of the party's propaganda and leadership. Among the masses there is a growing mood of conscious political indifference, side by side with a heightened interest on the part of some people in religion and Western propaganda; at the same time a crudely mercenary spirit and a crass consumerism are becoming widespread.

In the last few years these various moods among the masses have provided the ground for the appearance of several explicit political trends and groups, in what is now a continuing process. As a general rule, they proceed from a socialist viewpoint but try to interpret socialism and communism in their own way. For the most part they exist and are evolving *outside* the party, though they have their supporters inside it as well. Their development is largely independent of Marxism-Leninism, although some of them do not reject many of its most important propositions. Nearly all of them are oppositional in character, but on the whole it is a question of loyal opposition involving only ideas and convictions.

These diverse groupings—westernizers, ethical socialists, Christian socialists, legalists—are indeed a reflection of certain specific features of life in the Soviet Union. But they also mirror various movements now widespread in the world outside, everywhere confronting each other in acute ideological struggle. To some extent the new currents in the USSR are also a revival of certain prerevolutionary political ideas.

The largest trend consists of what may be called "westernizers." It is rather widely represented among scientists, scholars, writers, etc., and among some young people. The representatives of this trend are firmly opposed to dogmatism and Stalinism and try to reinterpret the history of Soviet society. But they fail to draw a proper distinction between Stalinism and the Soviet system as a whole, between Stalinism and Marxism. The rise of Stalinism is often viewed by them as something that followed logically from Marxism-Leninism, as a natural development of the dictatorship of the proletariat and the October Revolution. The postrevolutionary *temporary* limitations on freedom of the press, freedom of organization, direct suffrage, and other attributes of democracy, are regarded by them as inseparable from the dictatorship of the proletariat and Soviet power, so that degeneration is therefore inevitable. Isolated and regrettable excesses of the first years of the Revolution are thought to be its principal and most typical features.

Thus the westernizer attack on Stalinism is not based on Marxism-Leninism but is rather similar to the position adopted by certain groups of liberal intellectuals in the West. Our westernizers are clearly influenced by such modern theories as that of the postindustrial society, the new capitalist revolution, the managerial revolution, and also by the notion of "people's," or planned and controlled, capitalism. The westernizers have also been affected by new trends in social-democracy abroad.

Most westernizers are opposed to capitalism in its classical form and condemn the selfishness inherent in private ownership of the means of production. But many of them believe that contemporary capitalism has altered in a fundamental way, that regulated capitalism has many positive features and that we can learn something from it. They lose sight of the fact that the Western democratic states are in fact our political and ideological adversaries, they ignore or minimize the various symptoms of spiritual crisis in the capitalist countries—the loss of ideals and the collapse of moral standards. What attracts them are many of the charac- teristics of bourgeois democracy: freedom of speech, freedom of assembly and organization, freedom of movement, and the multiparty system. They also are impressed by the material security typical of Western countries, the appreciable rise in the standard of living of industrial and office workers during the last decade, as well as the high salaries paid to the majority of scientists, engineers, doctors, and many other groups in the population. They note the rapid technical prog- ress and high quality and low price of consumer goods. In the view of the westernizers, the major capitalist countries are not "decaying," but in fact are developing very rapidly—leav- ing the socialist countries behind in many areas. A distinction is of course made between the different capitalist countries. From the point of view of the development of democracy, preference is given to countries such as France, England, Italy, Switzerland, and Sweden. And in recent years there has been increasing interest in an Eastern country—Japan. Many westernizers support the idea of "convergence" in some form or other, usually assuming it to mean our assimilation of the positive elements in the way of life and culture of the West- ern world. (Among young people this sometimes finds a more primitive outlet—in a passion for Western films, dances, magazines, consumer goods, fashions, behavior, etc.) Al- though most westernizers use socialist terminology, in fact they start from the premise that Marxism-Leninism is already obsolete, bearing little relation to present-day developments in science, technology, and society in general. It is not, there- fore, a question of adapting Marxism-Leninism, since that doctrine can no longer, it is thought, be the basic method for resolving social conflict, and some new, more contemporary ideological theory must be found. The westernizers on the whole have no great hope that their point of view will be adopted by the Communist Party, and they do not believe in the possibility of the party's regeneration. Their ideal is a multiparty system.

As a group the westernizers are extremely heterogeneous. Some are in the first instance concerned about their *own* freedom, their own comfort, their own right to pleasure and travel. Giving little thought to the fate of the people, they display an egotism very much like that of the petty bourgeoisie in the West.

There are also extreme groups among the westernizers who are almost apologists for capitalism, openly admiring its virtues while disparaging or denying altogether the achievements of socialism. One of these groups calls itself the "Februarists" (i.e., they are in favor of the February and against the October Revolution). Another group calling themselves "democrats" have distributed a document in which they praise the great achievements of capitalism and maintain that "Eastern socialism" has nothing at all to its credit.[2] Thus we have an extraordinary paradox: the most extreme groups among intelligentsia and young people in the socialist countries, rejecting Marxism, take contemporary capitalism as their ideal, while their opposite numbers in the West denounce contemporary capitalism for its manipulation of people under the guise of democracy, and come out on the streets of Paris and Rome bearing portraits of Stalin, Trotsky, and Mao Tsetung.[3]

However, the overwhelming majority of westernizers have little in common with these extremists. Most of them come from that part of the intelligentsia which for many reasons is dissatisfied with the present situation in our country but sees no alternative to the "barracks" form of socialism other than the development of bourgeois-democratic freedoms. They make no distinction between genuine Marxism and the vulgarized form of it preached by *Pravda* and *Kommunist*. This attitude finds expression in a typical westernizer document by a well-known author (wrongly identified as Academician Varga), called *The Russian Road to Socialism*, which circulated widely in *samizdat* several years ago. There are also westernizing elements in Academician Sakharov's *Progress, Coexistence, and Intellectual Freedom*,[4] though of course the contents of this very interesting and important work can by no means be reduced to them alone.

Among the nonparty trends in our society, the westernizers are extremely significant and are growing rapidly, a process that is receiving remarkably little attention. There are many reasons for the spread of westernizer attitudes. In the first place, an increasing number of honest people are rejecting dogmatism, bureaucracy, and conservatism, whether it is a Stalinist or more moderate version. The extreme hostility felt by the majority of the intelligentsia toward all bureaucratic forms of socialism and perversions of Marxism-Leninism is transferred to the doctrine as such, not least because our propaganda constantly asserts that our present-day bureaucratic socialism completely conforms to the true scientific model. (The same lesson is hammered home by Western propaganda.) Secondly, the Soviet intelligentsia has been greatly impressed by the extraordinarily rapid scientific and technological progress made by Western countries during the postwar period. Although limitations on intellectual freedom do exist in capitalist countries, they bear no comparison—in the view of many of our scientists and writers—with those restrictions in our country that originated in the Stalin period and are still in force today. The growth of westernizer attitudes is also encouraged by different kinds of scientific and cultural exchanges and tourism. Our prolonged state of isolation more and more is becoming a thing of the past, on the whole a positive and progressive change. Without the growth of economic, cultural, and scientific links abroad, no country can count on rapid economic or cultural progress.

In present conditions westernizer political views also are sustained by intensive propaganda coming from the West, which in many cases achieves its purpose. The average Soviet citizen receives only inadequate and superficial information about all that is going on in the world. No educated person could possibly be satisfied, and the Soviet intelligentsia has a real hunger—there is no other word for it—for information. Our condition is such that everyone in the whole of this vast country of ours reads virtually the same bad and boring daily newspaper (though it comes out in different versions), listens to the same radio, and watches the same television programs. In the absence of any other intellectual sustenance, starved of official information on many topics of prime interest (and often denied truthful information of any kind), millions and millions of Soviet citizens tune in every day to the many Western radio stations which give them the news they crave but slanted in the way that one would expect.[5]

We publish many books by Western authors, scores of

Western films are shown on our screens, and Western plays are put on in our theaters. This can only be welcomed. Cultural exchange, as we all know, is reciprocal, and it also allows Soviet books, films, and plays to appear in the Western "cultural market." We have no means of judging the impact of Soviet propaganda in Western countries. But we can see only too well that here, on home territory, our stultified propaganda leaves people quite cold; it is so drab and old-fashioned in both form and content that it cannot compete with the flow of information and ideas from the West. It is significant that such magazines as *America, England,* and *France,** distributed here in small editions, are sold out in a matter of hours. And if there were no restrictions on publication and sale, their circulation would no doubt greatly exceed that of *Soviet Union* and *Ogonyok,* not to speak of *Kommunist* or *Agitator,* a substantial number of which would remain unsold were it not for the system of compulsory subscription.† Thus we see that as dogmatism and Stalinism continually lose ground, a large part of our young people and intelligentsia are joining the ranks of the westernizers—not least because of the favorable picture of its way of life given by the West in its propaganda to socialist countries. What it amounts to is that a hidebound form of Marxism is competing with various ideologies originating in the "bourgeois-democratic" West for the minds of our people on our own territory. The left-wing Marxist groups and the party-democrats on the other hand, deprived of access to the means of mass communication, have no way of reaching the majority of their fellow citizens. In the long run this is a very dangerous situation. Our dogmatists and bureaucrats see a solution in the jamming of Western broadcasts, the artificial restriction of tourism in both directions, a reduction in the number of people allowed to go abroad on scientific or other business, and a general cutting down of cultural and scholarly contacts. A senior official from the Political Department of the army recently gave a lecture in which he urged that the number of

* Journals published in Russian by the information services of the three countries concerned and circulated in the USSR in accordance with cultural agreements on a reciprocal basis.—Trans.

† Party members may be virtually forced to buy or subscribe to various publications.—Trans.

international industrial exhibitions in the USSR be reduced. But this approach is harmful and unrealistic. In our technological age, Western propaganda will always find a way to penetrate the USSR. Besides, in limiting contacts with the West, we would do enormous damage to the development of Soviet science, technology, and cultural life in general. Therefore the most effective way to counter the influence of Western propaganda would be to apply the principles of real socialist democracy, develop Marxism-Leninism in a creative manner, and wage a determined struggle against Stalinism, bureaucracy, and dogmatism, while at the same time assimilating some of the many attractive technical and cultural values of the West. Only in this way can there be a successful development of socialist society, of socialist and communist ideology and culture.

The trend that I shall refer to as "ethical socialism" is less widespread among the intelligentsia. Its exponents have been influenced by the ethical teaching of Tolstoy and Gandhi, and also certain social-democratic leaders who have maintained that morality is the basis of social development and has a decisive effect on economics, politics, and culture. They are passionate in their denunciation of all the abuses of the Stalin period and also have attempted a reappraisal of the first years of Soviet power, condemning all manifestations of revolutionary violence. In their opinion the central core of socialism is not the relations of production but rather the universal observance of certain ethical norms. If these standards do not prevail, there can be no question of true socialism. Revolutionary violence in their view always does more harm than good.

Ethical socialism in a rather peculiar way often overlaps with the westernizer trend. Many intellectuals condemn the past, criticize the present, and are attracted by the good features of contemporary capitalism, but when it comes to outlining some positive programme, they do not hold up the Western countries as an example. Instead they try to elaborate various models of ethical socialism. This is evidently so in the case of the "representatives of the Estonian intelligentsia" who sent an anonymous letter to Academician Sakharov. The authors of the letter argue that the political cataclysms of the twentieth century have resulted in the demise of Christianity as a basic ideological force and brought about the destruction of its moral values. But the new materialist philosophy could be no substitute for the values that had been lost. A moral vacuum was created, which ultimately led to all the excesses of Stalinism.[6] Therefore we now have the task of creating a new moral and philosophical teaching capable of guiding millions of people in their life and conduct.

Another programmatic document of ethical socialism is the essay by Lev Ventsov* called "Think!" The basic conflict in our society, he claims, is not one of "political doctrines, ideology, parties and classes, but something quite different, much more deep-rooted, more deep-rooted than anything else—it is a conflict between truth and lying as a matter of expedience; between honesty and self-seeking of the worst kind; between a sense of justice, warm human sympathy, and cruelty rabid in its cowardly vindictiveness; between a sense of law and the total lack of it; and finally between an awareness of personal dignity and a feeling of one's own insignificance raised to a principle of life. This historical clash of values takes place inside every individual, and everybody who has the capacity to do so is faced by the need to make his own choice. The scales of history are tipped by all those individual choices. It is nonsense to deny that the fate of the country and the world depends on the behavior of all the people who inhabit it. It is better not to take refuge in mendacious fantasy but rather to understand the measure of one's own personal responsibility . . . the conflict centers on the very foundations of morality and its essence can no longer be disguised by an ideological myth (as was the case in Stalin's day) nor obscured by incidental circumstances. In our present-day conditions, only a very benighted person can fail to distinguish truth from lies. By the same token anyone who is unable to recognize the roots of social evil today must be totally devoid of moral sense. The basic humanitarian values—truth and good—now stand clearly revealed for everyone to see if only because the regime as a whole is today no longer capable even of pretending to lay claim to them."[7]

In some of his writing, it seems to me, even Solzhenitsyn comes close to ethical socialism. Certainly what some of the

* Pseudonym of the philosopher Boris Shragin, who emigrated to the West in 1974.—Trans.

characters in *The Cancer Ward* say about ethical or moral socialism is not accidental.[8] Grigory Pomerants also expresses similar ideas in some of his essays (see "Man of Air," "The Moral Aspect of the Historical Personality," etc.).[9]

One cannot deny the importance of the problems raised by ethical socialism. Marxism-Leninism has in fact paid too little attention in the past to the ethical side of its teaching, to the clarification of its own ethical concepts. We have tended to have an oversimplified view of ethical questions, reflected particularly in the well-known formula, "Everything is moral that helps the revolution." But it soon became apparent that no stable ethical system could be built on the basis of such a formula. Who is to determine whether one action or another is useful for the revolution? And which interests of the revolution are relevant here—its immediate interests or its long-term ones? Lack of consideration for the moral aspect of revolutionary activity frequently led us to adopt the principle that "the end justifies the means" and to indulge in unwarranted violence. Rhetoric about lofty aims often in practice merely served to cloak the very base ones of certain individuals and cliques. Disregard for the ethical side of socialism has led to a number of distortions that for a long time were not exceptional but rather the norm of life in our society: failure to respect the interests of the individual disguised by fine words about the interests of the collective, a peculiar kind of party egotism that illegitimately identifies the interests of the party elite with those of the party as a whole (and then the interests of the party with those of the whole people, and the interests of the Soviet people with the interests of the whole of mankind), total indifference to certain elementary standards of justice, the restriction of people's spiritual freedom, the notion of people only as cogs in some kind of complicated social machine. All such perversions of socialism have done our movement and our country enormous political and moral damage. It would, however, be quite wrong on this account to jettison Marxism altogether. It would also be a great mistake to imagine that Marxism-Leninism no longer offers a basis for the development of a new system of socialist ethics capable of bringing about the general moral and cultural enlightenment of our people.

One characteristic feature of our cultural life has been

the rising interest among a considerable section of our intelligentsia in religion and the church, church history, and theological problems in general. It is not just that it has suddenly become fashionable to collect icons. We hear powerful voices demanding an improvement in the wretched condition to which the church is at present reduced. Many distinguished representatives of the intelligentsia are outspoken in their protest about the wholesale destruction of church buildings that took place not only in the early years of the Revolution and in Stalin's time, but also in the first half of the sixties. An intellectual who is a believer no longer arouses scorn but is more likely to inspire a certain respect. Religious attitudes are also to some extent spreading among young people.

There are many reasons for what would seem to be such an unexpected rebirth of religious feeling. Of course, for a great number of people an interest in the history of religion and the church expresses nothing more than a natural curiosity about their nation's cultural history, in which religion and the church were once a major element. Many others, though in no way religious themselves, view complete freedom of conscience as an important part of any real democracy. And if they protest against the many violations of freedom of conscience that still occur, it is out of democratic rather than religious conviction.

Naturally enough the church tries to take advantage of the disillusionment with former ideals experienced by part of our intelligentsia and young people. In so far as religion is the only permitted alternative ideology, it serves as a refuge for many oppositionally minded people. In the past, religion had a variety of functions; apart from giving solace to believers, it also played a social role, regulating relations between people and providing a channel of communication. Several of these roles are still relevant in our society—unfortunately we again have the sort of gulf between society and the individual that formerly prompted many people to turn to religion. A great number of people still feel the same need for consolation which, together with the craving for contact, forms the basis of religious feeling. Very many individuals, because of frustration in their lives, illness, hardship, or the loss of loved ones, seek relief not in political or social activity but in religion.

While the overwhelming majority of educated and thinking people certainly cannot regard the Bible and other such concrete expressions of religious belief as anything other than collections of myths rather like those of ancient Greece (this is evidently the reason for the "crisis of the churches" about which so much is heard in the West today), there is nonetheless a growing interest among part of our intelligentsia in the ethical side of different religious teachings. Furthermore many people see the church as a custodian of certain national traditions. The idea of God and the soul is felt to be of great philosophical and moral significance.[10]

This revival of religious sentiments among the intelligentsia is also a factor in the emergence of small groups and organizations advocating what they call "Christian socialism." (Many analogous groups and movements exist today both in Western capitalist countries and in countries of the third world. Of course in the East we find a peculiar blend of socialist ideas with religious systems other than Christianity.) Evidently the Social-Christian Party formed in Leningrad several years ago was an organization of precisely this kind. Its programme has not become available, but we do know about the very grim fate of this group—most of its leaders are now in prison. Recently the well-known advocate of Christian socialism in Moscow, Krasnov-Levitin, was arrested on the basis of highly questionable accusations. "I firmly believe," he wrote in his essay "At the Hour of Dawn," "that a powerful religious and social movement will arise leading to the nation's moral regeneration. This great moral upsurge can come about only as the result of a movement that will embrace all layers of society and give birth to a spiritual revolution throughout the world. It will burst forth and will transform the face of the earth. . . . Then we shall see the fulfillment of the prophetic words of Karl Kautsky, who defined socialism as organization in the sphere of industry and anarchy in the sphere of ideology." In another essay, Krasnov-Levitin wrote, "I am convinced, that the last word of Holy Russia belongs to Christian populism."

One must certainly mention among all the new trends the appearance of several groups (or people acting individually) which may be called the "legalists" (sometimes they are referred to as the "constitutionalists"). If the ethical socialists place prime emphasis on the development of moral consciousness and the creation of a new system of ethics, then the legalists see it as their main task to foster a sense of law in our society and particularly among the leadership. It is more than a question of familiarizing people with existing Soviet laws—this is now done through many official channels, including the mass circulation magazine *Man and Law,* which has been coming out in recent years. The legalists aim to bring about reforms in Soviet legislation, urging the removal of discrepancies between various laws and particularly between the Constitution and certain other legislative enactments (there is, for example, a clear contradiction between the Constitution and Article 190(1) of the Criminal Code passed in 1966).* Soviet society, as the legalists justly observe, is notable for its extremely poorly developed sense of law. Major areas of social life are not covered by special legal regulations. Thus, for example, to this day we have no press law, although its importance and the need for it were proclaimed in one of the decrees of the Soviet government signed by Lenin a few days after the October Revolution. It was only several years ago that basic legislation was passed on prisons, camps, and places of preliminary detention, i.e., the whole of what we generally refer to as the penal system. Needless to say, the legalists demand that all aspects of life in our society should be regulated in the same way. In 1967, for instance, one of the groups of legalists gathered signatures to a letter calling for a special law on the press.

Taking advantage of people's ignorance, certain of our authorities often flout even those laws and instructions that do exist. Numerous infringements of the law have been committed in the course of the political trials of recent years. In cases involving the use of psychiatry as an instrument of political persecution, there have been frequent violations of the existing directives on compulsory commitment and the procedure for psychiatric examination. The legalists regard the fight against such abuses as a central part of their activity. They also feel it is most important to make the United Nations Covenants on human rights as well known as possible.

For several years one of the legalist groups has been

---

* The "systematic dissemination of fabrications known to be false discrediting the Soviet political and social system."—Trans.

openly putting out a collection called *Texts from* Samizdat *Devoted to Social Problem*s. The editor's name, address, and telephone number are given on the cover. Recently, in November 1970, Academician Sakharov lent his authoritative support to the legalists when he became a founding member of the Human Rights Committee.[11] Of course one can only wish this committee success in its activity. But the role of law should not be exaggerated or turned into some kind of absolute. The campaign for strict observance of law and legislative reform is only one aspect of the struggle for democratization.

One trend has occupied a special place during the last six years—it is associated with the names of Grigorenko, Yakir, Litvinov, Bogaraz, Gorbanevskaya, Krasin, Yacobson, and several scores of their friends and people with similar views. There are possibly also several hundred or more sympathizers. The group began to be active after the Sinyavsky-Daniel trial* which aroused disapproval and anger among a large number of writers and scientists, as was reflected in the letters of protest against the trial signed by hundreds of people. The most vehement objections were expressed in the documents put out by several circles of young people and intellectuals, some of whom demonstrated on Pushkin Square December 5, 1966, demanding the observation of the Constitution and freedom for Sinyavsky and Daniel. Subsequent protests against the trial of Khaustov and Bukovsky (in 1967) and of A. Ginzburg, Galanskov, Lashkova, and Dobrovolsky (1968) led to the unification of several opposition circles into a distinctive movement with certain observable elements of organization.

However, emphasis has always been placed on functioning openly, legally, and not underground in the organization of demonstrations (on August 25, 1968, as a protest against the invasion of Czechoslovakia, and the yearly gatherings on Pushkin Square on Constitution Day), in the regular "publication" of the typescript journal *The Chronicle of Current Events*, in the organization of material help for victims of

* February 10–14, 1966. Two unusual features of this trial were that for the first time in Soviet history writers were tried *for what they had written* and, even more remarkable, that they refused to plead guilty.—Trans.

judicial and administrative persecution, and in meetings to plan actions and draft documents.

After the arrest of Grigorenko,* the most active members of this movement decided to take one more step toward formal organization by creating the Initiative Group for the Defense of Human Rights in the USSR. One of its documents states that: "The aim of the group is indicated by its name— the defense of human rights in the USSR. . . . Calling ourselves the 'Initiative Group,' we had something else in mind as well: without preliminary permission, to assert our right to free association. This is in accordance with the Universal Declaration of Human Rights adopted by the United Nations and is not incompatible with the Constitution of the USSR."

The ideological platform of this movement is extremely heterogeneous. Attracted by the possibility of real action, people of very different views joined it, although sometimes only for a short while; it includes both party-democrats and those who openly proclaim their opposition to Leninism and the Communist Party. It has attracted a few ethical socialists, as well as a certain number of Christian socialists and even some legalists.

The first programmatic documents were written very much under the influence of Grigorenko—the terminology was basically Marxist but at the same time reminiscent of certain documents and declarations made by the anarcho-communists of 1917–20. In various letters and appeals signed by Grigorenko we can see not only a vigorous protest against Stalinism in all its forms, but also a number of clearly anarchist proposals. There is the suggestion, for example, that because of their bureaucratic nature, almost all state organizations and institutions be immediately replaced by different forms of public control, a reform that, according to Grigorenko, is even possible in the Soviet army. He also advocates complete abolition of all organs of state security, which would then make possible the creation of necessary guarantees for full freedom of speech, freedom of the press,

---

* General Grigorenko was arrested in May 1969 in connection with his activities on behalf of the Crimean Tatars. After being confined for five years in psychiatric hospitals, he was released in June 1974.—Trans.

and freedom of organization. Unfortunately these documents bear witness not only to good intentions, but also to an extreme radicalism, a "leftism" resembling that of certain contemporary left-wing groups in the West; they also reflect a very superficial knowledge of the basic tenets of Marxism-Leninism or the social sciences in general. As a result Grigorenko and his friends have inevitably tended toward patent exaggeration, typical of any extremist opposition trend.[12]

With the arrest of Grigorenko and the death of Kosterin,* Marxist terminology almost disappeared from the documents of this movement, and it began to draw nearer to some of the trends described above—ethical socialism and legalism—while still retaining its own identity by virtue of a greater activism. "The Initiative Group," declares one of its statements written in May 1970, "is not engaged in politics. We are not proposing any positive solutions in the sphere of government. We only say: 'Refrain from breaking your own laws!' We have no policies of our own, but we cannot accept the punitive policy applied to dissenters. Opposition to lawlessness—this is the task of the Initiative Group. . . . The Initiative Group is composed of people who share certain fundamental views. All of us—believers and nonbelievers, optimists and skeptics, communists and noncommunists— are united by a feeling of personal responsibility for everything that goes on in our country, by the conviction that the basis of normal life in society is the recognition of the absolute worth of the human personality."

It would be difficult to object to that particular statement. However, in other documents of this group, apart from the radical extremism and exaggeration already noted, we also find a certain lack of discrimination which tends to alarm a large part of our left intelligentsia, on the whole inclined toward a more moderate opposition.

It must be noted in conclusion that this movement, as the most radical and best organized of the opposition trends, has suffered more than any other in recent years from judicial and extrajudicial persecution, which I believe to be both unwarranted and illegal. Not only Grigorenko but the majority of its leaders have been or are in prison or exile or are

---

* Old Bolshevik who spent seventeen years in the camps. He died on November 16, 1968.—Trans.

confined in psychiatric hospitals where they are subjected to compulsory "treatment."

Particular mention must be made of the different kinds of national and nationalist movements and trends that in the last years have played an increasingly conspicuous role.[13]

The Soviet Union is a multinational state. Therefore relations between the different national groups have always been one of the most important factors in the life of our country, though they have not always been ideal. One could expect, however, that after half a century there would no longer be grounds for national and nationalist movements. And so the fact that there has been a growth of national tensions in the last years, with the beginning of centrifugal nationalist tendencies in some regions of the country, has created a state of affairs beyond the comprehension of many of our theorists and political leaders. Some of them propose to ignore these movements and tendencies, so very unexpected and extremely disagreeable. Others seek a solution in administrative measures or even persecution, which can only lead to a further aggravation of the problems. These bureaucrats, unwilling to recognize the existence of new developments in the multinational life of our country, continue to condemn the influence of bourgeois propaganda and the remnants of bourgeois nationalism. There are in fact many very complicated causes for the increasingly troubled relations between national groups in the USSR. I shall discuss only some of them.

a) In a number of regions, problems go back to the Stalin period and either have not been solved or are still fresh in the memory of the population. Although most of the groups disgraced and deported under Stalin have been allowed to return to their native territory, Stalin's criminal actions have left a residue of injured pride and defiant nationalism. This can be observed in Northern Ossetia in the relations between the Ingush and the Ossetians, in the Chechen-Ingush area in relations between Chechens and Russians, and in the Kabardin-Balkar area, in relations between the Kabardians and the Balkars. As already noted above, a number of nationalities, despite full rehabilitation, have to this day not been allowed to return to their home territory, which to a large extent destroys their life as a nation. This applies in the first instance to the Crimean Tatars, the majority of whom are still showing great determination in their efforts to return to the land of their ancestors.[14] Many Volga Germans are also demanding the restoration of their native region and former national autonomy. They are supported in this by other Soviet Germans who once regarded the former Volga German Republic as their national home.

The fact of the matter is that the terrible oppression of Stalin's despotism, when the charge of nationalism could mean a life sentence to Siberia or death in the camps, caused many national problems and grievances to be driven underground—they found no overt expression. It is hardly surprising, therefore, that the end of Stalin's brutal system should have inevitably resulted in the open manifestation of tensions that had been accumulating during the Stalin years.

b) Under Stalin, the rights of all the Union Republics were seriously violated. But a typical feature of the period was discrimination in the treatment of various nationalities, putting some in a more advantageous position than others. Therefore the end of Stalin's rule, and the abolition of certain national privileges along with it, gave rise to discontent in a number of regions. It was not difficult to foresee that the exposure of Stalin's crimes would produce different reactions among the Ingush and Ossetians than among the Georgians and Armenians. However, the bureaucratic system was unable to make provision for this difference in initial response. Expressions of resentment were crudely suppressed, and in Georgia it even came to bloodshed. All this gravely complicated national relations in the Caucasus, and for many Georgians the question of Stalin became one of national prestige, which only played into the hands of the large contingent of neo-Stalinists in the Georgian party and state apparatus.

c) The growth of nationalist moods among the many different peoples of the Soviet Union is inevitably exacerbated by general factors, such as the discontent of a majority of the intelligentsia with excessive centralization and bureaucracy in government, science, and culture, and the resentment of many collective farm, office, and industrial workers of a standard of living still inadequate by modern standards.[15] Moreover, as a rule bureaucratic centralization makes it difficult to take many local peculiarities and traditions into account and often results in total disregard of national interests and attitudes that ought to be respected.[16] Many questions that could easily be solved in the capitals of the Union Republics must still be submitted to Moscow for decision or approval. This applies both to economic problems and to educational and cultural matters. There are great differences in the cultural levels of the nations concerned and in their history—for example, the time and circumstances of annexation to Russia (in some cases it was voluntary, in others the result of conquest). The size of a republic is also a relevant factor. A system of extremely centralized bureaucratic administration cannot adequately take account of all these peculiarities.

d) Rapid scientific advance and economic development throughout the world are accompanied by a degree of internationalization because, as a rule, economics, technology, and science are independent of certain qualities inherent in language and culture. And in the USSR, as a result of economic and scientific progress as well as because of various political and ideological factors, cultural integration is also taking place. A new community has been formed and continues to take shape, which we call the *Soviet people,* possessing a common *Soviet culture* based on values that are equally meaningful to all the nationalities of the USSR. Soviet culture does not deny individual national achievements—it becomes, rather, the repository of all that is best in the cultural history of all the peoples of the USSR. However, its primary form of expression, owing to certain historical circumstances, is the Russian language.

Economic and cultural integration often transforms traditional patterns and ways of life in the various republics. Change is particularly noticeable in the countryside. There has been a rapid increase in the urban population at the expense of the villages, which in the past had been the main guardians of the national tradition. While basically progressive, all these developments do, nevertheless, give an impetus to nationalist sentiment, with its emphasis on the need to preserve obsolete habits and customs. This was particularly so in a number of cases where the changes were carried out thoughtlessly and in undue haste, without consideraton for justified national demands or local tradition, as is inevitable where the system of administration is too centralized and bureaucratic.

Let us look at what is happening to modern architecture, for example—a field where enormous transformations are taking place, thanks to the use of new materials and construction methods, resulting in a fresh international style. This, however, is no excuse for building new and completely impersonal residential areas with standardized houses of identical design in Moscow, Baku, and Tashkent. What is appropriate for an industrial city may be out of place in the capital of a national republic. And what suits one capital does not necessarily suit another.

e) Certain demographic processes have also made national problems more acute. The industrial and agricultural development of Kazakhstan, Bashkiria, Buryat-Mongolia, and several other republics with large but underpopulated territories has led to a rapid increase in the number of Russians, Ukrainians, and other settlers. There are considerably more Russians in Kazakhstan, for example, than indigenous inhabitants.[17] In the Baltic republics, rapid industrial development has similarly led to a large increase in the Russian population.[18] Relations are strained between Georgians and Armenians in Georgia, between Azerbaidzhanis and Armenians in Azerbaidzhan. In certain regions and cities of the Ukraine, Ukrainians have become a minority.

In some southern republics—for example, Georgia, Azerbaidzhan, and those of Central Asia—rapid progress in the mechanization of agriculture has created a problem of rural overpopulation. The local cities cannot absorb the influx from the villages, but there are national and also social and psychological explanations for the fact that young people in the rural areas of these republics find it difficult to migrate to the rapidly developing eastern regions of the USSR.

f) One cannot ignore the process of natural Russification taking place in many republics, particularly with regard to language (and often the culture as a whole). Several nations of the USSR possessed a written language and literature long before the Russians or other Slavs. The Georgian and Armenian cultures, for example, are more ancient than the Russian. With their accumulated wealth of tradition and cultural values, their development of literary languages, their complex history, the Armenian and Georgian nations, along with many other peoples of the USSR, have every reason for wanting to preserve their national distinctiveness. Children from Georgian and Armenian families are usually taught in national secondary schools. In the majority of higher educational institutions of Armenia and Georgia, the native tongue is the language of instruction. And this, of course, is all to the good, since the development of their national heritage enables them to enrich the culture of the Soviet Union as a whole.

But the situation is very different in the case of many other republics and national minorities. A great number of the peoples of the old Russian Empire did not have a developed culture before the Revolution, and they often had no written language or literature of their own. Only after the October Revolution was it possible for more than forty small nations to create their own written language and literature, their own schools and theaters, etc. In the last ten years, however, the development of these young national cultures has been fraught with difficulties. It has often proved impossible for them to compete with Russian culture and the Russian language. With the growth of the mass media— radio, television, the cinema—and with the distribution of newspapers, magazines, and books in Russian, a number of local cultures are losing ground. In many cases Russian, instead of serving only as the lingua franca between different peoples, has in fact become a second native tongue. Nowadays Buryats, Bashkirs, Mordovians, and Chuvash frequently converse in Russian, not only with Russians or Ukrainians but with each other. Russian is the principal language of local radio and television. The local theaters put on plays mostly by Moscow or foreign authors, sometimes without even bothering to translate them into the native tongue. Some writers in these areas are beginning to use Russian in preference to their own language. Parents often choose to send their children to Russian schools and are demanding additional ones. In the national schools, the transition to Russian as the language of instruction now takes place earlier—in some republics the native language is used only through the eighth grade, in others through the seventh or even only the fifth grade. In certain regions children are taught in the local language just in primary schools and sometimes even only in the first two grades. In Kiev today, there are just a few Ukrainian schools left, and they have been able to maintain their enrollment only by introducing English as the medium of instruction in several subjects.

All these problems related to the development of national cultures, languages, and schools have created a confused situation in which some people tend to take an unjustifiably negative attitude toward their native culture, while others go to the opposite extreme by pressing for compulsory measures to ensure its survival.[19]

Intensive Russification is also taking place in scientific and technical literature, a process affecting all the republics of the USSR. Here, too, there have been conflicting proposals for dealing with the situation.[20]

g) Certain international events and processes have had their impact. Thus, for example, the growth of a nationalist mood in Rumania has complicated the state of affairs in Moldavia. Developments in the Middle East have considerably affected the Jewish question in the USSR: certain discriminatory measures against persons of Jewish origin have been intensified and there has been a comcomitant rise of Jewish nationalism.

In addition to nationalist trends in non-Russian areas, there is also the problem of Russian nationalism, now very much on the increase and, in certain circumstances, often taking on the features of "great power chauvinism."

Certainly the Russian people has reason to be proud of its great culture, its language, its history, and one can only have respect for certain aspects of the Russian national character. But in recent years in many articles and works of literature, we find that the words "Russian" and "Russia" are used in too broad a sense, almost in the same way as before the Revolution. Abroad it has always been standard practice to say "Russian" instead of "Soviet"—many people there evidently still find it hard to get their tongues around the words "Soviet" and "socialist." But such a confusion of usage is completely out of place in our own press.

Again, we have literature glorifying nearly all the Russian tsars, and also such tsarist generals as Skobelev and Yermolov, the "unjustly forgotten" conquerors of Central Asia and the Caucasus. The Russian people is once again often referred to as the "most outstanding nation" of the Soviet Union, the "elder brother," the "first among equals," etc.

In effect, we now have a new nationalist movement which centers around the clubs *Rossia* and *Rodina** and literary journals like *Molodaya Gvardia* and *Nash Sovremennik*. The movement includes several different groups. The most reactionary of them has a racist program which speaks of the "Russian race," the "voice of the blood," "the cosmic mission of the people," the "duty to our ancestors," and calls for the "sterilization of women who give themselves to foreigners." This program was summed up in 1965 by a leading official of the Moscow *Komsomol*, Valery Skurlatov, in his "Rules of Morality," duplicated and distributed among the activists of the Moscow City Committee and the *Komsomol* Central Committee.[21] The idea of a return to the "sources of the Russian nation" is set forth less explicitly in an article by Viktor Chalmaev called "Inevitability."[22] Chalmaev extols the doctrines of such extreme reactionaries as Vasily Rozanov and Konstantin Leontiev,† declaring them to be a most important part of the Russian spiritual heritage. The same line was pursued in an article by Yu. Ivanov called "Echo of the Russian People"[23] and in a number of others published in *Molodaya Gvardia* and *Nash Sovremennik*. The "Russite" trend takes on a more "cultivated" form in some of the works of Vladimir Soloukhin, for example, in his *Letters from the Russian Museum*, where he speaks, reasonably enough, about the wholesale, completely unjustifiable destruction of many monuments of Russian culture.

Some of the Russites and "neo-Slavophiles" make use of Marxist terminology in their arguments, but others reject it as "foreign ideology." In print, of course, they express themselves cautiously; but at gatherings in the privacy of their

---

* They were founded in the mid-sixties and dedicated to promoting the study of historical monuments and an appreciation of Russian history and culture. Members engaged in church restoration work on a voluntary basis.—Trans.

† Both men were prominent philosophers, essayists, and literary critics. Vasily Rozanov (1856–1919) was a political conservative who devoted much of his writing to sex and religion. Konstantin Leontiev (1831–1891) rejected European bourgeois democracy and sought the salvation of mankind in aesthetic values and Christian faith.—Trans.

homes these Russites openly declare that "the October Revolution was a mistake," that in the first years of the Revolution Lenin destroyed the "ancient foundations of Russian national life and began the work of destroying the villages, the Russian church," etc.

The majority of the Russites look backward, seeking what they feel to be of value in our culture mainly in the prerevolutionary past, in the deeds and actions of the Russian tsars and the Russian Orthodox Church, and in the Russian village. This has exposed them to criticism even from such a neo-Stalinist as Kochetov. As a result, our neo-Slavophiles have shifted their ground somewhat. In the first place, they are beginning to find good things to say about Stalin—for example, that during the thirties he supposedly restored Russian national values to an honored place. Secondly, the Russites now include in their assessment of the Russian heritage certain achievements of the October Revolution. But they do this in their own way, with a nationalist twist. A very clear example is S. Semanov's article, "Relative and Eternal Values."[24] He wrote:

I would like to stress, that it is not only monuments of the distant past, not only traditions and customs of ancient days that are in need of protection and preservation, but also what was created during the past five decades, and in particular, by our Great Revolution. For this Great Revolution is also part of our priceless national heritage. And we, Soviet citizens . . . are proud of the Great Russian Revolution, which opened up a new epoch in the history of our motherland and of the whole world. One cannot help being proud of a people who accomplished a revolution unprecedented in history, a people who barefoot and unfed created a giant industry, a people whose sons lay down with grenades under enemy tanks or who threw themselves bodily on enemy guns. It is in the light of such things that we must judge all that is happening in our society today. They provide the most important criterion, an absolute one, it seems to me: Does something help to strengthen our state system or not? That is the essential question.

Thus the October Revolution, industrialization, and even the victory in the Second World War are turned into achievements of the Russian people alone. And the main factor, we are told, in these historical accomplishments was not the existence of specific historical or economic conditions but some very special qualities unique to the Russian people. Today our first concern should be not the reaffirmation of socialist principles, not the development of socialist and communist social relations (which in particular presupposes a gradual decline of state interference), but rather the strengthening of our *Russian* state system. Semanov's article not only eulogizes Stalin, but also justifies all the conquests of tsarism—no hint here that Russia was once described as a "prison of peoples."[25]

The Russian nationalists have up to now been openly supported in such influential bodies as the Political Department of the army and the Central Committee of the *Komsomol* where their ideas are used for the purpose of "patriotic education." One may assume that in the face of growing political apathy among young people and soldiers, their loss of interest in the vulgar and oversimplified Marxism so inadequate for the needs of our time, many of the officials responsible for political education in the *Komsomol* and the army are falling back on an appeal to deep-seated nationalist sentiments and ideas. Internationalism goes by the board as they attempt to rouse feelings of national exclusiveness. In this way our youth is being taught a kind of patriotism most inappropriate for citizens of the first socialist country of the world.

The crudest forms of nationalist preaching by the Russites have been condemned in the party press,[26] and even in a special resolution of the Politburo. However, in other more veiled forms, the Russite movement continues to develop and to receive highly influential support.

V

One-party and Multiparty Systems under Socialism

Any discussion of socialist democracy must include the question of one-party and multiparty systems in a socialist society and during the transitional period that precedes it.

We know that in Marxist-Leninist theory, a one-party system was never assumed to be essential to the dictatorship of the proletariat and the building of socialism. Marx and Engels believed that the dictatorship of the proletariat could certainly exist in the form of a parliamentary democratic republic. "If there is something which is not subject to doubt," wrote Engels, "it is that our party and the working class can achieve hegemony only given the existence of some such political form as a democratic republic—which is only a specific form of the dictatorship of the proletariat, as was shown by the great French Revolution."[1]

Revolution in Russia inaugurated a new form of revolutionary power—the republic of soviets. From the first days of the new government's existence, it was assumed that there would be many parties whose democratic rivalry would ensure, in Lenin's view, the peaceful development of the revolution. As late as September 1917, Lenin wrote: "Having seized total power, the Soviets could still—and very likely it is their last chance—ensure a peaceful development of the revolution, peaceful elections by the people of their deputies, a peaceful contest between the parties in the Soviets, the testing out in practice of the various party programmes, and a peaceful transfer of power from one party to another."[2]

The armed uprising of October that overthrew the Provisional Government and transferred all power to the Soviets was the work of the Bolshevik Party alone. Yet at that time the Bolsheviks had no intention of creating either a one-party system or even a one-party government. Neither during the Second All-Russian Congress of Soviets nor after it was over did the Bolsheviks insist on the exclusion of the Mensheviks or SRs. On the contrary, they were even invited to participate in the first Soviet government, of course on condition that they accepted the October Revolution. "It is not our fault," said Lenin at a conference of representatives of regimental committees of the Petrograd garrison on October 29 (November 11), 1917,* "that the SRs and Mensheviks have walked out. We offered to share power with them, but they wanted to wait until the battle with Kerensky was over. We invited all of them to participate in the government. The Left SRs declared that they wanted to support the policy of the Soviet government, and they did not even make any statement expressing disagreement."[3]

Soon after the Second Congress of Soviets in Petrograd was over, negotiations about creating a coalition government began between the Bolsheviks and other parties who considered themselves to be socialist. On the eve of these talks the Bolshevik Central Committee passed a resolution stating: "The Central Committee recognizes the necessity for enlarging the base of the government and possible changes in its composition. . . . The government is appointed by the Central Executive Committee and is answerable to it. . . . The government confirms the decrees on peace and land."[4]

There is a legend to the effect that Lenin opposed the creation of a socialist coalition and categorically insisted on the formation of a purely Bolshevik government. But this was certainly not the case. Lenin was, however, determined that

---

* Until February 14, 1919, Russia adhered to the Julian (Old Style) calendar, which in the twentieth century was thirteen days behind the Gregorian calendar (long in use throughout the rest of Europe).—Trans.

there be certain strictly stipulated conditions for the formation of such a government, and he therefore condemned as unprincipled the concessions agreed upon during talks between other parties and the Bolshevik delegation, headed by Kamenev, Sokolnikov, and Ryazanov. Lenin absolutely rejected the excessive claims of the Mensheviks and SRs, who in fact wanted to put the new coalition government under their own control. But at the same time Lenin wrote, carried through the Central Committee, and published an appeal "To all members of the party and to the whole working class of Russia" in which he said: "We firmly stand by the principle of Soviet power, i.e., the power of the majority obtained at the last Congress of Soviets. We were willing, and remain willing to share this power with minorities in the Soviets, on condition of a loyal, honest commitment to submit to the will of the majority and carry out the programme approved by the entire Second All Russian Congress of Soviets—a gradual but steadfast and determined advance toward socialism."[5]

Although the Right SRs and the Mensheviks had walked out of the Second Congress of Soviets, nevertheless this Congress elected an Executive Committee in which out of 101 members, the Bolsheviks numbered only 62. There were 29 Left SRs, 6 Menshevik-Internationalists, 3 Ukrainian Socialists, and 1 SR Maximalist.[6]

In December 1917, the Left SRs agreed to enter the Soviet government, and were offered a number of important posts. Therefore until July 1918, the Soviet government rested on a bloc of two parties: Bolsheviks and Left SRs. Unfortunately this coalition subsequently became unworkable when the Left SRs indulged in criminal political actions (for example, the murder of the German ambassador von Mirbach) in an attempt to provoke war between Soviet Russia and Germany. The leaders of the Left SRs came out vehemently against the Brest peace and organized a number of armed attacks against the Soviet government.

And so one-party government has existed in our country from the summer of 1918 to the present day. However, in almost all other European socialist countries there have always been alliances between two or more parties, headed by communists, with several parties represented in the government.[7]

But it should not be thought that the only possibility

after a victorious socialist revolution is a coalition between several friendly parties or that the existence of any opposition parties or political organizations is ruled out on principle. The experience of Soviet Russia cannot in any way be used to support this view. Parties opposed to the Bolsheviks, after walking out of the Second Congress of Soviets, in fact took part in elections for the subsequent congress. Thus, for example, at the Fourth Extraordinary Congress of Soviets, in March 1918, representation was as follows: 675 Bolsheviks and 121 Bolshevik sympathizers, 275 Left SRs and their sympathizers, 64 Right SRs, 43 Mensheviks, 2 Bundists, 24 anarchists, Popular Socialists, and Labour Cossacks, and 22 nonparty representatives.[8]

Soon after the Revolution, the Soviet government outlawed only openly bourgeois and monarchist parties which had immediately begun to organize the overthrow of the new proletarian government. As for the Mensheviks, Right SRs, and some other opposition parties, until the end of 1918 they continued to exist legally, openly holding their meetings and publishing newspapers and journals in which they criticized many of the enactments of the Soviet government. Only at the end of 1918, in conditions of a bitter civil war, was the All-Russian Central Executive Committee compelled temporarily to forbid the activity of all opposition parties which in many cases had given aid to the counterrevolutionaries, White Guardists, and interventionists. However, at the end of 1919, when the petty bourgeois Menshevik and SR parties came out against the imperialist intervention—against Kolchak and Denikin—they were again permitted to function. Their further activity became impossible only after the Kronstadt revolt and certain other counterrevolutionary acts in which Mensheviks and particularly SRs played a large part. Illegal organizations of Mensheviks and SRs continued to exist for many years in certain cities and rural districts and in practice ceased all activity and completely disappeared only in the thirties.

There were many instances where the SRs, Mensheviks, and other parties opposed to the Soviet government overstepped the boundary line of *loyal* opposition and by their own actions forced the Bolsheviks to ban them altogether. It is also possible to argue that the behavior of the Bolsheviks in this period was by no means always irreproachable (for example, during the trial of the Right SRs in 1922). I am not attempting to examine here all the specific questions and allegations that arise in this connection. It is, however, an established fact that in the first years of Soviet power a legal opposition did exist within the Soviet government led by the Bolsheviks.

Similarly in the majority of the people's democracies, within the framework of a de facto dictatorship of the proletariat, not only did petty bourgeois parties legally exist, but also bourgeois parties and groups. Some of them even entered the government coalition, while continuing to form an opposition.

Today almost all the programmes of Western communist parties include a provision stating that after a victorious socialist revolution, all political parties that support a socialist policy will be able to participate in the government in *alliance* with the communist party. At the same time communists declare that they will respect and guarantee the legal rights of *opposition* political minorities, if their activity is carried out within legal limits. "For a long time we ourselves believed," wrote, for example, the leader of the Spanish Communist Party, S. Carillo, "that the dictatorship of the proletariat meant a one-party system and the denial of political freedom for the bourgeoisie. But this was in fact a departure from Lenin—it was the view of Stalin. We did not distinguish between the essence of the dictatorship and the concrete form that was adopted in Russia. Stalin's mistake, which we also shared, was that he generalized from the concrete example and gave it the status of universal law. Yet Lenin had pointed out in *State and Revolution* that the transition from capitalism to socialism will be marked by great diversity of political forms."[9] Identical sentiments have been expressed by leaders of other communist parties in capitalist countries.

This whole question is not only important but in certain respects crucial for the fate of the world communist movement. Without a correct and principled solution, it will be impossible to create alliances between communists and socialists or any new forms of a united or popular front. Even left-wing parties close to them often express the view that the communists' acceptance of the idea of a multiparty system under the dictatorship of the proletariat and socialism is nothing but a tactical maneuver to be abandoned after the victory of the socialist revolution, whereupon all other parties will be completely crushed.

Unfortunately, frequent pronouncements emanating from dogmatic groups in the CPSU are no help to communist parties in the West, since they undermine the confidence of potential allies in the sincerity of the new programmes. Thus, for example, in an article published in *Kommunist* (by L. Slepov and I. Yudin) one reads that after the victory of the socialist revolution, petty bourgeois and bourgeois parties may still exist because in this period there would still be a mixed economy. Under these conditions the communists, according to Slepov and Yudin, should conclude separate *temporary* alliances with the different petty bourgeois parties. As for the bourgeois parties, which "will always be in favor of restoring the old order and former social relations, there can be no other approach but a revolutionary struggle culminating in their utter defeat and complete expulsion from the political arena."[10] As we see, Slepov and Yudin do not allow for the possibility of an opposition in the proletarian state, operating within the legal framework. There is no indication that under certain conditions the struggle of the proletariat against bourgeois opposition parties might dispense with revolutionary means, i.e., the use of violence or the denial of political rights to the dispossessed bourgeoisie. But the choice of means should vary according to the nature of the revolutionary upheaval in question, depending on whether it was a peaceful process or not and also on a number of external circumstances (intervention by international imperialism usually makes a peaceful development of the revolution impossible).

In *The Ideology of Contemporary Reformism*,[11] we again find insistence that bourgeois opposition parties cannot continue to exist legally after the victory of a socialist revolution. The authors quote the provisional programme of the Japanese Party of Democratic Socialists: "We are for parliamentarianism not only as a means of gaining power; even after coming to power we will take account of the existence of antagonistic parties and welcome criticism from them." (It must be assumed that the word "opposition" was deliberately replaced here by the word "antagonistic.")

This statement by the Japanese socialists leads the authors of the book to expostulate as follows: "If it is not a question of playing games but really engaging in politics, let us look at what this statement means: surely the existence of antagonistic parties implies the existence of antagonistic classes, whose interests these parties represent. If the Japanese Democratic Socialists intend to struggle for 'socialism' while maintaining class antagonisms, then their programme is entirely logical. But in that case it has nothing to do with socialism."[12] One may well agree with the authors of this work that "the process of building socialism presupposes the destruction of antagonistic relations." But it may nevertheless be a very long and drawn-out process. Even in the German Democratic Republic today there are still private capitalist enterprises. One can also agree that "together with the exploiting classes, their parties will also depart from the historical scene." But there is no reason to assume that it will always happen simultaneously. Even if the bourgeoisie has disappeared as a social class, bourgeois political views may persist almost indefinitely among certain groups of the political minority. And it is by no means always a good thing to suppress such views by force. The same point, incidentally, is made not only by the Japanese socialists, but also in the programmatic statements of the Japanese communists, who for some reason are not mentioned in *The Ideology of Contemporary Reformism*.[13]

Above I have dealt with the fundamental issue of a multiparty system in the transitional period, i.e., during the period of building socialism. The question now arises, To what extent is it possible to keep a multiparty system in a society that is already socialist, when the transitional period has come to an end and the task is to create a mature socialist or even communist society?

Both in theory and in our actual practice, it is always assumed that in a mature socialist society there can be a social base only for the communist party. True, in some socialist countries of Eastern Europe, one or two other parties exist in addition to the communists. However, they recognize the leading role of the communist party, do not actually carry out any independent political activity, and have no real political platform of their own. They exist, then, only as a survival, a shadow of their former selves—"conveyor belts" for the communists. In other words, they are not parties in the true sense of the word. And in any case, Soviet theory assumes that the socialist countries of Eastern Europe are on a different level of social and political development than the Soviet Union.

In their new programmes, communists in Western Europe speak of political freedom for different parties, including opposition ones, not only during the transitional period but also in a full-fledged socialist society. Soviet theorists do not object on the grounds that for capitalist countries such a multiparty socialism would be a great step forward. But when it comes to allowing the re-emergence of some kind of opposition in socialist countries where it has been banned, the very idea is condemned as a totally impermissible step backward.

All the principal documents of the international communist movement acknowledge the importance of cooperation between communists and social democrats under capitalism and also during the first phases of the building of socialism. There are also provisions along these lines in the programme of the CPSU. "The communist parties," states the programme, "are in favor of cooperation with social-democratic parties not only in the struggle for peace, for the improvement of living standards of the workers, for the preservation and extension of democratic rights and freedoms, *but also in the struggle to win power and build a socialist society* [italics added]." But when there was an attempt to revive a social-democratic party in Czechoslovakia in 1968, it was denounced in the Soviet (and in part of the Czech) press as an antisocialist and counterrevolutionary move.

Such an approach to the problem of one-party and multiparty systems is unrealistic and ignores all the difficulties and complexities of socialist development. Looking at Soviet society today, we must not overestimate either its social or its political uniformity. There are still definite social and political differences between city dwellers and the rural population, between workers and intelligentsia, and between all of these and the bureaucratic elements that still exist in our state and party apparatus. And, moreover, there are still distinct layers and groups within the working class, intelligentsia, and personnel of the *apparat*. It is, in fact, these distinctions that provide the basis for the various political moods among the masses discussed earlier and that in turn are now giving rise to diverse political trends both inside and outside the party.

But any serious trend or movement contains within itself the potential of becoming a political party or organization, and those that have been developing in recent years in the USSR are no exception. It is often by no means easy to draw a hard and fast line between a political movement and a political party. We are accustomed to think of a party in the image of the CPSU, as a rigid structure with a fixed number of members holding party cards and paying monthly dues, with elected or appointed leaders, a party press, etc. But this kind of organizational structure is in no way compulsory for all parties everywhere. The Republican and Democratic parties in the United States work in a completely different manner. Political parties may in fact exist as groups of like-minded people, without formal organization, but supporting a more or less common platform and leaders who have not been selected by any formal process. Looked at in this way, several of the political trends in our country already contain in embryo all the elements of political organizations or parties. And were it not for the ban on all parties other than the CPSU, the transition from comparatively amorphous political movements to actual organizations would proceed much more rapidly. Yet even in the present situation, one cannot rule out the possibility of this happening.

It is a matter of historical experience that no political party is ever created on the initiative or by permission of some other party already in existence. New parties come into being only in response to specific political circumstances and social needs. Once the need exists, a new party will inevitably arise to meet it. The actual conditions of the moment may influence its form, tactics, methods, etc., but cannot prevent it from playing some role in the country's political life. A vast number of parties of the most varied kind have existed and still exist illegally in many parts of the world. And if their programmes are a direct response to some important social need, they will survive and gain support even in the most difficult circumstances. No amount of persecution or prohibition can entirely account for the disappearance of a party. For if it has firm roots in society, it will continue to exist in some form or other despite the cruelest efforts to suppress it. We have seen, for example, how the German communists managed to survive extremely vicious Nazi persecution, and then the wholesale purges of German political émigrés at the end of the thirties in the USSR. It would hence be wrong to explain the total disappearance of all former political parties in the USSR only as a consequence of Stalinist terror. It was of course the major immediate cause, but it was also true that they had lost their social base because the effect of the terror was so thorough, the transformation of the social structure had been so violent, that there were no longer social groups and political trends to sustain and support the former parties.

But the situation is now very different; political trends have again emerged that could be the starting points for political organization. Thus, for example, it is entirely possible that clandestine political groups will arise on the right, i.e., among the neo-Stalinists and nationalists of the chauvinist variety. It is possible that similar clandestine groups may come into being among nationalist circles in the non-Russian republics. Sustained by growing nationalist moods inevitable in conditions of bureaucratic centralism, both covert and certain openly existing clubs and associations will increasingly play the role of political parties. Secret organizations could also arise among extreme groups of westernizers, Christian socialists, and anarchists. The majority of the westernizers and party-democrats, who draw their support mainly from the intelligentsia, are likely to remain amorphous. But they will continue as trends of social thought, as social movements attracting more and more people and penetrating the party and state apparatus at various levels. Within them, furthermore, we shall see the constant formation of new focal points; programmes and codes of behavior will be devised, and they will throw up leaders whose example and advice will be followed not out of obedience to the rules of an organization but in response to the call of truth and moral conviction. In fact such a state of affairs could well be equated, at a certain stage in the growth of the movement, with the emergence of a peculiar kind of political party whose very lack of formal structure would serve as a protective device in the face of an omnipotent and centralized bureaucracy equipped with hitherto unprecedented means of surveillance and control. Its unorganized character could be a source of strength.

And so I believe that political "pluralism" is something that springs inevitably from our present situation. Within certain limits this pluralism will continue to develop over the next few years and perhaps will go on for another decade. Is this to be welcomed or not? There is no simple straightforward answer.

The first thing to remember is that the Soviet Union is a country where for many decades there has been only one ruling party. This party has virtually unlimited means for the propagation of its views through the press, radio, television, and many other channels; it controls not only the government of the country but also all branches of the economy, the whole educational system, and all scientific institutions, as well as trade unions, youth organizations, and associations of writers, artists, etc.; it supervises almost the whole of publishing, military and foreign policy, and also the security organs. Thus a new opposition party, even if sanctioned by the authorities, could not count on any significant political success. At best it would be able to attract a small proportion of the voters, thereby obtaining several dozen places in local representative bodies and a few in the Supreme Soviet. Even so, while not jeopardizing the socialist system as such or the leading role of the CPSU,[14] the very existence of a new political party or group of opposition parties would inevitably alter the whole political climate and the CPSU would find itself operating in rather changed circumstances. How would its leadership react to such a situation? There are two possibilities.

The first (which, if one is realistic, seems less likely but cannot be entirely discounted) is that there might be changes for the better in the attitude and policy of the CPSU. Having grown completely unaccustomed to waging a political struggle inside the country and conducting a normal ideological debate with opponents, the party would inevitably have to refashion its methods of political action and leadership. Within the top ranks of the party today there are practically no politicians worthy of the name, no ideologists or theoreticians, or even public speakers capable of talking on television for half an hour without reading from a prepared text; instead we find only a multitude of cloistered bureaucrats. But in conditions of open political confrontation on however small a scale, the party would have to bring into the forefront leaders of a very different type and caliber. The press and propaganda would have to be reorganized. Bureaucrats would have to make way for politicians in the true sense of the word. In time we might possibly witness the appearance of political personalities comparable in stature to the first leaders of our party.

Any political organization grows weak and decays without the stimulus of real political conflict, without opposition. If in capitalist countries the bourgeoisie generates and supports not one but as a rule two or more political parties, this is by no means simply to pull wool over the eyes of the "workers and peasants." The existence of two major parties in the United States reflects the fact that there are different political trends and opinions within the ruling circles of the country. Moreover, conflict between these two parties helps to promote the most capable politicians and administrators, highly proficient in their defense of the interests of capitalist society. As a result democratic bourgeois regimes to a large extent have proved to be far more stable than totalitarian ones. Socialist countries could well learn from the example of bourgeois democracy in the interests of their own further development. Unfortunately such a conclusion would scarcely appear logical to those bureaucratic elements that still dominate the leadership of communist parties in socialist countries.

Thanks to its enormous popular appeal in the first half of 1968, the new leadership of the Czech Communist Party, despite all the party's past political errors, was able to regard the appearance of small opposition groups and associations with relative equanimity. It saw no need to resort to repressive measures and relied instead on political and ideological arguments in this novel situation of political conflict. A leadership of this kind could not be seriously harmed even by an uncensored press full of various irresponsible and demagogic articles and assertions. The very existence of free discussion strengthened the ideological position of the Communist Party, which had been severely shaken by the rule of its former leader, Anton Novotny. Such tolerance, however, seems impossible for the present Czechoslovak leader Husak, who is extremely unpopular among the people and intelligentsia, as are his colleagues Indra, Bilak, Strougal, among others.

Nothing is more essential for our society at the moment than a liberalization of the regime. But what I have in mind is by no means the same process anticipated by some bourgeois experts who hope that it will ultimately undermine the position of the Communist Party. The point about open dialogue with dissidents is that it will strengthen communism and the Communist Party and facilitate adaptation to new conditions. The party must become more flexible and gain the capacity to counter ideological influences from outside. If it continues to ignore the spontaneous and irrepressible development of dissent which has been brought about not only by the reappraisal of our own past but also our greater exposure to external pressures; if it makes no response to new questions arising all the time and refuses to conduct political discussion within the country, contenting itself with a press swamped by boring cliché and an ideological output that is superficial, drab, and inept beyond belief; and finally, if it continues to isolate itself from the many new trends among our intelligentsia, the Communist Party will retain only the outward appearance of ideological strength. Its leading role will come to be preserved more and more in the form of naked power resting not so much on ideas as on administrative controls.

But if the party brings itself to permit an organized dissent with access to the press or even the legal functioning of opposition groups, would this not mean that it had ceased to be communist, having to all intents and purposes adopted the ideology and policies of social democrats?

"It is now the prevailing view in the West," wrote the well-known bourgeois specialist Z. Brzezinski in 1966, "that the communists will gradually become more moderate, eventually drawing near to social democracy. . . . The West above all counts on the erosive influence of time and on pressure for change within the communist countries themselves."[15]

Brzezinski has been quoted in support of a demand for tougher measures against communist "revisionists." However, what for our home-grown dogmatists passes as communism and Leninism is, in fact, a collection of political recommendations very remote from a genuine Leninist or communist approach to the solution of complicated new problems. Lenin was notable for his extreme flexibility in politics, for the way he was able to find new solutions in accordance with changing circumstances. The abrupt about-face that led to NEP* in 1921 is a most revealing example. At a moment when many dogmatists sought a way out of the existing crisis by means of repressive measures and a more brutal policy toward the peasants and even toward the workers (e.g., through state control of the trade unions), Lenin proposed a change-over to the "New Economic Policy." Every schoolchild is now familiar with its basic provisions and also knows that it was only NEP which saved the Soviet regime from catastrophe. Yet at the time much was written about the degeneration and erosion of the Soviets and the Communist Party; there was even a whole movement among Russian émigrés (the so-called "change of landmarks" movement)† in favor of supporting the Soviet regime as transformed by NEP. But Lenin was not in the least perturbed by all these prophecies and eager expectations among the enemies of communism— he was responding to the demands of a real situation in which any other policy would have led straight to disaster.

Only people of limited intelligence identify communism with demands for suppression of dissidence, the prohibition of opposition, and the establishment of a one-party dictatorship. These were mostly the attributes of Stalinism, which was not a form of communism at all. We must not, therefore, be unduly worried by Brzezinski's prophecies. The existence of diverse currents of thought in socialist countries is now an established fact. They can, of course, be dealt with by persecution and witch-hunts, but this can only further compromise

---

* Abbreviation for New Economic Policy, proclaimed by Lenin in March 1921 with the aim of restoring the economy, which had been devastated by revolution, civil war, and the policies of war communism. It permitted a limited degree of private enterprise in agriculture, trade, and small-scale industry while keeping the "commanding heights" in the hands of the state.—Trans.

† Former opponents of the Soviet government who in 1920 began to seek reconciliation with the Bolsheviks as the only party capable of governing Russia effectively and defending her national interest. They called their political philosophy "National Bolshevism" and welcomed NEP as a sign that Russia was entering a period of "normalization."—Trans.

communist ideology and weaken its influence in the contemporary world. The alternative is dialogue: not the peaceful coexistence of ideologies—that is an impossibility—but an open struggle of ideas between different trends of social thought with the aim of strengthening communism. This in no way implies that communists will be transformed into social democrats. It would on the other hand promote an effective rapprochement between communists and left social democrats as well as other left circles of the intelligentsia. Such a rapprochement is today vital to the prospects of socialist revolution not only in the capitalist countries but also in many countries of the Third World. I shall return to this in another chapter.

The second possibility, already foreshadowed by events in Czechoslovakia, is that the emergence of opposition attitudes and groups will lead in the next few years to changes not for the better but for the worse in the leadership of the CPSU. For most of the bureaucrats and dogmatists in the upper ranks of the party, open debate would spell political disaster. Over many long years these people have grown used to identifying themselves as the party—hence their tendency to equate the possibility of their own defeat with the end of socialism and the Soviet regime. This accounts for their extremely vicious reaction toward all attempts to promote socialist democracy in a real sense rather than just in words. We can be sure, therefore, that these bureaucratic elements will fight tooth and nail against the emergence of any opposition political parties or organizations. And if need be, they will be quite capable of sanctioning the use of mass political repression.

But at the present stage of the scientific-technological revolution, when democratization is the essential condition of progress, political persecution and restrictions can only make the internal crisis more acute both in the party and in the country at large. Some people may be intimidated by repressive measures but on the whole such things, far from halting the process, can only accelerate the growth of opposition moods and tendencies. This could lead to democratic reforms in party rule at a subsequent stage of political development. In that case the country will still find the right path, only at much greater cost.

But we must not close our eyes to the possibility that events may take a very different turn. If the forces of democracy inside the party prove too weak, if there is mounting pressure from various non-Marxist and anarchist groups as well as from antisocialist and centrifugal nationalistic elements, events could get out of control and culminate in the collapse of the present regime or even the disintegration of the USSR. Many of Amalrik's gloomy predictions would then come to pass.* Alternatively, in response to such uncontrollable mass movements, our party could once again fall into the hands of dictators and demagogues of the totalitarian-Stalinist variety. But they would be dealing with a situation entirely different from that of Stalin's day, and hence to preserve their power they would in some ways have to go even further than he did. And in that case we should find ourselves living in the nightmare world of George Orwell.

It is of course quite possible to prevent the worst of these various alternatives, but we should have no illusions about the amount of time at our disposal. An acceleration of historical processes has been taking place, and tomorrow it will be difficult to make up for the chance that was missed today. The only way to prevent the emergence of an extremely dangerous and uncontrollable crisis is a gradual and systematic development of socialist and party democracy. This would not mean the end of diverse social and political movements outside the party and possibly would not prevent the formation of political parties and organizations alongside the CPSU, as discussed above. However, in conditions of real socialist democracy all these non-Marxist movements, parties, and groups (the neo-Stalinists may be included among them) will be deprived of a mass base and therefore would present no threat to the future of socialist society. Allowed into the open, their activity can be kept within reasonable bounds by democratic methods. A process of normal political debate will only promote the development of Marxist-Leninist ideology

---

* Andrei Amalrik, historian, author of five plays, *An Involuntary Journey to Siberia* (London and New York, 1970), and *Will the Soviet Union Survive until 1984?* (London, 1970), in which he predicted war with China and the disintegration of the Soviet state. He was sentenced to three years in camp in November 1970 and is now in exile in Magadan.—Trans.

and the formation of a new, more capable generation of communist leaders.

Unfortunately we see that the movement toward "a tightening of the screws" still seems a more likely prospect than a systematic development of socialist democracy. Thus our task is not only to fight against the present dangerous trend in this direction but also, should we fail in this, to find the strength in any coming crisis to prevent a plunge into anarchy or a relapse into totalitarianism and terror—which in either case would mean the loss of all that our country has gained under socialism.

VI

Inner-party Democracy

According to its rules, the Communist Party is "the highest form of social and political organization, the leading and guiding force of Soviet society . . . which unites on a voluntary basis the more advanced, politically more conscious section of the working class, collective farmers, and the intelligentsia of the USSR."

It naturally follows from this that if there is no genuine democracy in the party, there cannot be democracy in society at large.

The preamble to the rules informs us that "the CPSU bases its work on unswerving adherence to Leninist standards of party life—the principle of collective leadership, the promotion in every possible way of inner-party democracy, the activity and initiative of communists, criticism and self-criticism." Defining the basic rights of party members, the rules proclaim the inalienable right of each party member to discuss freely party policy and activity at all party meetings, conferences, and congresses as well as in the party press and to express and defend his opinions openly—admittedly "only as long as the party organization has not come to a decision."[1] The rules also state that party members have the right to "criticize any communist, irrespective of the position he holds, at party meetings, conferences and congresses." Those who commit the offense of suppressing criticism or victimizing anyone for criticism "are responsible to and will be penalized by the party, and if need be, expelled from its ranks." A party member also has the right to "address questions and suggestions to any party body, up to and including the Central Committee of the CPSU, and to insist on a substantive reply."

The rules state that the party is organized on the principle of strict discipline and centralism, but that party discipline must be conscious and centralism must be democratic. This means, in particular, not only that "the decisions of higher bodies are absolutely obligatory for lower bodies," but that there must be "periodic reports of party bodies to their party organizations and to higher bodies."

Lenin always insisted on the fundamental differences between democratic centralism, bureaucratic centralism, and anarchism.[2] "It would be impermissible to forget," wrote Vladimir Ilyich, "that in defending centralism, we are defending democratic centralism only."[3]

Our party has always been based on strict discipline, and its leading bodies have always been invested with substantial powers. But the essence of communist discipline, according to Lenin, is that it is a "discipline based on trust, on total respect, a discipline that encompasses independence and initiative."[4]

These are the standards of party life established by Lenin, and they still underlie the party rules in their present form.

All these statutory provisions are very well known to every member of the party. However, for any person familiar with how the party actually works—whether it is a question of the process of discussion and decision-making, the formation of leading party bodies, or the real rights of party members—it is obvious that the most important provisions of the rules and Lenin's directions on party procedure are to this day either ignored or observed only in a nominal way.

Of course there have been a great many changes since Stalin and Khrushchev. Yet one can hardly say that the CPSU has now become a genuinely democratic organization which bases its activity on the principle of developing "in every possible way inner-party democracy, the activity and initiative of communists, criticism and self-criticism."

It is quite apparent that the rights of party members guaranteed in the rules and by the principles of democratic centralism are only to some extent observed in primary party organizations—at meetings and in elections to the bureaus of their party committees. And even at this level one can come across many instances of bureaucracy and empty ritual, but at least here there is the possibility of overcoming such negative features.

The same can by no means be said, however, of any party organizations from the district level upward. The ruling party *apparat,* consisting mainly of full-time professional party workers, still acts in the spirit of bureaucratic centralism, considerably restrained in comparison with the Stalin period but fundamentally unchanged.

At the district level, elections to the party committee are already an undemocratic formality. While at meetings of primary organizations to hear reports and elect new officials, there is usually a detailed discussion about the merits of candidates nominated for the bureau, nothing of the kind takes place at elections for the district committee. They are held at district party conferences once in two years, and the nomination of candidates is by a totally undemocratic process. One of the delegates to the conference reads out a long list of candidates prepared in advance by the permanent officials and approved by the outgoing members and the *apparat* of the next higher party body, usually the city committee. After this, another delegate generally reads out a further list of candidates to make up a delegation to the city party conference. Both lists contain something like 150 names in a Moscow district; in other cities and rural districts there would be about a hundred. Although the overwhelming majority of the candidates are completely unknown to the rank-and-file delegates at these conferences, no testimonials are read out as to the suitability of the candidates, and there is no discussion of their qualifications, nor could there be, in view of the large numbers involved. The secret ballot takes place after the nominations have been confirmed; each delegate receives printed lists of candidates for the district committee and the city conference and, after a cursory glance, drops them into the ballot box. It has been possible to establish from talks with participants at these conferences that over the last ten years in Moscow there has never been a single case of someone proposing a candidate additional to those on the lists prepared in advance or of any names being struck off them.

City and regional party committees are elected in a similar way at city and regional party conferences, and the same formalities apply to delegates elected to the party congress. We do not know of a single case where a candidate nominated by the *apparat* of the regional committee of the Central Committee as a delegate to the party congress was not elected.

To a large extent the right of party members to discuss questions of party policy freely and to criticize any communist, whatever his position, likewise exists only on paper. The facts of the matter are accurately described by the author of the anonymous article entitled "Disarmament and Democracy." "Ordinary party members," he writes, "are in practice excluded from the process of making political decisions. Almost no information is available to primary organizations about the working of party bodies above them, right up to the Central Committee. Political questions are rarely raised at party meetings, and if they are, then only *after* the issue in question has already been settled by a higher authority. But as we know, it is a basic principle of democratic centralism that once decided, a question can no longer be discussed—only implemented. It is hardly surprising, therefore, that all discussion at party meetings on questions already decided is an empty formality which generally takes place in an atmosphere of total apathy. As a result rank-and-file communists tend to be politically passive, indifferent to social problems. This passivity is in fact encouraged by the party *apparat,* which is quick to put a stop to any political initiative coming from below—goodness knows where such things might lead.

"To judge by the frequent appeals that appear in *Pravda* to develop inner-party democracy, one might think that the party leaders were very conscious of the importance of encouraging political activity among ordinary members. But since these empty words are never backed up by specific measures, their effect is nil or even worse—the discrepancy between words and deeds only creates cynicism and indifference."[5]

Party-wide discussion on specific political problems, as envisaged by the rules, has not in fact taken place for several

decades. And this despite the number of acute political crises
that have beset the party during these years. Public discussion prior to party congresses for the most part centers on the
directives for the new five-year plan. And even in this very
limited context, newspapers print no more than one letter out
of a hundred or even a thousand of those received. But it is
not a question of lack of space. I know of several scores of
letters, addressed to the Twenty-third Congress and to the
central press not only by rank-and-file communists but by
veteran party members and also prominent figures in Soviet
cultural life. These letters dealt with very serious problems,
but not one of them was published in the Soviet Union although several appeared in communist papers in the West.

The right of party members to criticize the leadership is
also still very limited. In local papers we find no criticism of
the local party leaders any more than we find criticism of
members of the Central Committee in the central press.
Adverse comment on party leaders appears only after they
have been removed from office and not always even then. The
most usual thing is for the name simply to disappear altogether from the pages of newspapers and journals. We know,
for example, that after the October Plenum a great number of
letters were sent both to the Central Committee and to
Pravda, criticizing such leading party officials as L. Ilichev,
V. Mdzhavanadze, A. Adzhubei, S. Pavlov, P. Satyukov,
V. Tolstikov, and several others. Not one of these letters was
published, although even in the Central Committee there
could have been no doubts about their validity. There are still
instances of individuals being punished for criticizing a party
leader.[6]

The right of each communist to address any party body
up to and including the Central Committee and to demand a
substantive reply is also quite meaningless in practice. An Old
Bolshevik from Kiev, S. B_____v, has in the last few years
sent several dozen letters to the Central Committee with very
well argued and constructive proposals for the development
of inner-party democracy. But he has never received any
reply that actually dealt with the question he raised. I could
fill pages with similar examples.

One is also bound to have serious misgivings about the
procedure for selecting and appointing leading party cadres

and the lack of proper control over their activities. And because of the leading role of the CPSU, the same procedures are followed in all other public organizations.

Innumerable books, articles, pamphlets, and learned dissertations have been written about how to select and assign cadres to their posts according to scientific principles. There have been many excellent resolutions on this subject by the highest party bodies. For example, the Twenty-third Party Congress formally adopted a Central Committee report which noted that "the growing scale and complexity of communist construction make great demands on the selection, appointment, and training of cadres. The qualifications for appointment to leading posts should be: dedication to the ideas of communism, a good knowledge of the work involved, and an ability to maintain constant contact with the masses and to organize them for the fulfillment of worthy tasks." It would not be entirely fair to say that these Leninist principles concerning the appointment of personnel, so often reiterated at party congresses, are merely a dead letter, since there are indeed many officials in the *apparat* who do meet the highest possible standards. But the fact remains that this does not apply to a host of others, and in crucial sections of the party and government machinery these principles are either totally irrelevant, or are observed only to a very small extent.

Unfortunately, to this day there is still no sound and rational machinery for the promotion and replacement of leadership cadres in party bodies and government institutions, and this explains many of the shortcomings that persist in the political and social life of the country. It hardly needs saying that under Stalin's brutal personal regime there could be no question of choosing the right people in a rational way. The principles applied were totally different, and they had nothing whatever to do with socialism or communism. There was no proper system of promotion under Khrushchev either, although some timid attempts were made in this direction after the Twentieth and Twenty-second Party congresses. Thus the basic principle of socialism—*from each according to his abilities, to each according to his work*—has no place in the administration of public affairs in our country. Frequently it is not ability that counts, but good personal or family contacts, loyalty to the right people, one's ethnic origin, or it may simply be a question of chance. As a result, not only at the first but also at the second levels of leadership, it is rare to come across men of outstanding talent, or impressive personality, or even the ability to speak in public. There is an old saying: "It is not the job that graces the man, but the man who graces the job." Yet in our society the reverse is true; once a man loses his seat of power, he ceases to have any importance in the eyes of society and no longer plays any role whatever in public life. For example, who today remembers A. Kirichenko, Khrushchev's once powerful favorite? What interest would there be today in the views of N. Mikhailov, now a pensioner, or former ambassador V. Stepakov? Yet only recently these men were enormously influential as the persons in charge of the whole of our press and propaganda.

It is all too evident that in their intellectual and other capacities our top leaders are for the most part only average and in a number of cases even less than that. Moreover the majority are past the age of retirement.[7] In capitalist countries, too, most professional politicians are rather mediocre— not everybody is a Roosevelt, Churchill, or Kennedy. But it must be admitted that in terms of their purely professional capabilities, many foreign political leaders surpass their counterparts in socialist countries. The same applies to many of our top economic planners in comparison with the equivalent "captains of industry" abroad. Very likely this explains why the socialist camp has been on the defensive in recent years in many areas of ideological and political competition and also continues to lag behind in the economic race.[8]

In order to create an appropriate system for the appointment and replacement of cadres, we need not only substantial structural reform but also an extensive programme of re-education to overcome the effects of Stalinism on the psychology of functionaries at all levels. There must be effective public control over government activity and an end to the secrecy that shrouds the work of all our institutions.

The excessive growth of the role and importance of the *apparat* presents another very serious obstacle to inner-party democracy and is a major cause of the rigidly bureaucratic handling of various political and economic problems. Originally created merely to *assist* in the work of elected party bodies, it now often dominates them instead. *Apparat* officials appointed in a strictly bureaucratic way frequently achieve self-sufficient status enabling them to exercise enormous influence not only in the drafting and adoption of directives but also in determining the actual composition of the ostensibly elective party bodies to which they are attached. The prime examples before our eyes are the vastly inflated administrative subdivisions of the party's Central Committee and Politburo.

It goes without saying that every member of the Politburo and every Secretary of the Central Committee (and many an ordinary member too) must be flanked by his own auxiliary staff, consisting of various technical assistants, researchers, and advisers. But these Central Committee *apparatchiki* have long since outgrown their merely subordinate functions.

This excessive growth in the size and power of the apparatus developed under Stalin when he stopped holding plenary sessions of the Central Committee and delegated most of its work to its administrative appendage. After the Twentieth Congress, measures were taken to remedy the situation. There was a return to the practice of holding regular sessions of the Central Committee and other elected bodies. Very soon, however, these plenary sessions and even meetings of the Presidium* began to assume a purely formal character. How could serious consideration be given to various important proposals and reforms submitted to the Presidium if its members received the relevant documents only a few hours or as little as thirty or forty minutes before the actual meeting? At the same time plenary sessions of the Central Committee were turned into gala performances, often with the participation of several thousand invited guests. The real work was done and crucial decisions taken behind the scenes among a narrow circle of advisers and aides in the *apparat;* all proposals were hammered out there and adopted by a kind of caucus consisting of trusted officials and even relatives.†

There was also a proliferation of new *apparats* under

---

* I.e., Presidium of the Central Committee, as the Politburo was called under Khrushchev.—Trans.

† Evidently a reference to the prominent role played by Adzhubei, Khrushchev's son-in-law.—Trans.

Khrushchev.[9] His crowning achievement in this respect was to split the regional and lower party organizations into two halves, one to deal with industry and the other with agriculture. This meant that every region now had two party committees, and that corresponding subdivisions were set up in the party bodies above them. The structure of the highest party organs became so complex that special diagrams had to be displayed in party educational centers to try and make it comprehensible!

A great deal changed after the fall of Khrushchev. The division of party committees into industrial and agricultural sections came to an end and, soon after, all the Central Committee's RSFSR Bureaus* were done away with. It is significant that scarcely anyone outside the central party *apparat* noticed the disappearance of these large and influential bodies. There was an improvement in the procedure for Central Committee and Politburo meetings, with better briefing for those taking part. But in other respects these supreme party bodies continued to function much as before despite the need for reform.

The *apparat* even today is excessively large—there are too many officials and too much subdivision. Therefore it inevitably begins to act as a substitute for many state bodies both executive and legislative, thus taking over a role that properly belongs to the government. For example, many laws or decrees receive much more than general consideration in the Central Committee *apparat*—they are discussed in very specific detail after which the *apparat* officials usually prepare an extremely precise and thorough document to be approved by the Secretariat, Politburo, or the Plenum of the Central Committee. Only then is the draft law or decree submitted to the Council of Ministers or the Supreme Soviet for their consideration, which at this stage, needless to say, can only be a matter of formal ratification, since any attempt to change or modify it would be regarded as an expression of lack of confidence in the Central Committee. Though the details of a draft law may often be worked out by government bodies such as a ministry, Gosplan,† or the Council of Minis-

---

* One of Khrushchev's innovations had been to create a separate party organization for the RSFSR. It was abolished in 1966.—Trans.
† State Planning Committee.—Trans.

ters, it is nevertheless carefully examined in the Central Committee and is approved by the Secretariat or Politburo before formal confirmation by the Supreme Soviet. Under this procedure, the Central Committee often unnecessarily usurps the functions of the Supreme Soviet or duplicates the work of the Council of Ministers or Gosplan. There have been cases when actual legislative enactments (as opposed to decrees on current problems) have not been formally passed by the Supreme Soviet but have simply come into effect by joint decree of the Central Committee and the Council of Ministers —the Presidium of the Supreme Soviet approves it retroactively. Finally there have been cases of a decree taking on the character of law although emanating from the Central Committee alone. An example of this was the division of regional party committees and regional Soviet executive committees into industrial and agricultural halves. And though this involved government as well as party bodies, only a decree of the Central Committee was published in the press —there was never any sign of a decree by the Council of Ministers or a session of the Supreme Soviet to pass a corresponding law.

The extraordinary expansion of the central party *apparat* often leads to its taking over not only the functions of the Council of Ministers and the Supreme Soviet but also those of many individual ministries as well. As long as there continue to be a number of specialized industrial departments within the Central Committee, their personnel will inevitably take it upon themselves to examine problems which should really be left to the competence of the relevant ministry or Gosplan. The Central Committee's large Department of Science and Education not only devotes attention to specific forms of party activity or the general problems of ideological education in scientific and scholarly institutions, but often, to the detriment of these main concerns, tries to decide a great number of concrete problems that would be better dealt with in the Academy of Sciences, the Ministry of Education, the Ministry of Secondary and Higher Specialist Education, or the State Committee on the Coordination of Scientific and Technical Research. (All of these, incidentally, are in any case usually headed by persons who are members of the Central Committee.) One could hardly imagine the work of Lunacharsky and Krupskaya* being interfered with in Lenin's day by some department of the Central Committee. At the beginning of the twenties, Lenin in fact stressed how wrong it was for the party to take over the work of Soviet bodies. "It is necessary," he said, "to make a much more rigorous distinction between the functions of the party (and its Central Committee) and those of the Soviets; to make the institutions and personnel of the Soviets more responsible and independent; and to see that the party exercises a general guiding role in the work of all state bodies instead of indulging in petty interference as happens all too often at present."[10] In Lenin's view this would not only have freed party leaders from the burden of minor administrative matters thus reducing the element of bureaucracy in the apparatus, but at the same time would have enhanced the authority of the Council of People's Commissars† and other government bodies. These remarks of Lenin's are still, alas, very much to the point today.

With the present system of duplication, it is quite impossible either for government and economic organizations or for the corresponding departments of the Central Committee to develop any sense of responsibility and independence. A ministry can always blame directives received from the Central Committee, while the Central Committee can claim that its directives were badly carried out by the ministry. It would obviously make more sense to let party members in the Writers Union make decisions on the development of Soviet literature rather than to rely on some department or literary section of the Central Committee. Because of the very nature of literature and art, it cannot be guided from outside by officials who are really capable only of undesirable interference. There was of course a time when things were quite different. Even under Stalin there was no department or section for literature in the Central Committee. If some directive was called for, a working group or commission was formed composed of party members in some way involved in

---

* Lunacharsky was Commissar of Enlightenment (in charge of education and the arts) from 1917 to 1929. Krupskaya (Lenin's wife) was a member of the Commissariat and was deeply concerned with the formation of educational policy.—Trans.

† As the Council of Ministers was called before 1946.—Trans.

literature. Later on, however, advisers and consultants on problems of literature and art made their appearance, and such apparently is the logic of bureaucratic evolution, that once this kind of adviser has become established in the higher reaches of the *apparat,* he soon begins to acquire a whole staff of his own—advisers and consultants breed more advisers and consultants. Thus a new "sector" gradually comes into being and before long begins to function independently, taking its own initiatives in the control of literature and in dealing with writers, only rarely reporting back to the head of the department as a whole. Neither literature nor art nor science can possibly gain from the activities of all these proliferating intermediaries. At first sight, however, it does seem easier to exercise control by such methods—so easy that neither knowledge nor ability is required, only skill in using the apparatus to good effect.[11]

Among the relatively less serious violations of inner-party democracy, one should mention that in recent years there have been an increasing number of expulsions from the party by the district or the city party committee without reference to the primary organization. This shows lack of trust in rank-and-file communists by members of the *apparat*, a fear of allowing any question to be taken up at the primary level. In other words, there is disregard for the opinions of the ordinary members, who are in fact the backbone of the party. Clearly expulsion that bypasses the primary organization is a gross violation of inner-party democracy.

All these examples of how inner-party democracy is flouted in practice should help to suggest ways of improving the situation. Thus, for example, fundamental changes are obviously necessary in the procedures for electing members of leading party bodies. Without this, and without greater respect for the electoral principle throughout the party in general, all the talk and all the plans for the development of inner-party democracy will remain nothing more than pious hopes.

Certain improvements could be made in the election of party officials even at the primary level. It is well worthwhile to look at the experience of the Hungarian Workers' Party: in its primary organizations both the secretary and the members of the party bureau have always been chosen by direct and secret ballot. Since the secretary of the party bureau is quite a powerful figure and is the direct link to the district committee, etc., this way of electing him enhances the contribution of the rank and file in the formation of their leadership.

To ensure that there is no longer any possibility of a mechanical acceptance of candidates, substantial changes must also be introduced in the procedure for electing the district and city committees and other leading party bodies. It would probably be possible to organize preliminary discussion of nominations for district, city, and regional party committees at lower-level meetings. Such meetings would provide an opportunity for members of primary organizations in a factory or group of factories or offices to give proper consideration to the qualifications of different candidates, thereby enabling them to select the most suitable person. Then the district or city party conference would only have to confirm the choice already made by the rank and file. At the conferences there need be discussion only about controversial candidates and also the appointment of permanent officials.

It has also been proposed that district and city party committees elect their bureaus and secretaries by a secret ballot instead of by a show of hands as at present, and that the Central Committee should elect its secretaries by the same method.[12]

A number of comrades have suggested a shift from the territorial to the production principle in the structure of the party.* The production principle now applies largely to primary party organizations, which is why they are more democratic, but at the next level of the hierarchy and above, the territorial principle prevails. The party committees of factories and institutes are subordinate to the district committee in whose territory they happen to be situated. This perhaps made sense during a period of war or revolution when the main concern of the district or city party organization was to mobilize all communists to carry out a variety of urgent tasks. But some party members argue that this system is now obsolete and is being preserved artificially. Almost every Moscow district contains a large number of the most diverse institutions and enterprises whose party organizations can be supervised by the district committee only in a very general way.

* I.e., from geographical to functional (place of work) criteria.—Trans.

How can a tiny science section of a district committee give ideological guidance to the party organizations of the Academy of Sciences or of twenty different types of important scientific research institutes? How can one district party official be expected to supervise the management of an enormous Moscow factory and *at the same time* look after its party organization? As a result, instead of serving as a channel for feedback from the primary party organization to the higher party leadership, the district committees only transmit directives and orders in the opposite direction—from the top downward.

The position would change fundamentally if the production principle were to be introduced even only at the next higher level. Under this arrangement, district committees would be replaced by branch committees composed, broadly speaking, of workers of the same type as in the primary organizations electing them. Indeed this system already operates in one or two places—for example, Moscow has an all-city committee representing all the transport organizations. The same thing should be done in the case of city and regional trade organizations, as well as for various categories of allied enterprises, scientific research institutes, educational institutions, etc. Thus, for example, the party committee of the Academy of Sciences should be chosen at a party conference of all communists employed in its many subordinate institutions throughout the whole city. Party organizations of educational, scientific, or research institutions would be subordinate to the party committee of the Presidium of the Academy of Pedagogical Sciences. Branch party committees would direct the work of party organizations in theaters and other places of entertainment in Moscow, etc. Such committees would have better knowledge of the needs and problems of the primary organizations within their jurisdiction and they would be less likely to yield to unqualified pressure from above. Of course to direct the affairs of the district as a whole there would still be the district Soviets and their executive committees, and corresponding district party committees would now represent the primary organizations of the service sector and other small enterprises within the territory in question. All these proposals seem to me very worthwhile and should certainly be tried out in one or two large cities.

As regards the higher party organizations, the main problem is to reduce as far as possible the excessive centralization that now afflicts them. The huge apparatus of the Central Committee must be gradually cut down. This could be done by a drastic reduction in all those sections that simply duplicate the work of government bodies.[13] Central Committee officials should cease to interfere in the day-to-day administration of government and the economy as well as in science, literature, and art. In all these areas party guidance must be left to party members employed in the various government, economic, and cultural bodies. I am, of course, far from advocating an end to the party's supervisory role. It is a question, rather, of changing the nature and direction of this role. In my view, the Central Committee should be a true political center which directs the building of communism on scientific lines. It is not the place to prepare specific economic measures or government enactments of one kind or another but should be, as it were, a general staff concerned with political ideas and methods and with the study and analysis of political moods among the masses; this would enable it to arrive at a party policy in the true sense of the word. This would require the enlargement of certain policy planning subdivisions in the Central Committee or the creation of new ones to replace all the very dispensable departments now concerned with government and the economy.

The Central Committee must be the principle center for scientifically organized agitation and propaganda, ideological work, and the training of cadres. It must be responsible for liaison with all other communist and socialist parties and with national liberation movements. Obviously here and in many other spheres we are faced with political and ideological problems demanding intensive study almost nonexistent today at the proper level, because the *apparat* of the Central Committee is overwhelmed by administrative and economic matters. Because of these preoccupations, its apparatus is for the most part recruited from among people whose careers have been in economic administration. Even the post of Central Committee secretary for ideological questions is held by a former expert in problems of the chemical industry. The present Central Committee secretary in charge of international affairs was until a few years ago a specialist in the design and production of automobiles. Whatever their abilities, such men do not have the kind of broad education suitable for devising and carrying out party policies on a truly scientific basis, and for developing a communist ideology adequate to the demands of the modern age.

If the Central Committee were transformed into a truly political body linked with the masses and sensitive to their moods and wishes, the party would be able to initiate a dialogue with the dissidents, i.e., with all the various new trends of social and political thought in the country. It would mean a confrontation of political ideas without recourse to any kind of administrative prohibitions or repressive measures. The Central Committee is just the place where the study of these different trends should be concentrated. And the experience would be of great importance for the selection and training of real ideologists and politicians able to win the support of the masses mainly by virtue of their political and moral authority. It is an iron rule, borne out time and time again, that human beings develop their capacities in any field only through practical activity. It is just here that a selection process goes on, separating the able from the less able. To become a real military leader it is necessary to fight in a war—this is the only test of one's ability to command. The same thing is true of scientists, engineers, administrators, and even literary men—all have to be tested in actual practice. In an identical way political leaders can only make their mark in the heat of genuine political contest if they are in constant touch with the masses. The period when our party was fighting against tsarism, or afterward during the stormy months of 1917 and the first postrevolutionary years as civil war raged in the country, was not the time to carry out normal elections or democratic discussions about the merits of candidates. In those days the most able party and government leaders simply emerged spontaneously. When a man is in the front line or near it, when he is in direct contact with the masses and not insulated from them by a large and unwieldy *apparat*, only then can he develop as a leader. Leadership means more than approving or disapproving suggestions and proposals prepared by the *apparat*. Often it involves reflecting on the political situation and seeking a way out of a difficult position with the leader himself making decisions, making mistakes, and learning from them. Only then can the party judge the capacities of different men and choose the best.

When there is an overgrown apparatus standing between leaders and the real world, the selection and promotion of cadres takes on an entirely different aspect. Most of the time only the lowest echelons of this *apparat* are directly in touch with ordinary life or have any contact with the masses. In the case of top leaders, years can go by without their having a normal encounter or conversation with an ordinary worker. Hence only at the lowest level is there any more or less intensive process of selecting personnel in accordance with practical capabilities. Yet officials at these lowest levels have no right to make decisions but are expected only to report to their superiors. As for the middle and higher levels of the *apparat,* practical abilities are often quite secondary. Other qualities are much more relevant for promotion, those that are regarded as being typical of a so-called *apparatchik.*[14] Frequently some chance event plays an important role in advancement. Thanks to a combination of accidental circumstances, a completely incompetent and even uneducated person may find himself at the head of a large and important *apparat,* where simply by virtue of being an *apparatchik* he will remain for rather a long time until some new chance occurrence brings about his downfall. This is why I am proposing a substantial reduction of the present Central Committee apparatus, so that it may become an active political body constantly replenished with the best people from the grass roots and the middle layers of the party.

It is important to understand that the origin and development of bureaucracy depends not only on the nature of the people who happen to be in power at a given period, but also on the kinds of institutions and the system of relationships and responsibilities already in existence. There are those who once in power assiduously devote themselves to setting up bureaucratic procedures wherever possible, giving their subordinates no opportunity to show initiative and encouraging red tape and fear of responsibility. Others are obsessed with concentrating maximum power in their own hands and to this end will establish unnecessary and harmful centralization, which ultimately leads to loss of contact with reality. And there is yet another type of bureaucracy involving middle-level officials who, while having every right to make independent decisions, prefer to avoid taking responsibility and refer everything back to their superiors. Bureaucracy has many faces. Often it turns out that not only middle-level officials but even very senior ones do not have the right to decide even the most seemingly unimportant questions. Such people can become bureaucrats, as it were, against their own will and inclinations and despite their practical and political abilities.[15] I could give many examples to illustrate this kind of transformation. Here is a typical one: Not long ago in Moscow an Old Communist, who had participated at many party congresses, died. His friends and comrades, also veteran party members, brought an obituary to *Pravda* signed by all of them. A member of the editorial board responsible for such things was at a loss what to do—he himself was unable to decide whether or not the deceased came into the category of persons about whom it was permissible to write in *Pravda*. In order to settle this "problem," he had to telephone the Central Committee, which gave him permission to publish. But then there arose a new, no less fundamental uncertainty. How should the obituary be signed—with the surnames of the friends of the deceased or without any names at all, using instead the standard anonymous formula "a group of comrades"? Here again this editor of *Pravda* did not have sufficient authority to make a decision. Once more he had to call the Central Committee and talk at great length with an official of the *apparat* (it was decided not to include the signatures). However absurd, this story illustrates the extreme servility and lack of independence that prevails throughout our party press although the press could and should become the most important instrument for the development of inner-party democracy.

Recently during the discussions preceding the Twenty-fourth Congress, a party member made a very important proposal that might well have been put into effect immediately. He suggested that district newspapers be made subordinate to the regional committee and no longer directly controlled by the district committee. "District newspapers in small towns and rural communities," he wrote, "play a terribly important role. But they function very much below their potential. The newspaper is the organ of the district party committee, which oversees the whole of economic and cultural life in the district; therefore the paper cannot criticize the most important, fundamental local shortcomings, since under the existing system the district committee is responsible for them and would be rather reluctant to wash its dirty linen in public. Sometimes it is even the case that the district committee itself is guilty of some fault. Of course even if the newspaper were taken out of its control, the committee would still be able to exert influence on the character of the paper through the editor and members of the editorial board, who would be party members. However, the vitally important thing is that if the paper were subordinate to the regional organization, the district party committee could not forbid publication of specific material or remove an editor not to its liking. The paper could become a platform for the airing of all kinds of local problems, a platform in fact for free discussion. Under a one-party system it is particularly important to have this kind of paper, where even if it is only a question of local issues it is possible to discuss them freely and to criticize the actions of the district authorities. It would make people more accustomed to examining different sides of a question and rouse the masses to active participation."

This proposal makes very good sense. It could be tested out in practice and after a year or two extended to regional party papers, which would then become the organs of either the Central Committee of the CPSU or of the relevant republican central committees and no longer subordinate to the regional party committees. The chief editors of the regional papers and members of their editorial boards would either be appointed by the Central Committee or chosen by special election at the regional party conference. This reform would mean a more democratic situation in the regions, with the possibility for a freer discussion of regional problems. And if the experiment were successful, and I have no doubt that it would be, the same principle could be extended to the central press as in the first postrevolutionary years. At the same time it elects the Central Committee, the party congress would choose persons to be in charge of the party's central press. The editorial board of *Pravda* would have to report periodically to the party congress, and editorial boards of republican newspapers to the party congress of the respective republics.

There certainly still would be party guidance of the press, but extreme centralization would be reduced with a more important role for the party congress.

The creation of a more independent party press would make it increasingly possible to debate the most varied problems of party policy. At present, party-wide discussion during the one or two months before a congress touches on only a very restricted number of questions. Because the period of time is so short, neither party nor other social-science journals can participate. Yet wide-ranging discussion should not be a temporary exception to the rule but a normal feature of party life. And for this purpose we need a regular organ modeled on the former "Discussion Bulletins,"* as well as the regular publication of special collections of materials. Party clubs should be set up in large cities where public debates could take place. There was a time when all this was envisaged in resolutions of party congresses and conferences. For example, in a resolution of the Ninth All-Russian Party Conference,† we read: "It is necessary to bring about more extensive criticism within the party of both local and central party institutions. The Central Committee is charged to provide an official instruction indicating ways of broadening the scope of criticism at general party meetings; to found periodicals with the aim of systematic and comprehensive criticism of the party's mistakes, for which purpose also special discussion bulletins should be issued as supplements to the Central Committee and city committee *Izvestia*."[16] The Tenth Congress similarly called for a "more regular publication of discussion bulletins and special collections of documents."[17] On the basis of its resolution, a network of special discussion clubs was set up in 1921 in Moscow and several other cities, and the debate was particularly lively in the Moscow one. However by now all these resolutions and proposals, intended at the time to become permanent features of party life, are completely forgotten. Not only are there no discussion bulletins, the *Izvestia* themselves long ago ceased to exist.

It is ironic, however, that one temporary resolution of the Tenth Congress, acknowledged by Lenin to be an exceptional measure in violation of democracy, is for some reason

* As in Lenin's time. See p. 62.—Trans.
† September 22–25, 1920.—Trans.

kept in the party rules to this day. This is the resolution
according to which the Central Committee can expel one of
its members by a two-thirds vote, with the same procedure
applicable in regional, city, and district committees. It is high
time that we returned to a correct procedure under which
members of the Central Committee chosen by the party congress cannot be removed except by a new congress, and
members of the district, city, and regional party committees
can be removed only by the respective party conferences.

Finally, one should mention the question of tenure of
office for elected party officials. Obviously where there is a
one-party system, a most important guarantee against abuse
or usurpation of power is the establishment of fixed terms of
office for every elective party post, and possibly for all important government posts as well. There must be exceptions to
any rule, and situations may arise making it necessary to
postpone the replacement of a certain leader. A man's services to the party may be so outstanding that, whatever his
position or even without any formal post, he will as before
have enormous moral and political authority in the party.
However, as a general rule, in conditions of the rapidly
changing world of today, there must be a regular procedure
for replacing political leaders. Certain measures were taken
in this direction at the Twenty-second Party Congress. Article
25 of the rules adopted at that Congress states: "The principle
of a systematic renewal of the composition of party bodies
and of continuity of leadership shall be observed in the election of those bodies. At each regular election, not less than
one quarter of the composition of the Central Committee and
its Presidium [Politburo] shall be renewed. Members of the
Presidium shall not, as a rule, be elected for more than three
successive terms. Particular party officials may, by virtue of
their generally recognized prestige and high political, administrative, and other qualities, be elected to leading bodies
for a longer period. In that case, a candidate is considered
elected if not less than three-quarters of the votes are cast for
him by secret ballot. . . . Party members not re-elected to a
leading party body due to the expiration of their term may be
re-elected at subsequent elections."[18] Similar procedures
were to apply at lower levels.

This was a very important decision. Of course a number

of points are open to criticism. The question of a time limit is extremely complicated and it is difficult to find a completely satisfactory answer.[19] It is also easy to understand why this article of the rules was not acceptable to many senior officials of the Central Committee and particularly not to the lower-level party committee members, accustomed to regard their positions as sinecures for life.[20] But of course the welfare of the party must come before any private interests. In comparison with the former procedure, there is no doubt that the new Article 25 was a lesser evil. Unfortunately this article was excluded from the subsequent version of the rules adopted at the Twenty-third Congress—this was the only major change in them. I believe it would be an excellent idea for the next party congress to reintroduce a provision for the regular replacement of party cadres. Clearly without some normal procedure of this kind, changes in leadership will happen not only very rarely but also in extremely traumatic fashion. At present it is always a question of political crisis fraught with danger for the country and the party. This is intolerable. The very pace of modern life demands the regular replacement of older leaders by younger and more capable ones. It is imperative to remove the great and sometimes insurmountable obstacles in the way of more rapid promotion. Secretaries of the Central Committee and ministers should not be "appointed" for life, and there must be regular replacement of people in all other leading positions.[21] It is by no means a question of demotion after the tenure of office expires. If an official has proved to be an able and efficient leader, work will always be found for him to fit his abilities and experience. For example, the Minister of Foreign Affairs, leaving his post, could be elected President of the Commission for Foreign Affairs of the Supreme Soviet. Or the Central Committee Secretary for International Relations could be appointed Minister of Foreign Affairs. Most senior officials could only benefit, in terms of their professional skills, by moving over to other positions in this way. A person leaving the Central Committee or some other party body because of the end of his term of office could also be re-elected after a lapse of several years. A similar principle gradually should be introduced in many other public organizations and government service.

In the past it was always obvious to socialists and com-

munists, dreaming of a more just social order, that all posts
in central and local government would be held only for a
limited period by persons chosen for their abilities and moral
qualities. Bebel, for example, wrote at the end of the nineteenth century: "All positions in the future society will be
held only temporarily. In this way persons occupying these
posts will not acquire that special quality of 'officialdom';
there will no longer be any question of those peculiar features we associate with prolonged tenure of office and a
hierarchical advancement in government service."[22] It would
be very rash to continue dismissing these very reasonable
proposals as the empty utopian dreams of nineteenth-century
idealists. On the contrary, they are today a most important
part not of utopian but of scientific socialism.

VII

The Soviets

The development of inner-party democracy as proposed in the last chapter would automatically lead to a more important role for Soviet *executive* institutions and representative bodies at all levels, from the Supreme Soviet right down to the local Soviets. In any large modern state the possibilities for direct democracy are extremely limited, so that the various forms of indirect representation take on vital significance—i.e., the people can exercise their right to participate in the government of the country only through freely elected and regularly replaced representatives. It is clearly just as crucial for a socialist country as for a bourgeois democracy that all elective bodies should function properly.

Yet one cannot ignore the fact that in the Soviet Union today representative bodies at all levels play only a very subservient part. This is particularly apparent in the activities of the Supreme Soviet, which are given comparatively extensive coverage in the Soviet press. The present chapter will be largely concerned with the Supreme Soviet. However, most of the comments and suggestions that follow can be applied to Soviets on all other levels (republican, regional, district, and city).*

* Soviets (councils) are the hierarchy of elected government bodies in the Soviet Union, forming a strict chain of command. Republican Soviets are bicameral, their structure similar in this and other respects to that of the Supreme Soviet. The degree of authority allowed to republican ministries and state committees has varied at different periods. Executive committees of local Soviets are subordinate to them but also to the executive committee of the

Under Stalin the Supreme Soviet gradually became a body that existed merely for show. Disregard for the opinion of the Supreme Soviet was such that budgets were submitted for its approval after they had already been in effect for half a year. Sessions of many regional and local Soviets were held simply in order to "elect" an executive committee, which then proceeded to deal with local affairs (under the guidance of the regional party committee); ordinary members had almost no further say.

The situation has changed to some extent during the last fifteen or sixteen years. Sessions of local Soviets have been held more regularly, and there have been more frequent meetings of the Supreme Soviet. The state budget is now usually ratified in December of the previous year. The various commissions of the Supreme Soviet have become more active, and their number has increased. Still, however, neither the Supreme Soviet nor its Presidium occupies anything like its rightful place in the government of the country as an organ of popular power. Although according to the Constitution the right to initiate legislation belongs not only to the Council of Ministers but also to the Supreme Soviet, the latter is not in fact encouraged to do so. In the whole thirty-four years of its existence not a single bill has been brought in by an individual deputy or group of deputies on their own initiative rather than on behalf of the Council of Ministers or some other state body. In all this time there has not been a single occasion on which its members have criticized any bill laid before it. Objections can be voiced only on minor matters of detail. The Supreme Soviet has never once rejected a bill or returned one for amendment. This should not be taken to mean either that the bills as submitted are perfect or that no deputies ever have serious doubts about them. Moreover, it is clear from the experience of the past ten to fifteen years that many bills "passed" by the Supreme Soviet have been ill-advised or seriously defective in some way or another. Sooner or later it has been necessary either to rescind them or to make substantial changes. But this has never happened on

---

next higher Soviet. They are concerned with local problems such as education, public health, local industry, the militia, etc. Voting for the Soviets is according to residential electoral precincts.— Trans.

the initiative of the Supreme Soviet or any of its commissions. In view of the fact that the Supreme Soviet usually meets only twice a year (and then only for five or six days), much urgent legislation is simply passed by its Presidium with virtually no discussion at all. The Supreme Soviet subsequently gives its formal approval, also without discussion. Not once has the Supreme Soviet refused to approve a decree passed by its Presidium, though the Presidium itself has often later annulled many of its own enactments as misconceived. Apart from the Presidium, there are also the commissions of the Supreme Soviet, which operate between sessions and have as their basic task the preliminary discussion of legislation. Presumably, proceedings in the commissions are more lively than in plenary sessions of the Supreme Soviet, but this can be no substitute for debate in the Supreme Soviet itself— the only body with full legislative authority and responsibility. Even more important, sessions of the Supreme Soviet are held *openly* whereas the work of the commissions or the Presidium are as a general rule not even reported in the press. Only occasionally are we given brief glimpses of what goes on.[1] Yet it is most important for any representative institution, particularly for the highest of them, to conduct its discussions of all major problems openly. The public should be allowed to know not only what laws are passed but also the arguments advanced both for and against them. Without this kind of wide publicity about the work of elective bodies it is impossible to foster a spirit of political activism among the people as a whole. Sessions of the Supreme Soviet continue to be an empty formality, so that nobody bothers to read accounts of "parliamentary proceedings" in Soviet newspapers.

We can see the purely formal nature of most plenary sessions by looking at the first session of the Eighth Supreme Soviet in July 1970. In the course of a *single day*, July 15, it got through the following agenda: 1) It elected a new Presidium; 2) the Council of Ministers (the government of the USSR), one hundred strong, was formed without any discussion whatsoever; 3) an All-Union bill concerning basic labor legislation was given its first reading, debated (short speeches were made by several delegates), and then approved (this evidently was the first comprehensive labor law since the 1922 RSFSR Code was passed; it would have been quite possible to have organized an explanatory debate about this extremely important enactment, but the entire discussion lasted only *an hour and a half;* no amendments of any kind were made, and what is more, the newspapers published only a short report written by V. Prokhorov but none of the speeches); 4) various questions of foreign policy were discussed and two resolutions approved—one concerning the situation in Southeast Asia and the other on the Middle East. This brought the joint session of the two chambers of the Supreme Soviet to an end.* All the questions on the agenda for the first session had been exhausted on the very first day, and the session was declared closed on the evening of July 15. (On the fourteenth there had been separate sittings of the two chambers—mainly in order to elect their respective controlling bodies and commissions.)

It is easy enough to show that present-day Soviet institutions are now far from enjoying the status they had in Lenin's time. During the early period of Soviet rule, each session of the Supreme Soviet was an outstanding historical event, rather more than can be said for most sessions of the Supreme Soviet today. Also in the first five or ten years after the October Revolution, the Central Executive Committee of the Soviets played a much greater part in government than its successor, the present-day Presidium of the Supreme Soviet. It is therefore at least in this respect rather early to start congratulating ourselves on a restoration of Leninist standards.

Lenin laid particular stress on the *election* of the Soviets at all levels. Marx and Engels long held the view that the dictatorship of the proletariat could take the form of a parliamentary republic. But Russia, of course, had never had a parliament or been a republic. In the Revolution of 1905, Russian workers created the first Soviets, and these were later re-established in 1917. Even before the October Revolution, discussing the experience of 1905, Lenin declared the Soviets to be the best possible embodiment of popular power. Later he added Soviets to the list of basic requirements for any

* The two chambers of the Supreme Soviet are the Council of the Union, in which each deputy represents a constituency of about 300,000 people, and the Council of Nationalities, in which Union and Autonomous Republics, Autonomous Regions, and National Areas are represented respectively by 32, 11, 5, and 1 deputies. The two chambers are equal in rights and responsibilities.—Trans.

socialist proletarian revolution ("Soviet power plus the dictatorship of the proletariat"), valid for any country in the world. At the same time he scoffed at the predilection of social democrats everywhere for a parliamentary republic and compared its characteristic division of powers unfavorably with a republic of Soviets. In this period all communist parties without exception included a demand for Soviets in their programmes. The prestige of parliamentary government after the First World War had markedly declined in all the countries of Europe, and Soviets were established by revolutionary movements that came into being as a result of October (in Hungary, Germany, Finland, etc.). Soviets also began to appear in China in the mid-twenties.

A great deal has changed since that time, however. Our own system of Soviets as a form of government has undergone considerable evolution. In the process many important aspects considered by Lenin to be most valuable advantages of the former system of Soviets have disappeared. For example, representation on the production principle has again been replaced by representation on the territorial principle, whereas Lenin so often said that the very fact of elections being held at places of work and in military units "gave [the Soviets] close links with the members of all the various professions and thus made it easier to carry out a wide range of fundamental reforms without bureaucracy."[2] Also a thing of the past are those close mutual links and interdependence between higher and lower Soviets that made it possible, in Lenin's words, "to combine the advantages of parliamentarianism with those of direct democracy, i.e., to unite in the persons of the people's elected representatives both legislative and executive functions."[3] Originally the workers, peasants, and soldiers elected deputies only to the local Soviets, which in their turn elected representatives to Soviets at the next level, and so on. In 1936 this system was replaced by direct elections in which the people of a constituency vote directly for deputies to local, city, and republican Soviets, and to the Supreme Soviet.

But of course what matters most about the Soviets is not the way they are elected or their structure. Even before 1936 the Soviets were "in a state of lethargic slumber and were dragging out a miserable existence."[4] Stalin had long since converted the Soviets from bodies of popular power at all levels into appendages of party organizations—they had become silent instruments for the fulfillment of party directives. Far from changing this situation the new Constitution perpetuated it, by stripping the highest representative bodies of all but nominal functions. The new electoral system undermined the mutual links between the Soviets and the factories and institutions, which now lost any possibility of effectively influencing the composition and activities of the Soviets. There was in fact a noticeable loss of contact between voters and their deputies. It became more difficult for the voters to follow the activities of a particular deputy and, if necessary, have him removed from office. Under the previous system of elections being held at places of work, voters were in a position to make informed judgments about their candidates and elect those best fitted to represent them; at present, however, there is no element of choice at all, since only one candidate's name appears on the ballot. The effect on a deputy's sense of responsibility toward his constituents is fatal. The voters are similarly affected, many of them quickly forgetting whom they have voted for. The Soviets at various levels are no longer effectively interdependent as they used to be. When local Soviets elected deputies to the next higher one, they were able to exercise some measure of control, but under the present system this is no longer the case—all pressures come from the top downward.

In short, while many advantages of the original system have been lost, the Soviets have not acquired any of the virtues of the parliamentary form of government. As a result, even among communist parties there has been a sharp drop in international regard for the Soviets as an institution. Almost all communist parties in capitalist countries have dropped the demand for a Soviet republic from their programmes. Reverting in effect to the view of Marx and Engels, they have concluded that the dictatorship of the proletariat will be best served by a parliamentary republic.

Some people believe that the shortcomings of the Soviets as representative institutions are rooted in the one-party system and the absence of a political opposition. They argue that under a one-party system the Supreme Soviet and Soviets at lower levels will never become public forums with genuine discussion of the basic problems of the country.

It is of course quite true that representative institutions are vitally affected by the existence of political opposition and a multiparty system. Under such conditions the party in power is compelled to justify its policies in the face of opposition criticism, answer questions, and defend its choice of candidates for government posts. As I have argued above, a socialist country has nothing to fear from the introduction of such a system, There are many situations in which an opposition may prompt the party in power to reform itself, strengthen its ranks, and put better people into positions of responsibility. A legal opposition can force a government— and this could be true in the case of a communist government—to adopt wiser policies, avoid obvious blunders, fight against abuses of power and corruption, and better protect the interests of the people. I believe, however, that even if the one-party system is retained in this country, it is possible to introduce many reforms that would substantially improve the position of our representative bodies, particularly the Supreme Soviet.

Of course it would not be enough merely to return to the form and structure of the Soviets as they existed in Lenin's time. This would be unrealistic and in some respects even unwise, since conditions are now rather different. At that time it was necessary to make a decisive break with the old order, to make revolutionary changes in thousands of established traditions and laws, simultaneously replacing them by new ones. If this tremendous task was to be achieved in the shortest possible time, any kind of permanent legislative body with regular sessions, long debates, and opposition arguments was clearly out of the question. More effective forms of authority were needed so that questions could be decided quickly, and the original system of Soviets met this need by combining executive and legislative functions. At that time All-Russian congresses of Soviets took place only once or twice a year. All basic decrees and legislative acts were passed by the *Sovnarkom* (Council of People's Commissars) or the Central Executive Committee. This was a necessary and suitable system at a period when parliaments were scornfully dismissed as mere talk shops.

But with the passage of time, the situation in the country changed radically. Soviet power was firmly established and the *quality* of its legislation now became an issue of prime importance. The urgent problem was to find ways and means of enabling representative bodies to exercise control over the activities of those in power. It was necessary to find an intelligent system for limiting the prerogatives of the executive and providing for more serious discussion of government legislation. In other words, there was an obvious need for a clear-cut division between executive and legislative power. The Constitution of 1936 appeared to make a small step in this direction by formally declaring the Supreme Soviet to be the sole legislative authority, with the right to adopt and confirm the laws of the country. In fact, however, it amounted to no more than a formal separation of powers. Since it met only one or two times a year and then only for short sessions, the Supreme Soviet could hardly become a *working* body and its real power was negligible, while in practice the executive was becoming even more omnipotent. With minor changes, this situation has lasted to the present day.

It is evident that the time has come to make a series of substantial changes in the functioning of the Supreme Soviet (what follows will also apply to the Supreme Soviets of the national republics of the USSR). In my view this means turning it into an effective working body with longer sessions at more frequent intervals. All legislative bills should be placed before it for discussion and there must be a more extensive right to initiate legislation. One can envisage the Supreme Soviet ultimately becoming a permanently functioning body which would go into recess only a few times a year for vacations and to enable deputies to visit their constituencies.

Such a reform would naturally require a very different type of deputy than at present. Many of them now are people who at the same time occupy top posts in the party and government, in the economy, and in the army, etc. They include ministers of the USSR, party secretaries from regional and large city committees, departmental heads from the Central Committee, chairmen of regional executive committees, commanders of military districts, directors of the largest factories, etc. These are all very busy people, hardly able to leave their normal responsibilities for long periods in order to attend sessions of the Supreme Soviet. It has even become the practice for heads of departments and Secretaries of the Central Committee to be elected chairmen of Supreme Soviet commissions. But inasmuch as nearly all the leading officials from the Central Committee, the Council of Ministers, and several other high-level executive institutions are members of the Supreme Soviet and head all its commissions, no wonder it has been turned into a body with strictly ritualistic functions! After all, what is the point of again discussing decisions and laws that have only just been considered by the very same people in the Central Committee or in the Council of Ministers?

Among the deputies there are, of course, also ordinary workers, collective farmers, clerks, teachers, doctors, artists, writers, etc. However, their position is clearly inferior. They are nominated, or rather selected, by a purely bureaucratic process in regional party committees. There is little sign here of workers in some factory or other choosing from a dozen or so possibilities the candidate they regard as the most suitable. As a result the ordinary people who find themselves "elected" to the Supreme Soviet scarcely feel themselves to be true representatives of those sections of the community to which they belong.

The time has come for the Supreme Soviet to be composed largely of *full-time* deputies. It is not simply that present-day legislative activity demands a great deal of time and effort, but also that the Supreme Soviet should be a truly representative body with deputies actually representing their constituencies. This is hardly the case at present, nor can it become so unless deputies are able to devote all their time to the job. Because of pressure of work, neither a minister nor a military commander can satisfactorily represent the electorate of a constituency and stand up for its legitimate interests. Therefore any person elected to the Supreme Soviet should be released from his normal duties during his term of service.

This is accepted practice, of course, in the parliamentary systems of many Western countries. It is true that ministers are also elected to parliament in these countries, e.g., England, though they do not necessarily attend all sessions. But in our country, with its one-party system, the top legislative body should be made up exclusively of deputies who have no duty other than that of representing their own constituents.

Ministers and people in basic positions of responsibility

in the government should be selected by the Supreme Soviet from among the most outstanding and capable men in the country. But if a person appointed to a government post happens also to be a deputy he should resign from the Supreme Soviet, and conversely, if a minister is elected deputy he should give up his ministerial office. Needless to say, the party would continue to exercise a decisive influence on the Supreme Soviet, since under our system the majority of deputies will certainly be party members or "sympathizers." But henceforth this influence would be indirect, channeled, as it were, through a kind of "communist faction" in the Supreme Soviet. On the other hand, the Central Committee would pay greater attention than at present to the views of deputies who are also party members.

It is quite possible that regional Soviets will also have to change to a system of full-time deputies, although it would not be justified to release deputies from their ordinary work at the district and city levels in view of their lesser resonsibilities. Here plenary sessions of the Soviet could be held less frequently; however a large proportion of the deputies should be elected from among ordinary people and given some time off from their normal occupations so that they could take part in sessions of the Soviet and carry out their representative responsibilities.

It goes without saying that all representatives to the Supreme Soviet must possess "parliamentary immunity," with the provision that a deputy may be tried in the courts only after a two-thirds majority decision of the Supreme Soviet and not just its Presidium. Only the voters should have the right to recall a deputy and deprive him of his mandate.

The changes that have been suggested would mean a more precise *division between legislative and executive powers* and also between representation on the one hand and government on the other.

If Lenin believed that a merging of legislative and executive functions was one of the main advantages of the Soviets, this was indeed the case during the first years after the Revolution. However, the further evolution of our state has clearly shown that the combination of legislative and executive powers within one institution leads over a period of time to the disproportionate growth of the executive, thus turning representative bodies into empty appendages, providing an opening for a regime of personal dictatorship, and creating a favorable atmosphere for the development of bureaucracy and abuse of power. The machine of state moves further and further beyond the people's control and becomes purely self-serving. It is therefore vital not only to separate party and state leadership (as was done at the October Plenum) but to effect a more precise division between legislative and executive power on the one hand and executive and administrative power on the other.

When enlarging the role of the Supreme Soviet, it is important not only to extend its right to initiate legislation but also to make it the highest supervisory body in the state. This task could be carried out by individual deputies, or by various commissions of the Supreme and lower-level Soviets which would take over a considerable part of the work dealt with so inadequately by the Committees of Party and State Control set up in 1962 (and subsequently renamed the People's Control Committees). Anyone who has had dealings with these People's Control Committees knows that they have rapidly turned into bureaucratic structures which in their terms of reference and approach are reminiscent of the former Ministries of State Control.* I believe that representative bodies whose powers and authority derive from popular election are the best agencies to exercise most supervisory functions.

Finally it must never be forgotten that the Supreme Soviet is a representative as well as legislative body; Soviets at lower levels also have a representative function. But at present a considerable number of deputies meet their constituents only once every few years, just before elections, after which almost no contact is maintained. These deputies can hardly

---

* Khrushchev set up the Committee of Party and State Control in keeping with his policy of fusing party and government administrative organs, although in practice party influence always remained dominant. It was a highly centralized structure, with (at least on paper) extensive powers of supervision and discipline at all levels of party and government activity. The People's Control Committee, which replaced it in December 1965, is a purely state body with no powers to check on party organs. The function of discipline in the party reverted again to the Party Control Committee.—Trans.

be said to *represent* those who elect them. A great many deputies not only of the Supreme Soviet but even of district Soviets have no regular procedure for receiving constituents. Thus the Soviets have virtually lost their representative character at all levels. This is intolerable. Deputies should have regular meetings with their constituents, give talks at large factories and public accounts of their activities, discuss important new bills of wide public interest and at the same time listen to the wishes of those who elected them. A concrete procedure must be devised for recalling deputies who have betrayed the trust of the electorate. (At present the right of recall is purely nominal.)

As long as the majority of deputies have no genuine opportunity to express the will of the electorate and moreover are so remote that they do not even know and seldom care about voters' opinions on particular questions, it hardly matters how many candidates are put up at elections—one or ten, it makes little difference. It is true, however, that the participation of several candidates in a lively electoral campaign would arouse the masses to political activity and promote the transition from pseudo democracy to genuine democracy.

Changes in the function and composition of the Supreme Soviet and the establishment of a system of full-time deputies would at last make it possible to introduce a system for electing representatives to the Supreme Soviet and all the other bodies in the Soviet system from among competing candidates.[5] The present electoral system under which only one candidate is nominated for each constituency is completely obsolete. There cannot be truly democratic elections if the voters do not have the opportunity to choose between at least two candidates. It is true that the existing r' gulations do not prevent the nomination of an unlimited number of candidates. The following sentence even appears on the ballot: "Leave the name of the *one* candidate for whom you wish to vote and cross out the remaining ones." But this is a perfect example of practice being completely different from theory.[6] If there is a second or third candidate it is almost always a leading member of the party or government who will subsequently announce that he wishes to stand only in one of the many constituencies that have nominated him.[7] Thus today's election campaigns have become an empty ritual, utterly tedious for canvassers and voters alike. If the aim is to educate people, election campaigns are either completely useless or even distinctly harmful both politically and morally. A large section of the population has by now completely lost interest in elections to the Soviets. Campaigning is carried out in a perfunctory manner and even candidates themselves show little interest in the proceedings. The nature of the system has resulted in a very minimal feeling of responsibility toward voters—a candidate knows perfectly well that if selected by a party organization and approved by the regional party committee, his election is a foregone conclusion. "I'll be elected all the same," a certain prominent Soviet writer cynically told members of the Kirov regional party committee when they reproached him for being drunk at meetings with constituents. Cases of candidates failing to be elected are in fact extremely rare and have occurred only during elections to local Soviets. The press for some reason has kept silent about these incidents, although they surely deserved to be written about in great detail.

Voters quickly forget the names of their candidates, often not even bothering to look at the ballots. A growing number of people are simply failing to vote altogether. At the same time infringements of the Electoral Law are becoming more frequent. Commissions in charge of polling places sometimes allow a daughter to vote on behalf of her mother, a husband for his wife, or one neighbor for another. It often happens that members of the commission themselves cast votes for people who are late or have failed to appear.[8] On election day "house managers" fill out and give to canvassers great numbers of fictitious forms to certify that people who have not gone to vote are either ill or out of town.* Thousands of members of electoral commissions and canvassers take part in this legalized confidence trick during each election campaign. Clearly electoral campaigns do little to encourage a spirit of truth and honesty among Soviet citizens.

* The role of canvassers is to ensure that voters actually turn out to vote. As each canvasser is responsible for a certain area, they ask house managers of large apartment buildings (*domoupravlenie*, roughly equivalent to a *concierge*) to provide documents exempting those who have not voted, thereby enabling them to account for these people to the electoral commissions.—Trans.

How can the present electoral system be transformed? Some socialist countries have already introduced certain changes. In Hungary, for example, a new electoral law makes it possible to nominate two or more candidates in elections both for local councils and to the State Assembly. It is true that in the election of 1967, when the new law was operative for the first time, only nine constituencies out of 349 put forward two candidates for the State Assembly. However in elections for local councils, 681 constituencies nominated two candidates while in five constituencies there were three candidates.[9] Four years later, in 1971, 49 constituencies had two or three candidates in the elections for the State Assembly and 3,014 in elections for the local councils, encompassing more than a million voters. Forty per cent of votes cast were for unsuccessful candidates. Re-elections were held for the State Assembly in three constituencies and for the local councils in 81 constituencies, where none of the candidates had received a clear majority.[10]

Interesting experiments have also been carried out in recent years in Czechoslovakia, Poland, and also in Yugoslavia. Which reforms could be adopted in the USSR? This question can be answered only after there have been experiments in the individual republics. Most experts who have seriously studied the problems of socialist democracy believe that it is now possible to introduce a system under which two or three competing candidates could be put forward in elections for local Soviets.[11] This system should first be tried in a few constituencies and then eventually extended until competitive elections are held everywhere for all Soviets up to and including the Supreme Soviet.

Many writers have proposed that we drop the system of elections on a territorial principal and return to constituencies based on places of work for elections to local and regional Soviets. V. Kotok, for example, in his doctoral thesis *Problems of the Development of Direct Democracy in the Soviet State* argues very convincingly in favor of this change. Yu. Shabanov suggests returning to the system of local Soviet elections that prevailed before the Constitution of 1936: "It will strengthen links between the Soviets and workers; it will increase the influence of the Soviets on the work of factories, mines, and other enterprises and will extend those aspects of the Soviets that are truly democratic. . . . If each deputy were genuinely to represent a specific workers' collective or group of collectives, voters would be much more interested in the person chosen as candidate and the level of political activity would certainly rise. The deputies so elected would for the most part probably be people who worked in the collectives in question, which would encourage a greater sense of responsibility on their part. Regular communication between deputies and their constituents would make it possible for the electors themselves, both individually and as members of their collectives, to keep a very real check on the work of their representatives in the Soviets. . . . Election to lower Soviets based on places of work and social collectives would greatly simplify the electoral system and increase its democratic element. Voting could be in secret, as already happens in the elections of their officials by party organizations and trade unions. All those attending meetings would have the right to nominate, discuss, and reject candidates."[12]

In constituencies dominated by one large factory or academic institution, etc., nomination of candidates could be organized by shop floors, departments, or faculties, followed by a meeting of all the voters at which the different candidates would be discussed and one selected.[13] Where constituencies are very large and include a great number of different enterprises, each separate factory or institution would hold a general meeting to select its candidate (with some element of competition at this stage) and also appoint representatives to a constituency electoral meeting where one candidate would finally be selected by secret ballot.

As far as pensioners and housewives are concerned, they could vote with a particular enterprise (where they used to work or where their husbands work). Or special constituencies could be set up on a territorial basis to enable persons of this category to vote.

We should also experiment (possibly in one of the republics) with the system of indirect elections that existed before 1936, but by secret rather than open ballot. In this way city or district Soviets would not only become bodies of local self-government but also would constitute an organic part, however small, of the whole state system, for it is the lower Soviets that would provide the personnel for those at higher levels. Under this arrangement, there would not be a single deputy in a higher Soviet who had not been first elected to a lower one.

It is interesting that in Hungary, which in many respects sets a good example of socialist democracy for other socialist countries, under the 1970 electoral law the organization of elections at the regional level is entrusted to city and village councils. This means that elections to regional councils are no longer direct. But on the other hand, lower representative bodies have gained in importance, which has encouraged citizens to be more personally involved and politically active. In the opinion of our Hungarian comrades, the system of indirect elections is ultimately more democratic.

Of course it is impossible to guarantee that any electoral system will be free of abuse. And this includes indirect elections. Both democracy and effectiveness can be lost unless an end is put to the bureaucratic practice of confirming all candidates *at a higher level* before they can be added to the voting list—particularly when they have in any case been "programmed in" by a system of "prior allotment."* If everything is predetermined from above, one cannot speak of voting or elections in any real sense. Obviously any higher state or party body must have the right to select its own candidates for election to Soviets. But the same right must not be denied in practice to workers in the factories and it must be possible for any group to defend its nominations at electoral meetings and at the elections themselves. It is also important that the voters at large have the right to put forward their own independent candidates as well. It should be possible for any group of citizens who collect the signatures of more than one hundred fellow constituents to put forward their own candidate for elections to the local Soviet, and with five hundred signatures to nominate candidates for elections to regional and republican Soviets. Nomination of an independent candidate to the Supreme Soviet could require a thousand signatures. Under this arrangement it would also be necessary to allow members of such nominating groups to participate in the work of electoral commissions. There should also be much greater guarantees than at present for secrecy during the voting process. The present system is quite intoler-

* *Razvyorstka:* The system whereby party officials fill places behind the scenes from their own lists of "suitable" personnel.

able: voting takes place in the presence of members of the electoral commission and representatives of the canvassers and can be done either by dropping the ballot directly into the ballot box or by going to the booths that stand a little to one side. However since there is just one name on the ballot, only someone who wishes to vote against by crossing it out enters a booth, which he must do under the gaze of those who have just noted him down on the electoral roll. This is a very strange way of ensuring a "secret" vote.[14] The procedure should be such that each voter, whatever his intention, has to enter a closed booth. Eventually it will also be necessary to make use of special voting machines.

Some authors have emphasized the importance of combining representative and direct democracy in various ways. It has been suggested that there should be more frequent conferences and symposia for the members of individual professions. These should not be mere show occasions, as in the case of the last congress of Soviet schoolteachers, but businesslike meetings where those taking part can really debate questions that interest them. Much more care should be taken in drawing up and adopting the "electors' mandate" and in seeing that it is in fact carried out.

One particularly effective form of direct democracy is the referendum. According to the Constitution, the Presidium of the Supreme Soviet is empowered to hold a referendum on its own initiative or at the demand of any one of the Union Republics. During the thirty-six years that the Constitution has been in operation, however, not a single referendum has been held. This despite the fact that the referendum is of vital importance not only to ascertain public opinion on a given problem but also to educate the masses politically and to increase their sense of responsibility in political matters.[15]

Referendums could be held not only at the all-Union level, but also in the republics or even regions. A referendum can be the best way of adopting constitutional reforms or basic amendments to the Constitution. Many other kinds of questions could best be settled in the same way. This problem was the subject of an interesting study by V. Kotov, published in 1964, entitled *The Referendum in a Socialist Democratic System*.[16] The eminent legal specialist N. Farberov also argues in favor of the referendum,[17] and these suggestions should not be ignored.

VIII

The Judicial System
and the
Security Forces

In a socialist democracy, it is crucially important that the legal system (courts, procuracy,* and lawyers) and state security services function correctly. To quote from a leading article in *Kommunist:* "It should be a matter of deepest concern not only for the government but also for party, trade union, and Komsomol organizations to reinforce the concept of law and order and to see that the workers have a better knowledge of the law. It is vital that we reach a stage where respect for the law has become the personal concern of every individual and is reflected in every action of people in authority."[1]

This same point is emphasized in the Central Committee's report to the Twenty-fourth Party Congress: "Attempts to deviate from the law, whatever the motive, cannot be tolerated under any circumstances. Similarly, infringements of the rights of the individual and encroachments on the dignity of citizens must not be tolerated. It is a question of principle for us as communists, as supporters of the highest ideals of humanitarianism."[2]

---

* Soviet procurators have a dual function. They prosecute in criminal cases but also are charged with defending the rights of the accused as part of their responsibility for the observance of the law throughout the judicial and penal system.—Trans.

Unfortunately it must be noted that at the present time there are many serious shortcomings not only in the actual work of the various bodies concerned with the administration of justice but also in their very structure. Our law courts, for example, are still insufficiently democratic. Everything said in the previous chapter about deficiencies in the system of election to the Soviets also applies to elections for the People's Courts*—there is no element of contest and little contact between "people's judges" and their electors. "People's assessors" are elected in factories, institutions, etc.; but the selection of candidates is generally done in a bureaucratic manner and discussion of the nominations at workers' meetings is superficial and lacks any element of real debate.

At the lowest level a court consists of a judge, who has specialized legal training, and two assessors, each with one vote. The verdicts of the court are reached by simple majority. This system has been subject to well-founded criticism in the press on a number of occasions (for example, in *Literaturnaya Gazeta*). It has been pointed out that the usual number of assessors is too small to justify the term "People's Court." There should, therefore, be a larger number of assessors with verdicts reached by a two-thirds or three-fourths vote rather than by simple majority. Under the jury system used in other countries, complete unanimity is generally required for a verdict of guilty.

The status of the legal profession in the Soviet Union is very low. In accordance with the Code of Criminal Procedure, a defense lawyer is admitted to a case only after the preliminary investigation has been completed and the case for the prosecution has been drawn up. Such a way of doing things is completely incompatible with the adversary nature of legal procedure. It is not only that the defense has far less time than the prosecution to prepare its case; the fatal defect of

---

* People's Courts have first-instance jurisdiction for all civil and criminal cases (except where codes of procedure indicate otherwise) and are set up in towns, municipal and rural districts. Their judges are elected by the inhabitants of their area of jurisdiction for five-year terms. (Judges of higher-level courts are elected by the appropriate Soviet.) Assessors are laymen chosen from a panel to which they have been elected. They have equal authority with the judge in passing verdict and sentence, but in present practice it is virtually unknown for them to disagree with the judge.— Trans.

this system is that in the majority of cases the defense lawyer is deprived of the opportunity to give the accused an explanation of his rights as a person who is presumed to be innocent. The lawyer has no chance of challenging the investigating officials' decision to order the detention of the accused before he is brought into court nor is he able to follow the course of the interrogation and prevent possible abuses (which unfortunately are by no means infrequent). For example, the majority of citizens who are faced with prosecution for the first time are ignorant of their right to refuse to make statements as laid down in the Code of Criminal Procedure. The same is true of persons detained on suspicion—although it is in violation of the Code, they are often interrogated as witnesses (who do not have the right to refuse to make statements). Clearly our system of legal representation, a vital element in the protection of the rights of the individual, is very much behind that of the bourgeois democracies. This situation is totally unacceptable in a socialist state.

Soviet citizens still have no means of legal redress in cases where they feel actions by state officials or organizations have been improper or illegal. Their only possible course is to protest through administrative channels, something that rarely results in a satisfactory response. Lenin wrote in 1903: "In order to stop highhanded behavior by officials it must be made possible for any person to complain directly to the courts. After all, what is the sense of complaining to the land captain* about the village policeman, or to the provincial governor about the land captain? The land captain will simply cover up for the policeman and the governor for the land captain, and what is more, the complainant will soon find himself in trouble. . . . We will only have redress against officials when every person in Russia has the right to complain to an elected court, talk freely about his grievances or write to the newspapers, as happens in all other countries."[3] Unfortunately, for the most part such a right does not yet exist.

---

* Land captains (*zemski nachalniki*) were officials appointed by the provincial governor to exercise administrative and judicial functions in rural districts, replacing elected justices of the peace. This reactionary change took place during the reign of Alexander III.— Trans.

We still have many cases of illegal interference by local or higher state and party bodies in court proceedings. There are also breaches of the rule that deliberations between the judge and assessors concerning the verdict must not be divulged to outsiders. Sometimes during the actual consideration of a verdict or in the intervals between court sessions judges even call the district party committee or some other nonjudicial body to ask for advice or for approval of a particular verdict.

It is quite intolerable that political cases should be heard in semiclosed or in effect fully closed courtrooms, when it is just these cases that arouse the greatest interest among the Soviet and foreign public. A good example of this was the trial of Sinyavsky and Daniel, which caused such a stir in 1966 and which was the first in a whole series of similar political trials. The courtroom was packed with hand-picked "members of the public," many of whom came not on their own initiative but under orders. But a number of writers and scientists who made persistent requests to be allowed to attend were not admitted, nor were foreign journalists—not even communists. Although "public accusers"* were there to testify, no "public defenders" were invited. It is hardly surprising, therefore, that both the proceedings and the verdict quite justifiably attracted much unfavorable comment both in the Soviet Union and abroad.[4]

The trials of Khaustov and Bukovsky in 1967 were also semiclosed, as were those of Litvinov, Bogaraz, and others (1968), Ginzburg, Galanskov, and others (1968), Grigorenko (1969), Gorbanevskaya (1970), Pimenov and Vail (1970), Amalrik (1970), Bukovsky (1972), and many similar trials which have taken place in recent years in Moscow, Leningrad, Sverdlovsk, Kaluga, and other cities. The trials of various groups of Crimean Tatars accused of breaches of the peace, as well as of Ukrainians, Armenians, and Estonians charged with nationalist activities were to all intents and purposes completely closed. The same was true of the trial in Leningrad (1970) where a group of persons, mostly of Jewish origin, were accused of planning to hijack a civil aircraft

* A "public accuser" is a person who supports the prosecution case on behalf of a "public organization" (e.g., the Writers Union, as in this case).—Trans.

in order to flee the country. Such cases not only arouse skepticism among the public about the way in which political trials are conducted but also undermine confidence in the legal system as a whole. Public opinion is alarmed not so much by the fact of the trials themselves as by the numerous infringements of legal procedure, by the secrecy, and by the one-sided and extremely incomplete reporting in our press. A short time before the trial of Ginzburg, Galanskov, Lashkova, and Dobrovolsky it became widely known in the Soviet Union and abroad that a group of thirty-one eminent members of the Soviet intelligentsia had signed a letter demanding that the case be heard in public. However not one of the signatories was allowed to attend the trial. Friends of the accused were also kept out, and the court even refused to admit a number of people whom the defense wished to call as witnesses. Furthermore there was no mention of the trial in the press until it was over; then several tendentious and misleading accounts finally appeared. Little wonder that the Western press mounted such an unprecedented propaganda campaign around this particular trial. It was also quite natural that many Muscovites and particularly people living in other towns sought information about the trial by tuning in to the BBC or the Voice of America. In the end considerable harm was done to the reputation of Soviet courts.[5]

The propaganda campaigns in the bourgeois press about the hijacking case and the Bukovsky trial were equally vociferous and by no means ineffectual in terms of their influence on Western public opinion. How can one remain indifferent when such serious damage is inflicted on the prestige of the party and the USSR in progressive circles in capitalist countries and among the Soviet intelligentsia!

There are also serious and well-founded misgivings about certain pieces of legislation that are very relevant to the problem of socialist democracy. For example, under our present laws, persons can be held criminally liable for "anti-Soviet agitation and propaganda." These are defined as activity "carried out with the purpose of subverting or weakening Soviet power or of committing particularly dangerous crimes against the state, disseminating for the said purposes slanderous fabrications which defame the Soviet state and social system, as well as circulating, preparing, or harboring for the said purposes, literature of similar content" (Article 70 of the Criminal Code).

Obviously every country must protect its citizens against slander and prosecute persons who incite others to commit particularly dangerous crimes against it. But the terms of Article 70 are extremely vague and imprecise: they are frequently applied to works containing even completely justified criticism of particular aspects of the political structure, usually survivals from the Stalin years which contravene the basic principles of socialism and the Soviet system. Materials intended to strengthen socialist democracy are thus denounced as "anti-Soviet agitation and propaganda." Similarly, entirely reasonable spoken or written criticism of the various shortcomings of Soviet life are made out to be "slanderous fabrications." Even a historical study of the abuses of power under Stalin was not long ago condemned in the following irresponsible way by certain very senior party authorities: "Under the pretext of criticizing the cult of Stalin the author has slandered the Soviet social and state system." In other words, the author should be arrested and tried under Article 70 of the Criminal Code.

Legal comment on Article 70 qualifies it in a number of important respects. For example: "A person can only be convicted of anti-Soviet agitation and propaganda when he has deliberately spread slanderous or defamatory views about the Soviet state and social order which he knows to be false. . . . There shall be no grounds for conviction if the person is honestly misguided in his interpretation of some aspect of Soviet reality or in his appraisal of various political institutions, etc. Such misguided judgment may, for example, be the result of mis-information. . . . An important criterion for the correct definition of 'anti-Soviet agitation and propaganda' is the subjective element, the presence of deliberate and specific intent on the part of the accused to undermine and weaken Soviet power. Intent is determined by the fact that the accused is aware of the danger to society and the possible consequences of his actions and was deliberately attempting to undermine or weaken Soviet power. . . . The absence of such awareness precludes the possibility of a successful prosecution under Article 70."[6]

These qualifications are evidence that Soviet jurisprudence has come a long way since the days when our prevailing legal theory maintained that there was no difference between objective and subjective behavior or activity. In other words, during the Stalin period, whether or not a person was in his own mind completely loyal to the Soviet system was irrelevant in the courtroom. If in the view of the party leadership he had in some way done harm to the dictatorship of the proletariat or supposedly aided the enemies of the country by means of an actual or alleged theoretical or practical error, then he should be made to answer for it no matter what his subjective intention.

Unfortunately, however, progress in legal theory is not always matched by corresponding improvements in the functioning of the legal system. During most of the political trials of recent years the courts have paid little attention to evidence concerning motivation. As a result people have been condemned almost entirely for views and convictions, arbitrarily and wrongly branded as anti-Soviet.

Public opinion has been severely critical of Paragraphs 1 and 3 of Article 190, recently introduced into the Criminal Code. Paragraph 1 is very much the same as Article 70. It is again a question of "the systematic dissemination of fabrications known to be false discrediting the Soviet state and social system." In legal comment on this article we read: "Isolated or repeated (not systematic) instances of dissemination of information known to be false which discredits the Soviet political and social system does not constitute a crime but rather provides grounds for intensifying political education of a preventive character." It goes on to state that "the subjective element of the crime as envisaged under Article 190 (1) of the Criminal Code assumes that the accused has an explicit intent knowingly to disseminate false information or documents, that he is aware of the systematic nature of his action and that he intends to act in a similar way in the future, i.e., that he will continue to slander the Soviet system. In cases where a person is not aware of the falseness of the information disseminated by him (for example, in the case of genuine error) there are no grounds for conviction under Article 190 (1)."[7]

Unfortunately, for all practical purposes this commentary has been ignored during most of the trials held in recent years under Article 190 (1). People have been convicted in spite of their sincerely held belief that the information or materials circulated by them were truthful and accurately reflected the facts of Soviet life whether past or present. There have also been convictions where the accused had not *systematically* disseminated information found by the court to be slanderous.

Paragraph 3 of Article 190 clearly contradicts the Constitution of the USSR. This paragraph defines as a crime "the organizing of or active participation in group actions which result in flagrant violation of public order or are combined with arrant refusal to comply with the lawful demands of representatives of authority or which entail a disruption of transport services, or the work of state or public enterprises or institutions." The adoption of this article in effect means a legal ban on any public demonstration involving several people which has not received previous sanction from the authorities. Even if a demonstration does not involve a "disruption of transport services" or "flagrant violation of the public order," it is always possible to charge people with "arrant refusal to comply with the lawful demands of representatives of authority."

Soviet legislation with regard to hooliganism also leaves much to be desired from a legal point of view. Abuses can easily occur because of the extremely summary way in which cases are heard without even the benefit of people's assessors. The police often bring a charge of "hooliganism" in order to obtain a rapid conviction under this simplified procedure where cases of a totally different kind are involved—such as attempts by Soviet citizens to enter the embassy of a capitalist country.

Our so-called "parasite" laws also give grounds for disquiet. Much of the wording of the Special Decree of the Presidium of the Supreme Soviet (May 4, 1961) is so vague that it has become the basis for a series of abuses. The most scandalous of these was probably the case of Joseph Brodsky in 1964, a gifted poet without regular employment who was sent to a northern region of the country where he was put to compulsory work. Unfortunately the new version of the law on parasites—the Decree of the Presidium of the Supreme Soviet of February 25, 1970—also has a number of serious flaws, following particularly from the fact that the term "parasite" remains exceedingly ill-defined from a legal point of view.

An extremely unfortunate aspect of our legal system is the legislation regulating the activities of psychiatric institutions. Psychiatric measures against dissenters—the certification of sane people as mentally ill or "psychopathic" and their consequent forcible committal to psychiatric hospitals of a general or special type—are nowadays resorted to more and more frequently. There are also cases in which the medical history of a person who may have suffered in the past from a relatively mild form of mental disturbance is deliberately misinterpreted to justify his committal to a psychiatric institution. According to my information, several dozen people have been illegally committed during the last few years. It is evident that forced hospitalization has become one of the authorities' favorite repressive measures against persons who have incurred their displeasure—a means of discrediting and intimidating dissidents. This abuse of psychiatry makes it possible to avoid normal court proceedings, the provision of evidence, and so forth. It is all too obvious that the use of psychiatry for political purposes poses an enormous threat to the future of socialist democracy in our country.

Of course this practice has existed since Stalin's time. Up to 1956 dozens of people were detained for political reasons in special psychiatric hospitals in Kazan and Leningrad. They were released after the Twentieth Congress and rehabilitated. In 1956 a state commission was set up under the chairmanship of a senior Central Committee official, A. Kuznetsov, to investigate illegal actions of this type. The commission included several eminent psychiatrists from various institutions. However its findings have never been made public.

Evidently after 1956, the process of partial democratization, with its greater emphasis on legality, put a temporary stop to the political use of psychiatry. There were signs of it again, however, in the early 1960's. Certain legislative measures and regulations were adopted at this time undoubtedly in order to make it easier to use psychiatry in this inhuman way, so incompatible with medical ethics. Up to 1960 the Criminal Code contained special articles that made doctors and psychiatrists liable to prosecution for ordering improper or groundless committal to a psychiatric hospital. This enabled relatives or the injured party himself to apply to the courts for redress. During the preparation of the new Code in 1961, however, these articles were dropped, and since that time there has been no way to lodge complaints about psychiatrists (or their superiors) in the courts. It can be done only through administrative channels via the district health department and eventually up to the Ministry of Health of the RSFSR and the USSR. Needless to say such an arrangement makes it very much harder to prevent or rectify cases of malpractice. And indeed, when some of the victims tried to complain to the courts about their illegal detention in mental hospitals, their applications were invariably rejected with the explanation that the actions of the psychiatrists or institutions concerned could only be challenged by an appeal to the Ministry of Health through normal channels.

At the end of 1961 the Ministry of Health in collaboration with the Ministry of Internal Affairs and the Procurator's Office adopted a special directive called "The Emergency Hospitalization of Mentally Ill Persons Who Are a Public Danger." Its basic provisions lay themselves open to severe criticism.

The directive appeared only in a specialized legal publication which was not made available to the general public.[8] In all cases of compulsory hospitalization known to me, the Health Department concerned has refused to show it either to the "patient" or to his relatives. Interested parties are also prevented from seeing many other directives, such as those regulating compulsory treatment, the procedure for psychiatric examinations, etc.[9] This makes it all the easier to violate official regulations, and certain psychiatric institutions take every advantage of the possibility. It should of course be pointed out that the documents themselves are highly dubious from both medical and legal points of view. None of them, for example, specifically defines what is meant by an action that constitutes a public danger. This gives rise to many abuses: "public danger" is applied to actions that do not constitute a direct threat to the life of the "patient" himself or those around him, but are perfectly normal manifestations of a critical spirit, such as the writing of dissident manuscripts, the putting up of posters, taking part in demonstrations,

expressing the wish to emigrate to another country, attempting to publish one's work abroad, etc. What is more, the
medical reasons mentioned in the directive as grounds for
emergency committal are deliberately couched in vague terms
which admit of a very arbitrary interpretation. This most
important section of the directive amounts to only *twelve
lines!* Among the symptoms indicating compulsory committal
are the following: "(c) a systematic syndrome of delusions
with chronic deterioration if this results in behavior dangerous to the public; (d) a hypochondriac delusional condition
causing an irregular and aggressive attitude in the patient
toward individuals, organizations, or institutions." One does
not have to be a psychiatrist to understand the inadmissibility
of such imprecise language. What exactly is a "hypochondriac
delusional condition"? Who can possibly establish what constitutes an "irregular and aggressive attitude toward individuals, organizations, or institutions"? If a Soviet citizen
criticizes an institution, takes it to court, exposes improper
activities on the part of those in charge of it—is this not likely
to cause the institution in question to turn to psychiatrists for
help? Yet the authors of the directive apparently felt that
even in such vague form the grounds for hospitalization still
did not offer enough scope, and they therefore added the
following caveat: "The grounds for compulsory hospitalization enumerated above are not exhaustive but only a list of
the most frequently encountered morbid states that present a
public danger. . . . The morbid conditions enumerated
above which can undoubtedly constitute a danger to the
public may be accompanied by externally correct behavior
and dissimulation." What this means, in effect, is that with
the aid of the police, psychiatrists may forcibly commit people
to hospital for reasons other than those listed in the directive!
The opportunities for abuse are appallingly obvious—it becomes possible for any unscrupulous psychiatrist to maintain
that a seemingly "normal" citizen is in fact mentally ill and
only simulating "normality."

One is also bound to have very serious misgivings about
Special Order No. 345/209 dated May 15, 1969, "Measures
for the prevention of socially dangerous actions by mentally
ill persons," signed by the Minister of Health, B. Petrovsky,
and the Minister for Internal Affairs, P. Shchelokov. This order

empowers both the police and psychiatric institutions to give a very broad interpretation of what constitutes a "socially dangerous act." The order notes that insufficient use is being made of the 1961 directive and urges that it be applied to "prevent dangerous actions by mentally ill persons." This means that since May 1969, not only *improper behavior* but even the *possibility* of improper behavior has been sufficient cause for compulsory hospitalization. As for persons who have already perpetrated socially dangerous acts (in the opinion of the police and the doctors), the new order makes it possible for psychiatric institutions to continue treatment even after the court order for committal has expired and to brush aside all attempts by relatives to secure the patient's discharge from hospital. The order introduces a new concept—"socially dangerous tendencies"—which is in no way defined or interpreted. It is not surprising that during 1969–70, after this order had been issued, there was an increase in the number of cases involving the abuse of psychiatry for obviously political reasons.[10]

It is particularly important for the healthy functioning of a socialist democracy that the role and responsibilities of the security forces be correctly defined. After an unlimited expansion had in effect placed them above all other state and party bodies, their power was in fact substantially reduced in the post-Stalin period. The security services were put under the control of the party, which meant that they ceased to have a punitive function—this was now made the sole prerogative of the judiciary. If in the past the security organizations held their own investigations, set up their own courts, reached verdicts, and carried out sentences, they were not restricted to their original role, that of investigation—and then only in certain types of cases. At present the courts alone have the right to try people, and places of imprisonment have also been removed from KGB control.

The main duty of the security services is to safeguard the basic interests of the state—to struggle against enemy subversion and espionage, to protect official secrets, to guard military establishments as well as members of the higher state and party leadership. After the Twentieth Congress the problems of dealing with such matters as "ideological subver-

sion" were entrusted to the Central Committee and a special
department was set up for this purpose.

The restriction of the KGB's functions led quite naturally
to a cutting down of its staff and the liquidation of some of its
lower-level divisions. For example, formerly each Moscow
district had its own KGB section but these were now abolished. Two years ago, however, these district sections in
Moscow were reconstituted, and their subordinate network of
special departments in factories and institutions was again
enlarged. To a great extent the KGB is now entrusted with the
struggle against "ideological subversion," as it is called. In
fact we are once more observing a growth of the staff and
functions of the security services, but this is certainly not a
response to any increase in foreign espionage activities.[11]
Rather it is a question of internal processes, particularly the
development of various political trends and the activities of
certain groups of dissidents discussed in Chapter IV. Because
there is too little democracy in our country, the security
organs have been given greater powers and larger staff—
measures that will only perpetuate the situation.

Obviously those in power should pay close attention to
the development of political moods and trends within a country. This is one of the basic and obvious responsibilities of a
political party. Lenin, we may recall, wrote that communists
"should live in the midst of the masses and know their every
mood." Under present conditions in our country, however,
where many elementary democratic freedoms are absent or at
best extremely limited—i.e., first and foremost freedom of
speech, freedom of the printed word, freedom of assembly,
and the freedom to demonstrate and organize—the study and
analysis of political moods and trends become exceedingly
difficult. New ideas evolve secretly, out of sight, and opinion
is formed somewhere far away from public meetings and the
official press. In this situation it is impossible for party bodies
to study moods and opinions at various levels of the community in the normal way, or to find out the attitudes of
various groups of workers toward important pieces of legislation—in short, they simply cannot keep abreast of basic social
trends.

In the early 1960's when various distinct opposition
currents of thought began to appear, the party made attempts
to study them through its primary organizations and special

departments of district party committees. Nothing came of this, however, since most members of the local party bureaus were either incapable of understanding or defining the real attitudes in their communities or else were reluctant to report on oppositionally minded individuals. It is hardly surprising therefore that in order to monitor people's thoughts and feelings the party leadership was increasingly obliged to fall back on the services of the KGB, which has its own methods of conducting "research" of this kind. In place of openly testing public opinion, they analyze reports from informers, a method that is naturally far more costly and ultimately much less reliable. A *samizdat* author has written, not without justification, that "first we spend vast sums of money to prevent citizens from openly expressing their opinions and then spend just as much trying to find out what they are actually thinking and what they really want." The security services are gradually becoming involved in the surveillance and study of developing trends not only outside the party but inside as well. I believe this is the major reason behind their renewed expansion in recent years. For the time being this process is still under the control of central and regional party bodies. Eventually, however, when the struggle between the various new trends is reflected at the higher levels of the party, the security organs could once more break loose and achieve an independent position which would put them above both party and government.[12]

Since the well-being of a socialist democracy depends on the nature of its judicial system and security services, it is particularly important to consider how it might be possible to improve their functioning. Here I shall discuss only some of the measures that could be taken.

It would seem desirable, for example, to increase the power and independence of judicial bodies and the procuracy. The Soviet Constitution states that judges are independent and subordinate only to the law; it also lays down that procurators shall be independent of all local authorities and answerable only to the procurator general. In practice, however, these provisions of the Constitution tend to be ignored and local organs exert considerable influence on both judges and procurators at the district level, even more so at the regional level—and at the republican level it is evidently overwhelming. This means that in Georgia, for example, before the republican procurator can institute proceedings against a highly placed bribe-taker, he must first obtain permission from the First Secretary of the republic's Central Committee. Nor is it by any means certain that this permission will be forthcoming, however much evidence there may be. It frequently happens (and not only in Georgia) that the procurator is instructed to drop the case at once. I believe, therefore, that it would be better for judges and procurators not to belong to local party organizations but rather to their own relatively independent ones, directly subordinate to the Central Committee in Moscow. Such an arrangement would be even more desirable for judicial bodies at district and regional levels.

It is vital that there be strict observance of the provisions of the Constitution requiring court cases to be heard in public. Sessions should be held *in camera* exclusively at the request of the defendant or the defense counsel, and even then only if the case touches on extremely intimate problems. But whenever it is a question of a political case, the trial must be absolutely open and take place in full public view. Anyone who wishes to attend should have the opportunity of doing so and if the courtroom is too small, arrangements should be made to relay the proceedings to adjacent premises or to televise them. In this kind of trial it is important that the court record be published, even if only in special editions, as long as they are freely available. This should also happen in the case of other trials of public interest.

M. Lebedev stresses the need as well to strengthen the supervisory powers of the procurator's office over central government departments, public organizations, and officials in very powerful positions. In Lebedev's opinion the procuracy "should be given the right to challenge all administrative acts that contravene the law."[13]

There is a need to substantially extend the competence of the courts to deal with infringements of civil rights, particularly on the part of the authorities. As things stand at present, Soviet citizens have no right to turn to the courts over a wide range of important matters such as those involving pensions, residence permits, illegal committal to mental hospitals, etc., etc., but may only complain through administrative channels. However such a procedure, as V. Chkhik-vadze correctly points out, cannot be compared with hearings in court, which would be public, more thorough and objective, and would entail participation by the interested parties or their representatives. A further advantage of court hearings is their educative function; they would encourage the growth of a sense of law and respect for the rights of the individual. Chkhikvadze advocates a system whereby citizens have a legal means of seeking redress in the courts against violation of their rights by any person in authority as an effective additional guarantee that there will be strict observance of the law, and one can only wholeheartedly agree.[14]

Several authors have discussed the question of creating a special Constitutional Court whose function would be to determine the legality, from the constitutional point of view, of measures taken by higher executive organs. The Crimean Tatars, for example, could ask a court of this type to re-establish their own national republic and make it possible for all those wishing to return to do so.

It is also necessary to make a number of radical changes in our statute books. For example, it is evident that the article making psychiatrists criminally liable for professional misconduct as described above should be reinstated in the Criminal Code.

Though it goes without saying that the interests of the state must be protected by law, nevertheless Articles 70 and 190 (1) and (3), so imprecise and open to abuse, should certainly be rescinded; or at least until this happens, examination of the accused in court should be concerned not only with objective facts but also with subjective intent. There are certain other articles of the law that need to be formulated in more rigorous language.

As regards the state security services, I believe it is quite possible to reduce the scope of their activities to a reasonable level while at the same time extending freedom of expression and access to information. In any event the intellectual world of Soviet citizens, their political views and convictions, their thoughts and opinions should not be the concern of the organs of state security. Other ways (research institutes, polls, etc.) must be found for the study of public opinion.

IX

Freedom of Speech and the Press

Almost all discussions of the problems of socialist democracy center around the question of freedom of information, which includes freedom of speech and the press, freedom for scientific research and artistic expression. This is only natural since intellectual freedom cannot advance without freedom to obtain and disseminate information. The degree to which this right exists is one of the most important indicators of genuine democracy in a socialist society.

The second edition of the works of Marx and Engels begins with two brilliant articles by the young Marx devoted to a defense of freedom of speech and the press ("Notes on the new Prussian Censorship Rules" and "Debates on Freedom of the Press"). It was with the struggle for freedom of the press, for freedom of thought and expression, that Marx began his career as a philosopher and revolutionary. And this, of course, was not just accidental. For as Marx wrote: ". . . without freedom of the press, all other freedoms are illusory. One form of freedom is the condition of another, just as one part of a body is dependent on the rest. When any aspect of freedom is called into question, freedom itself is thereby repudiated . . . and doomed to a phantom existence. . . . Unfreedom becomes the rule, and freedom the exception, a matter of chance and arbitrary circumstance."[1]

For all of the most prominent socialists and communists of the past it was always axiomatic that in the society of the future there would be absolute protection for freedom of expression and creativity. Intellectual freedom was an essential ingredient of their social ideal.

As August Bebel wrote at the end of the last century, in the future socialist society ". . . each writer will have the opportunity to show his worth, since he will no longer be at the mercy of publishers, commercial interest, or prejudice. His work will be judged solely by impartial experts whom he himself has helped to select, and should he find their verdict unjust, he will always be able to appeal to society at large. There is no such possibility today, with both newspaper editors and publishers concerned only with their own private interests. The naïve view that in a socialist society conflict of opinions will be suppressed can only be upheld by those who regard the bourgeois world as the most perfect social form; and, hostile toward socialism, they attempt to slander and belittle it. A society that rests upon democratic equality can never tolerate oppression in any form. *Uninterrupted progress is possible only where absolute freedom of opinion is a fundamental principle of society.*"[2]

In our country, however, during the Stalin period freedom of speech and the press ceased to exist altogether. A great deal has changed since those days; there is more freedom of expression, and science, literature, and the arts have much greater range and variety than they did fifteen or twenty years ago. Yet despite such evident progress, the situation remains highly unsatisfactory. There are still many completely indefensible restrictions on access to information, as well as on science and the arts in general.

And what is more, during the last few years there has been no improvement; on the contrary, violations of freedom of expression have grown even more frequent. Censorship intrudes more and more crudely in literature, science, and art. Many important aspects of life are ignored in the press and the very mention of a large range of urgent topics is again forbidden. Various crucial political, economic, and international problems are never examined even in our scholarly publications, and the jamming of foreign radio stations has been resumed. An ever-increasing number of books and journals are being withdrawn from general access in our libraries and transferred to the *spetskhran*. Even many issues of Western communist newspapers do not reach their Soviet subscribers and fail to appear on sale. Thus in recent years we have been witnessing a trend both retrogressive and totally unjustified.

There are those who try to show that under socialism freedom of expression is no longer a problem, since it is almost automatically guaranteed. "The socialist revolution," asserts, for example, N. Shamota, ". . . has eliminated the question of freedom for creative work in the sense that it was an issue in exploiting societies. For an artist who truly serves the people in a socialist society, the question 'Am I free or not in my creative work?' simply never arises. . . . In the Soviet Union an artist's freedom to create depends on his own capacities, on the extent, the depth of his insight into the inner laws to which his art is subject, and whether his talent and skill are sufficient to allow him to work within the limits of those laws. . . . What sort of reason can anybody have in our socialist conditions to pine for 'freedom of creativity'? . . . The reason can only be sought in philistine individualism, a mortal sickness distinguishable from the plague perhaps only in that outbreaks of it still occur. Anybody who feels himself restricted by his part in the common cause should look deep within his own heart: he will probably find a wretched individualist lurking there."[3] And these amazingly hypocritical pronouncements were published in *Literaturnaya Gazeta* five whole years after Stalin's death! One cannot help but be reminded of the words of Stalin himself at a meeting with a group of writers in 1932. When asked "What should we write nowadays?"—he replied: "Write the truth." Yet very soon hundreds of writers were to be arrested and killed precisely because they wanted to do just that.

Alas, we know only too well from the experience of our own society that socialism does not automatically guarantee freedom of creativity or freedom to serve the people with one's talent. The victory of a socialist revolution creates only the prerequisites for an unprecedented blossoming of intellectual freedom, for the development of the talents and abilities of all. However, we must also recognize that certain features of the postrevolutionary situation in our country worked against this. Very highly centralized government control not only over the means of production but also over the means of mass communication, the enormous growth of the role of the state in the life of society, the establishment of a one-party system—all these facilitated the development of bureaucracy and of massively organized and planned restrictions on freedom of expression on a scale quite unimaginable even in capitalist societies. If this is not to prevail there must be a ceaseless struggle by the party and the whole nation, by scientists, writers, artists, and political leaders against bureaucracy and against unwarranted bureaucratic restrictions on intellectual and artistic freedom.

Of course any such struggle to maintain freedom of speech and the press has to take account of existing social conditions, which themselves must be an object of continual study and analysis. It needs to be based on specific political and scientific principles and must be conducted in an orderly and rational manner. Thus, for example, in conditions of revolution and civil war, a revolutionary people may put certain restrictions on freedom of the press. However, during the following period, in the interests of the revolution itself, these restrictions should be substantially relaxed and after the consolidation of the new socialist order, reduced to the very minimum. But who is to determine even this minimum? And is there any need for it at all in a developed socialist society?

It is self-evident that freedom of speech and of the press, freedom for science and the arts are essential in a socialist society. But it is not enough merely to proclaim various freedoms. Specific mechanisms must be created to defend them and the rights of citizens against any possible abuse.

Everyone knows that the spoken and printed word are very potent, perhaps the most potent weapons of political and ideological struggle. The power and influence of the means of mass communication are greater today than ever before. But any weapon must be used according to certain rules. In other words, freedom of the press can never be absolute. And it is natural that in a socialist society too, there must be certain reasonable restrictions on freedom of expression. Indeed, some of those that presently exist in Soviet society may be put down to its credit. No doubt we will never quite achieve that "freedom" of the press that exists today in many capitalist countries, and this is no cause for regret.

Calling for freedom of expression, I am by no means suggesting that we should take as our model the situation that exists today in many capitalist countries. Of course it must be acknowledged that in these countries not only the bourgeois but also the workers' press (including communist papers) are comparatively free and, in a number of Western countries, enjoy enormous influence. Both the progressive intelligentsia and representatives of the working class have a very wide range of opportunities for expressing their views on almost any question of domestic or foreign policy. However, the greater part of the Western press is infected by a commercial spirit that produces distortion on a scale intolerable for any socialist society (this, quite apart from the ideological bias of the bourgeois press). In capitalist countries news agencies and the press are usually commercial enterprises whose first concern is profit. In order to increase their circulation, newspapers and magazines not only distort the truth but also violate elementary standards of decency and morality. Catering at times to the most primitive taste, they even allow undisguised pornography to appear on their pages. Intimate details from the life of some film star take up more space than crucial social problems. Interviews with criminals who have carried out particularly brazen robberies or committed appalling murders often appear on the front page of American papers; the memoirs of notorious gangsters are brought out in vast editions; there are anti-Semitic and Ku Klux Klan publications (not to mention handbooks on spiritualism and astrology). Obviously all this trash cannot be tolerated in a socialist society—on this we are all agreed. Of course propaganda in favor of racism or war is prohibited in our country, as is pornography. It is important that books, films, and television programs for children should not glorify criminals, gangsters, or those who commit acts of violence. Every government has the right to see to it that the press does not divulge state and military secrets and does not slander individuals, statesmen, or the state itself.

However, the question then arises, Who is to see to the enforcement of such essential restrictions? Should we keep preliminary censorship for this purpose? Hardly. In a genuine socialist society, preliminary censorship can only exist as a temporary measure in a state of emergency. The experience of all socialist countries has driven the lesson home that censorship, if created as a permanent institution, almost inevitably degenerates and is soon no longer a means of defending society but a weapon of arbitrary rule, whether overt or camouflaged.[4]

In literature, art, and science there is always a very relative dividing line between what is permissible and what is not, so that preliminary censorship can easily result in the prohibition of a very important work of literature, art, or scholarship. And in our country, anything can be declared a state secret! For decades everything related to the activities of the state security services has been put in this category—not only the methods of interrogation and the conditions in Stalin's concentration camps, but even their very existence were forbidden subjects. Surely it is significant that to this day not only the details of its work, but even the existence of a huge and elaborate censorship department is a state secret of which any mention in the press is prohibited. And although all authors are aware that there is censorship and often know the name of their own censor, receiving his comments and instructions through their editor, they can never meet him or complain to him directly or demand any explanations.

There is nothing that cannot be misrepresented and banned by the censors. Any reasonable criticism of obsolete dogma can be viewed as "revisionism" or even "ideological sabotage"; honest historical research scrupulously based on facts may be denounced as "slanderous"; an outstanding and original novel or story can be rejected as "anti-Soviet" or "ideologically harmful" and classical works of art described as "pornography"; a strictly scientific work on physics, chemistry, biology, or astronomy stands every chance of being labeled "pseudo science" or "idealism"; fair criticism of a government institution or individual leader may be viewed as defamatory, and the most sincere appeal for the reform and improvement of socialist society seen as a "disguised" call for its destruction, providing an excuse for attempts to silence all dissent.

And such things are not chance aberrations but are in the very nature of preliminary censorship. "The censors," wrote Marx, "are always trying to make the press feel that it, the press, is ill, and despite all its protestations of good health, insist that it must submit to treatment. But the censor is hardly a trained doctor administering different remedies depending upon the disease. He is more like a village surgeon who knows only one universally applicable cure—the knife. But he is not even a surgeon concerned with restoring health —he is an aesthete of a surgeon, who, convinced that anything disagreeable or displeasing to him on the body is superfluous, removes it. This kind of doctor is a charlatan, driving the rash inside so that it cannot be seen, totally unconcerned that it may affect the more delicate internal parts of the body."[5]

The long-standing domination of preliminary censorship inevitably has had very serious consequences for literature and art, for all the sciences (particularly for the social sciences), for the character and morale of the entire nation. As Marx pointed out, "A censored press only serves to demoralize. That greatest of vices, hypocrisy, is inseparable from it; and from this cardinal sin come all its other infirmities, none of which contains even a seed of virtue, not even the aesthetically most repulsive one, passivity. The government hears only its own voice while all the time deceiving itself, affecting to hear the voice of the people while demanding that they also support the pretense. And on their side, the people either partly succumb to political skepticism or completely turn away from public life and become a crowd of individuals, each living only his own private existence."[6]

But if preliminary censorship is to be eliminated, how can society exercise any control over the press? This would be done, first of all, by the editors themselves, when preparing material for publication. At the same time, state and party bodies and all individual citizens would keep a check on the mass communications media, publishing organizations, etc. —not by preliminary censorship but only *after* the work has come out—whether it is a scientific study, an article, a film, etc. The basic form of such supervision would be open criticism in the press.[7] Complaints from organizations or individuals would be lodged through the courts, but this could work only if there were special legislation on the press. Unfortunately we still do not have any press law, although Lenin's very first *Decree on the Press* stressed the need for it.[8] There is an enormous difference of principle between administrative control and control exercised by the courts, with the ultimate decision on the fate of a work coming not from some secret body but as the result of a democratic legal process conducted in public. For only an examination in open court can determine with any degree of reliability whether criticism directed at obsolete doctrine is constructive and fair or simply "anti-Soviet propaganda," whether criticism of some public figure or other is justified, a question of honest error, or deliberate slander. And only after both sides have been heard in court can there be a valid decision to withdraw a book or journal from sale, take a film off the screen, or close down a play. In a case of deliberate slander, the court could impose a fine or some other penalty. "A law on the press," Marx pointed out, "is very far from being a repressive measure against freedom of the press. . . . On the contrary, it is the absence of press legislation that must be regarded as depriving the press of freedom under the law, since a legally recognized freedom can exist in the state only in the form of a law. . . . A press law is, therefore, a legal recognition of freedom of the press. . . . My activity is examined by a court in the light of a given law: the censor not only punishes misdemeanors but also invents the very fact of their having been committed. When I am brought to trial, it means I have been accused of breaking a law, and if a law is broken, it must at least exist. Where no law on the press exists it cannot be violated. The censor does not accuse me of breaking an existing law. He condemns my opinion because it is not the same as his own or that of his superiors. Some open action of mine which I am prepared to submit to the verdict of society, of the state and its laws, is judged by a secret, purely negative power which, incapable of asserting itself as law, fears the light of day and is unrestrained by any general principles."[9]

Regrettably, however, it must be admitted that a transition from almost total censorship to relative freedom of the press cannot, in our conditions, take place in a rapid or revolutionary manner. It must be a gradual and controlled process. Otherwise our whole society and the machinery of party and state would be subjected to severe strains. It is not just a question of teaching all party members and all citizens how to make sensible use of freedom of speech and of the press—this would be a comparatively uncomplicated task. But it is necessary to train the entire party and state *apparat* to work in conditions of a free press with the gradual replacement of those officials who prove incapable of working in full public view—which would mean, as indeed Lenin proposed should be the case, that their every step is exposed for all to see without a system of preliminary censorship to protect them from criticism. This, however, is a much more difficult undertaking.

There is no doubt about the fact that the majority of the people and a large part of the intelligentsia are politically passive—indifference, or even a conscious rejection of politics, has become an ingrained habit, a form of self-protection. At the same time we have a massive state and party *apparat* possessing almost unlimited power; but because of the incompetence of many of its officials, both in professional and political terms, this vast machine is both inefficient and highly vulnerable to criticism. In such conditions, the sudden introduction of maximal freedom of the press is impossible in practice, since it could provoke a violent conservative backlash which, under the pretext of correcting "excesses," would proceed to abolish freedom of the press altogether, possibly throwing society back to the darkest ages of its history.

What first steps should be taken in the next few years toward establishing freedom of the press, toward freedom for science and the arts?

In the first instance, it is necessary to free all scientific and scholarly publication from any preliminary censorship. Lenin saw the need for just such a measure and on his suggestion a resolution was adopted exempting all Academy of Sciences publications from censorship. A special paragraph to this effect is still incorporated in the statutes of the Academy of Sciences. If nobody has so far dared to remove it formally, this is only because it was originally included on the personal initiative of Lenin. However, from the beginning of the thirties it has been disregarded in practice.[10] Yet it is absolutely clear that censorship has done enormous damage to the development of science in the past and continues to do so at present. We can easily see this, not only in the case of biology (whose tragic fate during the thirty years between 1934 and 1964 is rather well known), but also in that of mathematics (particularly cybernetics), chemistry, physics, and astronomy, not to mention the social sciences, where for decades there was almost no progress whatsoever—only regression of the worst kind.

The Soviet Union has a vast army of scientists at its disposal—they number about one million persons, i.e., more than one quarter of all the scientists throughout the world. However, as mentioned earlier, the productivity and effectiveness of their work is at a very low level. We are way behind many other countries in terms of the output of published scientific and scholarly work and in the number of inventions and discoveries by Soviet scientists. In the majority of the most promising areas of research, we are still very substantially behind the United States and Western Europe. Many reasons are given to explain this—the inadequacy of our equipment, a smaller outlay for science than in the United States, the inflexibility of the organizational structure of our scientific institutions, the insufficient number of scientific journals, etc. But in the end the basic reason for its backwardness is the absence of democracy in science—the authoritarian atmosphere and lack of intellectual freedom, the dominating role of the censor. And if we do not do something to remove these obstacles, our science will lag even further behind that of the capitalist countries in the next ten years. The dangers of such a situation in conditions of a scientific-technological revolution are self-evident.

The famous American physicist Robert Oppenheimer, explaining the comparatively rapid development of the natural sciences and physics in the United States, wrote as follows in an article entitled "Science and Freedom of Research": ". . . there must be no restrictions on freedom of scientific investigation—there is no room for prejudice in relation to new knowledge, new experiments, new truths. A scientist must be free to ask any question, to doubt any assertion, to correct any error. It cannot be otherwise. Whenever science has been used to create new dogmas, they could not exist for long if science was allowed to progress, and in the final analysis either dogma had to give way or science and freedom perished together. . . . an unprejudiced view, readiness to learn from example and argument rather than from authority—such is the legacy of the ages in the course of which science has changed the face of the Earth." These profound words fully correspond to the *spirit* of a true Marxist approach to science. Unfortunately this may be the theory but not the actual practice of our natural or social sciences.[11]

In the first years after the Revolution, our party, in defining its attitude toward the arts, invariably made a rigorous distinction between form and content. This meant that although the censorship would reject a work that was overtly anti-Soviet and counterrevolutionary in content, it would not impose a ban merely on account of form and style. As a result there was enormous variety in the arts, an intense search for new ways of looking at reality in painting, sculpture, poetry, etc.

Lenin very much disliked certain of the new trends in literature and art, although they often had the support of Lunacharsky. For example, Lenin found the early works of Mayakovsky extremely distasteful in form and style, despite the fact that the revolutionary youth of the period were wildly enthusiastic about them. In a comment, not intended for publication, on Mayakovsky's poem "150,000,000," Lenin wrote, ". . . arrant nonsense, stupidity, and pretentiousness." But Lenin never foisted his own personal taste on others as policy to be followed in the arts, and only on one occasion reproached the State Publishing House for Literature for printing Mayakovsky in excessively large editions. In his celebrated remarks on Mayakovsky's poem "Too Many Meetings," Lenin said frankly that he could not presume to judge the form of the poem (nor did he regard himself as competent to do so), but was in complete agreement with the political side of it.

This Leninist approach toward works of art was reflected in the Central Committee's famous resolution on literature, adopted in June 1925, which spoke of the need for "the greatest tact, caution, and tolerance," the need "to banish the tone of literary command and every kind of pretentious, semi-literate, complacent communist arrogance.* . . . With all the means at its disposal the party must eradicate attempts at amateurish and incompetent administrative interference in literary matters." The resolution particularly stressed that while carrying out a firm and definite policy vis-à-vis the

---

* "Communist arrogance" (*komchvanstvo*) was a term used very frequently in the twenties.—Trans.

content of works of art, the party must not express itself in a similar way on the question of form.[12] In other words, writers and artists were to have absolute freedom of choice when it came to form and style.

It should be borne in mind that in those days the policy of the Central Committee to a very large extent served to defend many traditional realistic styles. The October Revolution had received its most fervent support from those who represented what we nowadays call "modernism" in literature and art. Therefore, "modernists" occupied a leading position in many of the literary and artistic associations of the time. And their slogans were "Down with the classics!" "Clear our museums of all the old junk!" (by which they meant almost all the canvasses of famous artists of the past). But the party firmly resisted these demands and extreme modernist trends were denied monopoly in the arts.

The position began to change, however, at the beginning of the thirties. This was when socialist realism was proclaimed as a formula outlining the way in which reality should be reflected in art in a socialist society. In the statutes of the Union of Writers (created in 1934), we read: "Socialist realism is the basic method of Soviet literature and literary criticism: it demands of the artist a truthful, historically concrete depiction of reality in its revolutionary development. Moreover it must further the ideological education of the workers in the spirit of socialism."

In effect this definition of socialist realism is by no means unambiguous; its demand that reality must be depicted only in "its revolutionary development" leaves scope for a variety of highly tendentious and arbitrary interpretations. Unfortunately life around us is extremely contradictory, and "revolutionary development" is not always apparent. On the contrary, in some important spheres of social life, progress alternates with retrogression, when at least for a time the old prevails over the new. Therefore the demand for depiction of reality in "its revolutionary development" puts enormous limitations on an artist's freedom to apply his critical judgment and undermines the basis of such genres as satire—writers are compelled to refrain from portraying many aspects of reality, or alternatively, forced to embellish it or even resort to obvious fabrications. It probably would have been preferable, therefore, if the statutes of the Writers Union had given a much broader definition of socialist realism (for example, as "that kind of realistic art and literature whose task it is to promote the birth and evolution of the new socialist society").

It should be pointed out, however, that even in its narrower definition, socialist realism is described not as the sole but as the "basic" method of Soviet literature. Thus writers and artists were not in fact denied the right to depict reality by means of other forms and methods. But we know that by the middle of the thirties, almost every other approach was labeled "formalism" and in practice prohibited. And even within socialist realism, the range of possible styles and devices was continuously being restricted. Tendentious and abusive criticism began to be directed at some of the most eminent figures of Soviet culture such as Tairov, Meyerhold, Dovzhenko, Eisenstein, Zabolotsky, Aseyev, Kirsanov, Olesha, Vsevolod Ivanov, Fedin, Leonov, Ehrenburg, Kukryniksi, Shostakovich, Muradeli, Prokofiev, Khachaturian as well as scores of others. There were even critics who hurled abuse at Sholokhov's *And Quiet Flows the Don* and Tvardovsky's *Vasili Tyorkin*, calling them "insufficiently realistic."

Only after Stalin's death and particularly after the Twentieth Congress did some kind of "thaw" begin. Broader possibilities opened up for the development of earlier trends and styles of socialist realism that had once been repudiated wholesale. There was even a new possibility of experimenting with other methods, all rather indiscriminately lumped together as "modernism." Our critics began to make a sensible distinction between "socialist realism" and "socialist art." "Recently," wrote, for example, A. Ovcharenko and R. Samarin, "there has been a tendency to dissolve 'socialist realism' into the broader concept 'socialist art.' But the latter arose much earlier and is a much broader notion. It unites various distinct phenomena in art which have been associated with socialist ideas in the course of their historical development. . . . Socialist art, as the artistic expression of the builders of the new world, presupposes a continuous search in all directions, and it is called upon to extend its potential as far as possible in comparison with all preceding methods, movements, and trends; the forms of life itself are not incompatible with it and neither are romantic or invented forms, fantasy, fairy tale, allegory, symbolism, or the grotesque, if they aid the writer more profoundly, more delicately, more truthfully and expressively to re-create a picture of contemporary life in its complex transmutation from present to future."[13]

Unfortunately these most reasonable views have very little bearing on policy in the arts. By the beginning of the sixties, a certain indulgence toward various "modernist" tendencies gave way to crude campaigns of abuse; as a result, exhibitions of pictures and sculpture were prohibited. "Modernist" painters and sculptors were no longer accepted by their professional unions, and some of those who already belonged were even expelled—for many the normal pursuit of their art became altogether impossible. Criticism directed at different trends of Soviet abstract art was particularly crude and vicious. That the Union of Artists and other official bodies continue to persecute abstract art even today is one of the most scandalously absurd features of our life, not unlike the attacks on genetics and cybernetics in the not so distant past. It is perfectly possible that abstract art provides rather more scope for the activities of all sorts of charlatans and mediocrities than does classical realism. But it is impossible to deny the obvious fact that, along with many other forms of "modernism," it extends the potential of art and creates new ways of looking at reality. For example, abstract art has made it possible for painters, sculptors and, of course, composers (music, apparently, was always an abstract form) to express such nonconcrete and general concepts as fear, horror, hatred, the infinite (and even political ones such as fascism) where traditional realism is often inadequate.

Making an effort somehow to justify the harsh administrative persecution of "modernism" while pretending to take a thoughtful philosophical line, M. Lifshits in a really scurrilous article wrote: "Why am I not a modernist? Why does any trace of such ideas in art or philosophy arouse an inner protest? It is because in my eyes modernism is associated with the most dismal psychological phenomena of our time, namely: the cult of force, joy in destruction, love of cruelty, craving for an unthinking existence, and blind obedience." The absurdity of such accusations against "modernism" could not be more obvious. Of course one can only regret some of the statements made by extreme modernists and certain their actions, intended to achieve the "overthrow" of classical realism in art. But then we must remember that many militant supporters of realism played a rather active role in the forcible suppression of modernism. At least in our country it is the primitive forms of "socialist realism" which are bound up with the most "dismal psychological phenomena of our time." One may also recall that in fascist Germany modernism and abstract art were in fact subject to the cruelest persecution and abuse. The truth of the matter, wonderfully demonstrated by the recent example of the Cuban Revolution, is that the majority of those in favor of abstract art also passionately support the socialist revolution and are staunchly opposed to fascism, militarism, and monopoly capitalism. It would therefore seem natural that we, communists, should give serious attention to these trends in art and approach them with sympathy. Yet although A. Abalkin, for example, in his long article in *Pravda* (May 19, 1970) does not deny the anticapitalist and anti-imperialist character of most modernist and avant-garde trends in the West, insofar as these trends do not correspond to the aesthetic tastes of Abalkin and his friends, he quite groundlessly and categorically condemns them as "reactionary art." It is apparently irrelevant that many modernists struggle against capitalism and imperialism! "*In the final analysis* [italics added]," Abalkin asserts, "modernism serves the interests of the bourgeoisie."[15]

Certain Marxist theorists, trying to include the work of such eminent contemporary artists as Picasso within the body of works of art recognized by communists, devise various arguments full of sophistry to prove that ultimately Picasso is a realistic painter. Such concepts as "realism without limits" (*realisme sans rivages*) are defended by the French Marxist philosopher Roger Garaudy. But such an approach is also completely wrong. It would be much better for our communist movement to value Picasso's art for what it actually is— one of the most talented manifestations of contemporary modernism. Even where there is a real preference for socialist realism, communist parties—particularly in countries where they are in power—must allow writers and artists to have absolute freedom of choice when it comes to form and style.[16] This is the only conceivable policy that corresponds to the principles of socialist democracy in the field of literature and art.

There should be much wider possibility for the publication of scholarly, artistic, and political works written from a Marxist and socialist position, but whose authors represent different trends in Marxist thought. The international communist movement is today not monolithic, containing as it does a great number of different tendencies and groups; diverse currents of opinion also exist within our own party. With certain reservations, one can even speak of a crisis in the communist movement, of a crisis in Marxist thought. However, it is impossible to deal with it by means of censorship and repressive measures—they can only make the situation worse. The crisis in our ranks can be overcome; a new development of Marxism, a renaissance of communist thought, can take place, but only in an atmosphere where all the different problems that face us are freely discussed. We simply cannot go on avoiding a real confrontation of views within the party and within the framework of Marxism-Leninism. It is not a question of usefulness, but of urgent necessity. "The party cannot exist," wrote Engels, "without a great many nuances of opinion making themselves felt—and it is crucial to avoid even the semblance of dictatorship."[17]

It is impossible to ignore the fact, however, that precisely during the last five or six years our censorship has become even more rigid, further restricting what were already limited possibilities for the development of socialist science and literature.

Today there is a certain degree of freedom of the press only for the *moderate-conservative* trend that prevails in the party leadership. Many reactionary neo-Stalinist works are also published with comparative ease. At the same time, the most progressive trends in Marxist-Leninist thought are almost completely deprived of access to the press (the groups that in Chapter III I called the party-democrats). One could give a vast number of examples to prove this point.

In 1969 the monthly *Oktyabr* published Kochetov's defamatory and neo-Stalinist novel *What Do You Want?* with the full approval of the censor. At the same time, there was a ban on all discussion of the novel in the press. *Literaturnaya*

Gazeta alone received permission to print a completely superficial piece, but other critical reviews, including a very serious
and cogently argued essay by R. Lert (a party member since
1926), were turned down and could be read only in *samizdat*.
The censorship made no objection to two completely dis-
graceful novels by I. Shevtsov, which were published in 1970.
Yet the well-known Soviet writer Alexander Bek had been
trying unsuccessfully since 1965 to get his interesting and
very good novel, *The New Assignment*, published, even
though the novel not only had the backing of the prose section of the Writers Union but had been approved by a special
decision of the party committee of the Moscow writers organization. *Novy Mir* twice scheduled it for publication (in 1965
and 1970), but each time the censor, without explanation,
banned it in page proofs.*

In 1968 *Voyenizdat* (State Publishing House for Military
Literature) published the extremely dubious memoirs of
S. Shtemenko, which provoked serious criticism among the
reading public. And in 1970 the memoirs of air force marshal
Golovanov appeared, which were even more controversial
from the political and historical point of view. Yet a strict
censorship ban was placed on the military diaries of Konstantin Simonov (who is a party member). The poet
S. Smirnov had no difficulty in publishing his blatantly Stalinist poem, "I Myself Bear Witness," in *Moskva*, while the same
journal refused to print numerous critical reactions to it. A
critique of Smirnov's poem by B. Yakovlev, a member of the
party committee of the Moscow writers organization, was
rejected by the censor and then circulated in *samizdat*. And
such a distinguished poet as Tvardovsky, one of the greatest
figures in Soviet poetry, could not publish his new poem, "By
Right of Memory," in *Novy Mir* even when he himself was
editor-in-chief. One day this work will certainly be considered
one of the most outstanding achievements of Soviet poetry of
the sixties, but in 1969 it was on two occasions removed from
the journal in page proofs and was not included in the five-
volume edition of Tvardovsky's works. (Many other interesting poems and critical articles were also deleted from the
Collected Works in spite of insistent protest by the author.)

---

* It was published in Frankfurt in 1971, in Russian.—Trans.

S. Trapeznikov had no difficulty in publishing his large monograph on the history of collectivization, although it was entirely one-sided and very weak from a scholarly point of view, containing a number of assertions that were patently erroneous. But another large work on the same subject prepared by a group of competent party historians of the Academy of Sciences Institute of History, although twice approved for publication by the Institute's Learned Council, could not get past the censors.

Scores of veteran Bolsheviks, party members of forty or fifty years' standing, cannot publish their memoirs only because they include facts about crimes committed during the Stalin period. The memoirs of Evgenia Ginzburg, *Into the Whirlwind,* have been published throughout the world.* But in our country they are known only to a narrow circle who have read them in typescript. Even fewer people have seen the absorbing memoirs of S. Gazaryan, *It Must Not Happen Again.* In 1964 one publishing house agreed to bring them out, but a year later canceled the contract and returned the manuscript to the author. In spite of efforts by a number of prominent writers, the reminiscences of the former secretary of the Mogilev city party committee (in the thirties), Ya. Drobinsky, and those of the former secretary of the Eastern Kazakhstan regional party committee (also in the thirties), V. Kuznetsov, were not published anywhere. All publishing houses rejected the revealing memoirs of the former army procurator, M. Ishov, called *Years of Trial and Upheaval.* It turned out to be impossible to publish even some excerpts from the memoirs of one of the oldest members of the party, a participant in the first Soviet government, A. Spunde, *About My Life.* The list could go on and on.

In recent years our best literary-political journal, *Novy Mir,* whose role in the development of Soviet literature and social thought during the sixties would be difficult to overestimate, has had to work under extraordinarily difficult conditions. Finally a climax was reached with the dismissal of most of the editorial board and the retirement of Tvardovsky. Yet there is no doubt about the fact that in the course of the last fifteen years *Novy Mir* has consistently supported the policies of the Twentieth and Twenty-second congresses and as a

* The English translation appeared in 1967.—Trans.

general rule has approached Soviet life from a Marxist-Leninist point of view.

There is a most abnormal situation today in both our cinema and theater, where many films and plays completely consistent with a Marxist position are prohibited or withdrawn.

Because of the virtual ban on any comprehensive treatment of the past, we are deprived of the possibility of making any proper analysis of the present. On the whole it is now the case that the appearance of any significant work is becoming impossible in the official world of social science and the arts. (The creative process follows its own logic much the same as in physics and mathematics, and when one set of problems is not solved, our culture and our social science are then incapable of dealing with others.)

Of course some things do manage to get through the censored press, although this requires the use of Aesopean language, writing "between the lines," and speaking in hints. But even more frequently it happens that many leading writers and scholars (or those potentially so) simply give up altogether and abandon any attempt to express their ideas. Some of the works lost in this way would undoubtedly have been a valuable contribution to Marxist literature. The poet Voznesensky writes of this with extraordinary power and sorrow, in his "Lament for Two Unwritten Poems."

Different kinds of absurd censorship restrictions not only impoverish and emasculate literature and the press, they also encourage mediocrity. We cultivate drabness and monotony, we cripple talent. But inevitably the Soviet people are aware of a growing disparity between life and art. What happens in books or on the stage flies in the face of what they know from their own experience. And this gives rise to cynicism and indifference to politics, to ideas, and to social problems in general. For only art that tells the truth, that expresses in words and images the real life and real thoughts of millions of people, can excite, persuade, and educate.

It is clearly quite abnormal in a socialist society that men in the world of culture and scholarship, members of the party and people close to it, even Old Bolsheviks—all emphatically Marxist in their point of view—find it impossible to express their opinions freely in the press, to publish their works, to give effect to their ideas. This situation speaks for itself and it is scarcely necessary to stress how incongruous it is. Certain statements of the young Karl Marx on freedom of the press were quoted earlier. In fact the founders of Marxism held to these views until the end of their lives, by which time they had become acknowledged leaders of the workers' movement in Europe and America.

"It is a hard fate to be dependent—even on the workers' party," wrote Engels to Bebel in 1892. "But aside from the financial aspect, to be the editor of a paper belonging to the party is a thankless job for anyone who possesses initiative. Marx and I were always in agreement that we would never occupy such a post, and that we would publish only a paper that was financially independent, even of the party. Your 'nationalization' of the party press can have great disadvantages if it is taken too far. It is absolutely necessary for you to have a party press that is quite independent of the party leadership and even of the party congress, i.e., one that is free *within the framework of the program* and the tactics agreed upon to come out against any particular steps taken by the party and also, as long as it does not overstep the bounds of party ethics, to criticize the program and tactics themselves. You, as the leadership, should encourage or even, if necessary, create such a press. Your moral influence will be much greater than if it were to arise independently against your will. The party is outgrowing the limitations imposed hitherto by severe discipline—with two to three million members and a continual intake of 'educated elements,' there is a need for greater freedom of action than that which we have had until now and which at one time may have been sufficient or even beneficial in its limitation. The sooner you yourself and the party adapt to this changed situation, the better. And the first thing that is needed is a *formally* independent party press. It will certainly appear sooner or later, but it would be preferable if you were to help it into existence in such a way that from the very outset it is under your moral influence and does not arise in defiance of you and against you."[18]

Of course all of Engels' advice to the German Social-Democratic Party at the end of the nineteenth century is even more relevant today toward the end of the twentieth century and should be heeded by our Communist Party with its fifteen million members, including several million representatives of the intelligentsia. Unfortunately we do not have a formally independent party press or freedom of expression even for communists and Marxists. And it is safe to say that if, by some miracle, Marx, Engels, and Lenin were to appear among us, most of the works they might write analyzing our social conditions would not be passed for publication by *Glavlit*.

There is also the separate question of nonparty literature, of artistic and academic works by authors who not only are not party members but who on the whole do not subscribe to Marxism or communism (although some of them may call themselves socialists).

If there are still a great number of completely unjustified restrictions on members of the party, on different shades of Marxist and communist thought, the situation is even worse when it comes to various trends outside the party. Many works expressing nonparty ideas and attitudes are absolutely prohibited. For example, it is impossible for such an eminent writer as Solzhenitsyn to publish anything new or even any of his earlier writing. In the press and at meetings he is denounced as an "enemy" of the Soviet system. When he was awarded the Nobel Prize, which he certainly deserved (the criteria for the Nobel Prize, as everyone knows, are rather different from those, for example, for the Lenin Prize), a singularly inept propaganda campaign was launched against him. He was subjected to even cruder attacks when his *August 1914* was published abroad.* Unquestionably, this new novel was written from a non-Marxist, and in my view an incorrect, ideological position. But surely it could have been discussed and analyzed in a serious and dignified manner—it would not have been difficult to point out his many errors, particularly in his description of Russian life in 1914, the state of affairs in the army, the relations between soldiers and officers, his portrayal of the revolutionaries, etc. Instead, we are treated to empty and strident articles full of crude invective and deliberate distortions of the novel's meaning. And the amazing thing is that most of the authors of these abusive articles and reviews were not ashamed to acknowledge in print that they had not read Solzhenitsyn's novel and were judging it only on the basis of reviews by other persons, including reviews in émigré jour-

---

* The English translation appeared in 1972.—Trans.

nals. Recently in certain circles there has even been the demand to exile Solzhenitsyn abroad.*

The major works of Vladimir Maximov, although he is a member of the Writers Union, have never been published in our country,† nor have the interesting camp stories of V. Shalamov. To this day Pasternak's *Doctor Zhivago* has not been brought out in the Soviet Union; with all its shortcomings, it reflects processes in our cultural life in the fifties which simply cannot be bypassed or ignored. The poems and songs of A. Galich ‡ have been banned. Academician Sakharov's *Progress, Coexistence, and Intellectual Freedom* is still unpublished in the USSR; however controversial, it reflects the thoughts and attitudes of a significant section of the scientific-technical intelligentsia. As for the theater and cinema, directors who are not party members or who do not at least declare their adherence to Marxism-Leninism find it impossible as a general rule to stage a play or make a film.

It is true that these days we publish the works of non-Marxist Western writers on a large scale. We purchase Western films and show them in our cinemas. When it is a question of capitalist society being criticized, we are happy to listen not only to communists but also to persons of other political views. But when it comes to our own shortcomings we are usually unwilling to accept criticism from any source, whether from inside or outside the party.

The issue of nonparty literature has a long history, and a great number of rigid and distorted views have grown up around it. It has frequently been a subject of debate, of both wise and unwise decisions. Below I would like to look at only some aspects of this complicated problem.

Lenin's article "The Party Organization and Party Literature" is often referred to; it was written in 1905, when the bourgeois-democratic revolution had begun and censorship restrictions had been partially relaxed. In this period it became

---

* Solzhenitsyn was expelled from the Soviet Union on February 13, 1974.—Trans.

† Maximov was expelled from the Writers Union in the autumn of 1973 and left the Soviet Union on March 1, 1974. Three of his novels have been published in Russian in the West, and one of these, *Sem dnei tvorenia,* was published in English as *The Seven Days of Creation* in 1975.—Trans.

‡ Galich arrived in the West on June 25, 1974.—Trans.

possible to publish Marxist and party literature legally, and Lenin was concerned with the role of the party press in such conditions. His view is still relevant for our *party* literature today. But some present-day theorists deliberately misconstrue Lenin's words and maintain that in socialist countries only a party literature and no other can have the right to exist, which is not what Lenin had in mind. He was using the word "literature" in its broadest meaning to include both political and publicist works. In 1905 it was a question of appealing for some control over what was written under party auspices in order to set it apart from the flow of works by bourgeois and petty bourgeois authors and also those of other trends that began to appear after the abolition of censorship. He was certainly not demanding that the press of other parties and political groups be suppressed, and indeed at that period it would have been out of the question to advocate such a thing. Nor was he considering what the nature of literature should be in a future socialist society.

Lenin's letter to Gabriel Myasnikov* is also often quoted, in which he categorically rejected the slogan "freedom of the press," as well as Myasnikov's proposal to establish complete freedom of speech in Russia for all political groupings "from anarchists to monarchists." This letter was written in 1921. "Freedom of the press," Lenin declared, "while the RSFSR is surrounded by a hostile bourgeois world, means freedom of *political organization* for the bourgeoisie and their faithful servants, the Mensheviks and SRs. This is an irrefutable fact. The bourgeoisie (all over the world) is still many times stronger than we are, and to give it the additional weapon of freedom to organize (freedom of the press is virtually the same thing, since the press is the center and basis of political organization) means to facilitate the task of the enemy, to give it aid. We have no intention of committing suicide. . . . We clearly see that 'freedom of the press' *in reality* means that the bourgeoisie buy the services of hundreds and thousands of Kadet, SR, and Menshevik writers in support of their struggle against us. This is a fact. 'They' are richer than we are and will purchase ten times as much support as we can

---

* Myasnikov was a member of the Workers' Opposition and an ardent champion of freedom of the press; he was expelled from the party in 1922.—Trans.

muster. No. This we will not do. We will not help the international bourgeoisie."[19]

Yet this statement cannot be viewed in isolation from the specific historical circumstances of 1921, when our country was in a state of almost complete collapse and on the verge of famine, which undermined the authority of the party among the peasantry and the whole of the petty bourgeois masses and created a very serious political crisis. But all this was a long time ago. Today there is really no section of the population that can be described as petty bourgeois in Marxist sociological terms. The basic means of mass communication are in the hands of the party, and within the ranks of the CPSU there are thousands of able writers, journalists, and scholars. What have we to fear, therefore, from open polemic with different trends of socialist thought, or even with overt opponents of Marxism?

We must remember what Lenin wrote before October when proposing Bolshevik policy on freedom of the press: "Freedom of the press means that any opinion of any citizen may freely be published. . . . State power, in the form of the Soviets, will take over all printing presses and newsprint and distribute them fairly: in the first place, to the state in the interests of the majority of the people, the majority of the poor . . . ; secondly, to the large parties which have obtained, let us say, one hundred or two hundred thousand votes in both capitals [St. Petersburg and Moscow]; thirdly, to small parties and after that to any group of citizens with a certain number of members or supporting signatures. This system of distribution would be just, and under Soviet power could be put into practice without any difficulty."[20] Only the exceptional circumstances of civil war and subsequent collapse prevented this prerevolutionary Bolshevik programme on the press from being put into effect. However, Lenin did not give up the thought that as proletarian power became stronger, freedom of the press and freedom of speech should be extended. "With the publication of large Soviet newspapers," wrote Lenin after the victory of the Revolution, ". . . it will be completely feasible to assure that a much larger number of citizens are able to express their opinions— all groups, say, that have collected a certain number of signatures. Freedom of the press in effect would become much more democratic, incomparably more complete under such a reform."[21] Speaking at the first Comintern Congress, Lenin said that under socialism each worker "or group of workers of whatever size" will have and will avail themselves of equal rights to the use of publicly owned printing presses and paper.[22]

And we must not forget that when in 1921–22 Lenin came out against *absolute* freedom for the press, he had in mind only the explicitly anti-Soviet or counterrevolutionary section of it. There was a very different policy toward more moderate and loyal political trends. We need only recall how firmly the numerous errors of *Proletkult** were criticized or what the attitude of the party was toward the "fellow-travelers," i.e., writers who were not Marxists but who loyally supported Soviet power. It is enough to remind ourselves how the party treated the many bourgeois specialists and scholars who, although not accepting the basic tenets of Marxist philosophy, did much work of great value in their respective fields. If one studies the content of social-political, scholarly, and literary journals of the early twenties, it becomes quite clear that the party tolerated not only different literary and aesthetic trends, different shades of socialist thought, but also many publications and articles that were not socialist at all (for example, the books and articles of Kondratov, Chayanov, and others). It was Lenin himself who protected the "change of landmarks" journal *Novaya Rossia* when the Petrograd Soviet wanted to close it down.[23]

In the first half of the twenties there were many calls for a tougher policy toward literature. In 1924 one of the leaders of VAPP,† I. Vardin, declared at a meeting of the party Central Committee that even the most talented work, if ideologically inconsistent, is "the most harmful poison for the working people."[24] The "on guardists"‡ rejected almost the whole of fellow traveler literature as "hostile to the aims of

---

* Proletarian Cultural and Educational Organizations, founded in 1917 with the aim of producing a new literature created by and for members of the proletariat.—Trans.

† All-Russian Association of Proletarian Writers, founded in 1920 by writers who declared that literature must reflect the ideology of the proletariat and serve its interests.—Trans.

‡ From *On Guard,* a journal put out by the proletarian writers (VAPP). —Trans.

the revolution" and demanded that it be forbidden. Their list of "hostile" works included those of Gorky, Mayakovsky, Alexei Tolstoy, Prishvin, Sergeev-Tsensky, Leonov, Fedin, Malyshkin, Tikhonov, Inber, Chapygin, Shaginyan, Forsh, Shishkov, and scores of other important writers.

Of course the party rejected these preposterous demands. Lenin supported the creation of the journal *Krasnaya Nov (Red Virgin Soil)* edited by A. Voronsky, whose task it was to bring together all honest writers representing *different* literary trends from proletarian to bourgeois. It was intended that the journal would educate these writers by persistent efforts to enlist them in the struggle to build a new life and wean them away from bourgeois influences.

Krasnaya Nov of course was connected to the party. But at the beginning of the twenties such journals as *Vestnik Literatury* (Literary Messenger), *Letopis Doma Literatorov* (Chronicle from the House of Writers), *Zhizn* (Life), *Nachalo* (The Beginning), *Russki Sovremennik* (Russian Contemporary), and others, published in small editions, were independent of the party and reflected the views and attitudes of the old Russian intelligentsia.

In 1921 the Soviet government allowed the opening of private publishing houses and printing presses and by the following year there were more than two hundred in Moscow alone. On the whole, they published works expressing different nonparty trends in social and literary thought that were not openly directed against the power of the working class. And although the position of the Communist Party in society was then much weaker than today, it did not prevent the spiritual needs of the non-Marxist intelligentsia being met in this way.

During Lenin's lifetime and the first years after his death, on the whole there was no question of forbidding "dissidents" to express various views, particularly in the arts. If there was an attempt to guide literature and art in any systematic way, it was principally by means of persuasion and example. "Every artist, every person who considers himself to be one," said Lenin, "has the right to create freely in complete independence according to his own ideal. But, you understand, we are communists. This means that we cannot stand by, arms folded, and let chaos develop where it will. We must give full and systematic guidance to this process and shape its results."[25]

Many statements of Lenin's closest colleague, Lunacharsky, who played such an important role in formulating and carrying out the party's policy toward the arts, bear witness to its flexibility. "Suppose," wrote Lunacharsky in 1924, "a writer appears who expresses the mood of the most prosperous, 'semi-kulak' peasantry; or a writer who conveys the views of the noncommunist intelligentsia, or is a spokesman of the new bourgeoisie. . . . In view of the fact that more accurate knowledge of real conditions is so necessary for the party if it is to maneuver in the best possible way, how can one advocate silencing all these writers and allowing speech only to those who reflect the tendency of the vanguard proletariat and social groups close to it, i.e., the Soviet intelligentsia and the Soviet peasantry? Of course, for anyone wishing to know more about the real world from literature, this would be an enormous loss and would mean that the most valuable material would slip out of our hands."[26]

Some of our present-day authorities on the ideological front insist that the policy toward the press at the beginning of the twenties permitting a definite struggle of opinion both outside and within the party cannot serve as a model for our country today. At that time there really were different classes, it was the period of the NEP, and the whole people were not yet united around the party. Various nonparty trends were inevitable, and this had to be to some extent reflected in the press. But today, it is argued, the position is completely different—there is an unprecedented moral and political unity of the whole people. All classes and sections of Soviet society without reservation support the leadership of the party. Therefore there can be no nonparty trends that would not be blatantly anti-Soviet and antisocialist. The party and its leadership no longer have the need to maneuver—its authority is absolute and unshakable.

All this is a very good example of wishful thinking. We have not yet acquired a monolithic intelligentsia, with all its members thinking identical thoughts, any more than was the case in the twenties. Having experienced the Stalin terror as well as the subjective and "hare-brained" undertakings of Khrushchev, our intelligentsia is now very divided in its view of Soviet realities; it is impossible to ignore this obvious fact and go on trying to make everyone fit into the same pattern and accept a single approved point of view. Even supposing we wanted all Soviet citizens to share the same set of opinions, we would have to use different approaches toward different circles of the intelligentsia, allowing the broadest possible and comparatively free discussion in the process.

As I have described in the third and fourth chapters, many ideological and political trends have arisen based on different moods among various sections of the population. In the course of the next decade, these trends will develop, and they must be taken into consideration. They are all seeking self-expression: in the press, in literature, in the sciences, and in art. And it would be a grave mistake to forbid, as in the past, all publications, plays, and films that are not sufficiently orthodox. It would be terribly wrong not to carry out at least the policy that prevailed at the beginning of the twenties. The party urgently needs to know about the different attitudes of various groups in the working class, peasantry, intelligentsia, among officials and also youth. Today again the party must win the masses to its side not by decree but by argument. In politics there are no external and unchanging loyalties—they must be conquered afresh at every new stage. The only restriction, evidently, must be on the most extreme groups, without, however, resorting to repression when it is a question of views and not of actions.

Many people have something new to contribute; they want to speak out and they will have their say. At present there is no way of stopping them. Freedom of the press has come about spontaneously, by means of what has come to be called *samizdat*. Tighter censorship restriction cannot stop the flow of this literature (typed manuscripts without the censor's stamp of approval), which is exerting an ever-increasing influence on the minds of a growing section of the intelligentsia.[27] But the various restrictions on freedom of the press not only make uncensored writing a more hazardous process but also influence it in a negative fashion by directing it away from a Marxism that has become discredited by its own self-appointed guardians, the censors. In the final analysis this is an undesirable and dangerous process which can only be stopped by means of a dialogue as open as possible between representatives of different trends.

In refusing to publish "unacceptable" works, we of

course to some extent reduce their influence. But in the long run we only enhance their attractiveness while at the same time losing the chance to keep track of them. "In a country where censorship exists," wrote Marx, "any forbidden book . . . is an event. It has the aura of martyrdom. . . . Censorship makes each work, whatever its quality, an unusual one, while freedom of the press takes away all outward glamour."[28]

Obviously, unorthodox (i.e., not strictly Marxist or even completely non-Marxist) works can stimulate and enrich the whole of Soviet culture. The works of so-called fellow travelers in the twenties added very much to our literature and to the spiritual world of the Soviet people. Many of our most notable writers and artists came from the ranks of the fellow travelers. In any case, such categories as "fellow traveler" are very relative, as witnessed by the fact that for a long time Gorky and Mayakovsky were counted among them. The prominent historian Tarle was not a Marxist, but his works were an important contribution to Soviet historical scholarship. Such writers and poets as Bulgakov, Tsvetaeva, Bunin, Pasternak, Esenin, Mandelstam, and Akhmatova were neither fellow travelers nor Marxists nor adherents of socialist realism. Their works, however, enriched Russian and Soviet literature—often only after the deaths of their authors—and some have never appeared even to this day (at least not in Soviet editions).

The same thing may be said of Solzhenitsyn. He is not a Marxist; his novels and stories are not written in the spirit of socialist realism. No one could begin to argue that Solzhenitsyn criticizes the shortcomings of our society from a party or a Marxist point of view, and he himself would be the last person to make such a claim. Nevertheless his novels and stories have exerted a great influence on many very different types of Soviet writers, and there is no doubt that our language and culture are all the richer for them. His mastery and talent certainly make him the outstanding Russian prose writer of the last decades, and it will be impossible to give an account of Soviet literature during the sixties and seventies (or of the history of political thought) without considering Solzhenitsyn. And what do we gain by prohibiting the works of this very great writer and organizing campaigns against him, using the most unworthy means and even stooping to outright slander?

Addressing the Twenty-third Congress of the CPSU, the First Secretary of the Moldavian Central Committee, I. Bodyul, spoke about problems of freedom of speech. "As we all know," he said, "in our country every person who considers himself an artist has the right to work freely, to write as he sees fit, without the slightest limitation. But by the same token, our party and state institutions also enjoy full freedom in their choice of what to print." And these words have their own logic. Each organ of the press should have its own image. It would be wrong to compel *Pravda* or *Izvestia* to publish anything by Solzhenitsyn. But it is equally absurd to make all our newspapers and magazines identical, to demand that they approach problems in the same way. There are in fact by now discernible differences in the social-political and aesthetic positions of the various journals, and it would be a good thing to bring into being a still wider range of periodicals. I believe that at the present time it is not only possible but also would be extremely advantageous to have newspapers and magazines edited not only by *communists* of different trends, but also by people with noncommunist views. These publications clearly would not be organs of the party and so the party would not bear responsibility for them. Side by side with state publishing houses controlled by the party, a certain number of self-governing cooperative publishing houses could be organized by groups of writers themselves and function without any editors or officials assigned from above. In 1957 the well-known writer Alexander Bek proposed the creation of such cooperative publishing organizations, but unfortunately his suggestion was turned down. Yet there is an extreme need for just this kind of independent publisher in order to provide an outlet for the pent-up energies of nonorthodox writers.[29] In this way it would be possible to publish the works of Solzhenitsyn. Later on, journals could be founded with editorial boards that included such writers as Sinyavsky,* Daniel, and Shalamov. It is absurd to put writers in prison or labor camp for their artistic works (even if published abroad); this does not bear witness to the strength of the regime and does not in fact strengthen it. In

---

* Sinyavsky now lives in Paris.—Trans.

the Union Republics there could be journals with a specific nationalist bias; these trends also have to be given the opportunity for expression. The party has adequate means to counter them with more correct views.

My proposals are a call not for peaceful coexistence between opposing ideologies but for struggle between different views and ideas. The principal weapon of this struggle should not be the complete isolation of our people from all non-Marxist opinions and works but rather, critical discussion of them. A strict preliminary censorship, of course, prevents the expression of non-Marxist attitudes in the press. But in the first place, there can be no absolute barriers in the world of ideas, and secondly, censorship is also an obstacle to the development of Marxism itself, since the censor never distinguishes between development and distortions. By shielding Marxism from open confrontation with non-Marxist views and creating a hothouse situation, it encourages dogmatism and results in a loss of vitality. Robbed of its former militance, Marxism becomes very vulnerable to criticism and also to contamination from outside sources. If in the past the proletariat fought its battles under the flag of Marxism, this was because it was an ideology that had evolved and perfected itself in open struggle with its opponents. All the major works of Marxism-Leninism are polemical—they were not created in isolation protected by censorship from criticism; on the contrary, they were themselves subjected to the interference of various censorship bodies. By insulating Marxism and Marxists from all other ideological trends, we only ensure that Marxist thought falls into decay, thus virtually abandoning the field of battle to our ideological opponents. Undoubtedly this is why the development of Marxist thought in certain capitalist countries is far ahead of anything that socialist countries have to offer. True, the main concern is with the problems in those countries, but there is also interest in the strategy and tactics of the world revolutionary movement as a whole. At the same time there are a great number of complicated problems *in socialist countries* which could be solved by Marxists but which remain almost completely neglected.

Extraordinary theories are invented nowadays by opponents of freedom of speech. However, behind all their refined constructions one can sense not simply a fear of freedom of expression, but particularly a fear of truth, and of a press that tells the truth. That most eminent exponent of bourgeois democracy Thomas Jefferson always insisted that the press must be free from all restriction: "If democracy needs citizens able to read and write, then it follows that they must be free in their choice of what to read. Censorship of any kind destroys the very spirit of democracy, replacing despotic power over the body with tyranny over the mind."

Everyone, of course, pays lip service to the need for truth in describing reality. The literary critic Zoya Kedrina, only a few months before her appearance as public accuser at the trial of Sinyavsky and Daniel, wrote: "There very likely will be no argument about the proposition that the necessary and only possible way to educate people is by the truth, that lies, evasions, and omissions by teachers can hardly promote the moral growth of their pupils. Realistic art finds its meaning and purpose in being truthful to life."[30]

However, it appears that our writers and scholars do not stand united on this subject. For if we are all unanimously in favor of truth, then why has preliminary censorship grown so much stricter in recent years? Well, reply some of the critics, reviewers, and censors, we need the truth. But what is truth and *what kind* of truth do we need? Sometimes much of a writer's work is true, but it is not that "larger truth" of our life and our history which is needed by the Soviet people. It appears that truth has two dimensions: there is the "smaller truth" and the "larger truth," "truth of the isolated fact" and "truth of the age as a whole," "truth of the individual event" and "truth of the over-all phenomenon," truth that is only "apparent" and truth that is "real," etc. Furthermore, it turns out that it is not the readers who are qualified to distinguish between the two types of truth (one "necessary," the other not), but only the censors or officials in the ideological *apparat* of the Central Committee.

Reality is of course infinitely complex and can be seen from many different angles. But, ironically, theories about the duality of truth are at present used primarily as a means to justify banishing any faithful picture of life from our literature, cinema, and theater, in order to defend a one-sided and essentially false depiction of reality. "Marxism," wrote the critic V. Lakshin several years ago, "has always held that truth is concrete, assuming that while absolute truth exists, in historical and practical terms it is made up of an infinite series of relative, partial, and specific truths which tend toward the absolute but can never totally embrace it. To demand that an *artist* must not portray the 'smaller truth of isolated facts' but only the 'larger truth of the over-all phenomenon' is something new. As interpreted by some of our critics, 'larger truth' has come to stand for some mysterious absolute which can be spoken of only in the most general, abstract, and evasive terms. But let us try to put things plainly, without rhetoric or equivocation.

"What is really meant by 'larger truth' or 'truth of the age as a whole'? . . . More often than not it is a synonym for the happy life, for the general prosperity desired by all, while 'lesser truth' means the depiction of any shortcomings, difficulties, or hardships. Therefore as soon as anyone understands that art is serious and capable of affecting people most when based on the unadorned portrayal of problems and conflict, and then takes the risk of describing how things really are, he is immediately accused of being partial to 'smaller truths,' the 'truth of the petty fact.' "[31]

The important thing for dogmatist critics is that by thus dividing truth into "larger" and "smaller," they are able to subsume under the second category events and aspects of our life which are in fact of enormous importance. In recent years, for instance, many of the crimes and outrages of the Stalin period have all too frequently been written off as "lesser truth." How can anyone possibly argue that show trials and terror, torture and concentration camps had less impact on the life of our country than all the achievements in industry and education?

What we find in the works of Solzhenitsyn, or in the dreadful memories recounted in Shalamov's stories—are they really unimportant? And if the critic Dremov is right when he says that such things are outside the "mainstream,"* then it

---

* Dremov wrote in an unpublished report to a Soviet publishing house: "I believe it would be a mistake to publish *Stories from Kolyma.* It cannot benefit the reader because the naturalistic verisimilitude of fact, which it undoubtedly contains, is by no means tantamount to the greater artistic truth to life that the reader expects from any work of literature."—Trans.

can only mean that the same was true of the country as a whole during the times of which Shalamov writes. But if this is so, surely it is then doubly important for us to know everything written by Solzhenitsyn, Shalamov, Evgenia Ginzburg, Lydia Chukovskaya, and many others.

Furthermore in writing about the Second World War it is impossible, simply because it ended with our victory, to pass over in silence the serious defeats with which it began or the price our people had to pay.

Needless to say, most dogmatists admit that there are still isolated defects and shortcomings in our life, but they hasten to assure us that the general development of the country is proceeding correctly, that basically it was always moving in the right direction and that our achievements vastly outweigh the failings. And this must, it would seem, be the underlying assumption of any writer faithful to the method of socialist realism.

Still another favorite trick of our dogmatist critics is to allege that all writers or works they disapprove of are either "one-sided" or warped in some way. *"Into the Whirlwind,"* says one of the reports on it,* "is written with the heart's blood. It is a sharp, passionate, and moving account which makes a stunning impression on the reader. But it depresses and dispirits even old Chekists, not to speak of Soviet young people familiar with the 'black years' only by hearsay. The tragic events of the Yezhov-Beria period are portrayed by the author truthfully and powerfully; however, to a certain extent she is one-sided, as if she had only dark colors at her disposal. The universal spy mania, suspiciousness, repressions, the massacre of party, academic, military, and other outstanding cadres of the Soviet intelligentsia overshadow for the author the heroic deeds of the Soviet people and party during the same period: industrialization, the revolution in agriculture, the heroic deeds of Soviet participants in the Spanish revolutionary struggle," etc.

What is one to make of such a mentality? Of course we are all against one-sidedness—of the kind, for example, that might lead someone to reject an outstanding work of literature simply because it has a few minor blemishes. Or you might, say, have a novel portraying ten communists, one of

* Also an unpublished report to a Soviet publishing house.—Trans.

whom is a bribe taker, another a careerist, the third a coward and toady, the fourth a demagogue, the fifth a fool, the sixth a dogmatist, the seventh a tyrant, and so forth. Although all these types might well exist in the real world, this would certainly be an example of one-sidedness. But the novel would be no less one-sided if all ten were presented as the most excellent fellows, each of them a paragon of virtue, even though they, too, had not been invented but taken from real life. Such examples of tendentiousness are all too common, and when they occur in literature, the best way to deal with them is not by censorship but by reasoned criticism—not the most difficult thing in the world.

We should further bear in mind that there are different kinds of one-sidedness, and the term should not be used indiscriminately. Literature is a way of studying life. Therefore just as in science, there must be some degree of specialization. Each writer has his own theme, his work deals with subjects which particularly interest him. It is absurd to expect someone who writes about the working class to give a picture of the peasantry and intelligentsia as well, nor can one demand of a satirist that he describe only the virtuous. But it is no less absurd to insist that Evgenia Ginzburg, writing her memoirs of the "whirlwind" that swept up hundreds of thousands of honest Soviet citizens into Stalin's camps and prisons, must also pay homage to the feats of our industrial workers, our military exploits in Spain, the revolution in agriculture, etc. Of course accounts of camps or prisons may indeed suffer from one-sidedness, as we saw in B. Dyakov's story published in *Oktyabr*.* But Evgenia Ginzburg, it seems to me, has avoided that pitfall.[32]

When talking about truth in art, literature, and history, some of our critics and officials concerned with ideology often ask whether it is really necessary to speak the truth at all times and in all circumstances. They are, to be sure, against falsehood and misrepresentation, but is it really always a good thing to tell people the *whole* truth? May there not be

---

* Dyakov's story was published under the auspices of the dogmatists and intended to "counter" the effect of Solzhenitsyn's *Ivan Denisovich,* which had appeared a few months earlier. Dyakov also gives a horrifying picture of the fate of returned prisoners of war, but he is careful to emphasize the role of the party as eventually putting things right.—Trans.

occasions when it is better to wait a little before making certain "disclosures" about our past, however true they may be? If we are too open in our self-criticism, do we not give grist to the propaganda mills of our enemies abroad, still so numerous?

There are, of course, no simple answers. Circumstances vary, and there are certain things that should not be openly discussed, such as state, military, diplomatic or, say, medical secrets. Even nowadays there may be documents and other materials that it would be proper to communicate only to professional colleagues ("professional secrets") or only to members of the party ("party secrets").

The trouble is, however, that many of those in charge of literature, art, and the social sciences interpret the category of state or party secrets much too broadly; they declare it inopportune or inexpedient to discuss questions that are in fact crucial for the development and progress of our society. In the majority of cases the censor does not ban works that divulge state or military secrets, but enjoins silence where suppression is wrong and very much harms the development of social consciousness. Sometimes the truth is simply classified as secret (as happened, for example, with the commission's report on the Kirov murder or on the show trials of 1936–38); in other instances the study and investigation, even on a "restricted basis," of important historical questions has been forbidden (e.g., to this day there has been no official inquiry into the show trials of 1930–31—of the Industrial Party, the Union Bureau, the Toiling Peasant Party, and others). In recent years the list of such "undesirable subjects" has grown to such an extent that neither the Stalin nor the Khrushchev era is being properly studied, and as a result serious research in history and the social sciences has become altogether impossible. And this is happening in a society that one might have thought should develop on the basis of a thorough and continuing analysis of its own nature, its own shortcomings, its own laws of development. "Russia's past was wonderful," stated the chief of the gendarmes Benkendorf to Peter Chaadaev,* "her present magnificent, and as to her future—it is beyond the grasp of the most daring imagi-

---

* P. Y. Chaadaev, 1793–1856, philosopher profoundly critical of Russia's past.—Trans.

nation. This is the point of view from which Russian history must be written." Unfortunately, even today officials continue to give similar advice.[33]

There is a very obvious need for close scrutiny of the whole Soviet past so that we may be better able to chart our future. We cannot hope to develop Marxism-Leninism without studying its evolution during the last fifty years, including the difficulties, false turns, and zigzags on the way. And, needless to say, open and unrestricted research into the past would be enormously important as a means of averting a revival of Stalinism and "subjectivism." All the warnings that self-criticism may assist our enemies in their propaganda are simply not to be taken seriously. Our ideological adversaries are familiar enough with the major crimes and errors of past decades. Since they are primarily interested in the dark side of our history, the opponents of communism know far more about it than we do ourselves. Our self-criticism is less easily exploited than our silence, the reluctance to face up to mistakes and failings, the attempts to conceal the crimes of the past. The Stalin era has left a very deep mark on the whole of our social life, and by maintaining silence about many of the most important events of the period, we are in fact giving up vital territory to the other side without a struggle. In a word, we continue to allow bourgeois propagandists to trade on all our difficulties.

It would seem at least from their words that this is understood by certain leaders of the party. For example, there was an article in *Kommunist* in 1966 (No. 7) by the then head of the Central Committee's Department of Agitation and Propaganda, V. Stepakov, who wrote reasonably enough: "The strength of theory lies in its ability to make predictions about social life, to give scientific guidance to political activity. Yet those who work in the social sciences are still inhibited by a certain timidity, a fear of working out critical questions. And this often causes them to spend time on research into problems that have already been solved. Both the effectiveness and the prestige of the social sciences are thus diminished. They should be concerned with all the current problems of socialist reality, instead of shying away from them. . . . Silence on such matters has the most negative effect on the education of the Soviet people and particularly on the youth of the country. It must be remembered that whatever we neglect to discuss from a party position will be taken up by our enemies, but from a hostile point of view." Splendid words! Yet they were never acted upon when Stepakov was in a position to do so.

"Silence" is notoriously practiced not only with regard to controversial problems of the past but also of the present day. No objective study is being made of such things, for example, as the development of nationalism and great-power chauvinism or the great dangers for our society of bureaucracy in all its forms. There is almost no attempt to investigate the prevailing moods and trends among young people, the intelligentsia, or the working class. On the whole there are no surveys of public opinion in our country, no investigation of many vital social and economic processes. There are a number of other crucial political, social, and economic problems that to this day are still "forbidden" territory for our social scientists and writers. But of course none of these problems will simply disappear if we ignore them—they can only get worse as time goes on, particularly in view of the fact that in the absence of any discussion of them, there can be no public or party control over their development.

Each honest man and every nation as a whole inevitably strives toward and demands the truth. During the last decades, much in the party's ideology has lost its appeal and the party cannot hope to regain any ground by relying on propaganda techniques—it must learn to speak in the language of truth. Instead of parroting Lenin's words over and over again, we should take them seriously in our political behavior: "The bourgeoisie regards the state as strong only when it is able to use the whole power of the government machinery to manipulate the masses at will. Our idea of strength is different. We believe that the state is made strong by the consciousness of the masses. It is strong when the masses are informed about everything, make their own judgments, and act from a conscious position."[34]

The issues discussed above are intimately related to the problem of freedom to receive and impart information. I am concerned here not with freedom of expression but with the availability of facts, the most primary kind of information about events taking place in the Soviet Union and abroad. And in this respect we are faced with an absolutely unbelievable situation, particularly for a modern, developed society.

People are ill-informed on the simplest level about things going on in their own country and are even more ignorant about events in the world at large. The overwhelming majority of Soviet citizens have no available means of finding things out; besides being a source of irritation and discontent, this also results in an extremely distorted view of the world. Such staggering ignorance is typical not only of "ordinary" Soviet citizens but also of most persons engaged in science or the arts and has a highly adverse effect on their work.

Our newspapers and journals provide a pale reflection, a tendentious glimpse, of world events, neglecting all the shades and hues, the extraordinary complexity of what is going on. We are informed almost immediately about drought in Australia or Brazil but very rarely about drought or harvest failure at home even long after the fact. We know the amount of wheat purchased abroad by India or Pakistan but have no idea how much wheat and other agricultural products the Soviet Union buys from almost all the countries of the globe. We are told how many billions of dollars the United States spends on military aid to Israel, but the figures for Soviet expenditure on military and economic aid to Egypt or other foreign states are not revealed. In the summer of 1970 our newspapers were quick to report the epidemic of measles in Chile. But only after a two-and-one-half-month delay were we told about the outbreak of cholera in Astrakhan, Kerch, and Odessa, while incidence of the disease in Batumi, Volgograd, Tbilisi, and certain other cities went entirely unreported. Because they were not informed in time, millions of people had to cope with disrupted plans and ruined holidays.

Our press gave a detailed account of how three American astronauts died in the course of exercises on the ground. But we know nothing about the training of Soviet cosmonauts and were given no details about what caused four of them (V. Komarov, G. Dobrovolsky, V. Bolkov, and V. Patsaev) to die during flights in space. There has been no information whatsoever about those responsible for such catastrophes.

We are told about the growth of crime in the United States and how many murders and robberies take place annually in Washington and New York. But crime statistics for the USSR continue to be kept secret, and we do not even know how many serious offenses are committed each year in Moscow or Leningrad. We hear soon enough about mine disasters in Japan but were given no details about the catastrophe at the Minsk radio factory.* Our press gives us detailed information about the frequency of industrial accidents at enterprises in West Germany, but we publish no analogous data for the USSR. There are reports of strikes in Italy, but nothing about the serious labor unrest in certain large cities and industrial centers at home. What were the workers' grievances and were their demands met? We do not know. We read about the attitude toward the American army in Okinawa but are not told how ordinary Czechs feel about the Soviet troops stationed in their country.

We are regularly informed about the rise in prices and inflation in Belgium and England, but are not given the relevant statistics on price increases in the USSR or the rising cost of living during the last five or ten years. They tell us about the destruction of surplus fruit and vegetables in Italy and France but not about the way fruit and vegetables rot in the USSR because of inefficient transport.

Any citizen of a capitalist country has full access to an enormous amount of statistical data of a kind kept secret in the Soviet Union—information mainly related to shortcomings, problems, and mistakes. But concealment makes it impossible to mobilize the help of millions of people to overcome our failings.[35]

The secrecy around many aspects of our space program is quite ridiculous. No information is available about who created it, how much is spent on it, or who is now in charge. (The name of the chief designer of the Soviet spacecraft, S. Korolev, was made public only when he died.) Who built our rockets and their instruments? Who invented and constructed *Lunakhod I*? We have no idea. Even before the war, the names of those who designed military equipment were

---

* A poorly ventilated modern complex where accumulated fumes from inflammable paint caused an explosion; the concrete roof collapsed, killing several hundred people.—Trans.

known, and it was not the practice to award them decorations and medals secretly. Possibly at the very beginning of the space program such concealment made sense, but by now it has become an absurd anachronism and an insult to those responsible for our remarkable achievements in space as well as to the Soviet people as a whole. And furthermore, if the foreign press is to be believed, the identities of Soviet space scientists are known to Western specialists. From whom are we hiding these names?

Our citizens are also very poorly informed about events in other socialist countries. In the last ten years there has been less and less news on the situation in China. From a reading of Soviet papers alone, it has been impossible to understand anything about the December events in Poland* or the reasons behind them. Our press was extremely one-sided and biased in its reporting of the 1968–69 period in Czechoslovakia. There is little information about extremely important developments in Hungary—the recent reform of the electoral system, the evolution of socialist democracy, etc. Events in capitalist countries receive meager and prejudiced coverage.

Yet the information is available, in an enormous flow, from Soviet newspaper, radio, and TASS correspondents as well as from the many Western information agencies in the Soviet Union. But it is directed toward a few central receiving points and then distributed in highly uneven and arbitrary fashion to selected "consumers" but not, of course, to our daily press. The only rivals of Soviet papers today for drabness and lack of news are those of China and Korea. Readers of *Pravda* or *Izvestia* get much less information than readers of *Unità* or *Humanité,* although our newspapers have a better qualified staff and much greater means at their disposal. And when it comes to the French intelligentsia reading not only *Humanité* but two to three other daily papers as well, there is no point in even making a comparison. The Yugoslav *Politika* also gives its public much better coverage of world events than the Soviet press.

Readers of certain more specialized publications are only slightly better served. Take *Atlas,* for example, the weekly

* An allusion to riots by workers in Gdansk and Szczecin in December 1970 which led to the fall of Gomulka.—Trans.

bulletin of foreign news available to most party propagandists. It is not on open sale but can be found in most reading rooms of party organizations. It does provide more details about events in China or the Middle East; one can read the full text of important speeches by Gierek when *Pravda* and *Izvestia* have given only the briefest approximate summary, omitting the most interesting sections. The complete text of Janos Kadar's report to the last Hungarian Workers Party Congress was reprinted. There was a detailed description of the autumn events in Jordan. However even *Atlas* remains silent about a great number of important events, such as the Nobel Prize Award to Solzhenitsyn. Much essential information can only be found in special TASS reports, which are subdivided into three classifications and distributed only to restricted categories of recipients. The "green" or "blue" TASS reports are more accessible, while the most complete "white" TASS reports cannot be obtained even by most of the "instructors" and consultants of the Central Committee *apparat*. Yet not less than 90 per cent of the information contained in these "white" reports is readily available to the ordinary person in the West who reads several newspapers of different political complexions.

One must also mention that uniquely Soviet institution, the *spetskhran* (special depository), which exists in almost every large library with admittance on a very restricted basis. It contains an enormous and constantly growing collection of political and scientific publications and journals. Most foreign periodicals are kept there, although many of them have been available for the last ten years at almost any newsstand not only in Yugoslavia but also in Hungary and Poland.

A large number of important Western books on political themes are translated and published in very small editions— sometimes one or two hundred copies in all—and are distributed according to special lists to a very select number of people. The vast majority of social scientists either never see these "numbered" publications or come across them entirely by chance. This means that many of the people best qualified to use and evaluate such political and scientific literature do not know of its existence. And in the last few years there has been an appreciable decline in the flow of information even through these closed or semiclosed channels.

The main reason for all these restrictions on information is the desire within certain bureaucratic circles to preserve a monopoly on information as a means of augmenting their own authority. There is also fear of "undesirable" information that could undermine the position of many bureaucrats. But nowadays it has become very difficult to maintain control in this way. Many people do somehow manage to get at what they want without recourse to existing restricted sources. And it is also the case that the present system of bureaucratic control over information results in ignorance not only at the bottom but also at the top. An enormous amount of crucial data is distorted beyond recognition as it is processed through the bureaucratic levels of the *apparat*. Recent events in Poland showed clearly enough the extent to which the highest leadership could have an inaccurate picture of the mood of the people and the situation in their own country.

We are approaching the time when it will be impossible to put any kind of effective obstacles in the way of new information or ideas. Even now it is said that ideas know no frontiers, although this is still only relatively true. Large states have with considerable effectiveness been able to prevent the diffusion of what they consider to be objectionable views and information. However, given a more literate and educated population, a higher standard of living, and a simultaneous development of technology, it will become increasingly difficult to restrict the spread of views or ideas. As a general rule, no country can experience a rapid development of the forces of production without an even more rapid development of the most varied devices for receiving and distributing information, and these are becoming accessible not only to large institutions and organizations but also to individuals and groups of people. In a developed industrial state, no system of control can possibly prevent the penetration of information from abroad or its circulation within the given country. And as time passes, it will be more and more difficult to control the flow.

The typewriter has by now become a normal possession for most intellectuals in the USSR. Hundreds of thousands are sold annually to individuals, and as a result it has become common practice to distribute literary, publicist, political, and even scientific works in typescript.[36] The quality of a manuscript determines the extent of its circulation, with the size of its "edition" usually dependent upon the extent to which it corresponds to the attitudes and views of a specific group or political trend. And this advance in the availability of information can only accelerate. There have been enormous developments in photocopying processes and also the reproduction of microfilm. Microfilming makes it possible to photograph up to forty-eight pages of printed text on one sheet and then easily reproduce them. Many scholarly works and periodicals are already being issued by this process abroad. It has been predicted that there will be a rapid decline in the number of printed books. Very recently reports in the press described a new invention by two American engineers, a special type of "book" consisting of a plastic plate about the size of a postcard which contains a thousand pages of text, together with illustrations! This plate is then placed in a special apparatus that projects a clear image of the pages of the book onto a screen. The "pages" are turned by rotating the handle of a projector no larger than a portable typewriter. A very compact, efficient, and uncomplicated photocopying machine using ordinary paper has replaced the earlier, more cumbersome model. Such machines have now become a standard item of office equipment and in time, like typewriters, they will be owned by individuals for their personal use. And of course there are no works that cannot nowadays be reproduced on a tape recorder.

It has become impossible to achieve total obliteration of foreign radio broadcasts whether in Russian or other national languages of the USSR—there are now techniques for reducing the effects of jamming to a minimum. Knowledge of other languages also makes it possible to listen to numerous foreign stations, and the number of people who do know foreign languages is rapidly increasing. The potential of television is also developing. People living in our border areas easily pick up television broadcasts from Finland and Sweden. In East Germany, a great many Germans regularly watch television programs from West Germany. Experts predict that by the mid-seventies widespread use of space satellites for radio and television transmission will make it virtually impossible to stop the stream of information coming to the Soviet Union from abroad. The rapid growth of tourism both ways and also the growing number of scientific and cultural exchanges encourages an intensive sharing of ideas and information. Foreign radio stations broadcast and publishing houses distribute the works of Soviet authors which cannot be published in the normal way in the USSR because of irrational censorship restrictions. We can attempt to hold back this ever-increasing stream of information and ideas only at our peril, for it would mean retarding the technical and cultural development of the country.

Thus whatever the inclinations of those in charge of ideology, we must learn to live in a more open world where there will be a comparatively free circulation of ideas and information. Clearly this calls for a real transformation of our whole system of ideological work, our whole system of propaganda.

"The news is our weapon," declared A. Sylvester, a former public relations officer of the U.S. Defense Department.[37] Certain senior members of the Central Committee understand this as well. On June 14, 1967, the head of a Central Committee department, the late D. Shevlyagin, wrote in *Pravda:*

In present world conditions, when the very latest kinds of technological equipment are at the service of bourgeois propaganda, one cannot underestimate the significance of information as a crucial means of ideological influence. It is wrong to disregard the unprecedented growth in people's demand for information or the fact that they now have extensive new possibilities for obtaining it from different sources that cannot be controlled. Information that comes first makes the greatest impact. Timing is terribly important, as are selection and arrangement. The problem is to see to it that our audience receives its information from us *first* in as comprehensive and reliable a form as possible.

The deputy head of the Department of Agitation and Propaganda of the Central Committee, A. Yakovlev, recently wrote in *Kommunist:*

Information, apart from its direct propagandistic value, is of even greater practical assistance to the leading organs in the scientific control and study of public opinion and makes the masses more competent to observe, react, and criticize—one of the conditions for the effective participation of millions of Soviet citizens in the government of their country. It would otherwise be impossible to have a normally functioning socialist system or a growth of consciousness and social participation on the part of the workers.[38]

One can only agree with these words of wisdom. But they are very far from being realized in practice. Our propaganda is becoming even less effective and interesting, news takes longer to get through, newspapers grow more boring, and the pangs of the intelligentsia's information hunger grow ever more acute. Any person able to do so ignores Soviet sources and seeks his information elsewhere.

X

Freedom of Movement and Other Problems

The right to choose one's place of residence is an aspect of freedom essential to any democracy, whether bourgeois or socialist. Basic democratic freedoms were proclaimed to be among the universal rights of man in the Universal Declaration of Human Rights adopted by the General Assembly of the United Nations on December 10, 1948. They were again confirmed in 1966 when the UN, with the active support of the Soviet Union, approved the International Covenant on Civil and Political Rights. According to Article 12 of the Covenant:

Everyone lawfully within the territory of a state shall, within that territory, have the right to liberty of movement and freedom to choose his residence. Everyone shall be free to leave any country including his own. The above-mentioned rights shall not be subject to any restrictions except those which are provided by law, are necessary to protect national security, public order, public health or morals, or the rights and freedoms of others. . . . No one shall be arbitrarily deprived of the right to enter his own country.

In prerevolutionary Russia, the programmes of socialist parties always stressed the importance of freedom of movement and choice of residence. The Bolsheviks were particularly concerned to ensure this right for the peasants. In his famous "Address to the Village Poor," Lenin said:

Under serfdom a peasant could not leave his village without the landlord's permission. Today the peasant is free to go wherever he pleases, as long as the *mir** allows him to leave, as long as he is not in debt, as long as he can get a passport,† and if the governor or district police officer does not forbid his changing residence. Thus even now the peasant is deprived of absolute freedom to go where he chooses; he does not enjoy complete freedom of movement and is still half a serf. . . . The Social-Democrats demand complete freedom of movement and choice of employment for the people. What do we mean by *freedom of movement*? We mean that a peasant should have the right to go anywhere, to live where he likes, to choose any village or town without having to ask permission. This means the abolition of passports in Russia (as has long been the case in other states) and that no policeman will dare to prevent a peasant from settling and working where he pleases.[1]

The first programme of the RSDLP included the demand that there be freedom of movement for all citizens of Russia as a fundamental constitutional right in the future democratic republic.[2]

Immediately after the October Revolution, internal passports were in fact abolished. Among other freedoms, the Russian people at last acquired the right to freedom of movement. In the early twenties Soviet citizens were more or less at liberty to travel from one part of the country to another, from the provinces to capital cities and from village to town. This gave rise to certain problems but did not provoke economic disaster, since for a great many reasons the vast majority of the population were in no hurry to uproot themselves. During this period there was also a relatively simple procedure for obtaining foreign travel documents, whether for holidays or official business.

The situation began to change in the early 1930's. In 1932 passports were reintroduced, together with a strict system of registration for urban dwellers; at the time famine had struck the densely populated southern areas of the country,

---

* The village community in tsarist Russia.—Trans.

† Internal identity card; the term "passport" is always used in this sense unless there is specific reference to foreign travel.—Trans.

and millions of starving peasants were streaming into the cities where there was relatively more food available. Although within a year or two the famine was over, life remained extremely difficult for the peasants, and the internal passport system was retained, remaining practically unchanged to the present. Even today a collective farmer has no passport permitting him to leave the collective farm and move to another area of the country or find work in a factory. A collective farmer or his children can receive a passport only with the consent of the farm management and the local authorities—permission that is by no means automatically granted. And so, fifty-five years after the October Revolution, peasants are still *unequal before the law;* the passport system legitimizes and reinforces their inferior position.*

However, this is not the only limitation on freedom of movement within the Soviet Union. Many other factors also inhibit the Soviet citizen's freedom to live where he chooses. It is difficult to get permission to live in many southern districts, particularly holiday resorts. There are a great many restrictions on residence in nearly all the large cities, and this is especially true of the capital cities of the Union Republics. It is extremely difficult for someone living in the provinces to move to Moscow or Leningrad—permission must be granted at such a high level that it is practically impossible for an ordinary person to obtain it.

There have been many attempts to justify these limitations. The arguments usually refer to certain distinctive features of the Soviet economy. Since the standard of living in certain rural areas lags behind that of the cities, it is feared that freedom of movement would result in too great a population flow from country to town, which would in turn cause a breakdown in agricultural production and overcrowding in the cities. Some economists believe that an extension of freedom of movement would probably lead to a vast shift of population from the eastern regions of the country as well as from the Urals, Kazakhstan, and the far north to the more developed and "warmer" areas: the central region, the Baltic states, the Ukraine, Moldavia, etc. Others argue that if restrictions on residence in Moscow were lifted, the capital would be flooded with millions of new inhabitants from the

---

* According to new regulations published in 1974, peasants will be given passports within several years.—Trans.

provinces who would come and live with friends and relatives and make a solution of the Moscow housing problem even more difficult than it is already. Moscow would possibly become the most highly populated city in the world.

There is of course some justification for these anxieties. Over a long period of its development, the Soviet economy has depended on freedom of movement being seriously restricted, and so it is hardly surprising that this has become a condition of its normal functioning. In other words, specific economic factors do now exist that serve to consolidate and perpetuate restrictions on freedom of movement.

Today the negative, retarding effect of restrictions on freedom of movement is much more harmful than in the past. First of all, there is the very serious infringement on elementary democratic rights. With present-day developments in transport and communication, there is much more inclination and need to move about than twenty or thirty years ago. For many people, therefore, previously accepted restrictions are now becoming increasingly intolerable. After several visits to the city, the collective farmer begins to feel his own inferiority because he has no passport; this emotion persists, regardless of whether or not he actually wants to move to the town. The very existence of a right gives people a feeling of their own worth and reduces the danger of arbitrary behavior by the government.

There is also the resultant economic and cultural waste. Many people are not working where their abilities can best be utilized. Not only are gifted individuals being prevented from moving to Moscow, where of course it is easier to develop specialized skills, get the best training, and obtain information, but it is also the case that a person living in Moscow or Leningrad, afraid of losing his residence permit and his apartment, often refuses to move to the provinces where his particular abilities could be used to best advantage. There are many scientists and scholars working in isolation in provincial centers who have trouble in obtaining advanced degrees but who would have been able to progress much more rapidly in a large Moscow institute. On the other hand, many an ordinary engineer in Moscow would have become the head of a large enterprise in the provinces. One could multiply these examples almost indefinitely.

Clearly regulations that have been in force for so many

years cannot be changed overnight at the stroke of a pen; the restrictions on movement must be eliminated gradually but surely. There will be no economic catastrophe as a result. Population migration can easily be controlled by intelligent economic levers, with no need to fear that millions of people will leave Siberia and settle in Moldavia and the Kuban or that millions will descend on Moscow. Obviously there will always be a good number of people wanting to move to the capital, and economic and other incentives must be provided to encourage others to leave it. Surely if living in Moscow (or Leningrad) and the other "controlled" cities were no longer the privilege of a few, and if there were a guaranteed right to return and get accommodations equivalent to what one had before, hundreds of thousands of Muscovites would move to the provinces either for short periods or even permanently.

Together with freedom of movement and choice of residence, the Soviet people should also be given the right to travel abroad and even to change their citizenship if they are so inclined. At the same time, foreigners should be permitted to come to the USSR and become Soviet citizens. The Old Bolshevik S. Smirnov wrote in the article already referred to above (see Note 35 for Chapter IX):

Soviet citizens have in effect lost the right to travel abroad. This is humiliating; it leads them to break the law and, as a result, people are convicted for criminal offenses connected with attempts to leave the country. . . . Our socialist system as the prototype of the society of the future should encourage an increasing number of its citizens to live abroad, where they can advertise the Soviet way of life. Furthermore, as a counter to the American Peace Corps, we should set up our own distinctive socialist corps, which would provide much-needed cultural and educational aid to underdeveloped countries. They could also plant the ideas of socialism in the minds of workers beyond our borders.

Today most people might greet Smirnov's suggestions with a skeptical smile, and we are still a long way from putting them into practice. Unfortunately the majority of those requesting permission to leave the country and change their nationality are hardly motivated by ideas of advertising the

Soviet way of life abroad. Even so, the right to leave the Soviet Union should be substantially extended.

Evidently a decision was taken recently to allow Soviet citizens of Jewish origin to emigrate more or less freely to Israel. Not less than twelve thousand Soviet Jews received permission to leave in 1971, and the figure for the first four months of 1972 was five or six thousand.* This was certainly a wise decision, but one can only regret that although emigration to Israel has been made easier, it is still restricted and involves a number of degrading procedures—for example, the necessity to get a reference from one's place of work. Many people are dismissed from their jobs long before they leave for Israel and are often subjected to public abuse and insult.

Several thousand Soviet citizens of German descent have also been given the option of settling in the German Democratic Republic or West Germany, although most of their applications have not yet been processed. But these are all exceptions to the general rule that Soviet citizens are denied the right freely to leave and return to their own country, i.e., the right proclaimed in the UN Covenant on Civil and Political Rights. Those who have married foreigners also find it difficult to obtain permission to go abroad. This situation must be gradually changed.

We know that the possibility of allowing citizens to leave the country is now being considered at the highest level. But the purpose would be to rid the country of certain "undesirables," people with opposition views. Thus it would be a question not so much of freedom to go abroad but rather exile—a new form of punishment in the struggle against dissenters.† Such a measure did appear in legislation of the twenties and thirties but was later removed from the criminal code. The expulsion of certain dissenters would of course be more "humane" than semisecret trials followed by imprisonment or confinement in a psychiatric hospital. But any form of punishment for opinions or convictions flouts the basic principles of democracy. Therefore in advocating the gradual

* About 35,000 Jews emigrated in 1973, 20,000 in 1974.—Trans.
† Brodsky, Chalidze, Esenin-Volpin, Galich, Litvinov, Maximov, Zh. Medvedev, Nekrasov, Rostropovich, Sinyavsky, Shragin, and Solzhenitsyn are all now abroad, as well as others.—Trans.

introduction of the absolute right to leave the country and change one's citizenship, my motives are very different from those in authority. The right to choose one's place of residence within one's own country or abroad is now a generally accepted democratic liberty in most civilized countries of the world. Its introduction here would undoubtedly be a positive step and would have a healthy effect on the general political atmosphere within the country, not because certain "awkward" citizens would leave as a result, but because fear of a "brain drain" would force state and party bodies to take much more seriously all the democratic rights and freedoms that are formally proclaimed as belonging to all Soviet citizens.

Travel abroad in general is very difficult to arrange, apart from the problems of changing citizenship. Whether it is a brief vacation trip or participation at a scientific conference, there are many complicated and humiliating formalities. This is true of trips to socialist countries but even more so to capitalist ones. No accurate statistics on foreign travel are available, but it is certainly true that, during the last ten years, for every thousand persons wishing to go abroad, well under a hundred actually received permission. If one excludes repeated journeys by the same person, it is probable that no more than three or four million Soviet citizens have crossed the border during the last ten years. The official procedures for foreign travel not only offend against generally accepted democratic standards but also seriously affect the exchange of scientific, technical, and cultural information, to the great detriment of progress in these areas. Various aspects of the problems of foreign travel are dealt with in detail by Zhores Medvedev in his book *The Medvedev Papers*.* His criticisms of existing procedures are absolutely valid, and his suggestions would be enormously beneficial if adopted.

Finally, one may add that in most countries freedom of movement and choice of residence are constitutional rights. However they find no place in Chapter Ten of the Soviet Constitution, which deals with the "fundamental rights and duties of citizens." It is important, therefore, that the new Constitution (many years ago it was announced that work on it had begun) should include a special article with wording similar

* New York and London, 1971. Zhores Medvedev is the author's twin brother.—Trans.

to that of Article 12 of the International Covenant on Civil and Political Rights.

Unlike freedom of movement, the right of Soviet citizens to privacy of correspondence is provided for in the Constitution (see Article 128). Nevertheless, both internal and foreign correspondence are often treated as if this constitutional guarantee did not exist. Obviously the police must have the right to intercept certain letters and parcels in order to prevent or combat crime. But this should happen only with a procurator's approval, just as a search warrant is necessary to authorize intrusion on the sanctity of the home. It is generally believed that at present practically all foreign correspondence is checked by the postal censorship or customs authorities.[3] And although theoretically telephones can be tapped only with the approval of the procurator, many people have good reason to fear that both local and long distance calls are subject to official eavesdropping on an enormous scale, evidently without prior authorization.

Article 125 of the Constitution guarantees Soviet citizens the right to freedom of assembly, the right to hold street processions and demonstrations "in conformity with the interests of the working people and in order to strengthen the socialist system." In practice, however, this right scarcely exists. Soviet citizens have learned from experience that their right to assemble, march, and demonstrate is guaranteed only when it is a question of expressing *support* for some official measure or policy. Almost all demonstrations or even meetings held to *protest* against the actions of local or central authorities are usually regarded as illegal or a breach of the peace. On some pretext or other, they are stopped with the help of the police and *druzhinniki*.* For example, the peaceful demonstration held in Red Square on August 25, 1968 by eight people protesting against the invasion of Czechoslovakia ended in the arrest of all the participants, even though their means of protest had in no way contravened the Constitution. All the peaceful demonstrations against various political trials during the last five or six years have been dispersed, and some of the organizers have also been prosecuted. The traditional Decem-

* Voluntary militia.—Trans.

ber 5 demonstration on Pushkin Square held annually since
1965, usually with only a few dozen people taking part, is
always forcibly broken up and is apparently a cause of great
concern to the authorities. It lasts only a few minutes and
threatens no one, traffic is not held up and there is no
breach of the peace; yet there are always extraordinary "security" measures, with far more *druzhinniki,* police, and KGB
agents than demonstrators.*

Many attempts have been made to get permission from
local authorities to hold peaceful protest demonstrations but
they have invariably resulted in point-blank refusal or a total
unwillingness even to reply to such requests. Needless to say
this apprehensive attitude toward peaceful and restrained
protest is ill-founded and leads to unjustifiable actions by the
authorities. It would be absurd to maintain that all government actions are always correct; or that groups of citizens
might not feel dissatisfied even with basically commendable
measures. Long ago Lenin wrote that although we have a
workers' state, bureaucratic distortions still exist and workers
must always have the right to struggle against them. Peaceful
assemblies and demonstrations are important ways of pre-
senting demands to local and central authorities and are
recognized throughout the civilized world as means of expressing discontent.

The right of citizens to form different organizations and
groups should also be extended. It is ostensibly guaranteed by
Article 126 of the Constitution, and indeed there are a great
many different associations, scientific societies, cultural organizations, groups for young people, and athletic clubs. But in
practice the only kinds of organizations permitted to exist are
those which declare absolute allegiance to Marxism-Leninism
and the Soviet government and which support party policy in
their own special sphere of activity.

Yet even where all these criteria are satisfied, the freedom to form an organization is still very limited. What if a
group of scholars from various social science institutes, dissatisfied with the present state of Marxism-Leninism, decided
to set up a voluntary association, independent of party bodies
in their own institutions, in order to explore theoretical prob-

* The first demonstration had been organized in support of Sinyavsky
and Daniel.—Trans.

lems? Would such an association be allowed to function freely? Or would those taking part be dismissed from their jobs, expelled from the party, and forbidden to meet and discuss questions of common interest? The answer is obvious. And so one can hardly speak of freedom of assembly and association beyond the confines of orthodox views.

I do not know anything about illegal groups. There are, however, two small associations referred to above that exist legally, although not approved of by the authorities: the Human Rights Committee, which owes its survival entirely to the prestige of Academician Sakharov, and the Initiative Group for the Defense of Human Rights, most of whose members are now in prison or exile. Such fear of "dissident" groups is both wrong and unjustified (as has already been argued in Chapters IV and V above).

The principle of *equality* was an important part of bourgeois democratic doctrine at the end of the seventeenth century and the beginning of the eighteenth. However, it was usually only a question of legal relationships derived, it was thought, from the essential nature of man. All people were equal in the sight of nature, since basic human characteristics were thought to be identical "for each man and all of humanity at all times and in all places."[4] In the bourgeois democratic revolutions, therefore, the call for equality was as emphatic as the demand for "liberty, fraternity and democracy."

The overthrow of the feudal ruling classes was a tremendous step forward. Aristocratic and gentry power were curtailed and most hereditary privilege was abolished, opening the way not only for economic development but also for an extension of citizens' rights and liberties. But in the end, bourgeois equality meant only the formal constitutional equality of people who remained socially and economically unequal, and thus it was something of a sham. Bourgeois capitalist society never has provided nor ever will provide real equality and genuine democracy for the working classes; this is why they turn to socialism.

I have already discussed many of the notable achievements of the working class in socialist countries as well as some of the problems still awaiting solution. And among these, equality as an essential feature of socialist democracy requires special discussion. Briefly and only in a preliminary way, I would like to look at two central factors: wage levels and privilege.

Before the Revolution, almost all socialists and communists sought an answer to the question of how a fair wage would be determined in the society of the future. It was evident that there could not be one rate of pay for everyone during the transition period, and there was general agreement on the formula "equal pay for equal work." However, the basic principle of socialism, "from each according to his ability, to each according to his labor," suggested that there would be substantial inequality both in wages and standard of living. In his *Critique of the Gotha Program,* Marx wrote that equality under socialism primarily meant that in the distribution of rewards, "the amount will be measured by an equal standard—labor. But one man is superior to another physically or mentally and supplies more labor in the same time or can labor for a longer period; to serve as a measure, labor must be defined by its duration or intensity, otherwise it ceases to be a standard of measurement. This *equal* right is an unequal right for unequal labor. It recognizes no class differences because each person is only a worker like everyone else; but there is tacit recognition of unequal individual endowment and thus productive capacity. . . . Furthermore, one worker is married, another not, one has more children than another, and so forth. Thus with an equal performance of labor, and hence an equal share in the social consumption fund, one will in fact receive more than another and will be richer. . . ."[5]

The problem was not only the duration and intensity of labor (quantity) but also *quality,* i.e., the complexity of the work and skills demanded. How could equal pay be given for labor of the same duration and intensity which required differing degrees of professional competence? How should executive or managerial functions be rewarded, or work at different levels of industrial administration? Some who were more consistently egalitarian tried to show that payment for labor in a socialist system should be determined only according to quantitative criteria, ignoring the level of skill involved. Society, having provided the education and training, should be able to reap the rewards. "In a society organized on socialist principles," wrote Engels, "the cost [of specialized qualifications] is borne by society, and therefore the fruits, the greater value created by complex labor, belong to society. The worker himself has no right to claim higher wages."[6]

As far as office workers and civil servants are concerned, the Paris Commune established the principle that "the salaries of all state officials from the highest to the lowest shall be brought into line with ordinary levels of wages paid to workers."[7] This was in order to combat careerism and to avoid the emergence of socialist bureaucrats isolated from the people.

These then were the basic principles laid down by Marx, Engels, and Lenin on the nature of wages under socialism before the victory of the Revolution. But when the Revolution proved to be more than an ephemeral episode like the Paris Commune, it was obvious that nearly all these fundamental principles would have to be revised before they could be applied to the builders of socialism.

Clearly it was wrong and unfair to ignore qualifications or the complexity of the work involved when establishing wage levels. Even under socialism, society was only partly responsible for education or superior skills. To a large extent, these still depended on the ambition, determination, and efforts of the individual himself, and it was therefore quite fair to offer higher wages as a stimulus. The first Soviet wage scale established a ratio of $1:2.1$ between the lowest and the highest earnings. At the beginning of 1919, the gap between the two extremes was narrowed even more and became $1:1.75$.[8] This lasted until the beginning of NEP in the autumn of 1921; with the approval of the Central Executive Committee and the party Central Committee, the Council of People's Commissars passed a resolution that stated: "When setting wage rates for workers with different qualifications— office staff, middle-range technicians and senior administrative personnel—all thought of equality must be abandoned."[9] The new wage scale contained broad differentials according to qualifications, and divided staff into four groups: apprentices, workers with varying degrees of skill, accountants and office workers, and administrative and technical staff. The ratio between the lowest level and the highest (the seventeenth category) was set at $1:8$.

The question of payment for employees of state administrative bodies was dealt with in a different way. In the first months after October, the minimum subsistence wage based on the exchange rate and the level of prices was calculated to be eight rubles a day; this was confirmed by a decree of January 16, 1918.[10] Almost at the same time Lenin drafted a bill "On the Salaries of Senior Personnel and Officials," which soon afterwards was approved by the Council of People's Commissars with slight amendments. The text was as follows:

Since it is considered necessary to adopt the most energetic measures to lower the salaries of officials in all state, communal, and private undertakings and institutions, without exception, the Council of People's Commissars decrees:

1. There shall be a maximum limit to the salary of a People's Commissar of 500 rubles a month, with an allowance of 100 rubles for each child; the size of apartments is limited to one room per member of the family.

2. All local Soviets of Workers', Soldiers' and Peasants' Deputies are asked to prepare and implement revolutionary measures for the special taxation of senior personnel.

3. The Ministry of Finance and all individual Commissars shall make an immediate study of the accounts of ministries and shall reduce all excessively high salaries and pensions.[11]

Thus during the first months of Soviet rule the salary of a People's Commissar (including Lenin himself) was only *twice* the minimum subsistence wage for an ordinary citizen. Over the next years, prices and the value of the ruble often changed very rapidly and wages altered accordingly. At times the figures were quite astonishing—hundreds of thousands and millions of rubles. But even under these conditions Lenin made sure that the ratio between lowest and highest salaries in state organizations did not exceed the fixed limit—during his lifetime the differential apparently was never greater than 1:5.

Yet of course there had to be many exceptions in the interests of creating a socialist state. Not only were there special "shockworker" rates for certain categories of factory and office workers, the most serious retreat from the principles of the Paris Commune were the very large salaries paid to "bourgeois specialists" (*spetsy*) since it was necessary to "buy" their services until the working class could create its own intelligentsia. Speaking at the Seventh Moscow Provincial Party Conference on October 29, 1921, Lenin recalled the first months of Soviet power:

Even then we were forced to retreat on a number of points. For example, in March and April 1918, one issue was whether to pay specialists salaries that corresponded not to socialist but to bourgeois relations of production, i.e., rates which were not justified by the difficulty or complexity of the work but which conformed to bourgeois custom and would have been appropriate in a bourgeois society. Originally there had been no intention to provide such exceptionally high rewards for specialists (in no way exceptional, of course, in terms of bourgeois standards)—this would have meant contravening several decrees issued at the end of 1917. But at the beginning of 1918 the party directed that we must take a step backward and accept a certain degree of "compromise" (this was the word used at the time).[12]

High salaries for "bourgeois specialists" were retained during NEP, at a time when it seemed that there would be a prolonged struggle between capitalism and socialism. Lenin even advanced further arguments in favor of this policy. In a Central Committee resolution, "On the Role and Tasks of Trade Unions During NEP," drafted by Lenin himself and adopted on January 12, 1921, he stressed how important it was that the *spetsy* "live better under socialism than under capitalism, both in terms of standard of living and legal rights, that they enjoy a more comradely cooperative relationship with workers and peasants, and in the moral sense, that they are satisfied with their work and conscious of its social value independent of the mercenary interests of the capitalist classes."[13]

Such high salaries were paid only to specialists who were not members of the party. If a party member found himself obtaining a very high income, he became subject to a ceiling, and any money above that figure had to be given to the Party Finance Department for its mutual aid fund. This was the origin of the "party maximum," i.e., a limit to the salary a party member was allowed to receive.

These were the first basic measures taken by the Soviet government on wages and salaries. One can only speculate about what might have been if Lenin had continued to lead the country. Stalin, of course, particularly from the beginning of the thirties, was responsible for the fact that many of the basic principles of a socialist wage policy went by the board. The nominal pay of ordinary factory and office workers rose very slowly, which meant that millions of people earned wages or received pensions considerably below subsistence level (for the most part no longer even calculated in Stalin's time). Yet the salaries of senior party and state officials kept rising. The party maximum was done away with. Senior officials earned not two to five times but rather ten to twenty times as much as factory and office workers. At the same time the secret system of "packets" was gradually introduced—large monthly bonuses handed over to most so-called *nomenklatura* officials,* usually amounting to more than the regular salary for the particular post.

As for the top leadership—Stalin and the other members of the Politburo—no distinction was made between their personal expenses and needs of the state, and so in practice there was virtually no limit. It scarcely needs saying that this system was in flagrant contradiction of genuine socialist principles.

During the last twenty years the system of determining wage levels has been radically altered. Rates of pay for factory and office workers at the bottom of the scale have been substantially increased; the minimum wage and the minimum pension have more than doubled. At the other extreme, the practice of handing out "packets" has been condemned and abolished, considerably reducing the real earnings of high officials. There is, however, still a great deal to be criticized in the salary structure of the country. Teachers, doctors, certain other white collar workers, and members of the intelligentsia are all underpaid. Soviet economists and trade union officials virtually ignore the question of the "minimum subsistence rate" and neglect to measure the real earnings of all categories of workers by any such standard. Even today the ratio between highest and lowest rates of pay remains remote from the ideals of socialism. For example, in a small research institute concerned with the problems of training manual and professional workers (where I was employed

* *Nomenklatura* refers to a system of appointment lists, controlled directly or indirectly by the party, covering virtually all responsible posts in the country.—Trans.

for ten years), the difference between the lowest salary for a research assistant (60–70 rubles a month) and that of the most highly paid section head (he had a doctorate, was a member of the Academy of Pedagogical Sciences, and earned 800 rubles) was of the order of 1:13. In the larger institutes of the Academy of Sciences, the ratio between the salary of a laboratory assistant or a junior research worker with no degree and that of an academician in charge of a department is 1:15 or 1:20. In Soviet ministries and important military establishments, the ratio between the highest and the lowest rates of pay is also 1:20 or even 1:30, but if one takes into consideration the many services available to *nomenklatura* officials at public expense (food coupons, medical treatment, holidays, personal transport, dachas, etc.), the total value translated into monetary terms would make the ratio 1:50 or sometimes even 1:100. Obviously this is quite excessive for a socialist country.

How should the existing wage structure be changed? It can only be a gradual process taking place over a number of years. One writer makes a rather optimistic general prediction: "On the basis of continuing improvements in production which will affect the whole of society, along with a corresponding increase in consumer purchasing power, there will be a steady advance toward absolute eonomic equality for all members of society." Concurrently there will be progress in equality of educational opportunity, making it possible for more people to engage in the most complex forms of labor.

Several letters written by Old Bolsheviks and sent to the Twenty-third and Twenty-fourth Party congresses contained rather more concrete proposals. They called for a return to the principle of a party maximum, or at least to a maximum differential of 1:5 between the lowest and highest rates of pay. One thing wrong with these suggestions, however, is that they take the lowest existing wage rate as the bottom of their scale (now 60–70 rubles a month for certain categories of factory and office workers, while the average for this group is 115–120 rubles a month) rather than the minimum needed for an adequate standard of living. Of course it is necessary to decrease inequality, but not simply by gradually reducing the highest salaries. It is just as important to raise wages that do not provide a minimum standard; the required amount should be determined by scientific analysis. Given contemporary requirements in modern urban conditions, I believe this minimum should be around 100 rubles for each member of the family. Therefore for a family of four, including two working adults and two children, the monthly wages of one of the adults should be not less than 250 rubles and not less than 150 for the other. This in effect means gradually doubling the average monthly wage of factory and office workers. When ordinary workers receive 200 rubles, those more highly skilled should be paid, on average, 400–600 rubles. But top specialists and administrators should never be allowed to get more than 1,500–2,000 rubles a month, no matter how many posts they hold.

Aside from wage differentials, there is the question of special privilege, the fact that leading government officials have unique access to a variety of scarce goods and services. The original approach to this question, as everyone knows, was that there should be no special privileges for any members of the government. The first leaders of the socialist revolution were absolutely sincere about this; it was a natural reaction to the blatant injustice of the old order and at the same time certainly did attract the admiration of the masses as they rose up in revolt.

Memoirs about Lenin recall how on the day after the victorious uprising in Petrograd, he simply went by tram to rest in the apartment of one of his comrades. When he visited the Kremlin barber, Lenin insisted on waiting his turn and sat quietly reading a newspaper. He was very fond of strolling in the evening in the vicinity of the Kremlin without any special protection and categorically refused to have a bodyguard until after several attempts had been made on his life (he was seriously wounded on August 30, 1918). Even then he only agreed to let one Red Army soldier accompany him in his car. He still often drove to the countryside without a bodyguard and on one occasion was attacked by a gang of thieves who made off with his car. When Lenin moved into the Kremlin he occupied a small room which had belonged to one of the former servants. In *State and Revolution* he expressed the view that the leaders of the new state should not have their expenses paid out of public funds.

This absolute insistence on refusing almost all privilege

was typical of the majority of the leading figures of that time. Such an uncompromising approach was taken for granted by the first generation of revolutionaries, although sometimes it was not entirely wise. One can only regret, for example, that Lenin was so badly guarded during the early Soviet years that on several occasions he escaped death only by chance. Many of Lenin's colleagues died prematurely because they refused to rest and ignored their health. But those were exceptional times and need not be taken as a model for today. It is in the interest of a socialist society that its leaders have everything they need, since the prosperity and well-being of the whole people depend on the quality of their work. They must enjoy good health, have a chance to relax, and some of them must be constantly guarded. All vital information should reach them first. They are, in fact, representatives of the nation, and this function also requires additional expense. It is unthinkable that the head of the Soviet state should have to wait at the barber or to get tickets for a train.

A certain amount of privilege might be appropriate for various scientific institutions and also within literature and the arts. An individual's talent is not just his own personal possession but also belongs to the whole people, and society must nourish it with the care and attention it deserves. There can be no objection to certain privileges enjoyed by Deputies of the Supreme Soviet, or by Heroes of the Soviet Union and Heroes of Socialist Labor.*

There is the danger, however, that this whole system of special privilege can become self-serving and change from a means into an end. And it is often the case that privileges tend to multiply out of all proportion—the actual importance of the official concerned becomes irrelevant. When privileges are granted from above in the absence of public supervision, it is much easier for them to become excessive, leading to secret prerogatives and the abuse of high office.

During the Stalin period, *nomenklatura* officials not only received "packets" but also had access to a very extensive range of other privileges. Special "elite" apartment houses were constructed for them, along with exclusive dachas and sanatoria, none of which were available to ordinary factory and office workers. There was a system of "closed" clinics and

* Honorary titles.—Trans.

hospitals, and restricted shops where it was possible to buy foodstuffs and consumer goods otherwise in short supply. There were even cemeteries reserved for the favored few. As the number of people with the right to enjoy these special advantages inevitably increased, the entire network of "closed" institutions took on immense proportions, employing a vast number of carefully selected personnel. Powerful individuals seemed to be fencing themselves off from the people and either knew nothing or simply did not care about the difficulties of daily life for the man in the street. The inevitably corrupting influence extended beyond those in authority to members of their families and also to many of the people employed in the various establishments that serviced the elite.

Unfortunately many of these privileges still exist today for a large number of *nomenklatura* officials. There is also a disturbing new trend toward special advantages in access to higher education—sometimes more than half of the nominally available places are reserved *even before the examinations take place*. This means that certain selected pupils are admitted to an institute whatever their examination results, which leads to a decline in the quality of our officials in such fields as the foreign service and facilitates the rise of a hereditary bureaucracy.

Quite obviously most of these privileges could be abolished without harming society in any way or affecting the work of *nomenklatura* officials except possibly for the better. The most natural way to ensure certain benefits for leading officials is to pay them more; this is a much healthier method than the creation of restricted stores and other special institutions for their use alone. In his essay *Progress, Coexistence, and Intellectual Freedom*, written in 1968, Academician Sakharov says:

I would like to emphasize that I am not against the socialist principle of payment based on the amount and quality of a person's work. The payment of high salaries to proficient administrators and highly skilled workers, teachers and doctors, workers in dangerous occupations, scientists and scholars, people engaged in the arts (all of whom account for a very small proportion of the total wage bill) does not threaten society as long as it is not accompanied by concealed privileges. Higher wages, if properly earned, benefit society as a whole. After all, every minute wasted by a top administrator represents material loss for the economy, and every minute wasted by an artist or composer means that society loses that much emotional, philosophical or artistic capital. . . . But when it is a question of secrecy, there is inevitably a suspicion that something wrong is going on, that loyal servants of the system are being bribed. I believe that the most rational way to solve this "delicate" problem is not the setting of income ceilings for party members or some such measure but simply to abolish all privileges and establish unified wage rates based on the social value of labor along with an economic, market approach to the wage problem in general, while at the same time encouraging the role of moral factors.[14]

I certainly agree with Sakharov that there should be no concealed privileges.[15] Similarly any rewards for more qualified staff should come through higher salaries wherever possible. However, in present social conditions, certain privileges for senior officials are still necessary and should be retained —for example, priority to receive information, expenses incurred in the course of government duties, personal protection, transportation, etc. These and other types of official privilege can be reduced only very gradually since there would have to be simultaneous changes in salary structures and the pricing of certain types of goods and services.

Privileges tend to arise where there are shortages. Certain products are now available for practically the whole population while others are produced in a limited quantity which can satisfy only a small part of the demand. Under the Soviet price system, shortages either mean enormous queues or else distribution takes place via some other channel—personal contacts, *nomenklatura* privilege, or worst of all, bribery. There is no simple solution for this very complicated problem; sometimes it is imperative to regulate allocation by means of waiting lists—for example, in the case of apartments in state-owned (not cooperative) buildings. In other instances, there should be a market approach: if the prices of goods in short supply are raised, it will level supply and demand. This would go a long way toward removing various malpractices and black-market activities, and make it easier to close down many restricted distribution centers.

New kinds of goods and services are constantly appearing but inevitably become scarce almost at once, which means that only a few people can enjoy them. In certain critical situations even the right to live may be limited to a few. If a ship is sinking and there is only one undamaged lifeboat, who gets first priority? Will it be the most distinguished passengers or those with the highest salaries? Hardly. The most elementary moral code demands that children come first, although they have performed no service to society and receive no salary. There are of course less dramatic situations where other solutions are possible. But if medical research were to develop a means of prolonging life which was extremely expensive and could be used on only ten people in every million, how would those ten be chosen? It might be fairest to select five by drawing lots and five from among the most honored members of the community. One could think of various alternatives. As for the privileges of top state and party officials, the general approach should be that all really necessary privileges must be kept within reasonable bounds and not be allowed to create an impassable barrier between officials and ordinary workers.[16] Privilege must under no circumstance be secret and should exist only in order to make it easier for officials to carry out their obligations to society.

XI

Socialist Democracy and Socialist Economics

A very common prejudice shared by many officials in the government *apparat* and also certain social scientists is that basic economic problems should be solved before attention is paid to the question of democratization. A member of the Central Committee told Academician Sakharov: "Given the present state of the economy and the workers' inadequate standard of living, it is too soon to put through various measures to democratize society."

This very mistaken view is closely bound up with another misconception: that democracy is mainly relevant for the intelligentsia, or, to be more exact, those concerned with literature, the arts, and science. As for the workers and peasants, they are suffering not so much from a lack of democracy as from a lack of consumer goods, low pay, not enough meat and milk, and a shortage of housing. Party and state officials, therefore, should be concerned primarily with raising the productivity of labor and increasing the production of consumer goods and agricultural products. Democratic freedoms can be taken care of at a later date when Soviet society is better off and better educated.

There is, of course, a very small grain of truth in this line of argument. Many of the restrictions on democracy do have a particularly damaging effect on the work of the intelligentsia, and therefore the loudest protest comes from that quarter. But since a writer is not working for himself alone or for his friends, unjustified restraints on his freedom mean deprivation not just for a small section of the intelligentsia but for society as a whole. On one occasion Andrei Zhdanov* said that the party considered the publication of a good book to be just as important an event as the opening of a new factory. Although it is generally thought that Zhdanov himself did little to assist the development of Soviet culture, he was quite correct in his comparison and, taking it to its logical conclusion, it is also true to say that the suppression of a good book, play, or film is just as harmful as the wanton closing of a factory or railway.

Real political and cultural democracy would also encourage the development of economics as a science and thus would have a very beneficial effect on the Soviet economy. Many of the serious errors that occurred in economic policy were not only the result of practical miscalculation but also a reflection of obsolete dogma, some of which is influential to this day. Current Soviet economic journals may give the impression that there is now free discussion and frank exposure of problems and shortcomings. But this is far from the case. The situation in economics may be better than in philosophy or history, but the prospect of genuinely open inquiry is still remote. A great many interesting and important articles remain unpublished because of censorship, while numerous books appear only after extensive cuts have been made. Many writers find it easiest to stay silent. Much statistical data remains secret, inaccessible even to experts. And there is a lack of statistical information or analysis of certain crucial economic problems. Only recently *Glavlit* circulated a revised and considerably *enlarged* list detailing all the information not to be made public. Very likely much of it is economic material. It is also forbidden to write about the harmful effect of industry on the environment, if the facts refer to the USSR.

Obviously, democracy by itself cannot eliminate basic economic problems, which require political, economic, and

---

* Andrei Zhdanov (1896–1948), close aide of Stalin in charge of ideology and cultural matters; proclaimed the doctrine of socialist realism in 1934 and directed the postwar purge of the Soviet literary world.—Trans.

technical solutions combined. If farms do not receive needed machinery or fertilizer, if what they do get is of poor quality, if state procurement procedures are not improved, and if prices for agricultural products in many regions remain below cost, then making state and collective farms more democratic would do little to raise agricultural production figures. Nevertheless there can be no doubt that greater adherence to the principles of socialist democracy throughout Soviet society would make it easier to arrive at an intelligent response to the many economic, political, and scientific problems that face us. Only a democratic approach can ensure that crucial issues are properly examined and debated. Only democracy can become an effective safeguard against what we have come to call "subjectivism" and "voluntarism," the dangerous by-products of an undemocratic system which may have receded to some extent but are still far from extinct. "Democracy, by itself, can never lead to socialism," wrote Lenin, "but democracy must be seen in a context: it will affect the economy and help to transform it and will in turn be influenced by economic development. This is the dialectic of living history."[1] Lenin also wrote that "democracy is a purely political category." But he added that "any form of democracy, as political superstructure in general . . . in the final analysis serves production and is defined by the relations of production within the given society."[2]

The development of political and social democracy would create a heightened political consciousness among workers and thus encourage them to contribute more energetically to the economic life of the country. More than a century ago, in 1859, Nikolai Chernyshevsky* wrote about the connection between the political and economic aspects of a person's creative energies. "How can you expect a man to be vigorous at work when he has been conditioned to be passive in the face of oppression, even in defense of his own person? Habitual behavior cannot be channeled within limited spheres of activity: it influences every aspect of life. A man cannot be trained to be energetic when working in the fields, yet to stand silent in front of his master's steward."

But it is by no means only a question of the relationship

---

* N. G. Chernyshevsky (1828–89), publicist, literary critic, and economist, extremely influential among the radical intelligentsia in the 1850's and early 1860's; sent to Siberia in 1864.—Trans.

between political and economic man. What is needed today is the introduction of socialist democracy in all its forms into industrial production itself, particularly in basic decision making at all levels of administration. Without consistent democratization within the actual economic machinery, it will be impossible to overcome those most serious vices of the Soviet economy, negligence and irresponsibility, which result primarily from the absence of a *sense of ownership* on the part not only of many working people but also of management in industry and agriculture. At the December 1969 Plenum of the Central Committee, it was made abundantly clear that the lack of personal involvement was now a major cause of Soviet economic backwardness.

Political and economic problems under socialism have merged to such an extent that it is impossible to deal with either in isolation.[3] Some of these interconnections will be examined briefly below.

In an article called "On Authority," Engels wrote that even after the victory of the socialist revolution it would be necessary to retain the principle of subordination in industry:

Take, for instance, cotton weaving—before it can be used as thread, cotton has to undergo at least six successive processes, and each usually takes place in a different room. To keep operations running smoothly, an engineer is needed to take charge of the steam engine and mechanics are required to look after day-to-day repairs of the machinery; many other workers are needed as well, and . . . all of them . . . are obliged to start and finish work at times determined by the rhythm of the steam engine, which can make no allowance for personal independence. The workers must therefore arrive at an agreement concerning working hours, but once these have been established they must be compulsory for all without exception. Furthermore, in each room particular problems constantly arise related to the production process, the distribution of materials, etc., all of which must be dealt with immediately in order to prevent a rapid shutdown of the production line. Whatever the solution to these problems may be . . . it is bound to be authoritarian. The machinery of a factory is far more despotic than any petty capitalist employer. To abolish authority in a large factory is tantamount to closing it down, or doing away with steam in order to return to hand looms.

Engels also mentioned railways and ships as further examples where an authoritarian structure was essential, and concluded:

Thus we see that a certain degree of authority, whatever its origin, and subordination, regardless of the social structure, are inevitable in the presence of material conditions that give rise to industrial production and distribution. Yet with the development of large-scale industry and agriculture, the material conditions of production and distribution are bound to become even more complex, along with the tendency for authority to extend its powers.[4]

Of course Engels was completely right in his attack on the "anti-authoritarians." Modern industry cannot operate without firm management, whether the person in charge is a capitalist, civil servant, or director elected by the workers. There is hardly a role for democracy or autonomy, discussion or change when the factory is already constructed with conveyor belts in motion and delivery dates agreed upon. When grain is ripe or when trains or planes are scheduled to leave, work must follow a rigid timetable; the plan must be fulfilled, the train can travel in only one direction, and the aircraft must fly on course. Lenin wrote that "neither railways, other transport, large machines or enterprises can function correctly unless there is a unity of will binding individual workers into an economic body that operates like clockwork."[5] The actions of a worker in a well-organized factory are not determined by his own free choice but by the strict logic of the production process and must be planned many days in advance. Appropriate conduct for unexpected or emergency situations also has to be worked out beforehand. Similarly, once the plans have been confirmed and work has begun on a new factory or apartment building, there is little scope left for democratic discussion, and the better the construction site is organized and supplied with building materials and tools, the more disciplined the administration of that site should be.

It would be wrong, however, to see only this "authoritarian" side of modern industrial production. Wherever questions of change or innovation arise, and this now happens constantly, a democratic approach can help to solve most problems—whether or not to set up a new enterprise, produce a new product, or modify an old model. We must make a persistent effort to introduce genuine industrial democracy,

we must involve workers and office staff in the solution of
new problems and encourage them to state their views
frankly, for otherwise the alternative is total dependence on
one particular official, and no matter how competent he may
be, he is bound to make mistakes. As the economy and its
administration become more centralized, the administrative-
bureaucratic approach to basic economic decision making,
with inevitable lapses into "subjectivism" and "harebrained
schemes," will mean mounting losses as time goes on. I have
seen a report prepared at one of our institutes of economics
which contained an extremely detailed analysis of changes
that have taken place in the production process. It described
the emergence of new professions requiring intellectual ability rather than physical effort and the need to replace mecha-
nistic stereotypes by a creative approach that would enable
people to take the initiative in finding new solutions.

During the first decades of Soviet rule, economic policy
was implemented by means of a basically authoritarian and
arbitrary system. At first this had certain advantages, but the
subsequent preponderance of bureaucratic and arbitrary
methods led to serious errors which substantially retarded the
growth of the whole economy.

It would, of course, be wrong to blame the development
of a bureaucratic administrative system on the personal shortcomings of Stalin and Khrushchev alone. There were also
many objective causes. Industry in tsarist Russia was relatively weak and was disrupted and almost completely destroyed during the years of World War I and the Civil War. No
wonder, then, that much time was needed to restore industrial and agricultural production to prerevolutionary levels. In
a situation of capitalist encirclement, it was crucial for the
world's first socialist state to give priority to the development
of heavy industry, machine tools, and defense. It was also
imperative to set up new industrial centers in the eastern
areas of the country. The limited availability of internal resources and capital and the urgency of the situation created
the need for highly centralized economic management based
on a command system—directives from the center were inevitably more effective, and the state budget became the basic
source of finance. During that period circumstances justified
an administrative-command structure. It is now easy to criti-

cize aspects of the first stages of industrialization, which could probably have been different under more capable leadership. Soviet industry was often given unrealistic tasks, and too many large industrial plants were put under construction simultaneously. In a situation of scarcity meager resources were squandered, not to mention all the repressive measures taken against senior economic and technical experts, engineers, scientists, factory administrators, and building, railway, and farm personnel. As a result, the tremendous efforts and enormous sacrifices of the entire population produced far less than could have been expected.

In those days economic levers and democratic methods were almost never applied. Independent accounting (*khozraschet*)* was reduced to a minimum and profits were an almost insignificant factor since resources were distributed to branches of industry and enterprises by administrative decision. The law of value virtually ceased to be a regulator—emphasis was placed on gross output to the virtual exclusion of all other economic indicators. Products of heavy industry came to be priced at levels bearing no relation to real conditions, and by the beginning of the 1930's most enterprises in this branch of the economy had gone over to the planned-loss system and were subsidized by the state. At the same time state purchase prices for agricultural produce did not reflect production costs. Thus in order to balance government income and expenditure, it was necessary to raise the prices of certain consumer goods steeply, and the tax often was several times as great as the initial cost of production. This meant that there was little in the way of material incentives for urban workers, while collective farmers were obliged to labor almost without pay.

All this was the more or less inevitable result of the methods used to industrialize the country; they were originally thought to be a temporary retreat from socialist man-

---

* From *khoziastvenny raschet,* literally "economic calculation" but usually translated as "independent accounting" or "self-financing" —refers to the system under which an industrial enterprise finances itself without the aid of central state funds, involving a calculation of costs per unit of output—i.e., covering expenses with receipts.—Trans.

agement practice which had begun to evolve during the NEP. But unfortunately many government leaders began to view the temporary administrative-directive approach to planning and management as the only way to run a socialist economy. Even in theory the law of value was no longer considered to be relevant under socialism, since the idea of a market was held to be incompatible with planning. At this point socialist political economy ceased to develop as a science and was replaced by a system of dogmas that often contradicted each other. Applied economics also received little attention and all research in management studies came to a halt. Soon there was no longer any specialized training for senior economic administrators, and even the Industrial Academy* was closed down. Apparently it was possible to learn the art of giving orders without any special instruction or training.

Just before the war economic levers were partially applied in certain branches of the economy, but only as an experiment. However, the war demanded a return to the stringent command approach. Only the strictest centralization made it possible to mobilize resources and rapidly place the whole economy on a war footing. And in the immediate postwar years, the need to restore the nation's devastated western regions meant the continuation of very centralized planning and administration.

By 1948, however, the existing bureaucratic system had become an extremely inappropriate way to run the economy and was already noticeably holding it back. The country's economic structure had become far too complex to be administered from one center. New branches of industry were appearing one after the other, and hundreds and thousands of new factories were being constructed. A growing number of problems needed immediate solution, yet it was always necessary to wait for orders from Moscow. As the economy grew more complex, so inevitably did the system of administration. There was a proliferation of new ministries and departments of Gosplan, with large increases in the staffs of all central institutions. As before, however, jurisdiction was vertical, and at the local level it was possible to make only minor adjustments through the regional party committee. The drawbacks of this centralized command system are now

* *Promakademia.*—Trans.

very familiar: the endless demarcations between areas of competence prevented an integrated use of regional resources; the leadership, so far removed from the enterprises themselves, so remote from reality, was bound to be inadequate and insufficiently flexible. Feedback, as we would say today, from the enterprises to decision-making agencies became almost nonexistent. At the same time enterprises were unable to solve many often very simple problems on their own, constricted as they were by tens of thousands of usually obsolete directives and instructions. Because it seemed convenient or out of sheer incompetence, those in charge at the center ignored the most elementary economic considerations when allocating resources. Irrational crosshauls were common, the obvious cooperation that should have existed between neighboring enterprises was not encouraged, and so on ad infinitum. The result was an enormous loss of potential within the economy. At the same time agriculture went from stagnation to a state bordering on catastrophe.

After 1953 certain important measures were taken to deal with the agricultural problem, and conditions were ripe for an increase in the general tempo of economic development. It became increasingly obvious to members of the government as well as to professional economists that the economic system was outmoded and inefficient. Problems were piling up faster than they could be solved and were then either shelved or dealt with in such haste that mistakes and confusion inevitably prevailed.

At the beginning of 1957, Khrushchev, with his highly intuitive approach, came to the conclusion that certain changes were vitally needed in industry. However, discussion of potential reform remained totally abstract at the February Plenum of the Central Committee. Many were of the opinion that although a certain amount of decentralization was necessary, management and planning would still have to be organized along authoritarian lines. It simply amounted to whether decision making should take place in Moscow or in some new local economic administrative bodies. Obviously any new system of industrial management should have been thoroughly tested out in experimental form before being implemented at large, but this did not happen. However keen his intuition, Khrushchev did not possess any real knowledge of economics, nor was he patient enough to study a particular problem in detail or to take account of expert opinion. He was, in short, a perfect example of a "voluntarist." This sometimes brought him success in politics, but could not possibly work in economics. Only a month after the February Plenum, a new plenary session met and adopted a very detailed but ill-considered and badly prepared plan to reorganize the entire administration of the country's economy. The old system was to disappear at once and be replaced by a new one, although from the start many were skeptical about its presumed but unproven advantages. By June 1957, the setting up of regional economic councils (*Sovnarkhoz*) was basically complete. Decisions of immense importance were rushed through in a matter of days or even hours. After only very brief behind-the-scenes discussion during a session of the Supreme Soviet, various ministries (including those for oil and for defense industry) were abolished. There had been a proposal to set up certain interregional councils in view of the limited economic potential of certain regions and autonomous republics, but in practice only one council was established in each region. The entire process of reorganization was carried out in an extremely dictatorial way with complete disregard for democratic principles.

Of course decentralization made it easier to deal with certain local problems and to exploit local resources. There was much greater cooperation between enterprises in the same and in neighboring regions. Many problems at the enterprise level could be solved more quickly because of the proximity of those in charge. But the councils did not bring about radical improvement in the administration of industry, and within two or three years it became evident that the whole system was extremely inefficient. "Weak" councils— those in regions and republics with underdeveloped economies—became a problem. Difficulties arose around secondary branches of industry for which the councils had no special subdepartment. In practice many council departments were running five or six and sometimes up to ten different branches of industry at the same time, which meant that in most cases there could be no question of competent supervision. Industry was in chaos throughout the country. One council unnecessarily duplicated the work of another ("parallelism") or dealt with similar problems in a different way, which made it enormously difficult to standardize equipment and products. Parochial tendencies inevitably began to arise and many local decisions were clearly not in the interest of the country as a whole. Yet at the same time rigid lines dividing spheres of competence did not disappear—they actually multiplied because of the different departments within each council; this often disrupted cooperation between enterprises where there had previously been a close working relationship. Throughout this vast, unwieldy economic structure, communication was breaking down and conflict increasing—between enterprises and between regions and republics. Research and development went on in isolation, so that there was a great deal of unnecessarily duplicated effort in different institutions. No responsible center existed to ensure a unified nationwide policy for technological advance.

Many of the nation's leaders, including Khrushchev, were very soon aware of the new system's imperfections. However, since they were unwilling to abandon the economic councils and admit their mistake, they adopted a policy of piecemeal improvement. Unfortunately each new attempt in this direction was given as little thought and preparation as the original measures. For instance, in 1959 economic councils were set up for the RSFSR and for the Ukraine, but the powers and functions of these immense republican bodies were not clearly defined. According to one of the officials of the RSFSR Council, their motto was: "Give orders but don't answer for them." At times it was difficult for regional councils to distinguish between the activities of Gosplan and the republican council, as they had similar structures and dealt with more or less identical problems. Then, with no warning, the regional councils were amalgamated. A single council was now made responsible for the economy of several regions. For example, the Novosibirsk council took over the administration of industry in Omsk, Tomsk, Kemerovo, and several other regions. A new Economic Council *for the USSR* was created to coordinate the work of interregional and republican councils. But because it was empowered to deal only with industry but not with communications, transport, construction, services, or agriculture, it was decided to create yet another body—the Supreme Economic Council of the USSR!

The different council departments at various levels could scarcely cope with their basic supervisory tasks and had little time left to implement technological development in particular branches of industry. Research and development institutes were neglected. Then came the idea of creating special state committees in each branch of industry, and this was speedily put into effect. At first, these high-powered bodies were given very limited scope—they were only to make recommendations to enterprises and councils. But their role was soon extended: all research and development organizations were made subordinate to them and all plans for industrial production and capital construction had to be submitted for their approval. Furthermore, the new state committees had the power to designate priority lists of industrial products within the framework of plans, to replace outdated products with new types, and to determine an enterprise's area of specialization. They had by now taken over practically 60–70 per cent of the work of the former ministries; thus centralized administration had almost been restored but in rather worse form—with even more officials and more bureaucracy. As a result it was becoming extremely difficult to cope with a growing number of administrative problems. Decisions that once took two or three days were held up for months, and Moscow became crowded with regional functionaries. But since those in charge were hamstrung by the whole enormously intricate bureaucratic network, they in fact had even less control than before over the development of industry and agriculture, and as a result there was a substantial decline in the level of many economic indicators at the beginning of the sixties. The recommendations of professional economists had no influence on policy, although their discipline had made considerable progress during those years.

Serious disproportions in economic development came to light. As the economy became more complex, certain once-tolerable deficiencies now became completely unacceptable. As a direct result of a steady and unanticipated fall in the output/capital ratio, the country lost ten billion rubles' worth of production. Between 1948 and 1964, the effectiveness of productive investments in all branches of industry except electroenergy and metalworking fell two to three times, which had never happened since the establishment of Soviet rule. Although at the end of the Seven-Year Plan the list of goods in short supply was very large and continuing to grow, factories flooded the market with huge quantities of unsalable goods. The retail network had in stock a year's supply of all types of unsold fabrics, knitwear, clothing, and sewing machines, and six months' worth of toys. Many enterprises had warehouses packed with items rejected by the retail system. (There were also enormous inventories in wholesale warehouses.) In 1964, the value of unsold consumer goods (excluding food) piled up in retail warehouses alone was approaching 20 billion rubles, more than in the United States during recession years. Yet there was an increase in the amount of money in circulation, although real earnings were rising very slowly and among some sections of the population were even on the decline.

There is no doubt that the basic causes of such serious imbalances in the economy were poor management and inefficient planning and administration, combined with the absence of incentives. A vicious circle had been created: authoritarian and bureaucratic methods were perpetuated by the very nature of the system.[6]

Inefficiency also showed itself in a growth of unemployment. People were often unable to find jobs in the area where they lived. In certain cities of the old industrial regions, sometimes 20–30 per cent of the able-bodied population were unable to find work (this was partly the result of restrictions on the freedom of movement). This meant that a number of large enterprises in these regions were obliged to delay reorganization, technological improvement, and automation if these entailed reductions in the work force. Thus technical progress, productivity, and wages were all held back. These mounting problems gave rise to demands for a reconsideration of basic principles and methods with the aim of creating a more rational economic system.

It was only after the removal of Khrushchev that decisive changes became possible. Let us briefly look at the results of the economic reforms initiated at the September 1965 Plenum of the Central Committee. It was decided to abolish the economic councils and to re-establish industrial management via branches of industry. But this was not simply a return to the former system, because restoration of industrial ministries was accompanied by changes in planning and the provision of incentives, which in fact meant genuine economic reform. It was undoubtedly the most important revision of Soviet economic policy since the beginning of NEP.

In the first place, there was to be considerably more independence for enterprises. With this in mind, it was proposed to reduce the number of centrally set plan indicators. The index of total global output, which had been the main source for judging an enterprise in the past, would be abolished. In his report to the Plenum, Kosygin pointed out the inadequacies of the notorious "global-output" system. Not only did it fail to ensure the production of goods that were genuinely needed by the economy, in many cases it also prevented improvements in range and quality. Since enterprises were geared toward fulfilling the plan in terms of total global output, they often turned out low-quality products that were rejected by consumers and therefore remained unsold. Instead of the index of global output, he proposed several priority success indicators: sales, profits, and profitability, with a modest number of centrally set plan indicators for certain important articles. The wage fund alone was to replace four previous labor indicators (productivity, number of employees, average earnings, and wage fund). Most of the former indicators were retained in the economic plans of individual enterprises but no longer had to be confirmed from above and were not part of the compulsory plan for the relevant branch of industry. Still to be determined at the center were payments into and appropriations from the national budget, the extent of centrally planned capital investment, the commissioning of new productive capacity and fixed assets, targets for the introduction of new technology, and the allocation of materials and technical equipment.

One of the problems discussed in 1965 was how to increase the role of long-term planning. Up to then, it was the annual plan that dominated the activities of an enterprise and since it was never confirmed until the end of the preceding year, there was no way of knowing what the plan for the next year would be. In some enterprises even the current plan was revised two or three times in the course of a year. The starting point for a plan was invariably the "level attained" during the previous year and then a certain percentage was added to produce the new target. This system provided no incentive for optimal use of internal resources, since more often than not enterprises working below capacity came off best. It was now decided that individual enterprises should use a five-year plan as their basic planning format, with the most important targets indicated yearly. The plan was to be based on objective, scientifically determined standards and guidelines.

Enterprises would also have the right to dispose of a greater proportion of their profits—to provide material incentives, improve working conditions and living standards, and upgrade production technology. It was hoped that this would stimulate more efficient production, since the amount left to the enterprises would depend directly on how successfully they used their allotted resources to improve product quality and increase sales and profitability. At the same time there was to be more reliance on long-term bank credits instead of nonreturnable government grants. In order to make enterprises behave more responsibly toward each other, it was proposed that fulfillment of all mutual obligations be strictly enforced by financial sanctions. The September Plenum also significantly revised the whole policy of capital investment. Under the previous system, investments were allocated almost exclusively according to the central plan, with a considerable proportion spent on new construction. Many enterprises already in operation lacked adequate means to replace outmoded equipment. It would now be possible to do so from special funds set aside out of profits. Part of the amortization payments earmarked for the full replacement of fixed assets would also be contributed to the production-development fund. Until 1965 that part of the amortization payments was allocated on a centralized basis for financing capital construction, and enterprises could not dispose of these funds themselves. It was estimated that by 1967 the production-development fund would amount to some four billion rubles —a sevenfold increase over three years.

One of the most important reforms was the introduction of a charge for capital provided by the state. Before 1965, funds for capital investment simply came out of the budget, gratis. The managers of enterprises had little reason to care, for example, how much the reconstruction of an enterprise cost or what the effect of additional capital investment would be. There was almost no attempt to make the most efficient use of available funds or to build up surpluses, since enterprises could not really be called to account for the way in which such allocations were used. It was hoped to change all this by adopting a system of financing capital construction by long-term bank credits. The budget would no longer replenish the working capital of an enterprise free of charge—instead there would be short-term credit facilities. Deductions from the profits of an enterprise into the budget would henceforth be dependent on the value of the fixed and circulating assets assigned it, i.e., the deductions were presented in the form of payments for productive assets. These payments would be established for a long period at a level that would allow a normally functioning enterprise to be left with sufficient profit to set up incentive funds and cover planned expenses. It was expected that the new capital charges would eventually become the most important part of state revenue, and correspondingly the role of other payments, such as turnover taxes, would be reduced.

The reforms envisaged a considerable increase of material incentives for both the enterprise as a whole and for individual workers, as performance improved. Before the reforms, most bonuses came out of wage funds and not out of profits. Amounts were insignificant and made up a very small percentage of wages, and there were many enterprises with no bonus system whatsoever. Thus any increase of profits and profitability had practically no direct effect on the wages of employees within that enterprise. Under the new system, an enterprise's ability to increase the remuneration of its staff would be determined by the growth of production, increased profits, greater profitability, and improved product quality. Although enterprises had no authority to increase basic rates of pay, they could add part of the profits to the wage fund. It was further decided that such deductions from profits should take place over a number of years and according to standard norms, which meant that the size of incentive funds would be directly dependent on sales, profit, and profitability.

By giving all employees an immediate interest in the efficiency of the enterprise as a whole, they would be made to feel more responsible for every aspect of its work. But this created the objective conditions for the growth of democracy in our enterprises and also made it even more essential. In the resolutions of the September Plenum it was stressed that the economic reforms "provide the economic prerequisites for wider participation by the masses in the running of production." Kosygin's speech at the time also emphasized the importance of the development of economic democracy: "Better management is impossible unless it becomes more democratic and unless the participation of the masses is considerably extended. Employees within the factory should have a greater role in the solution of planning problems, the mobilization of internal resources, the evaluation of results, and the provision of incentives. Every worker should be made to feel that he is one of the owners of the factory."

These, then, are the main outlines of the proposed reforms. The planned economy itself was of course never called into question—the intention was rather, by means of a shift to economic levers and a more democratic approach, to improve planning and create a more flexible, self-regulating mechanism.[7] This did not, of course, mean the complete abolition of "administrative methods," but their scope was sharply reduced and, most important of all, they were now to be strictly in accordance with economic criteria, i.e., scientifically determined. The reforms were aimed at maximizing "intensive" development: more efficient management, technological progress, and improved labor utilization and productivity.

It was pointed out at the September Plenum that the reforms would have to be implemented gradually in view of the amount of change envisaged in management and administration. Hundreds and thousands of officials would have to be taught a new approach, and a great many established ways of doing things would have to be revised. For example, in many branches of industry, wholesale price formation as it evolved over the years was not based on economic criteria. It would be necessary to review and no doubt correct or abolish many standard directives. None of this could be done very rapidly. And even once the reforms were in progress, problems would inevitably arise requiring discussion and study. It was the very principle of gradual change that distinguished these reforms from all the impulsive maneuvers of the preceding decade. Only a few hundred industrial enterprises were to go over to the new system beginning in January 1966.

Their number would be gradually increased and come to include almost the whole of Soviet industry by the end of the five-year plan. The new economic principles would then be applied step by step in building, transport, and the service sector. It was said at the Plenum that the implementation of these reforms would lead to further ones which would extend and develop the basic principles laid down in 1965.

At present, the first and most difficult stage is over. The reform of planning and incentives has been introduced in nearly all industrial enterprises. Whole branches of industry have been working under the new system for several years. It is therefore possible to make a preliminary assessment.

Certainly a great deal has been achieved. Planning procedures have been changed both at the center and at the enterprise level. Material incentives have been substantially increased and there has been more investment to develop production. A great deal has been done to establish wholesale prices that reflect basic economic realities. As a result the number of enterprises working on planned loss has been sharply reduced, and there are none at all in several branches of industry. The new prices better reflect the capital intensity of goods, and enterprises therefore have a greater interest in technological progress. The profits of most enterprises (as well as the percentage they are allowed to retain) have increased, with a consequent growth of self-sufficiency. At the same time, quality has definitely been improved by the fact that credit and the market are playing a greater role. Labor productivity has risen appreciably, and in many enterprises other important economic indicators have also shown change for the better.

One cannot fail to notice, however, that the economic reforms have come up against various obstacles—objective and subjective—many of which still remain to be overcome. Even certain basic principles have not been fully implemented. What is more, among a section of state and party officials, economic administrators and economists, there appears to be a regressive tendency to revise certain basic aspects of the reforms with the aim of gradually abolishing them altogether. This approach has already done serious damage and has retarded the pace of economic development. The various obstacles encountered in attempts to apply the reforms in practice can be divided into three categories: economic, organizational, and political.

It became apparent, for example, that it was necessary to extend the new incentive arrangements not only to enterprises or production associations* but also to ministries and similar bodies. As long as ministries bore no direct financial responsibility for the consequences of their various decisions and directives, there would always be a large element of bureaucratic and administrative inefficiency, with inevitable ill effects on individual enterprises. In the past, neither supply organizations nor the railway system were answerable for their dealings with enterprises, which meant that the latter were frequently held responsible for losses that were not their fault, with no possibility of recovering them from the guilty parties. This problem is now being dealt with, although far too slowly. It is a question of making all administrative and supply organs operate on the basis of independent accounting (i.e., covering expenses with receipts). Ministries would henceforth bear direct financial responsibility for the results of their directives and this would give ministry officials and economic administrators a real incentive to encourage efficiency in the enterprises under their control.

During the last five years the familiar pattern has continued of enterprises being told to make frequent changes in both the volume and assortment of their planned output. In many instances, enterprises were prevented from setting up production-development or incentive funds and were forced to contribute a much larger share of their profits to the state budget than the original guidelines allowed for. Enterprise independence was often restricted even when it came to dealing with internal problems. Long-term planning over five or ten years within individual enterprises has progressed very slowly, which has meant instability and an absence of clear perspectives in the functioning of enterprises as well as of whole branches of industry. Evidently the state has run into completely unforeseen expenditure as a result of various complications abroad (the Middle East, Czechoslovakia, and the Far East). All this has combined to reduce the maneuverability of resources within the economy and has led to greater

---

* *Obedinenia:* enterprises, producing related products, that have been amalgamated into vertical trusts or horizontal combines.—Trans.

deductions from the profits of enterprises than were originally anticipated.

Economic reform has only recently begun in the building
industry, still one of the most backward branches of the
economy. There is an enormous amount of uncompleted
capital construction, and as a rule plans for most construction
sites are never met. It takes anywhere from seven to fifteen
years to build many large industrial enterprises while similar
operations in capitalist countries are completed two to five
times faster. It is hardly surprising that certain enterprises
have become obsolete even before they begin production. Factories and plants have still not been given stable guidelines
regulating the creation of incentive funds. For many enterprises plans are still based on the "previously achieved level,"
even though officially these enterprises have gone over to the
new system of economic stimuli. Naturally in such cases
there is little interest in the judicious use of internal resources.

Because they have little confidence in the efficiency of
the supply system, many enterprises still hold excessive reserves of materials and commodities, including those in short
supply. Various experiments (including the Shchekino
scheme*) have shown that improvements in production and
labor productivity are often linked with the need to reduce the
work force at an enterprise and pay correspondingly higher
wages to those who remain. But in many regions of the
country where there was a labor surplus, attempts to implement the Shchekino scheme met with great opposition. And
even in towns with an acute labor shortage, many enterprises
keep on superfluous workers in order to obtain as high a wage
fund as possible. This stems from the fact that even now
enterprises are not allowed to change basic wage and salary
rates. Clearly independence and initiative at the enterprise
level are still, if not directly, then indirectly, curtailed by
"petty tutelage" and totally unwarranted regulation from
above. Many economists have urged that further work be done
to improve the wholesale price system. A large number of
price-setting functions could be passed on to enterprises them-

* The "Shchekino scheme" was an experiment first carried out at the
  Shchekino Chemical Combine in 1969: bonus funds are increased
  for workers out of funds saved by laying off excess labor.—Trans.

selves, with the retention of central control to the extent that it is necessary.

It has also been suggested (and certain measures are now being taken in this direction) that wholesale trade should be expanded to include the means of production. A gradual changeover is envisaged from the system of centralized allocation of producer goods to their sale through a wholesale market network. If trading partners can make agreements on the spot without reference to higher bodies, this should substantially increase the maneuverability of resources. It would also encourage enterprises to stop hoarding superfluous reserve supplies, which today account for many billions of frozen rubles. A system must be devised to make an enterprise concerned not only with its own efficiency but also with that of the enterprises consuming its products.

Some economists and planners see our nationalized socialist industry in its *ideal* form as some enormous but precisely structured mechanism in which all the component parts and units are rigidly adjusted to each other and which in principle can be regulated from a single center. And so they concentrate their efforts on optimizing *centralization* and removing chance factors. If such an objective were attainable, the result would be a vast economic machine by means of which several hundred or several thousand people armed with computers could regulate and control the entire production process. Is there any room for democracy in such an autocratic administrative system?

But the economic life of a socialist country is rather more complex than the above model. An effort should certainly be made to gain the maximum benefit from centralized planning and to reduce the effect of accidental and unforeseen factors, but this can hardly be the only economic objective. The problem is not just that for the time being our vast economic machine is not adequately integrated or adjusted. It can never *in principle* be a completely integrated whole, precisely regulated down to the very last detail. In real economic conditions it is impossible to predict in advance the different problems that are bound to arise. Consumer tastes and fashions change, local and national conditions change, unplanned inventions and discoveries are made, and accidents, conflicts, and unforeseen natural disasters occur. The international political and economic situations are in a constant state of flux. Furthermore, the dimensions and complexity of modern economies are such that they defy total control even by all-powerful central institutions equipped with the most advanced computer technology in existence.

Therefore even in a very highly centralized economy, apart from rigid channels that permit only predetermined, virtually automatic reactions, there should certainly also be a more flexible structure to leave administrators room to maneuver and freedom to display initiative and independence. Some degree of freedom of choice should remain, as well as the genuine possibility of healthy competition. While it must avoid excessive stock-piling of reserves, a socialist economy should have sufficient supplies of all kinds at its disposal. Lower levels of the hierarchy as well as the central administrative bodies should bear considerable decision-making authority. In other words, the problem is how to combine centralized management and decentralization in the best possible way.

Lenin once said, "Our first concern is to centralize." On another occasion he wrote: "Communism demands and presupposes the maximum centralization of heavy industry throughout the country. Therefore the center must unquestionably be given the right to make all the enterprises of a given branch of industry directly subordinate to itself."[8] These principles still hold good. It is precisely centralization of the economy on a nationwide scale (or of several nations combined) that permits us to realize in practice the many advantages of socialism based on public ownership of the means of production. However, at present our second major preoccupation is how to combine centralization with rational decentralization of economic management.

If centralized management entails a more rational overall use of the nation's resources, decentralization leads to more efficient exploitation at the local level. The present Soviet economic machine is enormous, hundreds of times larger than in the early 1920's, and a vast amount of planning is required to make it function properly. The extraordinary size of the state plan means that usually only one variant is ever prepared, and economists are by no means satisfied that the best decision is taken in every instance. But

with intelligent decentralization, with the creation of relatively autonomous economic substructures, it becomes possible to develop several variations of the plan with the aid of
computers and then to choose optimum solutions.

One economist has summed up the drawbacks of the
highly centralized Soviet economy as follows: "Socialism is a
single-track, almost closed system—there are no efficient
automatic correctives to bring us back to minimum cost,
which is a great advantage of the capitalist system." Such a
general indictment of socialism is completely unfair. A properly constructed socialist economy must certainly include
corrective mechanisms that function more economically and
efficiently than under capitalism. But this presupposes, apart
from anything else, a relatively decentralized economy. In his
extremely interesting and informative article "Problems of
the Marxist Theory of Organization," P. Yakovlev writes:

It has been argued, of course, that the introduction of computer
technology means an almost infinite increase in man's capacity to
assimilate information, but paradoxically this does not affect the
desirability of decentralization, which is necessary not only due to
the limited capacity of the human brain but also because of other
objective factors—particularly social and psychological ones. Excessively centralized administration eliminates the sense of personal responsibility—the result is a mood of indifference within
the *apparat* and more often than not leads people to adopt a negative attitude toward the organization for which they work. Thus
the devolution of decision-making authority means no more than
to create the conditions needed to ensure efficient management
(all other things being equal) and to give psychological encouragement to *apparat* officials in the achievement of their targets. The
absence of such a reform means that there is a constant danger
of reversal to "personal rule," and it also explains why functionaries are always operating by fits and starts, trying and ultimately
failing to exercise direct control over too wide a range of problems,
switching all the time from one to another.[9]

One of the most obvious ways to bring about a devolution
of decision-making authority is to increase responsibility and
autonomy at the enterprise level. This was indeed envisaged
in the 1965 reforms and confirmed in the new "Statute on the
Socialist Enterprise" ratified after the September Plenum. It is
quite apparent, however, that although the powers of industrial and agricultural enterprises have been appreciably ex-

tended during the last seven years, both in theory and in practice, many of them have simply not been able to make full use of their new possibilities. This is largely because most individual enterprises are of negligible size by present-day economic standards. Of course even today there is a need for enterprises with different capacities—there can be no uniform pattern. In many cases the rationalization of production has led to the splitting up of enterprises into smaller, more highly specialized and relatively independent units. Specialization is certainly a step in the right direction, but at the same time there should also be an increase in cooperation and concentration. In other words, a more determined effort must be made to encourage further consolidation, the creation of larger enterprises, trusts, specialized firms, and industrial complexes possessing a higher degree of autonomy and independence. In many cases research and development institutes should also be included within a combine. These larger industrial units would be able to take better advantage of the rights and freedoms granted to enterprises under the 1965 reforms; they should be given an even wider range of powers.

As was stated in the Central Committee's Report to the Twenty-fourth Party Congress: "The setting up of productive associations and combines based on independent accounting should proceed more rigorously; in the future they will be the mainstay of the nation's industry. When they are created, it is of vital importance that overlapping areas of competence and administrative boundaries do not impede the introduction of a more efficient form of management."

A considerable amount of concentration has been achieved in certain branches of industry, particularly in nonferrous metallurgy.[10] In most other branches of production, however, amalgamation is proceeding very slowly. It was pointed out in *Kommunist* that in the five-year period from 1966 to 1970 only some two hundred new production associations were set up and approximately as many again disbanded and reorganized for various reasons. The author of the *Kommunist* article, V. Gromov, gave the following explanation:

As a rule individual enterprises did not initiate the move toward amalgamation and in many cases even opposed it. The directors of enterprises very often wanted to retain their own independence.

This attitude was reinforced by the fact that relevant departments of the industrial ministries frequently ignored the larger new structure and, bypassing the general directorate, continued to have dealings with the original individual factories. This could not but have an adverse effect on amalgamation into production associations. There were also cases where local bodies were determined at all cost to keep particular factories as independent units, particularly if amalgamation were to mean putting them under the administrative jurisdiction of another district. This kind of motive caused many viable combines to be disbanded in 1965 and 1966. Finally the creation of production associations is held back by the fact that central planning and finance organs still set basic indicators for each enterprise individually, thus emphasizing their autonomy even though they may now be a part of a larger economic unit. In the past three or four years this has led to the setting up of combines in which enterprises have retained their economic and legal independence. . . . But in such cases instead of becoming a primary industrial unit, the combine has essentially turned into an administrative-managerial structure which to a considerable extent simply duplicates the functions of the ministerial departments.[11]

Thus instead of an extension of economic democracy we sometimes find an even more highly bureaucratized form of management.

The amalgamation of collective farms is also proceeding very slowly. This reform is needed not so much to increase production as to achieve other goals. Interfarm combines can act jointly to set up food-processing plants, construct roads, supply electricity lines, etc. There could be effective mergers of agricultural and industrial enterprises as has been demonstrated in Moldavia by the initiative of large factories that process agricultural products. Experience has shown that there are many other possibilities for cooperation between agricultural and industrial enterprises including temporary or purely financial arrangements, and so far not enough is being done in this direction.

It is time for a reappraisal of the whole problem of management at the enterprise level, in branches of industry, and in the economy at large. Management can no longer depend only on such qualities as experience, resourcefulness, intuition, or strength of character. Engineering or technical training alone is also not enough. Important decisions are often so complicated that the amount of information and experimentation involved requires the services of scientific research institutes. Over the past decades the art of management has become a very important and broad field of specialization. Clearly the director of a large or medium-sized enterprise should be required to have taken basic courses in management studies. In recent years there has been considerable development of this field in capitalist countries, where there are many academic centers devoted to the study of management problems as well as hundreds of firms that act as consultants to industry. The training and retraining of managerial personnel is carried out on a large scale, with the United States leading the world. It is not only superior technology and labor productivity that keeps the United States in first place among the world's industrialized countries, it is also skilled management throughout the whole of its industry, whether in small firms or vast corporations. Soviet enterprises and combines, it must be confessed, are not nearly so well managed as their American counterparts. The Soviet Union is substantially behind America, Japan, and other capitalist countries as regards basic management methods, automation, the development of modern means of collecting, storing, and processing information, and also in the training of personnel to run our industry. In 1970 there were all together only five departments in institutions of higher education devoted to the preparation of future administrators and planners. The State Committee of Science and Engineering has only recently established an Institute of Economic Management in Moscow. This is clearly just a beginning. Over the next ten years there should be a considerable expansion of management training facilities. Otherwise it will simply not be possible to cope with the many enormous problems confronting our socialist economy.

The extreme complexity of contemporary economic life demands a radical departure from the "administrative command" style of management that prevailed in the past; changes should take place in two basic directions. The first is to make the widest possible use of economic levers in management. Academician Rumyantsev* has written:

---

* A. M. Rumyantsev is a former editor of *Pravda* and now a vice-president of the Academy of Sciences.—Trans.

As our economic system becomes increasingly intricate, as the volume of production grows and the division of labor intensifies, the more imperative it becomes to balance administrative methods with economic levers in a truly scientific way. Today it is simply not enough to make vague pronouncements to the effect that there is a trend away from administrative forms of management toward the broadest application of economic stimuli, that in the long run the command approach will be reduced to a minimum. Management studies must give more specific answers. What exactly should be the relation between centralized management and economic autonomy that best corresponds to the level of development of productive forces today and in the foreseeable future? But even if the optimal relation is clearly defined, the Soviet economy will not move forward unless the restructuring of industrial management in practice is carried out on a scientific basis.[12]

Management can also be made more efficient through the automation of many of its functions and the application of mathematical expertise and computer technology in industry, agriculture, transport, communications, and the service sector. That computers have a role in management is now universally accepted. It is worthy of note that the first lecture delivered at the Institute of Economic Management was devoted to the automation of management processes by means of computers, economic levers, and improved communications. Of course the personal, subjective factor in management remains very large, particularly in the course of reorganization, the manufacture of new products, etc. But in normal circumstances the personal factor should be reduced with reliance on automated computer-based administration.[13] The changeover to computers very much restricts the scope of bureaucratic functioning and will lead to a reduction of the administrative *apparat*, particularly at the middle level.

There have been very important advances in recent years in the automated gathering, storage, and transmission of information at various levels of planning, administration, and decision making. Yet despite the view of many sociologists that a socialist society is better able rapidly to assimilate new accounting methods or automation, the use of computers in management has so far progressed with much geater speed in capitalist countries. It is vital that we overcome our backwardness in this area during the next decade. It is not only a question of increasing efficiency and competence at the enterprise level. The various steps taken in the direction of

partial decentralization and the creation of large, more autonomous productive associations would limit the role of central
administrative bodies. At the same time the quality of their
work should improve, with decisions based on scientific evidence and economic reality.

A nationwide socialist centralized economy does of
course have enormous advantages. It is easier to avoid industrial anarchy, to mobilize the country's resources, and to solve
crucial technological and economic problems more rapidly.
As the sole proprietor of industry throughout the country, the
Soviet state can, for example, ensure the development of the
northern and eastern regions of the country. It can undertake
necessary projects where there is no question of quick re-
turns, carry out various economic or technological experiments, and encourage innovation.

There are also drawbacks, however, which cannot be
ignored. If administration is incompetent, forms of industrial
anarchy may appear that are simply unthinkable in decentralized systems. When "harebrained schemes" or "subjectivism" occur within a single enterprise, the damage is not
very substantial. But when a whole assortment of unsuitable
projects and dubious reorganizations originate at the center
and are supported by the authority of the whole state machine, the resulting chaos can do more harm and cause
greater losses than all the disharmony and competition
endemic in the capitalist system. A centralized economy is
more open to the dangers of bureaucracy. If it is badly managed, it can lose its necessary flexibility—administration becomes unwieldy and ineffective.

Rumyantsev has written that ". . . in a socialist society
. . . the despotic nature of management typical of capitalist relations is totally impossible."[14] It hardly needs saying
that this is not so. Under both Stalin and Khrushchev, not
only in politics but also in economics, decisions were taken
and carried out in an extremely despotic manner. Inevitably
this involved error, distortion, and loss on a scale inconceivable in any more or less viable capitalist system.

Experts are unanimously of the view that management
today is becoming more and more the province of professionally trained personnel who must base their decisions on exact
and accurate information. Yet with all the reliance on cyber-

netics, it is far too soon to discount the importance of human qualities: professional knowledge and skill, moral and political judgment. Therefore it is particularly important to create an appropriate system for selecting and promoting the most able and conscientious administrators. An inept or dishonest bureaucrat in charge of a large modern institution can do far more damage today than was ever possible in the past.

A major obstacle to reform has clearly been the absence of any regular procedure for the promotion and replacement of senior party and government functionaries. The economic reforms quite obviously demand a determined changeover to new methods. Factory directors and ministry officials must adopt a different approach to their work. One article on the subject puts it this way:

The reforms call for managers of initiative and resourcefulness. Their outstanding quality should be a desire to take responsibility, an inclination to make independent and self-reliant decisions while at the same time showing concern for the effect on other people (including subordinates) and the country as a whole. Before the reforms, the ideal official was of a different type—the main thing was the ability to obey orders. It is therefore hardly surprising that many are finding it difficult to liberate themselves from old habits and it is crucial to retrain and re-educate them, and at the same time to promote new officials. Naturally those who remain technically or psychologically inflexible must be replaced.

Yet there has been virtually no shakeup of cadres during the last five years, and this seems to be the main reason why the command approach to management still prevails in the Soviet economy. Relapses into administrative methods and "subjectivism" have been all too evident in the behavior of many factory managers as well as ministers and highly placed party officials. It is therefore vital, if economic reform is to advance, that more suitable procedures be adopted to remedy this situation.[15]

Another important change that is needed is an increase in the role played by workers themselves in the management of industry. Management problems cannot be solved merely by promoting more capable, better-trained administrators. A great number of issues will never be dealt with successfully until there is real participation by the masses. Economic democracy can of course take various forms, and the different possibilities must be studied and explored.

Lenin urged that every worker be made to feel "not only that he is proprietor of his factory but also a representative of his country."[16] ". . . while preparing the masses for participation in all aspects of governmental and economic administration, while encouraging the most detailed discussion of current problems so that they may arrive at correct solutions independently, we should at the same time distinguish strictly between two kinds of democratic procedure: on the one hand, there is discussion and meetings, and on the other, the establishment of a system that holds officials strictly accountable for their actions and demands an absolutely disciplined, zealous execution of instructions and directives so that the economic machine can run like clockwork."[17]

Trade unions occupy a special place among workers' organizations. As long ago as 1919, the party program stated: "Participation by trade unions in running the economy, the way in which they involve the broad masses in this process, is one of the best means of combating the spread of bureaucracy in the economic *apparat* and exerting genuine popular control over industrial production." A resolution of the Tenth Party Congress on the role and tasks of trade unions declared: "There is a vital need in the present situation for trade unions to participate more directly in the organization of production, not only by sending delegates to economic organs but also by acting as a body. Real success on the economic front can be achieved only with the cooperation of the working masses organized within independent and active trade unions." The basic tasks of trade unions in Soviet society were seen to be as follows:

By playing an immediate role in the elaboration and implementation of a unified economic plan, the unions become the organizations that draw the broad working masses into the management of the economy. . . . Among their tasks are: 1) methodical study and summary of the work of economic organs; 2) inspection and control; 3) participation in the preparation of the economic plan, allotment of economic targets, and the setting of production programs; 4) study of labor processes from a technical point of view; 5) participation in the formation of economic organs; 6) supervision of the allocation of labor resources, specialists, equipment, and raw materials; 7) development of ways and means to combat infringements of labor discipline, absenteeism, and the use of working time for private gain; 8) the study of technical improvements suggested at meetings of delegates' committees and individual groups of workers, with the view to their immediate adoption by the economic organs . . . ; 9) without setting up organizations parallel to the central administrative network, trade union departments should have their own efficiently functioning technically trained *apparat;* 10) fulfillment of the above functions presupposes the creation of special economic departments (starting with production units at the factory committee level) whose boards will be made up of representatives of economic bodies as well as elected union delegates.[18]

It is easy to demonstrate that many of the duties envisaged at the Tenth Congress are no longer part of normal trade union activities. The situation today is of course very different from that in Stalin's time, when unions were completely taken over by the state and there were no longer even any nationwide congresses. After 1956, the rights of unions were considerably extended, and during the last decade a real effort has been made to increase their role and significance in industry. This was reflected in the statute recently passed on the rights of factory, plant, and local trade union committees.[19] At most enterprises there are, under union supervision, regular "production conferences" whose participants include workers, office staff, delegates from union shop committees, representatives of management, the party and the *Komsomol,* and also from local primary organizations of scientists, inventors, and specialists in production efficiency. The composition of these conferences is determined at general meetings of factory and office workers, and delegates retain their role for the duration of the enterprise union committee's term of office.

Yet it must be pointed out that in many enterprises even today group activity is restricted and controlled by a small coterie that usually decides all basic production and other issues in advance. Even V. Chkhikvadze, in his book *The State, Democracy, and Legality,* has to admit that "workers' participation in management remains ineffective even though there are a large number of different organizations within the enterprise at their disposal."[20]

Trade unions continue to occupy a subordinate role. And they too are hamstrung by interminable bureaucratic restraints. This is apparently why they do not seem to be very concerned about such obviously relevant questions as their members' standard of living, the minimum subsistence wage, or the rising price of consumer goods. Unions make little effort to raise wages in relation to increases in the cost of living—at union meetings such matters are quickly disposed of without open discussion. Thus trade unions today are hardly functioning as schools of communism, economics, and government, although Lenin considered this to be their most important role.

I believe that we should experiment with worker self-management. Workers' councils could be set up in at least some Soviet enterprises. The principle of elected representation should be extended, with procedures devised for electing rectors of institutes of higher education, directors of scientific research institutes, and school headmasters; they could be elected, for example, by the district Soviet. Certain types of officials have, in fact, been elected—for instance, work superintendents on construction sites. These experiments should be analyzed and expanded. The party program states: "The elective principle and accountability to representative bodies and to the electorate will gradually be extended to all the leading officials of state bodies." Unfortunately today, ten years after that program was approved, the implementation of this most important paragraph has not progressed beyond a few restricted experiments, and only several isolated articles have appeared on the subject.

More participation by workers in the running of production has become an objective necessity. Today's factory and office workers are far better trained and educated than their counterparts before the scientific and technological revolution began—a crucial prerequisite for the extension of industrial democracy.

In his extremely interesting pamphlet "Working for Oneself," A. Volkov quotes the views of a Soviet economist, assuring us that they are shared by a section of the economic leadership. The argument is that even under socialism, labor still is and should continue to be a commodity that is purchased on behalf of the state by its management officials. Furthermore, at the present level of the development of production, socialist conditions do not yet exist that would justify worker self-management or their direct control over public property. Volkov totally refutes these assertions. He writes:

Obviously with the development of science and technology, production becomes more specialized with workers carrying out increasingly narrow tasks. . . . Does this mean that communication will become so difficult that people will be unable to act together to solve the basic problems of the economy? Nobody is calling for a ballot to decide how to manufacture nylon or how much fertilizer is needed per hectare of plowed land. The kind of question we have to ask is: Should we produce nylon cardigans if no one wants them? Should we waste fertilizer on a crop where climatic conditions are unfavorable? Can production be entrusted to a person who is unqualified or negligent? How can better quality be achieved? These are just a few of the problems of good management that can and should be solved by collective discussion and always, of course, on a scientific basis. . . . Some decisions, like the choice of basic crops, are virtually self-evident. In other cases specialists might be needed to suggest various possible alternatives and point out the consequences in each case. According to the logic of the views described above, scientific and technological progress are slowly but surely destroying the possibility of democracy. This is a very delicate issue but it must be faced: to deny the right of the majority of workers to participate in management means not only a rejection of *industrial* democracy but also of democracy in general, because the relations of production are the basis of social life. Civil freedom, as Marx convincingly showed, begins with the liberation of labor.[21]

For many years even capitalist enterprises have been making efforts to increase job interest. The motive, of course, is to intensify exploitation and raise productivity. Nevertheless there is also a certain amount of objective need for this "paternalism." In many capitalist countries, firms employ a profit-sharing system and devote much attention to "human relations." In this way the bourgeoisie strives to encourage a fuller integration of the workers and rouse their interest in the profitability of the enterprise. Capitalists employ various methods to stimulate the inventiveness of their employees and engage their help in rationalizing production—they even hold talent contests with large prizes for the winners. Other widespread paternalistic practices include industrial pensions, factory housing, factory rest homes and sanatoria, sports organizations, amateur theatrical circles, etc. And recently there has also been the idea of "participation in management." In a 1965 memorandum by Swedish businessmen, we read: "Greater cooperation between staff and management is a very important way of raising productivity and arousing personal interest and satisfaction among all who participate in the work of the enterprise and can actually see the result of their labors." Even de Gaulle in the summer of 1968 proclaimed the doctrine of "participation." He said that France had embarked on the creation of a new society that would be neither communist nor capitalist. A typical feature of this "new" society would be extensive participation by workers in all discussion and decisions about basic economic, social, and political questions. In some large capitalist firms, employers encourage factory newspapers in which workers are able to publish letters complaining about faults in the production line, the rudeness of foremen, etc. In another section, "Following Up Workers' Comments," management reports what has been done to sort these things out.

Capitalists are of course simply using the policy of "social partnership" to give the appearance of actual worker participation in management. However, what is merely appearance in the capitalist system must become *real* in the Soviet socialist economy. Volkov is right when he says:

Fundamental questions that vitally affect the activities of the entire collective and the maintenance of labor discipline should be decided with the full participation of all those who work in the enterprise. The manager must be a person with special ability to organize, and his major role will be one of coordination. Only technical questions will continue to be settled by "one-man decisions." Thus there will still be differences in the degree of participation in management, but they will not be substantial ones.[22]

The whole question of industrial democracy is closely bound up with the form of ownership of the means of production; ownership to a very large extent determines the kind of management that is to prevail. In the abstract, there are three basic types of ownership of the means of production: private, cooperative, and state. But of course many mixed forms also exist such as state-capitalist or state-cooperative. A large enterprise can be the property of one individual, many shareholders, or a small group of capitalists who possess a controlling number of shares. There are many kinds of cooperative ownership where the proprietors are not capitalists or share-holders but the workers themselves. Certain differences also exist among enterprises that are the property of a socialist state. In capitalist countries, there is private ownership of the means of production although cooperative and state enterprises exist as well.

Yugoslavia has rather originally attempted to structure her economy on the basis of a unique form of state-cooperative ownership. Industrial enterprises have, as it were, become the property of their workers' collectives. Yugoslav theorists point out that in this way groups of workers have direct control over the means of production and are themselves responsible for the production process.* They do not have the right to convert productive capital into consumption funds but do make decisions about capital investment and plant modernization. Wages in Yugoslavia depend on the achievements of the section, shop, and enterprise as a whole and not just the efforts of the individual employee himself. The state does not plan production or determine costs or profits. Nor does it absorb enterprise profits into the central budget. The state plan is devoted to general economic conditions—for example, the creation of a more favorable environment for those branches that need to be developed, protective tariff measures, provisions for credit, a turnover tax, etc.

Soviet critics of the Yugoslav system often quote Lenin: ". . . any direct or indirect legitimization of workers' ownership of their factory . . . or of their right to undermine or interfere with government directives constitutes a total denial of socialism."[23] It is quite clear, however, that enterprises in Yugoslavia are run on a joint state-cooperative basis (in which the state is predominant). In this respect they bear some resemblance to Soviet collective farms, which in their present structure are also a distinctive form of cooperative and state property combined. But although we usually refer to collective farms as cooperatively owned, it is nevertheless assumed that they are socialist institutions.

Any large Soviet enterprise can serve as an example of how state socialism functions. The enterprise forms a definite link within the nationwide industrial system, and its key

* I.e., they allocate the capital.—Trans.

planning and production indicators are decided by central government organs (ministries, Gosplan, etc.).

Advocates of each of these three basic forms of ownership and management quite naturally criticize the others. But although I myself am convinced that in a socialist state preference should be given to the development of state ownership, this is not to say that other types of ownership have no advantages. In order to examine the pros and cons more easily, let us look at the different alternatives in their abstract or "pure" form.

"Pure" capitalism possesses the virtues of speed and flexibility of operation. A capitalist can accomplish reorganization much more rapidly because there is no need to seek the approval of a higher authority. He can simply decide whether to change the product, the technical process, or the salary of a manager. As the owner, he has maximum opportunity to use his own initiative. Competition is an important stimulus to industrial development—it eliminates inefficient enterprises. Less resourceful owners are driven to bankruptcy, while incompetent managers are very soon replaced. The vices of a "pure" capitalist system are very well known: workers have no rights and are cruelly exploited, there is anarchy of production on a nationwide scale, as well as unemployment, cyclical crises, and business failures. As capitalism develops, these weaknesses retard its further progress. It would be wrong to ignore the fact, however, that an attempt is being made to overcome them. Modifications have occurred and are continuing, sometimes even in the face of opposition by certain groups of capitalists, which increase the viability of the capitalist system and temporarily smooth over its contradictions. One can even say that without changing its basic nature, capitalism is to some extent trying to borrow certain elements from other economic systems. Also the struggle of the working class has served to restrict arbitrary exploitation and has led to a higher standard of living. The development of technology in capitalist countries creates a demand for workers who are better educated. The number of well-paid and highly skilled workers, engineers, technicians, and scientists is increasing rapidly. With the growth of monopolies, capitalist industry is gradually becoming more centralized, which makes it possible to apply certain elements of economic planning on a nationwide scale. The regulating role of the capitalist state is also expanding—machinery is being set up to prevent crises or to reduce their disruptive effect, and we see the creation of social services: employment benefits, social security, allowances for mothers with large families, grants for needy students, etc. The paternalistic policies of some enterprises have already been referred to above. One should not underestimate the effectiveness of these developments for the temporary consolidation of capitalism as a stable and viable system.

Under Yugoslav self-management and semicooperative ownership, effective decision-making is also possible, since approval from above is not required. Workers in such enterprises apparently have a very strong sense of ownership and as a result feel much more responsible for all their activities. This tends to encourage both factory and office workers to display initiative and actively participate in discussing important problems and making suggestions. Enterprises compete in an attempt to outdo each other. Workers' control also prevents the growth of bureaucracy. It is made effective by the power of workers' councils to appoint and replace all managerial staff within the enterprise. This system does, however, have many drawbacks. Enterprise autonomy carried to the extreme leads to a lack of coordination and a certain degree of anarchy at the national level. Enterprises can make unsound decisions to raise prices, thereby causing problems for their customers and ultimately boosting the cost of living. It is possible for an enterprise to go bankrupt. If not regulated from above, reduction in the work force at individual enterprises leads to unemployment. At present, up to a million Yugoslavs are working in Western Europe, creating surplus value for European capitalists. Decisions by workers' councils are often preceded by long discussions which have an adverse effect on speed and efficiency. Nor does the fact of participation by many people guarantee a correct policy. It is more difficult to set up large industrial enterprises, combines, and trusts on a nationwide scale or to distribute labor between enterprises, etc. Economic crises can even take place as in 1967–68. Worker self-management in Yugoslavia is therefore an incomplete socialist experiment; it is still too soon to make a final judgment or to rush to imitate it in other socialist countries.

The advantages of state socialism in the abstract have

already been described above. However, at present it is much easier to see certain of the drawbacks of this system, its inflexibility and inefficiency, the strong tendency toward bureaucratic methods, particularly when participation and supervision from below are frowned upon. Inevitably in an extremely rigid, centralized system the rights of both managers and employees will be restricted. Although the workers of a socialist country in theory are the owners of all the plants and factories, and therefore are proprietors of their own enterprise, in practice the sense of ownership hardly exists among ordinary workers—instead, there is a growing feeling of alienation. Where there is state monopoly and no competition, both workers and management often become conservative and reluctant to try out new ideas. There is less stimulus for scientific and technological progress. Many enterprises are apathetic about the introduction of new technology and are unconcerned about improving product quality, rationalizing production, or increasing output. Many inventions are ignored, and often innovation is initiated only after it has been applied extensively abroad.[24]

It was precisely in order to overcome such problems in the Soviet Union and other socialist countries that various types of economic reform were introduced. They envisage greater reliance on the market as a regulator, an increase in enterprise autonomy, and a closer connection between the remuneration of employees and the enterprises' performance as a whole. Although the implementation of the reforms has come up against strong opposition from conservative elements, it is likely that the claims of economic development will ultimately be the deciding force. In any case, the decisions of the Twenty-fourth Party Congress point toward the continuance of reform.

I do believe that a centralized socialist system, modernized in accordance with the basic principles of the reforms, is the most effective way to run large-scale industrial enterprises. In capitalist countries, big companies and monopolies are subject to various kinds of state regulation, and even bourgeois economists are advocating the nationalization of basic heavy industries (as well as defense, railways, the telephone system, etc.). Many large companies were nationalized in 1945–46 in a number of Western European countries as a result of internal political pressures at the time, and most of these nationalized enterprises continue to function successfully.

Of course in socialist countries, even within very large industrial enterprises, there should also be elements of self-management. Workers could profitably discuss such topics as day-to-day conditions, incentives, promotions, certain aspects of wages, etc., but would be less concerned with matters directly related to production. After all, what could be "decided" about a large power station that had already been designed and constructed?

There is much more scope for self-management in medium-sized and small-scale industrial enterprises, in collective and state farms. Here it would be possible to draw on the Yugoslav experience, although under Soviet conditions the concrete forms would of course be very different. Some of the best collective farms have experimented successfully with self-management, and state farms could benefit from a similar approach. Workers' councils could be set up in a number of smaller enterprises, if only on a trial basis. This would be the best place to introduce the right of the collective to influence the selection of senior management personnel and to maintain a constant check on management efficiency. It could be a very important step for many reasons. There are now thousands of medium or small enterprises in the Soviet Union, whose structure and activities were ordained long ago when far fewer of them existed and production was on a very different scale. But this is a good illustration of the Marxist principle that quantitative change turns into qualitative change. Clearly the state can no longer maintain effective control over such an enormous number of smaller enterprises—hence there are many more cases of embezzlement and abuse, bad workmanship, obsolete technology, low labor productivity, etc., at this level than in large factories and plants. In these smaller enterprises, therefore, the collective should be given wider powers and responsibilities. Worker control would supplement that of the state and act as an intelligent corrective, encouraging the fullest use of internal reserves and resources.

As for the smallest enterprises, consisting of a few dozen workers or just several persons working in a single room, here it would be most appropriate to inaugurate cooperative rather than state ownership. In most cases it would be co-operative ownership in its "pure" form. This kind of enter-prise should be encouraged by the state because there are many areas of production, particularly at the juncture be-tween industry and the service sector, where small coopera-tive units could become immensely important links. There were at one time a great many urban *artels* which were transformed into state enterprises, although there was no economic rationale for it. Like the decision to abolish many small rural industries, this was very much a mistake. In the service sector and certain other branches of production *artels* would be extremely practical—at present and for some time to come. With the rapid expansion of services of all kinds and the increased output of consumer goods, including durable ones, there would be great advantages in transforming small state enterprises like the existing television repair workshops, apartment maintenance centers, watch or shoe repair fac-tories (with a wide network of outlets) into *artels* or coopera-tive organizations. There should also be encouragement for rural workshops to which larger enterprises could farm out small orders. In a June 1971 pre-election speech, Brezhnev himself said:

There are many people—pensioners, housewives, the disabled—who would be pleased to put their talents to work in the service sector, possibly on a cooperative basis. The Soviets should be en-listing the efforts of these people, drawing them into socially use-ful employment. Obviously their activity would have to take place within the framework of the law, and where appropriate legisla-tion does not exist, it must be enacted. The main thing is to give the strongest possible support to initiative where the object is to benefit society and improve the functioning of the service sector. It would not be a bad idea for Moscow to take the lead. For in-stance, it might be worthwhile to get each district Soviet to organize several tailoring workshops, snack bars, or similar enter-prises. It would thus be possible to test out the pros and cons and on the basis of this experience to extend the scheme.[25]

This was an excellent suggestion but for some reason there does not seem to have been any particular rush to put it into practice, either in Moscow or in other cities where the ser-vices are often in an even worse state. Nor is the creation of a legal framework to regulate such new enterprises, as suggested by Brezhnev, proceeding very quickly. The press has mentioned many examples of various independent cooperative organizations being set up in different cities, such as *Fakel* (Torch), *Novator* (Innovator), and others which, acting as "middle men," perform the role of introducing technical innovation into production in return for a fee. There is a tremendous need for many more such independent cooperative enterprises. Yet several of them have had to close down because of interference by tax agencies.

It must be realized that enormous enterprises and service organizations cannot by themselves meet all the needs of a modern economy. Large-scale mass production satisfies stable and basic demands, but there are a great number of minor secondary needs that vary with taste and local conditions, and it is practically impossible for a centralized system to take account of or satisfy them. This is where very small enterprises, sometimes created only for a limited period, could provide invaluable assistance. Secondary schools should be encouraged to form small self-financing workshops to produce articles for local consumption and also to work on commission for local industrial or agricultural enterprises. It should even be possible to stimulate research institutes and laboratories to be more enterprising—in addition to financing their own experimental requirements, they could engage in production on a commercial basis. For example, institutes need a wide range of chemical or biochemical preparations but only in very small quantities, which makes it uneconomical to produce them in factories. The institutes could prepare certain chemicals in their own laboratories and sell the surplus to other institutes or exchange them for different ones. And so on.

It is certainly possible for individual economic initiative to exist and be encouraged within the framework of a socialist society—for example, in the form of a one-man or one-family enterprise. There is no reason to be any more apprehensive about this than about farmers' private plots or garden allotments for urban workers. Private traders and independent handicraft workers are still needed within the highly complex Soviet social and economic structure to deal with many problems that larger state enterprises cannot handle efficiently. A whole range of jobs and services would profit from a greater degree of personal initiative, including the repair of domestic appliances or photographic equipment, copy typing, apartment maintenance, commercial flower growing, the manufacture of certain kinds of souvenirs, tailoring, and finally, medical practice, to name just a few. Soviet law does not forbid this kind of private activity, and there are many private doctors, tailors, and typists who work perfectly legally in our large cities. A great deal of private tutoring goes on in foreign languages or to prepare young people for entrance to institutions of higher education. But unfortunately this kind of occupation in most cases is simply not profitable because of heavy taxation (according to scales set during the later years of NEP). While people are giving up their leisure hours to engage in private work, the resultant evenings are taxed on the basis of a full working day and at a comparatively high rate. For this reason most "private enterprise" is conducted illegally. And many individuals who could easily devote some of their spare time to a useful trade or could provide services for others refrain from doing so because they are not in a position to pay the high tax and are reluctant to break the law.

It is certainly my view that as social life grows more complex and leisure time steadily increases, private and socially beneficial economic initiative on the part of individual citizens should be actively encouraged. Instead of paying heavy rates of progressive taxation, it should be possible to buy an inexpensive permit to engage in a particular activity for one to three years. Apart from those mentioned above, there are other kinds of "private enterprise" that could be promoted: bookbinding workshops, taxi services, hairdressing salons, the manufacture of made-to-order furniture, agencies for accommodation and other services, etc. Prices for these services at present are extremely high, since on the whole they operate illegally. The state is unable to maintain control or collect any income tax. Therefore it would be advantageous for both the government and the public if fundamental changes were introduced.[26]

It is of course a well-known fact that almost all forms of private and commercial activity tend to expand. It is possible that any emergence of private initiative could give rise to a certain number of small capitalist enterprises, but this is not likely to happen in a socialist country. Moreover, the state could easily combat such manifestations of capitalism not only by means of intelligent taxation but also by encouraging cooperative ownership in the service sector and in the case of small factories. These small cooperatives could in the first instance be allocated necessary materials, spare parts, tools, and other items. Certain "futurologists" have predicted that by the end of the twentieth century the Soviet Union will have a mixed economy composed of state, cooperative, and even private capitalist enterprises. This is highly improbable—the development of private capitalist industry in the Soviet Union is undesirable and almost certainly out of the question. But under Soviet conditions, it would be appropriate and undoubtedly advantageous to develop a number of small cooperative enterprises, as well as private ones to provide various services.

The state and the public would benefit enormously from a combination of state and private enterprise in the service sector and the element of competition this would provide. The development and encouragement of private and cooperative initiative without the exploitation of hired labor will be an important factor in the democratization of the economy and will facilitate a more rapid improvement in the material well-being of the entire working population.

XII

The National Question

Socialist democracy, if consistently put into practice, would create a much more favorable climate for finding a just solution to the increasingly urgent national question in the Soviet Union. A more democratic Soviet state would promote the development of national minority cultures and at the same time encourage closer ties between the nations that, taken together, make up a new historical entity: the Soviet people.

The problems of democracy and nationalism converge at various points. I will now briefly look at certain aspects of the national question that are specifically related to important aspects of the problem of making our country more democratic.

In Chapter IV, I described the appearance of certain national and nationalist movements and trends in all the Union Republics (including the RSFSR) and also in many Autonomous Republics.* Since there are fundamental objective and subjective causes for this phenomenon, it is obvious that socialist democratization will not mean the end of these

---

* The USSR is made up of 15 Union (constituent) Republics. Some of these contain Autonomous Republics, Autonomous Regions, and National Areas, all based on the existence of homogeneous national groups. Thus most nationalities are at least theoretically granted a degree of self-government and cultural autonomy within a hierarchical structure: Union Republics have their own constitutions and the nominal right to secede; Autonomous Regions have more powers than National Areas.—Trans.

nationalist movements but rather the beginning of a dialogue with them. For without open and frank discussion it will be impossible to deal with accumulated grievances or to discourage at the very outset the growth of centrifugal tendencies.

Certain aspects of the way personnel are appointed in the Union Republics need to be revised. In the last few decades the basic trend has been to appoint nationals from the indigenous population to chief positions in the administration. Until the mid-thirties there were relatively few Tadzhiks, Kirghiz, Kazakhs, Turkomans, or Uzbeks among the ranks of the highest party or government leaders in the Central Asian republics. This situation changed with the rapid spread of education and culture among the peoples of the non-Russian republics, and native officials now predominate in all responsible posts. This process of "indigenization" also went on, although more slowly, in most of the Autonomous Republics, and it was, of course, a progressive step. As a general rule, all those engaged in public service at any level should come from the majority nationality. And when a member of another national group occupies such a post, it is essential that he be able to speak the local language, whether he be a post office clerk in Georgia, a shop assistant in Turkmenia, or a taxi driver in Minsk.

In the light of recent developments, however, it is time that certain changes were made in the selection of leading officials at the republican level. A new situation has been created by extensive economic progress and integration, the voluntary and reciprocal assimilation of national minorities, the adoption of Russian as a *lingua franca* and also as a second mother tongue, and finally, the growing numbers of non-Russian nationals living in Russian towns while many Russians have moved to the republics.

In each republic there should be greater opportunities not only for nationals of the indigenous population but for local minorities as well. For example, it is absurd for a Tadzhik film studio automatically to choose a Tadzhik for a part that really calls for a Kirghiz actor. It was certainly unwise for the Dovzhenko film studio in Kiev gradually to get rid of all its non-Ukrainian directors. Today half the population of Tbilisi is made up of Armenians, Kurds, Russians, Jews, and Azerbaidzhanis. Before the war it was traditional for an Armenian to be elected first secretary of the Tbilisi city party committee. This post is now always held by a Georgian, which of course is the way it should be. It is also quite obvious that the chairmen of the Presidium of the Supreme Soviet of Georgia and of the Georgian Council of Ministers should both be Georgians. But surely among the other national groups living in Georgia there are many who are perfectly competent to play leading roles in the administrative, economic, and cultural life of the republic. It would be just as wrong to keep them out as it is to pass over non-Russian nationals in Moscow or other predominantly Russian cities.

Discrimination against Soviet citizens of Jewish nationality is particularly objectionable. Obviously it would be foolish to give positions of authority to persons who wish to emigrate to Israel—they should simply be permitted to leave the country. But all other Soviet Jews, most of whom have been virtually assimilated into the surrounding Russian or Ukrainian population, should have absolutely equal rights. The policy of excluding Jews from the party and military *apparat*, the KGB and MVD, the foreign service, senior posts in government and economic administration, publishing houses, and even certain scientific institutes clearly is ridiculous; it is damaging in its effect on our economic and cultural development and lowers the prestige of the Soviet Union in the eyes of the world.[1]

Changes must be adopted which will encourage the promotion of wiser, more capable and experienced personnel. This is what should concern those responsible for selecting leading officials; all criteria of "racial purity" are not only morally corrupting but also quite clearly detrimental in a practical sense. It is time to do away with the "nationality" inquiry on passports and official forms—information of this kind should be confined to the census.

Certainly there should be a fundamental extension of the rights of the Union Republics, particularly with regard to a whole range of local problems; these could easily be dealt with at the republican level, yet consultations in Moscow are still required before any final decisions are made. A typical example of contempt for the rights and competence of the Union Republics is the existing system for awarding and confirming academic degrees and titles. No Union Republic has the right to appoint senior lecturers or professors or award the degree of Candidate or Doctor of Science.* This prerogative is enjoyed solely by the Supreme Examination Board of the Ministry of Higher Education in Moscow. But in view of the enormous expansion of higher education, this system inevitably leads to red tape, bureaucracy, and a tremendous waste of time and energy on the part of candidates. Many are obliged to make several trips to Moscow and only after a number of humiliating appeals are they at last given a decision. Needless to say, red tape always creates fertile soil for corruption, and the reputation of the examination board is not very good in this respect. It would obviously make much more sense to decentralize the process of awarding degrees by providing each Union Republic with its own examination board. There are undoubtedly men of learning in each of the republics who are no less capable than their Moscow colleagues of judging the qualities and shortcomings of candidates. The All-Union Board should be retained merely to carry out spot checks and to deal with possible complaints. The academic councils of the older universities and of the foremost twenty or thirty institutes of higher education should be given the right to confer degrees without confirmation by the central board.

The Union Republics should also be given more extensive responsibility for the curriculum and timetable of secondary schools. In each Union Republic up to 1,000 or 1,200 hours are devoted to studying the native language and literature, which leads to an overcrowded programme. But until now only the Baltic republics have been permitted to increase the period of secondary education to eleven years.

Very often questions arise about the form of state system appropriate for a particular nation. In the first decades of Soviet rule, national development was generally accompanied by a rise in status, i.e., many Autonomous Republics achieved the status of Union Republics while various Autonomous Regions became Autonomous Republics of the RSFSR. For the first ten years after the Revolution, the

---

* The Soviet *kandidat nauk* (Candidate of Science) is really closer to our doctorate, while the Soviet doctorate is a more advanced degree than the western Ph.D.—Trans.

Mordvinian people, for example, had no government structure of their own at all. A National Area was formed in 1928,
then an Autonomous Region in 1930, and finally an Autonomous Republic in 1936. Kirghizia became an Autonomous
Region in 1924 and a Union Repbulic in 1936. There are only
two cases of status being lowered: the Abkhaz Union Republic, formed in 1921 and linked with Georgia by federal treaty,
was in 1930 reconstituted as an Autonomous Republic within
the Georgian Union Republic; the Karelo-Finnish Union Republic was set up in 1939 but became an Autonomous Republic after the war. (I am not concerned here with the illegal
abolition of the state structures of certain national groups—
this has already been discussed above. Clearly it is about time
that national autonomy was restored to the Crimean Tatars
and the Soviet Germans, with boundaries in accordance with
the wishes of the majority of those peoples.)

One result of intensive economic development is that the
indigenous population of some republics within the RSFSR
has dropped to 15–25 percent of the total. It might be desirable, therefore, to reconstitute certain Autonomous Republics
into Autonomous Regions, which would mean a considerable
reduction of the administrative apparatus. There are many
cases where republics with small populations, such as the
Adzhar and the Nakhichevan Autonomous Republics, possess
an *apparat* almost equal to that of such large regions of the
RSFSR as Chelyabinsk or Sverdlovsk.

The right of nations to self-determination requires
special consideration. As everyone knows, Lenin himself insisted on inserting a specific clause in the party programme
giving nations the right to self-determination, including the
right to secede. Lenin insisted that this right must be retained
after a democratic and even after a socialist revolution in
order to make it clear that membership in the union of socialist nations was equal and voluntary. At the same time,
Lenin did say that, while defending the principle of national
self-determination and opposing any attempt to exert pressure by force or unjust means, the Bolsheviks were primarily
concerned with the unity and solidarity of the proletariat of
all nations. According to Lenin, Bolsheviks should only in
certain circumstances support demands "aimed at creating a
new class state or replacing a single political entity with a

weaker federal one." The important thing for Bolsheviks was that the *right* of self-determination be guaranteed, not that self-determination actually should be put into practice.

The idea for the creation of the USSR in fact came from Lenin. The new Union was to combine the federal principle with that of strong central authority, essential in view of capitalist encirclement. There is an article of the Constitution that gives each Union Republic the right of self-determination up to and including secession from the Union. However, no right can be genuine unless appropriate machinery exists to guarantee its effectiveness in practice. How could the Ukraine, for example, inaugurate the actual procedure for leaving the USSR? Neither the Soviet Constitution nor those of the Union Republics offer any enlightenment on this point. And who could even place the question on the agenda for discussion, when any public statement in support of Ukrainian independence is considered to be enemy propaganda subject to criminal charges, in defiance of both common sense and the teachings of Lenin![2] If it cannot even be talked about, how can secession be called a constitutional right? This is a case where the absence of effective guarantees reveals an obvious gulf between word and deed. The virtual ban on broad public discussion of this and many other acutely disturbing and controversial issues is one of the reasons for the present increase of national tension (in addition to those discussed in Chapter IV).

The founding principle of the Soviet Union as embodied in the Constitution should be taken more seriously. It is time for the formulation of a new constitutional law giving Union Republics the right of self-determination, including the right to secede and form an independent state, and indicating the procedure by which this could take place.

I myself would strongly oppose the secession of any republic from the Union. Even in the capitalist world, there is a trend today toward greater integration; the technological revolution leads to the setting up of larger economic (and in the future, political) units than are possible within the framework of most existing nation-states. It is even more vital to achieve economic, political, and technological integration within the USSR as well as within the whole socialist camp. Therefore the secession of a Union Republic would be neither in its own interest nor in the interest of the Union as a whole. However, our state should be a voluntary union of nations, with respect for the right to self-determination not only in theory but in practice.

The best way to guarantee this right would be to institute a compulsory referendum in every republic at least once every ten years. Obviously this presupposes absolutely free discussion of all national problems, as well as the inevitable appearance of groups and movements in favor of secession. The referendum should be conducted by secret ballot under the supervision of special commissions composed of representatives from the other Union Republics. The Supreme Soviet of each Union Republic should also have the right to hold a referendum in exceptional circumstances before the expiration of ten years, but not within one year of the next regularly scheduled referendum. Certainly a vast majority in all the Union Republics would vote to remain in the USSR. But if a republic were to secede, there should be a further compulsory referendum after ten years on the question of whether or not to rejoin the Union. It could be held earlier if the population demanded it.

Possibly there is an element of risk in holding national plebiscites on this question. However, our whole nationalities policy is worthless if we are not willing to test it in this way. Furthermore, the holding of referendums would have a healthy effect on all aspects of the national question throughout the Soviet Union, while the dangers would be minimal. The results of a referendum can be predicted in advance by means of modern methods of testing opinion, and this would make it possible to influence final voting since preliminary polls would reveal the causes of existing discontent and appropriate action could be taken.

If the right of self-determination were *genuinely* guaranteed, this would facilitate any future expansion of the USSR. The question of other socialist countries voluntarily joining the Union will inevitably arise as a result of economic integration throughout the socialist camp. The development of political and economic democracy within the USSR would also be an influential factor. A first step could be open borders, making it possible for all citizens of socialist countries to travel freely from one to another. It is absolutely intolerable,

even insulting, that it should still be so much more complicated for a Soviet citizen to travel to Poland, Czechoslovakia,
Hungary, Bulgaria, or Rumania (and vice versa) than it is for
a Frenchman to travel throughout Western Europe.

We have unfortunately lost the flexibility of relations
between the republics that existed when the Soviet Union was
first established. This will make it much more difficult to
attract any new republics to the Union.

XIII

Foreign Policy

We are living today in a world of enormous complexity and contradiction, and in many respects the situation grows increasingly confused. Mankind continues to be divided into capitalist and socialist military-political alignments, and at times the tension between them assumes critical dimensions. Leaders of all countries, both large and small, have never before had to bear such grave responsibilities.

At the same time there has been a rapid development of the industrial productive capacity of most countries, huge advances in the manufacture of weapons of mass destruction and their means of delivery, an unprecedented "demographic explosion" in underdeveloped countries, and many other processes that have brought humanity to a point where the solution of basic world problems requires the concerted efforts of all nations, cooperating with each other in an atmosphere of trust. It is now crucial to preserve world peace and avert the nuclear war that would bring disaster to the whole of mankind. All the developed countries are faced with the problem of coordinating and increasing their aid to the poorer nations of the Third World as they enter what appears to be the most critical period of their history. There must be a united effort to work out a sound demographic policy on a global scale.[1]

We are all confronted with the immensely important task of protecting the earth's environment and natural resources. Neglect up until now has caused a substantial degree of pollution of most of the world's rivers, lakes, seas, and oceans. If the development of industry and power engineering proceeds uncontrolled, it is liable to accelerate the exhaustion of natural resources and cause irreparable damage to the structure of the earth's atmosphere, formed in the course of millions of years. Experts believe that in the foreseeable future this could lead to such a steep increase of ultraviolet radiation that most plant life on earth would be destroyed.

At the present stage of the development of the forces of production, a new, more effective international division of labor is possible. Cooperation in carrying out various worldwide projects could bring about a universal improvement in human living conditions. But unfortunately the present climate in world affairs hardly favors a solution to the urgent problems that face us.

No single country or group of them can be blamed for existing world tensions, although of course it would be quite easy to demonstrate that certain countries were more responsible than others for aggravating the atmosphere of the "cold war." But since all major countries and several smaller ones did play a role, it is now appropriate for them all to participate in the search for ways to bring about a new environment in which the efforts of every nation can be directed toward constructive goals.

In this context we cannot ignore the close relationship between a state's domestic and foreign policies. Clearly democratic trends are not encouraged, whether in socialist or capitalist societies, by the cold war, by more intense confrontations between the great powers, by the continuous military buildup or interminable local conflicts constantly threatening to develop into nuclear war on a global scale. The posture of confrontation between the great powers, by making the already difficult economic and political situation in the third world even worse, encourages the rise of totalitarian regimes which then become a threat not only to their neighbors but to everyone else as well.

It is of course equally true that a country's domestic situation influences its foreign policy. There can be no doubt about the fact that surviving elements of totalitarianism or authoritarianism in the USSR, the United States, and other great powers, the existence of ideological intolerance and artificial restrictions on scientific, economic, and cultural cooperation all act as an obstacle to relaxation of the cold war;

instead there is confrontation, power politics, and mutual distrust, which hardly facilitate a policy of détente. Since I am primarily concerned here with the Soviet Union, I shall now look more closely at the relationship between our own domestic and foreign policy.

I am absolutely convinced that a thoroughgoing, comprehensive democratization of Soviet society would not only have an enormous influence on life within the country but also on foreign policy and the position of the Soviet Union in the world at large. Socialist democratization could affect foreign policy in several different ways. As pointed out earlier, democratization would make government policy subject to public scrutiny. The Soviet people, better informed about world events, would have the opportunity if not to participate directly in affairs of state, at least to exert an indirect influence by openly expressing views and opinions.

Of course foreign relations, like military matters, require a certain degree of secrecy. For the time being we cannot avoid secret diplomacy altogether. But there are many aspects of foreign policy that should be open, with information available to the people and to their representatives in the Supreme Soviet. For example, there is the question of economic and military aid to other countries. Soviet citizens know far less about this than Americans do about their country's foreign aid programs.

The whole process of decision making in foreign affairs should become more democratic. Although *the very nature of these problems* often means that final decisions can be taken only within a narrow circle or sometimes by one person alone, there should be preliminary debate about options, the possibility of a clash of views, and full discussion even if only within the relevant department. Various issues should be considered at plenary sessions of the Central Committee, within commissions of the Supreme Soviet, and at conferences of specialists, with absolute freedom for all points of view to be expressed. Given the tremendous complexity of the present world situation, research institutes that specialize in international affairs and strategic analysis should be expanded. One cannot avoid the impression that actions are often committed without adequate advance scrutiny.

A greater element of democracy within the Soviet Union

would strengthen the position of communist parties in capitalist countries. It is quite apparent that the constant display of undemocratic behavior in the Soviet Union—political trials, the persecution of dissidents, scurrilous "campaigns" in the arts, discrimination against national minorities, etc.—are all very damaging to the prestige of both the Soviet Union and the whole communist movement. The Soviet Union is not only the world's first socialist country, it is also the basic source of strength for the socialist camp, and quite naturally anything that happens in our country attracts a great deal of attention and has global repercussions. This must not be forgotten. The fact that progress along the path to democracy has been extremely slow, with frequent relapses into the methods of the past, has had a negative effect on the development of the communist movement; it has retarded revolutionary processes throughout the world by creating hostility toward communism and the Soviet Union among potential allies. It becomes extremely easy for bourgeois propagandists to present such distortions of communist theory and practice as typical of the doctrine in its true form.

Clearly, serious reasons lie behind the failure of most communist parties in capitalist countries to become mass organizations or to attract young people, students, or intellectuals. And the communist parties that do hold the strongest positions in Western Europe are those that not only carry on a self-sacrificing struggle on behalf of the workers but also regularly criticize Soviet domestic and foreign policies (while of course supporting positive achievements). All these considerations make it obvious that the Soviet Union cannot carry out its international obligations without extending the role of democracy at home. Democratization within the Soviet Union would undoubtedly make it easier for communist parties to collaborate with socialists and social democrats, particularly with their increasingly influential left wings.

In its present form social-democratic ideology is alien to Marxism-Leninism. Yet one cannot deny that it enjoys considerable support not only among the petty bourgeoisie and intellectuals but even in the working class of Western countries. This is why communists, as is stressed in all the programmatic documents of the world movement, must attempt to arrive at agreement and unity of action with social democrats wherever possible. On June 17, 1969, the Moscow International Conference of Communist and Workers' Parties agreed on a final resolution which urged the need for working class unity and advocated communist cooperation with socialists and social democrats.[2]

In an article called "New Perspectives," the well-known Soviet journalist Ernst Henri has written:

Only communists can bring dynamic vitality to coalitions of the left. . . . However it is almost always true that a left-wing front cannot function without socialists, as they continue to be supported by millions of factory and office workers, sections of the petty bourgeoisie, and many intellectuals. . . . The capitalist world, in view of past experience, bases most of its strategy on the assumption that such cooperation is ultimately impossible. But is this still the case in the 1970's? The problems of the world have become so enormous, so urgent that it is inadmissible, even criminal, to use outmoded criteria as a guide or to seek answers in past experience. Solutions can be found only through united actions by workers' movements.[3]

Henri is absolutely right. It is true, of course, that in Western Europe social-democratic parties are stronger politically than communist ones. They have 9.5 million members, as against the communists' 2.5 million. In the mid-sixties the social democrats polled 36 per cent of all votes cast in Western European elections, while the communists obtained a little over 8 per cent.[4] In many countries, governments are headed by social democrats or by a coalition that includes them. Clearly by the end of the seventies, socialist parties will be the dominant political force in Western Europe and Japan. One can say, therefore, without exaggeration, that the fate of socialism in these crucial parts of the world will depend on the nature of the relationship formed between socialists and communists.

Right-wing social-democratic leaders are well known for their anticommunist views. But it would be a great mistake to think that this was the only stumbling block toward establishing a unified workers' movement. For a variety of reasons a process of differentiation is now going on within the ranks of the socialist parties and as the left wing grows in strength, this is reflected in the composition and policies of the leadership. The swing to the left is in the first instance bound up with the logic of the class struggle within capitalist countries. However, communist party policy also exerts considerable influence. The communist movement should certainly go part of the way to meet the socialists. It is by no means a question of opportunism; for some time to come there can be no other viable communist strategy. It would be completely wrong and unrealistic to demand that all concessions must come from the socialists, that they must accept *all* basic aspects of communist policies and *all* the domestic and foreign policies of the Soviet Union. It will be impossible to agree on unity of action if there is insistence that communists must have the leading role. Unfortunately certain aspects of communist policy are very much an obstacle to unity of action—above all, the inability to come to terms with the Stalinist past, along with current instances of undemocratic behavior within the Soviet Union. Our reluctance to break with Stalinism once and for all and condemn all signs of relapse, our fear of proceeding further along the path of socialist democratization—this is what stands in the way of unity of action between socialists and communists.

At present the speeches and articles of European social-democratic leaders devote a great deal of attention to the problem of how democracy can be developed and extended.[5] They believe that democracy should be the central political concern of socialists in the 1970's. Their understanding of the concept is of course hardly the same as for the communists, but it is wrong to view their programme as mere social demagogy, because it does in fact reflect widespread popular attitudes within the working classes and among intellectuals. This is why it is so vital to seek rapprochement.

In the 1960's a new political movement emerged in many capitalist countries and grew very rapidly, particularly where there were no strong socialist parties (as in the case of the United States)—it became known as the "new left." It was basically composed of students and intellectuals and encompassed a wide range of tendencies and groups. But although ideological and tactical positions vary and slogans change, particularly from country to country, members of the new left nevertheless share certain basic convictions including a rejection of capitalism and opposition to war. They are staunch supporters of democracy and repudiate all forms of totalitarian government. In an analysis of the new left, the Soviet political theorists Yu. Zamoshkin and N. Motroshilova have written:

As a movement it is constantly evolving, with different subgroups emerging all the time. While some of them love to protest by staging anarchic, nihilistic demonstrations (particularly in the arts) and have a taste for utopian revolutionary bravado, the often courageous actions of others are being guided by a growing sense of social responsibility. Their role and influence is continually increasing as they display a capacity for self-criticism along with intellectual maturity, clear-sightedness, and the ability to identify their movement with the real problems of their country. Although their approach may appear to be narrow, these new left groups are an important factor in the class struggle and their activities serve to broaden the democratic anticapitalist, anti-imperialist front.[6]

It is becoming vital for communist parties to find a way to cooperate with various new-left groups. A. Rumyantsev is right in saying that "at the present time, when a process of polarization is taking place on a vast scale between the forces of democracy, peace, and progress and those of authoritarianism, militarism, and chauvinism, it is terribly important to take advantage of every opportunity to win over democratic public opinion in bourgeois countries."[7] In many countries (including the United States) unity of action with the new left is just as important as with left-wing socialists. The difficulty here, however, is that most new-left groups are extremely anticommunist. They make superficial and inaccurate generalizations about various events of the Soviet past and object to the strict discipline typical of communist parties. Communism is simply regarded as a form of the totalitarianism they hate so much.[8]

The Soviet Union must make an effort to convince the youth and intellectuals of Western countries that they are wrong in identifying communism with Stalinism. It is even more important to demonstrate that communism is not inevitably totalitarian—it is a social system which is meant to create the necessary preconditions for the full development of the personality and the maximum satisfaction of the material and spiritual needs of all working people; under communism there will be genuine democracy. Unfortunately, existing socialist countries still lay themselves open to attack by violating the democratic rights of their citizens and preserving elements of totalitarianism.

It would undoubtedly be much easier to find solutions to many complex international problems, such as disarmament, if Soviet society were to become more democratic.[9] We must remember that the various undemocratic trends in our political life, the persistent efforts of extremely influential groups to revive Stalinism and rehabilitate Stalin himself, do not merely tend to sow discord between communists and the non-communist left. Undemocratic behavior at home and ill-considered actions abroad (which often seem to be an extension of domestic policy, as in the case of Czechoslovakia) assist the growth of right-wing forces in capitalist countries. Forty years ago, Soviet domestic and foreign policy in conjunction with sectarian Comintern tactics (against social democrats) helped to bring about the victory of fascism in Germany. This fatal error must not be repeated. Nor can we ignore the fact that bourgeois propagandists are able to skillfully exploit and exaggerate undemocratic aspects of Soviet life in order to effectively turn large sections of the working, middle, and lower-middle classes away from communism and socialism. Most of these people do not sympathize with the new left either. But a growing number of individuals from intermediate levels of society and even from politically less aware sections of the working class are now giving their support to the "new right." In the United States this can be seen in the popularity of the racist politician George Wallace and the rapid rise of various ultra-right-wing organizations, along with the fact that a number of influential trade unions have swung to the right. When New York building workers attacked a students' demonstration in May 1970, it was an extremely dangerous symptom and not a chance event.

The Soviet Union does not approve of either Democratic or Republican policies. We rightly criticize various undemocratic actions by American authorities and relentlessly condemn their aggression in Vietnam. But it must be remembered that in spite of its imperialist role, the contemporary American state is not fascist, which means that it is possible for us to reach agreement on certain questions. The most reactionary ultra-right wing is not in power. The Soviet Union must make sure that its policies do nothing to make it easier for this element to seize control. A victory for fascism in the United States would have far more terrible consequences for the whole world than the rule of Hitler in Germany. For this reason the USSR must do everything in its power to prevent a right-wing fascist takeover in the United States.

It would also be wrong to underestimate right-wing tendencies in the Third World. With growing confrontation between the great powers (particularly the United States and the USSR), there is an acceleration of the arms race which absorbs an ever-increasing proportion of available resources. This not only holds back the economic development of the great powers (and certain other capitalist countries as well), it also imposes strict limits on the degree to which developed countries can supply economic, cultural, scientific, and technical aid to the Third World. Poverty, unemployment, and illiteracy among the young are all rising in underdeveloped countries, and millions of people are being driven to despair. The slow pace of economic development combined with the "demographic revolution" is creating the very real threat of famine for tens and hundreds of millions of people in many areas of the world. It is easy to see how this simultaneously encourages the rise of despotic right-wing regimes and extremist left-wing movements. There are also appeals for a struggle of the "world village" against the "world city": it is argued that the overpopulated Third World should seize the wealth of the developed countries by force. The aggressive attitude of China toward the Soviet Union is an extremely dangerous symptom of this approach. Although consistent democratization within the USSR would not solve all these problems, it would at least create a more suitable climate for devising ways to improve the situation. By creating a rich and technologically advanced and truly democratic society, the Soviet Union could provide the Chinese people with a model to be followed after their own "Twentieth Congress"—which must surely take place in the not-too-distant future.

XIV

Bureaucracy under Socialism

Bureaucracy is with good reason often regarded as the principal enemy of socialist democracy, the most important element standing in the way of democratization throughout the Soviet system. Let us therefore briefly examine this curious phenomenon, which is like a malignant growth on the body of Soviet society.

The terms "bureaucrat" and "bureaucracy" have many different meanings and are used in a number of ways. The expression "bureaucratic apparatus" sometimes refers in a general way to the entire machinery of government, and all government employees are called "bureaucrats," not necessarily in a pejorative sense. In this usage, "bureaucrat" is just a synonym for "administrator," and bureaucracy has a positive role in the sense that no state, whether capitalist or socialist, has as yet been able to function without administrative machinery at various levels. This rather vague notion of bureaucracy can even be found in the writings of Lenin. In notes he jotted down before the Tenth Party Congress, Lenin described the party apparatus as "a *good* bureaucracy" which would be at the service of policy.

Bureaucracy is sometimes used to refer only to higher officialdom, the upper levels of government, and the military and political elite. But it would be more accurate to define bureaucracy as a structure whose main characteristic is the absence of accountability from the top down, i.e., an authori-

tarian system of administration. In such a system any signs of
initiative or criticism from below are ignored or suppressed;
power is exercised exclusively from above. Inevitably this
gives rise to certain secondary patterns that include a lack of
consideration for individuals, a profusion of red tape, the primacy of form over content, and ineffective leadership, since
paperwork becomes more important than any real activity.
Bureaucracy in this sense always means that its servants are
badly informed and blindly obedient to authority, often to the
point of worshiping it.

In a bureaucratic machine the most important cog is the
official. He gives little thought to the needs of the people or
the lower levels of the population, although he probably rose
from there himself. Above all, he is concerned with his own
career, his own position and the material advantages and
rewards that it brings. He is not particularly interested in
doing his job but rather in keeping it, along with his privileges, his authority over subordinates, and the approval of his
superiors. For this reason a bureaucrat more often than not
carries out his duties in a perfunctory way without getting
down to essentials, conducting his business by shuffling
papers at a desk. The terms "bureaucracy" and "bureaucrat"
are used below in this narrower and more precise definition.

Bureaucracy has many faces. An official who tries to
make everyone subordinate, takes too much power into his
own hands, decides everything himself and brooks no opposition—such a man is a bureaucrat. But a functionary who
avoids responsibility, takes no independent decisions, and
tries not to interfere even in matters that most require action
on his part—he too is a typical bureaucrat.

There is a strong interrelationship between the personality of the bureaucrat, the structure of power and institutions, and the general social and economic conditions and
traditions of the country. The prerevolutionary autocracy in
Russia was essentially bureaucratic. Even officials who possessed the highest personal qualities were almost always
transformed into bureaucrats under the tsarist regime, because if the metamorphosis did not take place the individual
in question was very soon rejected by the system.[1]

Before the October Revolution the organization of
Soviets was extremely democratic—they were almost entirely
nonbureaucratic structures. But after the victory of Soviet

power, bureaucracy re-emerged and soon began to penetrate every pore of the new Soviet and party organizations. It was clear that even after a socialist revolution a considerable amount of authoritarian administration was unavoidable, given the size of the country and its economic and cultural backwardness. The population was predominantly peasant and petty bourgeois whose inadequate educational level deprived the Bolsheviks of potential support. But the bureaucratic mentality was not confined to bourgeois specialists or former tsarist officials employed by the new state in lower and middle levels of administration. Even former revolutionary leaders, finding themselves in power, were most of the time forced to resort to authoritarian methods; they simply gave orders, often in a high-handed bureaucratic way. It is often said that the first generation of revolutionaries could never have become bureaucrats, but this is simply not true. Because of Russian conditions at the time, even proletarian revolutionaries had no alternative.

More than anyone else in the party, Lenin was aware of the problem. He believed that bureaucracy was the greatest threat there was to decent government, although at the same time he accepted the fact that a certain amount of bureaucratic distortion was inevitable in the functioning of the young Soviet state. He was also convinced that the future of the new state would depend on the efforts of the party and in the first instance on the behavior of senior party officials— either the state would degenerate or democracy would prevail and succeed in overcoming bureaucratic tendencies.

Although he regarded bureaucracy as an inevitable evil in the first stage of the Soviet state's development, Lenin did not believe it to be insurmountable, and he constantly battled against all visible signs of bureaucratic conduct within the *apparat*. The party program of 1919 declared that the party was waging "a most resolute struggle against bureaucracy" and advocated a number of measures in order "totally to eradicate this evil." Lenin was often heard to say, "Bureaucracy is our chief enemy." He also made the point that the struggle against bureaucracy was extraordinarily complex and could only be successful if there was "tremendous persistence over a lengthy period" and "only if the whole population, every individual, participates in governing the country."

Lenin's attitude toward "Soviet" bureaucracy clearly

emerges from his conversation with Klara Zetkin; he admitted that bureaucracy did exist in the Soviet Union, and then added: "I detest it with all my heart, although of course certain individual bureaucrats may well be efficient workers. But I do hate the system. It creates paralysis and disorder both above and below. The decisive factor in overcoming and eradicating bureaucracy will be the expansion of education."[2]

Many of Lenin's articles, speeches, letters, and notes reveal his hatred of bureaucracy. In 1922 he wrote to one of his deputies in the Sovnarkom: "We have all sunk into a rotten swamp of bureaucratic departments." In one of his last articles, dictated from his sickbed when he was seriously ill, he said, "Our new Rabkrin,* it is to be hoped, will be free of . . . those absurd affectations, those ridiculous airs so dear to our entire bureaucracy. . . . May it be said, by the way, that bureaucracy is with us not only in Soviet institutions but in party organizations as well."[3]

Even after Lenin's death the party did devote a great deal of attention to the problem of overcoming bureaucracy and encouraging the masses to be more active. But as Stalin's power and influence grew, the struggle against bureaucracy became more a question of empty words and had relatively little effect. With the establishment of the cult of Stalin, unlimited power was backed up by terror. The working class and the population at large had no control over the leadership, and most of those at the top succumbed to a process of bureaucratic degeneration. Stalin and those around him isolated themselves from the people—they were no longer in any way accountable for their actions and began to abuse the power entrusted to them. Thus they ceased to be representatives of the people and in fact had become usurpers. As a result Soviet society experienced a profound contradiction between on one hand the forces of production, the socialist character of the relations of production, and on the other a bureaucratic terrorist form of government.[4]

During the years of the Stalin cult the power of the state became an autonomous force. Passivity was cultivated not

---

* Commissariat of Workers' and Peasants' Inspection, which existed from 1920 to 1934 and was intended to check on the administrative apparatus and guard against bureaucratization at a time when many non-Bolshevik officials still occupied important positions in government. The first commissar was Stalin.—Trans.

only among the masses but also within the ranks of the party and all initiative from below was disregarded or suppressed. Powerful individuals or small groups of senior officials took decisions and gave orders—government guided by rational considerations was out of the question. Promotion into the ranks of the leadership did not of course depend on such qualities as intellect, ability, or devotion to the people; it was rather more important to be devoted to Stalin or one of his lieutenants and to possess other traits appropriate to the times—cruelty and the capacity to carry out any order without demur.

After the Twentieth and Twenty-second congresses and again after the October Plenum, a great effort was made to remove bureaucratic distortion at all levels of government. But the job was not done thoroughly enough and the masses were not properly involved in the process. In other words, the struggle against bureaucracy was carried out by bureaucratic methods. There was probably no other way in the immediate post-Stalin years (it was rather a question of "set a thief to catch a thief"). And the new leadership did manage to prevent the transfer of power to adventurers and political criminals like Beria, Molotov, Kaganovich, and others. But there was little attempt to deal with the "gentler" forms of bureaucracy and administrative abuse of power: voluntarism, harebrained schemes, the exercise of personal authority with insufficient supervision from below, the rejection of rational methods—all, unfortunately, still with us. The cultural level of the population is incomparably higher than in the first decade of Soviet rule and today the masses do exert a certain influence on administrative bodies, although largely at the lower levels of government. There is still very little impact at the top. Bureaucracy becomes more apparent as one progresses up the hierarchy, whether in industry or in the party. Officials in the highest echelons of the *apparat* (state, party, economic, and military) by virtue of their power, standard of living, and legalized privileges, are cut off from the people and are extremely remote from their subordinates in the administrative pyramid. This inevitably is reflected in the way they think, their attitudes at work, their psychology and social habits.

It cannot be denied that our leaders work very hard. How could it be otherwise in view of the degree of centralization that still prevails? There are far too many things that could be handled perfectly well at middle levels of administration, yet are still decided at the top. But given the conditions and circumstances that must be part of any bureaucratic system, many of these administrative endeavors are quite superfluous or even negative in their effect. As we all know, Khrushchev spent fourteen to sixteen hours a day working on the details of his numerous reforms.

In the higher reaches of the state machine there is often a very slow rate of efficiency, with certain sections virtually running idle. At the same time the leadership pays little attention to the crucial social change taking place in our midst. Bureaucracy is still the most serious obstacle to the advance of Soviet society.

There is yet another danger characteristic of bureaucracy that should be stressed. With its interminable instructions, prohibitions, and technicalities, there is bound to be an increase in illegality, bribery, and corruption. Since real life is constantly changing while regulations remain static, there is a natural tendency to circumvent them by any available means. It is sometimes the case that a perfectly legitimate need can be satisfied only in a not entirely honest way. The examples of private doctors, typists, and tailors have already been mentioned.

The author of the essay "Words Are Also Deeds" is quite right in his view, that

of course when we say that bureaucracy is the guiding principle of the party and state *apparat,* we have no right to assume it applies to *all persons* in positions of authority throughout the country. One cannot ignore other relevant factors: There is the powerful moral legacy of socialist ideas, the grandeur of social goals still proclaimed to be the objectives of our society. A slow, restrained but quite steady replenishment is taking place within the ranks of the bureaucracy—new elements exhibit quite different qualities, allowing nothing to be taken on trust (this is particularly true of those energetic specialists who themselves have suffered under the bureaucratic yoke and cannot abide the absurdity and clumsiness of the machine). Thus more and more the ruling *apparat* merges with the scientific and technical elite and cannot but absorb certain progressive tendencies in the process. The overwhelming demands of real problems tend to crack the monolithic structure of the *apparat* and even dyed-in-the-wool bureaucrats are forced to seek other ways out. And finally, there is the latent pressure of public opinion which today cannot be eliminated in the Stalinist manner with the arrest of several thousand or even tens of thousands among the educated—by now there are simply too many of them.

It is wrong to underestimate the role and importance of the bureaucratic elite in a centralized socialist state, but neither should it be exaggerated. Western writers have for some time maintained that there is a new ruling class in the Soviet Union which developed in the course of Stalin's rule— some describe it as composed of the highest party, state, economic, and military leaders, while others include the most eminent scientists, writers, and figures in the arts as well. It has even been suggested that the Soviet "new class" embraces most party members. In the postwar years this idea was taken up by certain former communists; for instance, there is the particularly detailed treatment in Djilas' *The New Class*. Djilas asserts that the highest echelons of the bureaucracy in the USSR not only possess unlimited control over all nationalized property but are also the real collective owners of all the assets of the state. He declares that "Contemporary communism is not only a party of a certain type, or a bureaucracy which has sprung from monopolistic ownership and excessive state interference in the economy. Above all else, the essential aspect of contemporary communism is the new class of owners and exploiters." Djilas tries to support this and similar statements with a great deal of very complicated but unconvincing argument, and it simply is not true.[5]

In the first place, there can be no comparison between genuine communism and the travesty of the Stalin period. Genuine communism cannot coexist with rule by a bureaucratic elite. Secondly, although there are groups within Soviet society that might with some justification be regarded as a bureaucratic elite, they do not constitute a class in the socioeconomic sense of the word. It is perfectly obvious that they do not own the means of production or the land, and that they are not able to bequeath their rights, privileges, or positions to their children. In many respects the situation of these people is much less stable than that, for example, of those in the higher levels of the Church hierarchy. Of course the power of

Soviet leaders is considerable, usually greater than that of their opposite numbers in capitalist countries. But a guardian, as everybody knows, does not himself inherit the property.[6]

"The superiority of the bureaucracy in socialist countries," writes a foreign student of the subject, "rests on nothing more solid than the political equilibrium. In the final analysis this is a far more fragile basis for social supremacy than other forms of property relations sanctified by law, religion, and tradition."[7]

It should also be borne in mind that the position and authority of the highest leaders depend less on the army, the party, and the secret police (all of which in the final analysis have an ancillary function) than on the trust invested in it by the majority of the people, including most ordinary members of the armed forces, the party, and the security organizations. It is a question of confidence or even simply of faith, an assumption by the common people and rank-and-file officials of the *apparat* that those in charge are pursuing a correct policy, that the leadership is composed of people best qualified to interpret Marxism—the doctrine that fifty-five years ago was accepted by the most active section of the Russian proletariat as a guide to action.

Lenin and his colleagues were supported by a proletariat that gave them just this kind of trust. Stalin also relied on it to facilitate the use of terror, which in turn became the *second* mainstay of his power. When the Twentieth and Twenty-second Party congresses shattered all confidence in Stalin and his entourage, they did not on the whole undermine the Soviet people's trust in the party and its leadership. As the initiator of "de-Stalinization," Khrushchev acquired considerable political capital only to lose it very rapidly as a result of his extremely incompetent policies in nearly all spheres of public life. The October Plenum in 1964 was only partly successful in overcoming the crisis of faith that had materialized in 1963–64 among the people and within the *apparat;* confidence in the party leadership had been impaired and to some extent this second exposure of a "great leader" only made matters worse. This problem must be faced squarely without any illusions. At present none of the top leaders enjoys very much *personal popularity,* an obvious disadvantage in political life. On the whole the masses have only a vague image of many members of the Politburo or Secretaries of the Central Committee. There is still trust in the highest bodies such as the Politburo, the Secretariat, the Central Committee, the Council of Ministers, and the Presidium of the Supreme Soviet. But it should be remembered that this trust is by no means as boundless as our propaganda makes out. There are many definite indications that the crisis of faith in the leadership continues to grow, particularly among young people and the intelligentsia. Although the regime still has large reserves of strength, there is always the possibility that if it came to the worst, some in the leadership might be tempted to resort to "strong measures." However, in today's conditions, this inevitably would lead to even greater disenchantment, undermining the stability of the regime. It would be a dangerous course.

The alternative and the only correct approach is to seek popularity and political authority by introducing a democratic programme that would be supported by the people and the intelligentsia. This would certainly require the promotion of new men, who would govern the country together with many of the present-day leaders.

While I do not believe that the bureaucracy can be described as some kind of new class, I am forced to agree that those in charge of Soviet society now constitute a definite stratum sharing certain customs and rules of conduct. This group, with all the peculiarities of its social psychology, requires special study. That senior administrators should form a separate and clearly defined estate is not in itself an ominous development—the problem is that, having grown arrogant and out of touch with other strata and classes, this estate has passed beyond the control of society. The alarming thing is that advancement is largely dependent on personal patronage, on friendships or family connections—political and professional qualifications are secondary. How else can one explain the fact that a man who invariably is the subject of scorn and ridicule in scientific circles has for seven years been head of the science section of the Central Committee? In a conversation with a prominent figure connected with the arts, the Central Committee Secretary for Ideology said: "If you have any problems, come straight to me. Never mind those idiots." He was referring to one of his subordinates who headed a department of the Central Committee. A senior party official who has been working in Minsk finds jobs in Moscow for those who assisted him in Belorussia, while a different leader, who was in Moldavia, assiduously pushes his colleagues from Kishinev up the administrative ladder. In this way extraordinary "spheres of influence" and "private domains" are formed within the apparatus of government—with "one of our boys" in charge. Individuals are often referred to as "so-and-so's man."

Then there is the problem of technocracy. It is well known that bureaucracy does not overburden itself with excessive learning. E. Gnedin points out that "bureaucracy rests on a hierarchy of privilege rather than knowledge, and so it is hostile to science. This rather peculiar trait at a time of scientific and technological revolution aggravates the harm done to socialism by bureaucracy." Having obtained a position thanks to personal contacts rather than ability, a bureaucrat will attempt to continue advancing in the same way.

However, life is becoming more and more complex and bureaucrats are constantly pursued by failure. This is the reason why scientists and specialists are being drawn into the *apparat;* committees and commissions of experts are being created, but at the same time undemocratic methods of administration remain intact. In other words, the bureaucrats are being replaced by knowledgeable and more efficient technocrats. This process is developing rapidly in the economic *apparat,* in the army and security organs, but very much less so in the party, or in the press and propaganda departments. Conflict is inevitable between the bureaucracy and technocrats who are far more capable of applying the fruits of scientific progress to the business of administration. Very possibly the major development of the next ten or fifteen years will be the transition from bureaucracy to technocracy. But technocracy, as a distinctive form of "socialist managerialism," cannot resolve the basic problems of Soviet society. There is only one way to deal with them, only one acceptable alternative to bureaucracy, and that is genuine democratization.

XV

The Intelligentsia

The intelligentsia is the section of our society most sensitive to violations of democratic rights and freedoms. Representatives of different subdivisions within the intelligentsia have been the most energetic advocates of a genuine development of socialist democracy. Therefore it is particularly important to examine the intelligentsia as a specific social group.

Until recently, Marxist literature defined the intelligentsia as a particular stratum serving the interests of a given class—meaning a feudal, bourgeois, or proletarian intelligentsia. In the simplest terms, persons whose work implies some kind of original intellectual activity are considered to be members of the intelligentsia. Those who perform different kinds of physical labor are workers (in industry) and peasants (in agriculture). White collar workers primarily carry out various tasks involving repetitive and mechanical forms of mental work that do not demand a high level of education.

Counted among the intelligentsia are scholars and scientists, writers, artists, teachers in schools and institutions of higher education, doctors, engineers, lawyers, as well as certain others—individuals whose work embraces more complicated kinds of mental labor demanding considerable independence, creativity, and a high level of general or specialized preparation. However, a diploma or degree is only a formal indication and is by no means obligatory for all members of the intelligentsia, many of whom have never completed technical school. At the same time not all specialists with higher or particularly with technical secondary edu-

cation can be considered to be part of the intelligentsia—
some of them would more accurately be classified as white-
collar workers.[1]

This, then, is a very general description of the intelligentsia; however, within this category there are a vast number of very different types and groups, many more than in
other classes and strata of society. Not only under capitalism
but in a socialist society as well, there is all the difference in
the world between the head of a large university and a
modest rural schoolteacher, between an academician and a
young scientist, between a popular and successful writer and
his less talented and less successful fellows, between a factory director and an ordinary engineer, between a theater
director and a humble extra. Yet all are equally members of
the intelligentsia. Of course it is true that today we find substantial gradations within the working class as well. In England a highly qualified metalworker is rather different from
an unskilled immigrant laborer.

There are also a great number of intermediate groups
between the intelligentsia and all other classes and strata of
society, and for this reason all definitions are subject to criticism. For example, what about the various technicians who
fall somewhere in between engineers and workers? Maurice
Thorez in his *The Concept of Class and the Historical Role of
the Working Class* (1963) has called them one of the constructive elements of the working class. There is the nurse—
midway between doctors and medical orderlies. Many intermediate groups exist between the intelligentsia and those
described above as "bureaucrats." But the intelligentsia is not
exceptional in this respect—"pure" social strata and classes
do not exist. As a general rule, there are no clear-cut divisions
in society. It is well known, for example, that in tsarist Russia
there was an extensive semiproletarian category that included different types of half peasants, half workers, far
exceeding the numbers of the proletariat proper. Even in
feudal society many intermediate groups existed in between
the landowners and their serfs. The social boundaries between the large capitalist landowner and the independent
farmer are even more blurred. And there are obviously many
intermediate groups between the working class and the bourgeoisie.

In a socialist society it is particularly difficult to define the social boundaries of the intelligentsia because of the efforts being made to overcome the distinction between mental and physical labor. The process is a very complex one, and a detailed examination of it is beyond the framework of this book. The changing relationship between physical and mental labor is a result of the scientific-technical revolution and affects many aspects of social relations in our society.

When speaking of the working class in the traditional sense of that term—primarily manual laborers—it is necessary, of course, to note that in all the industrially developed countries this class is still the major producer of material wealth, the basic productive force of society. The historical services of the working class have been enormous, and the hopes that Marxism places in it have turned out to be fully justified. For it is the working class, the proletariat with its labor in the factories and its struggle against capitalist exploitation, that advanced the development of society and its productive forces. Not only in Russia but also in a number of other countries (benefiting from the Russian example), the working class, united with the peasantry under the leadership of the communist party, has succeeded in coming to power and laying the basis for a socialist society, ensuring at the same time an accelerated development of the forces of production.

Our working class, faced with the enormous task of social reconstruction, enlisted the best elements from among the bourgeois intelligentsia and eventually created a new Soviet intelligentsia, devoted to the building of a socialist and communist society. In many other countries although the struggle of the working class has not yet brought about a socialist revolution, it has nevertheless been able to promote social progress, accelerate the development of the forces of production, and help to strengthen democracy. In developed industrial countries it has led, albeit still within the framework of capitalism, to an improvement in the standard of living and the cultural level of the majority.

It is not only for workers that material and cultural conditions have changed. Scientific and technological progress in all developed countries has led to a rapid decline of the peasantry, both in absolute and relative terms. Although many capitalist countries export a substantial portion of their agricultural produce, the peasantry in those countries makes up less than 10–15 per cent of those gainfully employed. Moreover in developed capitalist countries, where sophisticated machinery and other scientific achievements are employed in agriculture, the general level of farm laborers comes very near to that of the working class. In socialist countries a convergence between peasants and workers in terms of various social indicators is also taking place, as well as a reduction in the number of people working in the agricultural sector.

Scientific and technological progress at first leads to the rapid increase of the working class, both numerically and in relation to other groups in society. At the same time a growing number of people are employed in offices and the service sector. Thus, for example, in the USSR in the postwar years, the numbers of industrial and office workers have increased annually by two to three million. However, in the next stage (and we can see this from the experience of the more developed countries of the West), there may be a tendency first for a relative and then for an absolute decline in the numbers of the working class (i.e., in the original meaning of this term, those doing physical labor).

As the Soviet sociologist E. Arab-Ogli writes:

It has been predicted that by the end of the century in the most highly developed countries less than 5 per cent of all workers will be left in the agricultural sector and approximately 10 per cent in industry—the remainder of those gainfully employed will be concentrated mainly in the "third sphere": in science, education, government, transport, trade, and the social services. In other words, one result of the scientific-technological revolution is that, with the passage of time, there will be more teachers than peasants, more scientists than construction workers, more doctors than miners. . . . If the symbol of the industrial revolution was the power-driven machine, used to manufacture various objects, then the symbol of the scientific-technological revolution will be electronic computers producing information. Within several decades it is in the "third sphere," above all in scientific and experimental activity and in the educational system, that the basic wealth of society will be created. Knowledge in all its diversity, science in the broadest sense of the word, just as Marx predicted, will become not only a direct part of the productive process but indeed the predominant productive force of society. The distribution and consumption of knowledge will acquire greater social and economic significance than the distribution and consumption of goods.[2]

These processes are most evident in the United States, but they are also discernible in the USSR. Thus, while the number of factory and office workers increased by 7.45 times in the Soviet Union in the forty years from 1928 to 1968, in approximately the same period (1928–70) the number of people employed in science and in auxiliary scientific activity has grown more than forty times, and in 1970 amounted to about four million persons. In 1940 for one scientist there were thirty industrial workers; in 1966 this ratio had become one to ten. By the beginning of 1970 there were more than 16 million specialists with higher or secondary education and during the five years of the ninth Five-Year Plan it is intended to prepare nine million more. In 1928 for each engineer or technician there were twenty-seven or twenty-eight workers; in 1966 there were only seven or eight. By 1975 this figure will decline to four or five. Thus both the peasantry and the working class are historically transitional social classes. The idea that communism would be built by manual laborers was clearly an oversimplification; it does not correspond at all to the complexities of the last years of the twentieth century.

The greater role and significance of the intelligentsia results not only from the new importance of engineers, technicians, scientists, and teachers in industry. The enormous growth of the productive forces during the last twenty to twenty-five years has led to a substantial increase in the manufacture of consumer goods. And the rapid increase of production has been achieved in the developed countries despite an appreciable shortening of the working day with a corresponding increase of leisure time. In this situation, the problem of satisfying the needs of the spirit takes on ever-increasing urgency—there is a rapidly growing demand for education, culture, art, etc. The general rise in well-being can be shown by production statistics not only for clothing, furniture, and housing, but also for television sets, radios, tape recorders, cameras, motion-picture cameras, and many other objects that are the basis of what has come to be called mass culture. It has become easier for citizens of the developed countries to care for their health, to raise their children, etc. This is just where the intelligentsia plays a vital role in the satisfaction of cultural and intellectual needs. Thus the last fifteen or twenty years have witnessed a dramatic growth in both the size and the social importance of the intelligentsia—scientists, writers, artists, etc. The number of doctors and teachers has increased several times over.

It is important to note that in our socialist society, the growing ranks of the intelligentsia are recruited not from certain privileged sections of the community but from among the people as a whole. The enormous growth in the demand for their services has brought about a real democratization of the intelligentsia. A similar process has taken place in capitalist countries, where there has been an appreciable increase in the availability of both secondary and higher education for working-class children.

In the USSR and other socialist countries the development of universal secondary education, along with correspondence courses and night schools, is raising average workers to the level of the intelligentsia—i.e., to the level of engineers and technicians. For certain jobs an engineering or technical diploma is even becoming a formal requirement.[3]

In the most developed capitalist countries there has been a growing demand for workers to have a skill and a relatively high standard of general education. In many branches of production our workers also are doing a larger share of mental labor. Thus here too the working class and the bulk of the intelligentsia are increasingly acting not as antagonists but as allies, both in the production process and in the struggle to rebuild society.[4]

By the end of the seventies, according to authoritative forecasts, the size of the intelligentsia will exceed that of the peasantry and by the end of the eighties will be greater than the number of workers engaged in industry and transport. This compels us to seek a new approach in defining the intelligentsia as a specific social group. Today the intelligentsia can no longer be described as a *stratum* serving the interests of the working class. And what kind of social "stratum" will it be when it comes to outnumber the so-called "basic" classes?

A number of recent Soviet publications on the subject are full of oversimplification and bear little relationship to the

real world; they argue that in antagonistic societies, the interests of people engaged in mental and physical labor are in
fact opposed to each other, that they represent hostile social
groups.[5] Yet some sociologists have come to define the intelligentsia as a part of the working class, stressing that it is the
most conscious and advanced section of that class.[6]

"The intelligentsia," writes R. Kosolapov, "is visibly
merging with other categories of industrial workers and turning into an intellectual branch of the working class."[7] In a
different, unpublished article we read that the intelligentsia
"expresses the essence of the working class, that class which
embodies the actively creative power of humanity, its most
profound inner potential, its future." It has become increasingly fashionable to quote Marx on the "all-round worker" in
support of this view. Describing those employed in the factory, Marx divided them into three categories: 1) those who
work directly at the machines; 2) auxiliary workers "who
simply feed the machinery"; and 3) "along with these main
categories there are a relatively small number of people who
regulate the machinery and see to its maintenance and repair, for example, engineers, mechanics, joiners, etc. This
higher half-technically-educated, half-artisan stratum of
workers stands outside the circle of factory workers but is
associated with them. This division of labor is purely technical."[8] And of course Lenin often referred to the "engineering proletariat."

There is nothing wrong with all these definitions, but at
present it would be more accurate to approach the problem of
the role and place of the intelligentsia rather differently.
Although the word "worker," as is obvious, comes from the
verb "to work," it is generally understood to have a narrower
meaning in common usage, i.e., a person who does manual
labor or primarily manual labor or at least work in which
physical labor occupies an appreciable place. Therefore to say
that not only engineers and technicians but also teachers,
scientists, and scholars, etc., are now all new detachments of
the working class hardly makes sense.

For the intelligentsia is not a new social class. We would
be seriously contradicting Marxist doctrine if we tried to show
that a new class called the "intelligentsia" has appeared in
our society. If only because of its enormous heterogeneity, the

intelligentsia cannot be defined in this way. It is not difficult to see that engineers and actors stand in very different relation to the forces of production.

Marxist doctrine proceeds from the assumption that under socialism classes will disappear and that communism means a classless society. This must be our premise when defining the social role of the intelligentsia. A classless society does not mean that there is only a single working class. What takes place is not the transformation of one class into another but rather a complex process in which all classes merge into some new, higher community embracing all those engaged in any kind of work or labor. An important part of this new social community will be those whom we now call the "intelligentsia." By the end of the twentieth century there will no longer be peasants or workers or office workers or intelligentsia in the original sense of those terms. The population of our country will consist largely of well-educated, cultured human beings who will be engaged in industry, in agriculture, in science, in the provision of services, and in cultural activity. They will also participate in the management of their enterprises and institutions, as well as in government and public affairs, both locally and nationally. They will to some extent or other play a role in the creation of the material and spiritual wealth of our society. Of course the assumption is that this will be a society in which the democratic rights and freedoms of all citizens will be strictly observed.

At this stage it will be less a question of socialism than of communism. It is completely possible that by the end of the twentieth or the beginning of the twenty-first century we will arrive at a society which is communist *in its basic parameters*. But it would be a grave mistake to suppose that this mainly depends on technological progress or an increase in the productivity of labor. Much will hinge on how seriously and persistently we carry out the process of democratization.

In the world described above, there is an obvious need to revise the old formula according to which "the working class leads the intelligentsia." This approach was quite correct in the twenties and thirties but it is hardly appropriate today, let alone in the future.

In an article in *Pravda*, R. Kosolapov and P. Simush maintain that the Soviet intelligentsia is still in need of the "guiding and educative influence" of the working class and also of the "party of the working class."[9] It should be recalled, however, that the present rules and program of the CPSU no longer refer to the "party of the working class" but rather to the "party of the whole people." The views of Kosolapov and Simush accord ill even with simple statistics on party membership.

At present party membership is as follows: workers— 40.5 per cent, collective farmers—14.8 per cent, white collar workers—44.7 per cent. And among white collar workers, more than two-thirds are engineers, agronomists, teachers, doctors, scientists, writers, and artists.[10] It is not difficult to imagine the way in which the composition of the CPSU will change in the future.

However this is not to support the completely opposite argument, that today under both capitalism and socialism the intelligentsia is in fact the ruling class. For example the liberal American economist John Galbraith writes: ". . . it is safe to say that the future of what is called modern society depends on how willingly, rationally, and effectively the intellectual community in general and the educational and scientific estate in particular, assume responsibilities for political action and leadership."[11]

Although Galbraith is right to stress the responsibility of the intelligentsia and its growing influence in politics, I cannot agree with his view that political leadership is the prerogative of the intelligentsia. In any case, Soviet society is in a transitional phase and there is no basis for singling out any one class as the "leading" one. Political leadership is at present the task of the Communist Party, which according to its rules must be recruited from the most progressive and politically active representatives of all classes, strata, and groups of Soviet society.

XVI

The Methods of Struggle for Socialist Democracy

This final chapter will deal with methods—how can we act to bring about democratization in the USSR?

The following observations can only be very general because the situation is constantly changing, which means that certain tactics used by the democratic movement at the beginning of its activity are no longer appropriate; on the other hand, new possibilities are constantly suggesting themselves.

At the outset it must be stressed that, in our conditions, the struggle for democratization must be a political one. It is unrealistic to suppose that neo-Stalinism, bureaucracy, and dogmatism can be overcome without a political fight. This is the only way that democracy can be achieved. However, we must make sure all our activities are strictly within the framework of the Constitution. In fact, the struggle has already begun at every level of society, taking different forms according to circumstances. And what is more, one can predict that with each extension of democratic rights, the political struggle will gain momentum, often reaching acute proportions. The transition from any authoritarian regime to a democratic one is always accompanied by an intensification of political passions and pressures.

There is no doubt about the fact that democratization is an objective necessity for our society. Its inevitability is related to economic and technical progress, the scientific and technological revolution and changes that have taken place in the social structure. The country cannot be governed in the old way, and this is beginning to be felt not only by many young government officials but also by certain seemingly dyed-in-the-wool bureaucrats. Yet the fact remains that democratization will not come about automatically nor will it be handed down "from above." It will occur only as a response to objective demands and determined efforts.

It is also unrealistic to suppose that a limited amount of democracy can be introduced which would apply to only one or two "approved" political trends or movements. Certainly all political groups, including all the conservative and reactionary ones, will try to use democratic freedoms to increase their own influence. The more circumstances seem to be turning against them, the harder they will struggle to maintain their political position. Therefore the presence of political conflict contains an element of risk, but risk is inevitable if there is to be a transition to a new and higher stage. Only the experience of struggle can foster the political activism and initiative of the masses and encourage democratic habits throughout the social fabric.

In democratic conditions, political struggle presupposes a comparatively free confrontation between different points of view, which obviously would provide a much better education in civic responsibility than does the present show of ostensible unity. We must only see to it that the political struggle is waged responsibly in forms that reasonable people can accept. Mutual destructiveness should be avoided; there must be a basic tolerance for those with whom one disagrees. Only this kind of open political contest can offer our people a proper political education, teaching them not only to express their own opinions but also to heed the views of others. This is the only way to establish a convention of ethical behavior in politics, to eliminate uncompromising sectarianism, intolerance, and elitist complacency. Only in conditions of overt political struggle will it be possible for genuine political figures to emerge, men who are capable of guiding the construction of a developed socialist and communist society in an

efficient way. Thoughtful foreign observers who are sympa-
thetic toward our country understand this very well. "Soviet
society," wrote G. Boffa, the Italian communist, "stands in
need of the establishment of democratic methods. The experience of the post-Stalin decades has shown that this cannot
come about without political struggle, a struggle against those
individuals and groups who openly or in secret have resisted
and obstructed the policies initiated at the Twentieth Congress, a struggle against their theories and attitudes. But at
all times there must be scrupulous regard for democratic
principles. The words 'political struggle' evoke uneasiness in
the Soviet Union, an out-of-date reaction, as if there were
some real threat to the unity of society. But surely periods of
political struggle are the greatest source of progress in both
thought and action."[1] This is an entirely reasonable view. If
socialist democracy is to be firmly established, it must be
defended by the whole people, possible only after all have
passed through the school of political struggle by actually
participating in the fight to extend and strengthen socialist
democracy.

I speak of struggle and pressure coming from the people
and particularly from the intelligentsia; however, this does
not exclude the possibility of initiative appearing at the top. If
moves toward democratization were taken at the higher levels
of party and state it would be an important guarantee that
subsequent controversy involving so many difficult political
problems would take place in the least painful manner and
would be kept within bounds. But for the time being we do
not have such a leadership; fine words about socialist democracy are not supported by actions. Yet the experience of
Hungary, where over a period of years there has been a
process of real democratization directed from "above," does
show that cooperation between those "above" and those "below" is a perfectly viable possibility. Something similar happened in Poland in 1971–72 but only after a very bitter and
dangerous political crisis, which could have been avoided by a
more rational leadership. The Czechoslovak experience of
1968–69, its achievements and failures, must also be carefully studied.

It is by no means impossible that pressure from below
could lead to various changes in the apparatus of power, to

the appearance of influential groups that would support democratization. I have been criticized for expressing this view. One response to a preliminary version of this book was an accusation of utopianism: "You believe that the leadership would support a certain degree of democratization. But this would amount to the leadership liquidating itself, and the whole of political history confirms the unreality of such an expectation. No government withdraws of its own free will. . . . Your ideas are harmful, because they create illusions about the ease with which your proposed programme of reform might be realized. You suggest that because of changing social and political conditions, fresh forces will become part of the *apparat* and transform its bureaucratic style. But this only encourages the false idea of an automatic and spontaneous process—in reality these fresh forces will inevitably encounter fierce resistance."

Of course I know that democratization cannot come about automatically and have no illusions about the difficulty of the struggle. But all the same, it is wrong to exclude the possibility of an alliance between the best of the intelligentsia supported by the people and the most forward-looking individuals in the governing *apparat*. The author of "Words Are Also Deeds" writes:

Because the language of the party-democrats' programme is loyal and will not shock, it can and should appeal to "consumers" within the party and state *apparat*. Our words can become their deeds, particularly in view of the growing emphasis on science and technology in the higher reaches of government. . . . Those endowed with expert qualifications, energy, and practical sense must be encouraged to revolt against the ignoramuses, scoundrels, and idlers who have no business being where they are.

But he also suggests that "we must promise a special approach to the problem of expropriating the exploiters within the bureaucracy, an approach that would on the whole avoid abrupt dismissals, let alone reprisals, but would rely instead on the mobility brought about by democratic reform."

The realization of a serious programme of democratic change must be a comparatively slow and gradual process. The actual time period will be determined by many factors, but it should take not less than ten or fifteen years. First of all, the democratic movement in our country is still too weak and would be unable to achieve rapid political changes. Secondly, we are still very much in the process of formulating political programmes. Therefore as the democratic movement evolves, there must also be a development of socialist political thought, the creation of new political doctrines on the basis of Marxism-Leninism which will analyze our changed political and economic circumstances. Without this kind of theoretical preparation, without a serious programme—even if it is discussed only in a relatively narrow circle—any kind of rapid political change would inevitably create overwhelming contradictions and disarray. Overhasty reform can also cause problems within the socialist bloc (as the experience of Czechoslovakia has shown). Improvisation in politics can easily result in anarchy. But although diametrically opposed to authoritarian abuse of power, anarchy offers little prospect for elementary human rights and freedoms.

Reform must also be gradual because of the peculiar nature of bureaucracy. As Lenin often pointed out, there is no way to "lance the bureaucratic boil, to wipe bureaucracy from the face of the earth"—the only possibility is cure. "Surgery in this case," wrote Lenin, "is absurd, it cannot work. There can only be a slow healing process—other alternatives are fraudulent or naïve." This advice should not be forgotten. It is essential for us to work out a democratic platform. But at the same time we must make an effort to accumulate information, educate people and win them over, step by step. And it all will take time.[2]

There is now a very widespread feeling that the way we live and work has become untenable, and this applies not just to the intelligentsia but also to much of the working class, white collar workers, and perhaps some of the peasantry. But there is still no mass movement demanding change or democratic reform, and without this it is difficult to count on any rapid transformation of our political system or on a change of attitude at the top.[3]

As for the ways and means of political struggle, they must be absolutely legal and constitutional.[4] There are certain extreme groups that believe in the use of illegal methods including, for example, the organization of underground printing presses. Several years ago one group did manage this, not far from Moscow, and they succeeded in printing one or two leaflets. But very soon the press was discovered and its organizers arrested. Some dissident circles become involved with very dubious foreign groups and even tolerate indirect links with an émigré anti-Soviet organization like the NTS,* distributing journals and books published by them. In certain provincial cities popular discontent led to isolated acts of violence which can only be condemned. The use of unscrupulous means must be avoided at all cost, as a matter of principle and also because in practical terms it plays into the hands of the neo-Stalinists and reactionaries, making it easier for them to discredit absolutely valid demands in the eyes of public opinion. Of course we do not yet possess many of the most important rights and freedoms obligatory in a genuine socialist state which would make it easier to struggle for democracy. However, it is to some extent the case that we still have not learned to make the most of those rights and freedoms that really do exist already.

There is an indissoluble link between means and ends in the struggle for democratization, writes Valentin Turchin in *The Inertia of Fear:*

There must be an open and honest discussion of all problems, an appeal to reason and conscience for mutual understanding, and of course a rejection of all forms of violence and dishonesty. . . . We must learn to observe our own laws. We must bring our deeds into line with our words. The Constitution of the USSR guarantees basic democratic freedoms, and so let us claim them as our right. . . . We must avoid false starts and oppose moves that would alienate people or sow mistrust or fear. We must argue, explain, persuade, and compel people to think—and yet again—explain, demonstrate, and attempt to convince.

Turchin is undoubtedly right—truth is a very special weapon of the democratic movement. The honest word has become the greatest source of strength for the civically minded intelligentsia.

The author of "Words Are Also Deeds" argues that "future revolutionary change in our country to a decisive extent may be dependent on *words*. Ideas that take posession of the masses are now almost directly capable of becoming a 'material force.' "

* Popular Labor Alliance, émigré organization based in West Germany.
    —Trans.

Forty years ago the following six precepts were very popular among the timid rank and file of the party: "Don't think. If you think, don't speak. If you speak, don't write. If you write, don't publish. If you publish, don't sign. If you sign—recant." It is hardly surprising that Stalin's abuse of power met no opposition in such quarters. But times have changed and there is a new generation. Many people now live according to a very different code. We must think and think again, seek the truth, publish it, even if only in typescript, and circulate our ideas and suggestions although even today it is sometimes necessary to remain anonymous or use a pseudonym, and this must not be condemned.

It is understandable that in the first stage of our democratic movement literature and art played a major role in the diffusion of truthful information and honest views. It was a way of reaching the widest public and was also the most flexible means of influencing people's intellect and emotion. It is somehow easier to begin questioning commonly accepted dogmas with the help of images rather than theoretical generalizations. In the period just after the Twenty-second Congress, many of our progressive writers, directors, and people in the world of art were in the first ranks of those opposed to Stalinism and dogmatism.

However, it has become increasingly obvious that there is now a need for specialized philosophical, sociological, political, historical, and economic studies from a Marxist position which reflect the enormous changes that have taken place in the world during the last fifty years. In his essay "From Intellectual Ferment to an Intellectual Movement," A. Antipov calls for an intensive exchange of ideas:

It has now become a matter of urgency—we must undertake a fearless examination of our social organism. This can only be done together, in conditions of free and lively discussion. We have mastered the art of speech—it is time to learn how to write.[5]

A. Mikhailov in an article called "Thoughts à propos of the Liberal Campaign of 1968," stresses the need for serious theoretical work:

The regime will not continue for very much longer in its present form. Our task is not to finish it off at any price as rapidly as possible, but rather to prepare the way for an acceptable successor.

When it comes to theory, however, the opposition is almost as impotent as the government. If this situation continues right up to the turning point (one way or another it will come, whatever the behavior of the opposition and most probably within the foreseeable future), the results could be deplorable. . . . The public should be given a very clear idea of what is meant by democratic socialism. . . . We must have an explicit programme that deals with such questions as the organization of production, the political structure, the distribution of income, the regulation of social processes, etc.

"Our society," writes yet another author, K. Korostelev,

is in need of a positive platform that will unite people ideologically and politically in the struggle to democratize the party and the whole structure of government. An alliance between the party-democrats and the progressive elements of the intelligentsia cannot be based on anti-Stalinism alone. It is essential to spell out a realistic and genuine socialist programme. . . . Let us have no illusions—it will be a protracted, stubborn fight which will most certainly claim its victims. . . . For this reason it is crucial that the basic aims are clearly understood.

The author of "Words Are Also Deeds" explicitly calls for a new "Marxist Library," which would include a programme, theoretical works, and propaganda materials to support the broad ideological struggle.

We might be able to do no more than carry out this theoretical task, but this would be no mean achievement. Then in a situation of developing crisis, a programmatic document could be submitted to the leadership of the party and to public opinion in the name of a *broad* circle of authoritative representatives mainly from the academic, scientific and party intelligentsia *with a demand for all-party discussion*.

In this way, he argues, the means of transformation become one with the goal, foreshadowing the democratic standards that will come to prevail in the country and in the party. Discussion is the only way to ensure that social change takes place without fundamental breakdown. He envisages the need for "a resolute struggle against even the smallest hint of antisocialist or simply antisocial attitudes bound to surface in certain sections of the party and particularly in the press, radio, and television." Once democratic forces began to prevail, new policies would be consolidated by an *extraordinary party congress* followed by specific legislation.

Alternatively he suggests a second possibility—that a less severe crisis would result in discussion only at the top.

If in the end a majority favored reform, there would be a certain extension of freedom and it would be our role to make the most of it. . . . As the discussion developed, it would inevitably reach the limit of what was allowed and then pass beyond that point. If restrictions were to follow, we would return to the original position with all the obvious consequences that this entailed.

A third variant would be the defeat of the democratic or even of the technocratic trend, with subsequent political repression on a vast scale. I believe, however, that this is unlikely (the first scenario is also improbable).

This brings us to the question of Stalinism: To what extent is there still the possibility that political terror *on a massive scale* will be revived? There is also the matter of Stalin worship, but this is secondary because a mass repression of dissidents could take place without any official glorification of Stalin.

In the most general terms, there can only be an affirmative answer. Yes, a revival of Stalinism is possible, because we are still without any guarantees for the maintenance of the rule of law and without stable government machinery, supported by the whole people and capable of preventing the abuse of power. But how likely is such a development? In order to answer this question it is necessary to examine various factors that will either promote or alternatively act as an obstacle to antidemocratic trends. This will entail a certain amount of repetition of what has already been said above in other contexts.

First of all, there are the elements that favor the development of neo-Stalinism:

1. Stalinism has never been completely eradicated from the political and social life of the USSR. After the Twentieth and Twenty-second congresses the extreme forms of arbitrary power and despotism were removed. But at the time the people and the party were told just a small part of the truth about Stalin's crimes. The majority of those who played an active and deliberate role have not been brought to justice

either in the courts or before the party. Many prominent party members who became Stalin's victims have not been rehabilitated, and almost none of those who survived and were rehabilitated and returned to their families, including some of the party's oldest members, have been allowed to participate actively in the political and social life of the country.

2. As we all know, even after the Twentieth and Twenty-second congresses, there were still many cases of illegal administrative, party, and judicial repression; arbitrariness and subjectivism also continued in economic, cultural, and foreign policy. In fact, a regime of personal power was established with the beginning of a new personality cult. After the October Plenum there was a substantial reduction of arbitrary behavior in the economy and foreign affairs, yet even today the economic situation of the country is still extremely unstable. In recent years there have been more frequent instances of illegal administrative reprisal and punishment and an intensification of censorship, not to mention the deliberate campaign in certain circles aimed at a rehabilitation of Stalin.

3. As in the past, it is still the case that a majority of the people, the party, and the intelligentsia are politically passive. On the other hand, extreme economic and political centralization has been preserved. The bureaucratic element is still far too strong in all the organs of power, and there are no effective mechanisms for supervision from below; the authorities remain cut off from the people. There is also a dangerous dissociation between the leading strata of party and state and the most influential circles of the intelligentsia.

4. A large number of *apparat* officials are not in favor of democratization; they support "firmer" leadership and seek a way out of growing economic and political problems through greater centralization and a tightening of the screws.

5. In recent years, conservative military leaders have had a growing influence on domestic and foreign policy—they also give overt support to the campaign for the rehabilitation of Stalin. The role of the security organs has also been increasing, and their staff has been considerably enlarged.

6. The neo-Stalinists and conservatives in pursuing their goals are trying to exploit isolated manifestations of the "ultra-left": nationalist, antisocialist, and anarchist positions that do exist among a small section of our youth and intelli-

gentsia, usually as the response of politically immature but completely honest and sincere people to the crimes of Stalin.

7. There has been a growing anti-Soviet mood abroad, even in many traditionally friendly countries. Communism, in its present Soviet version, has become more isolated morally and politically. This has had the effect of encouraging insularity in Soviet ideological bodies, an impatience toward criticism or dialogue, a rejection of normal forms of ideological struggle.

Thus in recent years we have witnessed an obvious shift to the right. But I do not believe it is an irreversible trend or that it will last very long, because within our country and in the world at large there are many very crucial factors exerting an influence in the opposite direction. I shall list only some of them:

1. The scientific-technological revolution, which has begun to come into its own even in the USSR, inevitably brings about changes in the social structure and its economic base that are incompatible with Stalinist or neo-Stalinist forms of political leadership. Stalinism obstructs the free exchange of information, prevents the advancement of the most able and gifted individuals, and is an enormous impediment to the development of the productive forces of society. In the final analysis this growing contradiction can be resolved only if the political superstructure is brought into line with the material base.

2. A rapid growth is taking place in the numbers and influence of the intelligentsia, a group that cannot work effectively without freedom of information and freedom of discussion, i.e., without intellectual liberty. Moreover, as the structure of our economy becomes more complex and hence more sensitive to incompetent interference, it is no longer possible to liquidate tens of thousands of technical specialists and administrators in one year and replace them with Stakhanovite workers,* very worthy individuals, perhaps, but entirely inadequate in terms of their technical and political qualifications. Therefore a mass repression of the intelli-

---

* Aleksei Stakhanov, a miner who exceeded the established output quota many times over, became a symbol for the official drive to raise labor productivity in the mid-thirties (the "Stakhanovite movement").—Trans.

gentsia is today fraught with danger—it would mean an enormous brake on economic development, and the USSR would remain far behind the advanced countries.

3. The arms race is becoming an increasingly onerous burden. Growing military expenditure damages the economy, and this makes a change in foreign policy objectively necessary—there must be improved relations with Western countries and with Japan. But stable changes in foreign policy necessitating a display of greater tolerance can hardly come about in the absence of similar concessions at home.

4. The scientific-technological revolution inevitably raises the cultural and educational level of the whole population. And this in turn leads to the growth of an interest in politics, and of participation, by the working population as a whole.

5. There is a slow, still hardly perceptible, but irreversible process of change taking place in the psychology and consciousness of the public. A new "spirit of the times" has gradually evolved, an atmosphere in which certain political ideas, even if authorized and disseminated by the authorities, cannot have very great appeal. For example, after the collapse of two "personality cults," it would be rather difficult to create a new cult of some new personality successfully, however much effort was exerted by the official propaganda machine. Even at the top there are misgivings about any individual becoming too powerful or influential. But it would be extremely risky to embark on a course of mass political repression without preparing the people first by means of a preliminary propaganda campaign, and a cult figure is essential for the right kind of atmosphere.

6. Neo-Stalinism in all respects is a much more unattractive proposition than the original Stalinism was. Coming forward as the heir to Lenin, Stalin could exploit widespread post-October political enthusiasm; he was able to deceive and win over many able and talented persons who in turn made the final victory of Stalinism easier. It was not only a question of political terror, it was also a demagogic system that in many respects functioned with absolute success. At any event, a large proportion of the intelligentsia and youth were a source of rather solid support for the Stalinist system of power. The neo-Stalinists do not have any popular, tal-

ented, or able people on their side. Their faction is headed by persons who are both morally and intellectually inferior.

7. Particularly among the intelligentsia, certain nonconformist scientists, writers, and artists have become very popular figures. A number of social and political trends opposed to Stalinism and neo-Stalinism have come to the fore. We have begun to witness the appearance of "society" (in the very special meaning of that word—i.e., numerous unofficial centers of intellectual and moral influence that already have an effect on public opinion and will play an even greater role in the future).

8. A steady intensification of the international division of labor is going on in today's world, embracing both socialist and capitalist countries. This makes the development of the most varied economic, cultural, and scientific contacts with all countries of the world even more necessary. Therefore we cannot ignore world public opinion, since to a certain extent it will determine whether or not such contacts are effective.

9. The position of the CPSU in the international communist movement has also changed. Even many of those communist parties that continue to recognize the leading role of the CPSU in the world revolutionary movement are no longer inclined to give blind support to everything that takes place within the USSR. Undemocratic actions by the Soviet authorities are frequently subject to sharp criticism in the press controlled by these communist parties, criticism that cannot simply be ignored by the leadership of the CPSU.

10. At present an international system of mass communication is coming into being based on new technical achievements. Ideas and information penetrate state boundaries with ever greater ease, and no developed country can isolate itself from this constant flow coming in from all sides. Thus with the development of technology, freedom of speech is becoming a real fact to be reckoned with, and this very much restricts the possibilities for arbitrary rule.

I am convinced that in time this second group of factors will gain the upper hand in the political and social life of our country.

When it comes to theoretical work and the creation of new programmatic documents, we inevitably must examine the contemporary state of Marxist-Leninist theory. Marxism emerged and developed as the scientific ideology of the working class in the middle and second half of the nineteenth century—i.e., before the appearance of imperialism and the era of proletarian revolutions.

From the beginning, Marxism was always a doctrine with many different aspects: it included political economy, philosophy, and a theory of scientific communism (socialism). However, in that period the chief task of Marxism was to analyze the nature and internal mechanisms of capitalist society, capitalist exploitation, and the class struggle between the proletariat and the bourgeoisie. These were the problems to which Marx and Engels devoted most of their attention. But the founders of Marxism always stressed the continuously creative character of their doctrine, that it was incomplete and would have to be constantly perfected and developed. And in Lenin's words: "We in no way regard the theory of Marx as something finished and inviolate; we are convinced, on the contrary, that it only laid the foundation stone of that science which socialists must develop further in all directions if they do not want to be left behind by life."[6]

For any social scientist this approach to social theory is self-evident. Every theory originates from a more or less simplified model of reality; without such simplification it would be impossible to have any theories at all. Marxism also contains many deliberate simplifications. Models of reality involve abstraction from certain concrete situations and are bound to be simpler than reality itself. Thus, discussing the concept of the future society in the works of Marx and Engels, it was none other than Lenin who wrote: "It is . . . society in the abstract which can only be realized by way of a number of diverse attempts to create one kind of socialist state or another."[7] It is hardly surprising that all attempts to put into practice what was recommended by Marx and Engels led to results that partly corresponded to theoretical prediction but in certain respects were different. It is also natural that the followers of Marx should introduce certain refinements and elaboration of the theory in accordance with their own subsequent experience. It is not a question of the revision but of the development of Marxism.

We know that this process was to some extent already taking place in the works of Plekhanov, Kautsky, Mehring,

Bebel, Lafarge, and a number of other disciples and followers of Marx. However, side by side with the development of certain aspects of Marxism at the end of the nineteenth century, there were also instances of opportunist distortions of it. Genuine development of revolutionary Marxism is primarily associated with the name of Lenin. Leninism is in varying degrees a development and continuation of all the basic aspects of Marxism. In accordance, however, with the specific contours of his own time, Lenin placed special emphasis on the theory of socialist revolution and the dictatorship of the proletariat. The international significance of Leninism is that it is in fact Marxism of the *era of the beginning of imperialism and proletarian revolution*. However Leninism, like Marxism, is not a finished doctrine. As in the case of any other theory, it too is in need of constant improvement and development. Therefore it is wrong to be dogmatic about the universal applicability of Marxism and Leninism, ignoring the fact that any scientific theory or ideology has inevitable limitations.

Leninism did not, of course, arise in Russia accidentally; at the beginning of the twentieth century Russia became the center of the world revolutionary movement and then the first country in the world to experience a victorious socialist revolution. But the very circumstance, that Leninism came into being and evolved in Russia, naturally meant that along with certain universal truths it would include propositions largely applicable to Russia alone, and not very appropriate for conditions existing in the developed countries of the capitalist West or in the backward noncapitalist areas of the world. Lenin himself often made this point. It is entirely obvious, for example, that "the peasant question" in England or the United States, where capitalist relations were dominant and those working in agriculture were a minority of the population, was rather different from Russia. But the peasant question in China or India was and remains no less dissimilar— the peasantry included the overwhelming majority of the population, and the weight of foreign exploitation and feudal survivals was even more oppressive than in Russia.

Another limitation of Leninism comes from Lenin's inevitably having been influenced by the circumstances that existed in the first quarter of the twentieth century, both within Russia and throughout the world. Many of the later problems of the revolutionary movement could not have been foreseen and certainly cannot be resolved by Leninism, although they are often no less complicated or fundamental than those that Marx and Engels and then Lenin had to deal with many decades ago. It also must be remembered that Leninism as both an ideology and a scientific theory did not and could not include a general analysis of all contemporary social problems without exception. And so, guided by the doctrines and methodology of Marx and Lenin, scholars must continue and extend the analysis. Unfortunately this task has not always been carried out as well as it might have been.

One cannot but observe, moreover, that both the passage of time and further scientific study have revealed a degree of inaccuracy and even error in certain statements and assertions by Marx, Engels, and Lenin. For example, a number of positions assumed to have universal validity have proved to be applicable only to given periods and situations. Indeed some of their views and judgments were inadequate even at the time.

Of course mention of the limitations of Marxism-Leninism refers here to the classical texts. As a whole frame of reference, as a scientific theory, Marxism-Leninism extends beyond the works and writings of its founders and must be developed and expanded to overcome those anomalies inherent in any scientific theory. Marxism can in this respect be compared with Darwinism (Engels was very fond of this analogy). As everyone knows, Darwinism provided the foundation and starting point of scientific biology. But afterwards it was only natural for other scientists and pupils of Darwin to develop the theory rapidly in all directions. As a general rule, a study of the history of human thought shows us that only unscientific theories and doctrines retain their original form for centuries, becoming the basis of some kind of religious belief.

Unfortunately, during the last fifty years there has been little development of Marxism-Leninism. Therefore it would be rather easy either to misrepresent the doctrine or to turn it into a system of dogma very much resembling a new religion. Marxism-Leninism did in fact suffer extensive distortion during the years of the Stalin cult. As a result, the ideology of our party and the theory of Marxism-Leninism are out of touch with rapidly changing conditions in the modern world. This has resulted in an enormous gap between theory and practice in many areas.

Therefore the most important task that now faces the communist movement is that of sifting out all the perversions and distortions that have become part of Marxism-Leninism since the death of Lenin. We must also develop the theory in all directions. For social scientists in socialist countries, this will entail the creation of a broad and comprehensive theory of socialist society, the study of its specific features and short-comings and the ways in which it can be improved. We must analyze the changes in our society at different stages of its development. The political economy of socialism must be given more depth, economics made more concrete, while political science grounded in Marxism-Leninism will in effect have to be created from scratch. There must be serious study of the political and social problems of the socialist common-wealth. How can socialist democracy be developed? What difficulties arise in the creation of state and party structures under socialism? In many of these spheres we still have only the outward semblance of a truly scientific approach.

Then there are the capitalist countries, and here Marxist social scientists must analyze those social and political changes that have taken place as a result of the scientific-technological revolution, the breakup of colonial empires, and the rise of an international socialist bloc. There should be more serious study of the present situation and probable evolution of the Third World. Of general concern for all Marx-ists are the problems related to mutual relations between socialist and capitalist countries and also between advanced and underdeveloped areas of the world.

Lenin himself developed and perfected Marxism in ac-cordance with the conditions of his own time. It was he who resolved many of the new problems that arose in the first quarter of the twentieth century, when Marx and Engels were no longer alive. Therefore until 1924 and perhaps even later to some extent, one can speak of Leninism as the contempo-rary form of Marxism. But the fact remains that more than half a century has gone by since Lenin's death. During this period the world has been transformed to a much greater degree than in the forty years between the death of Marx (1883) and the death of Lenin. If Marxism, after the death of its creator, needed so much elaboration, then how much truer it must be for Leninism. But the task has never been carried out. Therefore the cliché that represents Leninism to be Marxism of the *present* is essentially inviting us to accept a Marxism of *yesterday;* it simply turns Marxism and Leninism into a system of dogma. Unfortunately, *there is no such thing as Marxism and Leninism of the present day*. Contemporary Marxism consists of separate strands that bear very little relation to each other.

One should also mention the fact that Lenin did not concern himself with all the problems dealt with by Marx and Engels. Certain questions, so urgent in the middle of the nineteenth century, seemed less so by the beginning of the twentieth. Yet some of them have again become extremely relevant today: the question of democracy, for example—how to implement and develop it. Of course our party has had very little historical experience in this area. Statements by Lenin on the subject are inadequate, often one-sided and applicable only to a very limited period of our history. And it can even be said that some of Lenin's views on democracy are open to question. Therefore we must turn for guidance to the works of Marx and Engels themselves. Restricting ourselves to Leninism alone implies an impoverishment, a limitation of the theory.

In order to develop Marxism-Leninism we must overcome the tendency toward opportunist distortion. In my view, there are today two basic types of opportunists. One group calls for a revision of the basic tenets of Marxism-Leninism and in this way would emasculate it. The representatives of this trend are bent on belittling the achievements of socialism while exaggerating the positive qualities of contemporary capitalism. A variety of this "right" opportunism made its appearance in Czechoslovakia in 1968, although it was in no way a major component of the "Czech experiment."

However, I believe that the main danger confronting the communist movement is opportunism of the "left": Maoism in China and neo-Stalinism in the USSR (and also certain "gentler" forms of our own domestic dogmatism). This is the chief threat because it springs from very influential circles within Soviet communism and usually is disseminated through the mass media. Of course both the neo-Stalinists and the Maoists are attempting to wage a struggle against those whom they call "revisionists." But their opposition is based on reactionary and dogmatic positions and does not promote the development of Marxism-Leninism. They usually uphold obsolete theory, all that is most in need of reconsideration and development. And even more frequently they defend ideas that were never either Marxist or Leninist but were only camouflaged by Marxist terminology. Therefore the dogmatic critics who attack "right" revisionism do not achieve their goals; they offer no convincing refutation and their efforts are often counterproductive, promoting the development and popularity of revisionist doctrine. Today dogmatism only serves to discredit Marxism, particularly in the eyes of the intelligentsia and young people.

Dogmatic critics brand as opportunists not only people who really are maintaining opportunist positions, but also those who are striving for a development of Marxism-Leninism in complete accordance with its underlying spirit and methodology. Thus dogmatism (not to speak of retrograde neo-Stalinism) works to prevent the evolution and modernization of Marxism-Leninism and very much weakens its standing in the contemporary world. Therefore our fundamental theoretical task is not only to develop Marxism-Leninism but also to struggle resolutely against every variety of dogmatism, neo-Stalinism, and also "left" and "right" opportunism. This is the essential meaning of the decisions taken at the Twentieth and Twenty-second Party congresses.

Of course the struggle for democratization in our country is not only a matter of theory. Concrete tactics are also immensely important: how shall we deal with cases of abuse, with violations of democratic standards and contempt for the rights and freedoms of citizens? Unfortunately, such manifestations of arbitrary bureaucratic behavior are still very frequent both in Moscow and in the provinces and cannot be ignored by public opinion. And even though protests are very rarely effective, this does not mean that we should give up all hope. Perhaps it would be appropriate, however, to reconsider the forms of protest. The peculiarities of each individual case should determine the way in which disagreement can best be expressed, without exposing the still extremely weak democratic movement to too much risk. At the same time it must be remembered that silence could be disastrous. In his article on the liberal campaign of 1968, A. Mikhailov criticizes its naïveté: "Liberal-romantics without a positive programme engaged in protest. Their approach was largely negative." Although there can be no doubt about their good intentions and moral courage, they often acted irresponsibly and in this way helped to discredit the idea of opposition.

I cannot agree. Of course there were blunders and mistakes, understandable in view of the inexperience of the movement. However, it evoked a profound response and had tremendous moral significance (although I believe it is inappropriate to repeat exactly the same form of activity today). Mikhailov argues that until a viable alternative to the regime has been devised, isolated protests against injustice are pointless and sometimes harmful. But the whole campaign of protests, starting in 1966, stimulated and continues to encourage the creation of positive programmes by different political trends.

On the question of organization, a memorandum by A. Slavin called "Some Notes on the Soviet Democratic Movement" (1970) circulated in *samizdat;* it criticized existing forms of the movement in defense of civil rights and appealed for the formation of a conspiratorial organization that could "carry the masses with it." An anonymous leaflet appeared in response, rejecting Slavin's views. Called "Against an Underground Party," it was a very strongly worded protest against the creation of any kind of conspiratorial group or organization. The author believes (and not without foundation) that today's highly developed techniques and methods of detection leave little hope for the success of a conspiratorial organization, inevitably the work of a few amateurs.

Obviously the party-democrats should maintain links. And not all of their activities should immediately become public knowledge. However, at present one of the main rules of the democratic movement must be a commitment (in a moral sense, of course) not to use unconstitutional or illegal methods of struggle in support of its aims. This does not exclude the possibility of creating legal organizations such as the Initiative Group or the Human Rights Committee already discussed above.

In his article "Obstacles in the Way of Democratization

and How to Overcome Them," E. Gnedin proposes the creation of a voluntary association whose task it would be to work
out problems connected with the rationalization and democratization of political and social life. He writes:

Since in all areas of social life we are at a new stage that requires
democratization, and in view of the fact that bureaucratic distortions affect every aspect of our life, the membership of the pro-
jected voluntary association should include representatives from
different professions; the results of its work could in fact prove to
be valuable even for various state and party institutions. Discussion in such a society would be open. The results of its investigations would be published and available for general use.

Gnedin believes that such an association should be created
not in secret but with the permission of the appropriate
authorities. Although this is a rather dubious proposition
today, in the future, if a certain amount of change takes
place, such an association could be formed and would play a
very useful role.

Speaking in the name of the party-democrats, we of
course should think about the relation of our movement to
other opposition trends and groups. It is unrealistic to think in
terms of a common programme uniting all the opposition
trends (as A. Mikhailov has suggested), because it would
have to appeal both to Marxists and to members of the Orthodox Church, and clearly this is not possible. The important
thing is that the whole movement, united by a single democratic purpose, despite differences in approach, does not
waste vital energy on mutual squabbles and infighting; this
could only be to the advantage of some future Bonaparte.

An anonymous *samizdat* article called "The Ethical Approach" urges communists and social democrats not only to
seek common ground with all those fighting for freedom of
thought and national rights, but also to strive to understand
the truth of others as they see it. The unknown author also
makes the following crucial point:

. . . it is particularly important to try to understand the enemy.
Antihumanism grows out of real soil and is nourished by the same
reality as humanism . . . we must discover, therefore, the underlying motivations, we must understand its "truth" and unmask it
in order to deprive the enemy of its source of strength.

Coming to the end of this book on socialist democracy, I would like to compare our society and ideology with a building that continues to grow taller despite its antiquated, decayed, even rotten foundation. There are still firm supports, but they are becoming less reliable. One hardly needs to stress the dangers of such basic social and ideological weakness. There are, however, a number of people in the leadership who prefer to ignore all the cracks in the foundation of our social structure and all the flaws in our ideology. They tend simply to evade all difficult problems, dreading change and refusing to countenance repairs to the foundation of the house in which we live. Others in the leadership try to salvage and restore to their previous position in the structure totally rotted supports in the shape of dogmas long since discredited. And there are some who see only minor defects in our social fabric and attempt to put them right, but far too late and far too slowly. This means that new cracks constantly appear in the edifice even faster than existing ones can be eliminated.

There are, however, some bold spirits, well aware of all the faults of our society and ideology, who demand the *immediate* removal of all the flawed or weakened props that shore up our social system, even though they still have nothing with which to replace those dilapidated parts of the foundation that continue after a fashion, however badly, to support the enormous and still growing structure above. They can propose nothing better than to prop it up by makeshift, untried means, apparently untroubled by the possibility that the whole building might come tumbling down.

Finally, there are people who have no desire whatsoever to live in this particular building and would prefer to move to another one. They are therefore not interested in strengthening the foundation of our society or reconstructing it at any level. Such people should be allowed to change their place of residence.

But I cannot myself share any of these attitudes. Without being blind to the shortcomings and flaws in the very foundations of our social structure and ideology, we should fairly quickly, but also with the utmost caution, remove all the decayed elements at the base of the structure, replacing them with something much more durable. At the same time attempts must be made to improve conditions on all levels higher up. The whole process must take place gradually, step by step. Something new can only be fashioned out of what has come before in previous stages of social development. This painstaking and difficult task must, in my opinion, be the main objective of the democratic movement, which has arisen in the healthiest section of the party and includes a constantly growing number of honest individuals.

It is in no way a question of destroying the values of the October Revolution. Rather we must restore and purify them; they must be reinforced and built upon. Only if there is a systematic and consistent democratization of the whole of our political and social life on a socialist basis will our country be able to regain its role and influence among the progressive forces of the world.

Notes

I. The Soviet Union During the 1960's

1. Electric power increased from 292 billion kilowatts in 1960 to 740 billion in 1970. During the same period, oil production grew from 148 to 353 million tons; gas, from 47 to 200 billion cubic meters. Coal production went up from 510 to 624 million tons. Steel output in 1970 totaled 116 million tons, as opposed to 65 million tons in 1960. The production of mineral fertilizer quadrupled—from 14 to 55 million tons; production of synthetic resins and plastics increased fivefold—from 312,000 to 1,672,000 tons; of synthetic fibers almost threefold—from 211,000 to 623,000 tons; of metal cutting machines from 156,000 to 202,000 per year. The capacity of turbines almost doubled. In 1970 our industry was equipped with 579 new complete automatic and semi-automatic production lines for the manufacture of tools, as against 174 in 1960. Equipment for automation worth 3,102,000 rubles was manufactured in 1970, as against 1,182,000 rubles' worth in 1960. Production of equipment for the chemical industry more than doubled. There was a significant increase in the manufacture of machinery needed by the oil industry; also of rolling stock, of diesel and electric locomotives, trucks and passenger cars, tractors, combines, excavators, and almost all other kinds of equipment and machinery.

The production of cement increased from 45.5 to 95 million tons and of reinforced concrete used in building from 30 to 85 million tons. A substantial amount of housing was constructed, making it possible for more than 100 million persons to be given better accommodations. The total amount of living space available in the cities grew from 858,000,000 to 1,592,000,000 cubic meters.

The production of fabrics of all sorts increased from 8 to 10 billion meters as measured by length; knitwear garments of all kinds from 964 to 1,338 million items, leather footwear from 584 to 1,236 million pairs. In 1970, 22 million wrist watches were manufactured, as against 16 million in 1960. The production of radios and record players increased from 4 to 8 million, television sets from 1.7 to 6.7 million. In 1960 slightly more than 500,000 refrigerators were manufactured, and in 1970 more than 4 million; 900,000 washing machines were produced in 1960, and in 1970 5.2 million. There was an appreciable increase in the production of almost all other consumer goods, including food, books, toys, etc.

2. Even from the incomplete information published in the Soviet press it is possible to see that the targets of the 1966–1970 Five-Year Plan

were not met for such basic indicators as gas production (200 billion cubic meters in 1970 instead of the 225–40 billion planned), coal (624 million tons instead of 665–75 million), mineral fertilizers (55.4 rather than 62–65 million tons). In 1970 1.67 million tons of plastics and synthetic resins were produced instead of 2.1–2.3 million tons, and 623,000 tons of synthetic fibers instead of the planned figure of 780,000–830,000. The production level for all types of fabrics reached 8.7 billion square meters by the end of the five-year period instead of 9.5–9.8 billion, and 1.2 billion items of knitwear were produced instead of the planned 1.65–1.75 billion. The plan for capital investment was overfulfilled as a whole but underfulfilled with respect to the capacity of new enterprises and equipment. The annual growth rate of productivity in industry and building also failed to reach planned targets. Planned figures for return on investment and many other important indicators were also not met. And this by no means exhausts the list of failures to meet various targets.

3. *Problemy mira i sotsialisma* (Problems of Peace and Socialism), 1971, No. 1, p. 58.

4. According to the ninth Five-Year Plan, by 1975 we should reach the 1970 gross production level of the United States. If the present rate of growth is maintained in both countries, this would allow the Soviet Union to catch up with the United States in terms of gross output by the end of the 1970's and by 1985 in terms of per capita production of most traditional goods. However, given the general level of labor productivity and production efficiency and judging by key technical and economic indicators, it will not be possible to catch up with the United States even by 1985. It has been calculated that the Soviet Union is now economically and technically five to ten years behind the major countries of Western Europe and fifteen to twenty years behind the United States. We may possibly hope to catch up with Europe by the early or middle 1980's (assuming the best possible management of the economy). But there can be no question of reaching the level of the United States before the year 2000. We must be realistic and avoid consoling ourselves with vain illusions.

5. Expressed in percentages, it rose in 1955–60 to 6.7 per cent and then decreased to 2.2 per cent in the period of 1960–66 (*Ekonomicheskaya gazeta*, 1968, No. 27, p. 9).

6. Although the Soviet Union was already considerably behind the capitalist countries in the productivity of labor, it actually regressed even further in this area during the sixties. In the 1950's the average annual increase was 7 per cent, in 1961–65 it declined to 5 per cent and in 1966–70 to 4.5 per cent. In the United States, according to Soviet statistics, in 1961–65 the productivity of labor rose on an average of 4.6 per cent per year, in West Germany 5.2 per cent per year, and in Japan 10 per cent per year.

7. Lenin, *PSS*, XXXIX, p. 21.

8. The following figures will give an idea of the development of agriculture as a whole in the course of the decade: gross agricultural production increased from 59 to 80 billion rubles (to take the average annual figures for 1956–60 and 1966–70 for all types of farms); production of grain increased from 121.5 to 167.5 million tons; raw cotton, from 4.36 to 6 million tons; sugar beets, from 45.6 to 81 million tons; sunflower seeds, from 3.7 to 6.4 million tons; flax fiber, from 438,000 to 458,000 tons; potatoes, from 88 to 95 million tons; vegetables, from 15.1 to 19.3 million tons. There were 11.6 million tons of meat as opposed to 7.9 million at the end of the fifties. Milk production increased from 57 to 80 million; eggs, from 23.6 to 35.8 billion; wool, from 317,000 to 397,000 tons.

The average annual yield for the same two five-year periods rose as follows: grain from 10.1 to 13.7 centners per hectare;* cotton from 20.5 to 24.1; sugar beets from 184 to 228; sunflower seeds from 9.1 to 13.2; potatoes from 94 to 115; flax from 2.6 to 3.4; vegetables from 101 to 132.

The supply of mineral fertilizer to the farms rose from 11.4 million tons in 1960 to 45.6 million tons in 1970 (i.e., from 12.2 kilograms to 47 kilograms per hectare of plowed land). The number of head of cattle grew during the ten years from 74.2 to 95.2 million; pigs, from 53.4 to 56.1 million. Tractors used in agriculture (calculated in fifteen horsepower units) increased from 1,985,000 to 4,343,000.

9. *Voprosy ekonomiki*, 1970, No. 2, p. 76.

10. *Ekonomicheskaya gazeta*, 1969, No. 6, p. 29.

11. *Voprosy ekonomiki*, 1969, No. 12, p. 62.

12. For example, in 1967–68 in the USSR, 35.1 kilograms of fertilizer (expressed in terms of the percentage of its nutrient content) were applied on one hectare of sowing land as against 62.5 in Yugoslavia, 173.1 in Czechoslovakia, 82 in the United States, 224 in Britain. Moreover the quality of our fertilizer is still much inferior to the best foreign products. The output of herbicides and other chemicals to protect plants should have, according to the plan, reached 800,000–900,000 tons in 1970 (with a calculated demand of 2 million tons). In 1970, it in fact amounted to less than 400,000 tons. (*Voprosy ekonomiki*, 1969, No. 12, p. 62.)

13. *Voprosy ekonomiki*, 1971, No. 7, p. 49.

14. See the statistical yearbook *Narodnoye khozyaistvo SSSR*, 1970.

15. *SShA* (USA), 1972, No. 2, p. 27.

16. According to data published in the Soviet press, the U.S. retail price index for the 1960's rose by 37.4 per cent, taking prices for 1957–59 as

* One centner equals 220.46 pounds; one hectare equals 2.471 acres. —Trans.

the base (see the magazine *SShA* [USA], 1971, No. 4, p. 73). In the same period the cost of living index in West Germany (including consumer goods and services) rose by approximately 20 per cent, in England by approximately 40 per cent, and in Japan by 65 per cent. Similar information about the Soviet Union is not published or made available to the public or trade unions. Unofficial calculations show, however, that the rise in the cost of consumer goods and services in the USSR for the period 1966–70 alone was not less than 25 per cent and for the whole decade not less than 50–60 per cent.

17. *Voprosy ekonomiki,* 1971, No. 11, p. 22.

18. According to official Soviet statistics (see the 1970 statistical yearbook of the Central Statistical Board), per capita income in the USSR in 1970 was $1,325. Soviet economists calculate the equivalent figure for the United States to be $2,819, for Switzerland $2,010, for Sweden $1,820, and for Canada and Denmark $1,780 and $1,760 respectively. The Soviet Union is also behind such countries as West Germany, Norway, Australia, Luxembourg, France, Holland, and Belgium but ahead of New Zealand, Finland, Japan, Britain, Austria, and Italy. However these calculations cannot be accepted at face value. In the first place, Soviet statistics are based on the official exchange rate (one ruble equals 1.2 dollars), which obviously inflates the value of the ruble and bears no relation to its actual purchasing power. The authorities have been forced to acknowledge this by introducing the so-called "certificate ruble" and by opening special shops in major Soviet cities where only certificates or foreign currency can be used. Secondly, a disproportionately large share of Soviet national income is accounted for by the means of production and armaments. Therefore the relatively high per capita income figure tells us little about the actual standard of living, which clearly is lower than that of New Zealand, Austria, Britain, Finland, or Japan. Finally, statistics for the GNP from capitalist countries include the service sector. The United States per capita income for 1970, including the cost of services, was in fact about $4,000. Soviet statisticians calculate the GNP on the basis of industrial production alone. In view of the growing role and importance of the service sector, Western statistical practice seems more realistic.

19. According to data from the Institute of Soil Science of the Academy of Sciences, in European Russia alone more than 50 million hectares of arable land are subject to water erosion, while wind erosion is removing the most valuable elements of the soil (those that aid fertility) from 35 to 40 million hectares, largely in parts of Kazakhstan, the Volga region, and Siberia (*Voprosy ekonomiki,* 1970, No. 2, p. 82). The terrible dust storms that raged in the spring of 1969 in nearly all parts of the Kuban and the center of the black-earth region caused multibillion ruble losses to collective and state farms and demonstrated yet again how ill protected Soviet agriculture is against natural disasters.

20. There was a series of important government measures in the early 1970's dealing with protection of the environment. It is to be hoped that they will be rigorously enforced.

21. All data on the increase in crime and alcoholism in the USSR is considered secret, which serves to indicate the gravity of these problems. Data published in *Voprosy ekonomiki* gives indirect confirmation of alcoholism on a massive scale. According to calculations made by B. Kolpakov and A. Semenov, meat, milk, dairy products, eggs, and honey account for 34 per cent of all food consumed in the Soviet Union, bread 9 per cent, cereal products and various types of pasta, sugar, and confectionery 11 percent, while beer, wine, spirits, and liqueurs amount to 24 per cent. This means that in the Soviet Union, *one quarter* of the total expenditure on food is for alcoholic beverages. That is the average for the whole country—in some families it comes to more than half.

The following figures are also of interest: calculated in terms of per thousand of the population, during the 1960's the birth rate dropped from 25 to 17.4, the death rate increased from 7.1 in 1960 to 8.2 in 1970, the number of divorces doubled in the decade, and the number of marriages dropped sharply from 12.1 to 9.7.

22. The General Secretary of the Italian Communist Party, Luigi Longo, wrote in August 1969: "Our Czech comrades embarked on a course that excluded the possibility of returning to authoritarian, bureaucratic repressive methods. They were above all concerned to develop inner-party democracy, democracy for the workers and for the people. . . . Not only did military intervention fail to solve the complex problems that exist in Czechoslovakia, it also offended national feelings and aroused deep resentment. It was a blow to democratic aspirations and opened the way for further activity by internal and external enemies of socialism" (*Unità*, August 21, 1969).

23. The appearance of various trends and ideological conflict within the communist movement is in certain respects not a sign of weakness but of health, the only way that dogmatic and sectarian attitudes can be overcome. The unity of the world communist movement can be achieved only if its ideological and political principles are renewed and developed. And this cannot happen without dialogue and conflict. Unfortunately, mutual criticism within the movement is often excessively bitter—argument can be crude and in bad faith, as we have seen in the virtual split between the CPSU and the Chinese Communist Party; also various individuals and groups have been forced to break with communist parties as a result of disagreements that could easily have been resolved within the framework of the world movement.

II. *The Development of Socialist Democracy*

1. Lenin, *PSS*, XXXVII, p. 244.

2. *Kommunisticheski internatsional*, 1919, No. 1, p. 14.

3. Lenin, *PSS*, XXXVIII, p. 74 (italics added).

4. Lenin, *PSS*, XXVII, p. 253 (italics added).

5. Lenin, *PSS*, XXX, p. 128.

6. Certain students of Soviet society maintain that once basic social and economic rights have been ensured for the workers, political and civil liberty will follow almost automatically. For example, A. K. Uledov writes: "For the individual, the socialist revolution means liberation from exploitation and oppression. In the new society people work for themselves, for their country, and they are free. Once economic rights and liberties have been established, *other individual rights and liberties become fully operative*—there will be the opportunity to take part in the political and cultural life of society and freedom to discuss and pass judgment on it" (see *Obshchestvennoe mnenie sovetskovo obshchestva* [*Public Opinion in Soviet Society*], Moscow, 1963, pp. 138–39). It is obvious that things are not quite so simple as Uledov imagines them to be. Surely the experience of the Soviet Union shows that the workers can be freed from economic exploitation and oppression without receiving their full share of other rights and liberties in the process. In practice it appears that even though a socialist society is more able to organize the immense material resources needed to provide all old people with a decent pension and all young people with a decent education, it finds it very difficult indeed to provide its citizens with genuine freedom of speech, freedom to discuss, freedom of the printed word or association. This is in spite of the fact that the establishment of these political and civil rights would involve practically no material sacrifice, while their restriction requires the setting up of vast and expensive structures such as the censorship and the system of secret informers to monitor the mood and opinions of various groups and sectors in the community.

7. The American philosopher Scott Nearing convincingly describes the limitations and speciousness of many democratic freedoms in the West in his book *Freedom: Promise or Threat*. However, carried away by his critique of bourgeois freedom, he begins to denounce freedom in general and contrasts the idea of "freedom" with that of "social discipline." He regards Soviet society as a model, where freedom is not viewed as "an end in itself," and is based, in his view, on principles of reason, justice, and social discipline. Nearing commends the Soviet example of "restricted liberties" to the young countries of Asia and Africa, whose problems he sees as depending "not on freedom, but on the decisive transformation of a social order which perpetuated their dependence and enslavement." It is as if political freedom and democracy were not a prime condition and powerful weapon for the solution of economic and social problems even in poorly developed countries. In a primitive apologia for the Soviet historical experience, Nearing writes: "Freedom in itself is insufficient. An age of violence stands in need not so much of free men and women as of disciplined people who are devoted to the interests of society and who possess a highly developed sense of

responsibility. The interests of the future, moreover, the interests of survival itself, will not be best served by free nations, but by peoples who desire and are able to subordinate national interests to peace, justice, and general well-being throughout the world."

It is not surprising that Nearing's book was published in the USSR under the general editorship of such an outstanding Stalinist as Academician F. V. Konstantinov, who was personally responsible for the death of many Soviet scientists.

Replying to Scott Nearing, the Soviet philosopher G. Shakhmazarov has written: "One cannot agree that the progress of socialism is connected with social discipline alone. Such a formula reveals a lack of faith in the creative power of the masses and in their political consciousness. . . . Experience shows that as a socialist society becomes more mature, there is a corresponding growth in its need for democracy and an extension of free relationships in the economic, political, and all other spheres of public life. It is not simply the fact that freedom is of itself one of the aims of communism—and not merely an end in itself. To minimize the role of freedom means, in crude terms, putting the cart before the horse and giving up the powerful instrument for progress represented by the creative force of popular initiative. . . . One can only shiver at the thought of the future stretching out infinitely ahead of us, which Nearing prophesies for mankind. In effect he is talking about life under absolutely totalitarian conditions in which the relations between society and the social group on the one hand, and the individual on the other, are those of master and slave. And what is worse, the slave is satisfied with his position and receives sufficient material benefits in exchange for his exemplary service and uncomplaining subordination. Nearing not only sees this state of affairs as inevitable but also to some extent justifiable. . . . But this substitution of discipline for freedom is entirely wrongheaded. In actual fact only people who are free, who are able to make conscious judgments and feel in control of their own lives are in a position to maintain discipline in a responsible and reasonable fashion. Whether Nearing intended it or not, his conclusions sound like he is ringing the death knell of freedom." (*Novy mir*, 1967, No. 2, pp. 255–57).

8. *Programma KPSS*, Moscow, 1961, p. 101.

9. The Czech philosopher R. Richta has written: "Inasmuch as science is becoming a productive force, the development of the creative powers of every individual is becoming a decisive factor in the development of the material base of civilization, previously determined by the availability of capital and labor." Richta believes that a member of a socialist society cannot and should not merely carry out other people's orders. The progress of society depends on how actively all the workers take part in decision making, in social life, in carrying out the various functions of technological, organizational, scientific, artistic, and all other kinds of creative activity involved in human development. This is because "overall success in transforming the world depends on the absolutely indispensable contribution of the individual personality. The possibility of active fulfillment and participation in the progress of

civilization would be assured by the very nature of human existence under socialism" (*Voprosy filosofii*, 1970, No. 1, pp. 70, 77).

10. The majority principle is accepted in theory in socialist countries, but it is not always observed in practice. As we know, Lenin by no means regarded victory in the October Revolution as having been conditional on winning over a majority of the population. It was necessary to have majority support only in certain key political centers and regions of the country. Lenin thought the winning over of the majority elsewhere could be left until after the revolution. He argued most convincingly that in a country like Russia, with its rural, poverty-stricken, uneducated, and multinational population, a socialist revolution could be successful only if it was the work of a revolutionary minority organized and led by the proletariat. At the time this view was openly expressed. Up to 1937, it was even reflected in our electoral system— voting was not secret and representation was indirect and unequal, with one worker's vote being equivalent to those of several peasants. It was assumed, however, that with the building of socialism, our party would rapidly gain the support not only of the revolutionary minority but also of an overwhelming majority of the people, including the peasants. We know that in actual fact the minds and hearts of a majority of the people were won over after the October Revolution. Unfortunately this trend was later overshadowed by the growth of an undemocratic regime based on the cult of personality. It would, however, be a mistake to reduce Stalin's regime merely to political terror and violence. Stalin relied not only on force and deception; he also fed parasitically on the faith put by the majority in socialism and the Communist Party—a faith that had resulted from the social reforms carried out after the October Revolution. Though of course to a different extent, this extremely complicated and incongruous state of affairs continued to exist under Khrushchev. Many of the measures taken by his administration were actually supported by a majority of the people, although in some cases Khrushchev disguised his rash and often utterly erroneous decisions by having recourse to such pseudo-democratic hoaxes as campaigns for "nationwide discussion" of his various "reforms."

11. *Problemy sotsialisticheskoi demokratii v period stroitelstva kommunizma* (Problems of Socialist Democracy in the Period of Building Communism), Minsk, 1969, p. 73.

12. In the memoirs of an old member of the party we come across the following passage about majority and minority views: "Since the majority view, based on its political experience, is closer to objective truth than any individual can be, it follows logically, as one knows and can foresee, that future practice will justify the majority line and that sooner or later the individual will come to think the same way. For the good of the party a person suppresses his inner resistance (however natural from a psychological point of view) because reason tells him that all such resistance will later disappear in the face of the logic of events. . . . The unity of the party does not rely on uniformity of

opinion, which is impossible in any voluntary association of thinking people, but on conscious and honest submission to the decisions of the majority. But this must not be accompanied by obligatory breast beating and penitence which reduces party activity into a kind of religious ritual in the manner of Muslim self-flagellation."

But it is by no means a foregone conclusion that the opinion of the majority will be borne out by subsequent events. The opinion of the minority can and often does prove to be correct. Furthermore, if the party really does respect the right of a minority to stick to its point of view and defend it, then it is always very much easier at a later stage to reverse a majority view that proves to be wrong. When democracy within the party was destroyed, when the minority not only had to submit but was forced to recant under the threat of punishment or expulsion (obviously this does not include cases when the minority really was won over by sheer force of argument), it proved extremely difficult to correct mistaken decisions. The adoption of a preferable policy was extremely painful and difficult for both majority and minority in cases where the one had just succeeded in crushing the other. What is more, both majority and minority are very often proved wrong by events, making it necessary to seek middle ground between them. But the "unity of views" achieved by compulsion will impede the search for any compromise solution.

13. Strange as it may seem, even such an active supporter of genuine socialist democracy as Valentin Turchin takes strong exception to the use of the word "opposition." In his interesting unpublished study, *The Inertia of Fear,* he writes: "We should begin by being honest. We have the right to honesty and must defend that right. Let us recognize that the responsibility for lies and for hypocrisy rests with ourselves. We must fight the virus of lies and hysteria with the antibody of honesty and self-possession, proselytizing honesty as a doctrine, as an article of faith. Each convert must carry this faith to another and he must not pass by anyone who has retained even a drop of humanity. A conspiracy, you may say? Yes, if you like—a conspiracy against lies, propagating no other idea than that of honesty. Do you believe that Stalin was a 'wise father and teacher'? That all his victims really were 'enemies of the people'? Very well. You have the right to think that way, but I don't agree with you, so let's talk about it. Do you think that we have freedom of speech? Splendid! Or you believe the contrary, but that it isn't necessary? Excellent! I don't agree with either statement, but this too I'm prepared to discuss. You might even convince me. The only thing that I insist on is that you believe what you are saying, that you make your case honestly and let me have my say.

"Everyone must give his word that he will observe the following elementary principles. Never under any circumstances directly or indirectly to help to spread false information, lies, or slander! Never to vote at any meeting for resolutions whose wisdom one doubts; never to vote at an election for a candidate of dubious integrity.

"This is not a political programme or an 'opposition platform.' I wish to warn our intelligentsia and particularly the young against setting up any kind of 'opposition.' There is nothing more disastrous

for society, when instead of thinking in terms of truth, duty, and freedom, people begin to think only of the interests of 'us' and 'them.' This
inevitably serves further to encourage hatred and the breakdown of
communication and trust. The dividing line between good and evil
runs not between one man and the next but through the heart of every
individual. Therefore our urge toward good must first and foremost be
directed within ourselves—each must begin with himself. This is a
great and profound truth, borne out by the whole of history."

It is interesting to note that these ideas expressed by Turchin in
1968 are very like the views put forward by the American sociologist
Charles Reich on what he calls "consciousness three." His book *The
Greening of America*, first published in 1971, was largely directed
toward young people. It rapidly became a best-seller, particularly among
the "new left." The important point, however, is that if Turchin's proposal were put into practice it would inevitably lead to the emergence
of very rigid majority and minority trends, i.e., in effect to the very
"opposition" which he, for some reason, considers to be disastrous.

14. *Ideologia sovremennogo reformizma* (The Ideology of Contemporary Reformism), Moscow, 1970, p. 444.

15. *Problemy mira i sotsializma* (Problems of Peace and Socialism),
1971, No. 8, p. 19.

16. Some friends have suggested that since the word "opposition" has
supposedly been discredited by our political experience, it would be
better to replace it by the word "dissent." It is true that under Stalin
"opposition" took on a sinister connotation that still lingers on in
people's minds. However it would be more appropriate to keep the term,
restoring the normal meaning it once had. One friend has written
that in defending the right to opposition, it is necessary to advocate a
constructive and civilized form of it and to condemn nihilism, extremism, and anarchism. But who is going to draw the dividing line? In
normal circumstances when freedom of speech and of opinion are
assured, it is inevitable that a constructive and civilized opposition will
prevail. Nihilists and extremists will never command more than an
insignificant minority. Since we are talking here about the expression
of opinions and not about actions, restrictions should be absolutely
minimal, especially since it can also be of some use to have extreme
views expressed. Extremism and destructive anarchism, on the other
hand, turn into a very real danger under totalitarian conditions when
all criticism and opposition are banned under the pretext of a struggle
with "enemies of the regime."

17. An Austrian Communist, F. Fürenberg, wrote in the journal *Problemy mira i sotsializma* in 1971: "There is no political movement more
prepared to discuss issues than communism. Even though communists
are fully aware that class struggle rather than talk is the moving force
of history, they nonetheless believe that discussion is able to open the
eyes of millions to their class situation and help them to realize the
nature of their true interests and how to defend them. In this way
discussion becomes a means of continuing the struggle with capital-

ism. Marxists have never maintained that they know everything; they are ready to learn from 'dissenters' and have done so many times over the decades. As we know, Lenin often stressed that one can even learn from the enemy" (1971, No. 4, p. 80). Such views, of course, bear little relation to the actual history of the communist movement at many stages.

An eminent member of the Italian Communist Party, G. Boffa, was much closer to the truth when he described internal conditions in the USSR in his book, *After Khrushchev:* "Soviet institutions and the Soviet press cannot be made less rigid because of an attitude never openly formulated but implicit in political life, which sees all disagreement as hostile, especially disagreement openly expressed. It is one of the survivals of the Stalin period difficult to overcome. Although no longer regarded as treason, disagreement is still seen as a hindrance and impediment to progress and is treated with suspicion. The duty of each person is to work, to build and to create; anyone who dissents, stands on the sidelines, or 'gets out of step,' is failing in his duty as a citizen. It is still not accepted that disagreement is potentially useful as a positive stimulus, as a means of providing a warning of unsolved contradictions and problems both large and small. . . . But when disagreement is given no scope, there can be no solutions to the very problems around which it revolves. This has led to a very tense situation in the international movement. . . .

"A change in the political life of Soviet society would appear to be inevitable at the present time. Does it make sense that in a huge country such as the USSR, top leaders should be so carefully shielded from criticism until the moment that they fall from power, when accumulated dissatisfaction is suddenly given expression in a torrent of abuse? It could not be otherwise when the cult of personality reigned supreme; but at the present time it scarcely enhances the authority of those who govern the country."

It is true that complete unanimity may give society or a political party considerable strength at certain moments of their existence. But times and circumstances change, and it is far more often the case that denial of the right to disagree, instead of being a source of strength, leads to weakness and fragility in the machinery of social and political life, rendering it incapable of withstanding the sudden shocks and strains of our complex political realities. Lenin's views on the problem of opposition will be discussed later. For the moment it suffices to quote one sentence from Lenin's letter to Bukharin and Zinoviev which has evidently not yet been published in full: "If you get rid of all the clever but not particularly obedient people and keep only the obedient fools, you are absolutely sure to bring ruin on the Party" *Stenograficheski otchet VI kongressa Kominterna*, Vypusk I, Moscow-Leningrad, 1929, p. 614).

II. Trends Within the Party and the Question of Party Unity

In the anonymous essay "Words Are Also Deeds," which analyzes various current political trends, the author writes: "The Stalinism of

the 1930's and '40's was the work of scoundrels who relied on the blind
enthusiasm of the majority of the people and the selfless support of the
best, most honest and loyal elements among the new generation of
party officials. Today's Stalinism is as before the work of scoundrels,
but it flounders in a sea of popular apathy or mistrust and no longer
has the support of the younger party officials. This does not mean to
say, of course, that Stalinism is completely alien to the popular mind.
A part of the workers are still retrograde in their thinking, nostalgic
for the absolute, indisputable, and deified master whom they saw as an
all-powerful protector against oppressors at the local level, as one who
visited justice on all their enemies, particularly thieving bureaucrats
and administrators. To a certain extent Stalinism embodies the under-
dog's dream of retribution with the aid of a higher justice, however
cruel, against all those who humiliate him in his daily life. Impotence
seeks the protection of a supreme avenging power. But this kind of
'Stalinism' is an implicit criticism of bureaucracy, an expression of
hatred for it. There have been many cases in history of progressive
social moods originating in the guise of reactionary utopias. Like a
filthy animal devouring its own excrement, Stalinism is now feeding on
its own excretion, on its own waste products; the masses take refuge
from its basic deformities and dire consequences in recollections of the
golden age of Stalinism now become legend."

2. The success of neo-Stalinist propaganda is visible in the reactions of
cinema audiences to the appearance of Stalin on the screen in such
films as *Ambassador of the Soviet Union* and *Liberation*. In many
cinemas, including those in working-class areas, the audience breaks
into applause. This happens for a variety of reasons, including discontent with the current situation in the country and the desire to protest
against hardships and unfulfilled promises. We have good reason to
speak of "the Stalin *cult*." It was a religious phenomenon as much as a
political one, a peculiar Soviet form of worship. The eradication of this
religion among the masses will need a prolonged campaign of education. But for six years now almost nothing has been done to expose the
Stalin cult and the fearful crimes associated with it. Can we be sur-
prised, therefore, that this cult is beginning to revive? Today's young
people, students, and older schoolchildren know almost nothing about
Stalin's crimes and have only a very general idea of the decisions of
the Twentieth and Twenty-second congresses. We have even less about
Stalin in our school textbooks than they do in West Germany about the
crimes of the Nazis.

3. An interesting article by the Soviet sociologist N. on the problems
of socialist democracy also refers to the connection between neo-
Stalinism and of the country's economic situation. N. writes: "In the
years that immediately followed the Twentieth Congress, the country
began to pick up economically as well as in the political, ideological,
and cultural spheres. For this reason the idea of rehabilitating Stalin
and returning to old ways found scarcely any influential supporters, as
we saw in the Twenty-second Congress. If a decline gradually set in, it
was due to the half-heartedness of de-Stalinization, poor economic

organization, and the serious mistakes committed by Khrushchev. With the fall of Khrushchev, there was an almost immediate resurgence of serious trends in favor of bringing back the old methods along with attempts to rehabilitate Stalin. These attempts were temporarily frustrated by the introduction of the economic reforms which were essentially incompatible with the return to harsh administrative methods. Unfortunately inconsistencies in carrying out the reform have again led to renewed difficulties in recent years, and many people see the only way out in a return to the 'order' that prevailed under Stalin, in the hope that economic inefficiency can be eliminated by stern measures and by silencing malcontents. Brezhnev referred to such attitudes at the December Plenum and was right to comment that a return to the past would lead to new and even greater problems. One of the reasons for the revival of Stalinism is that after the Twentieth Congress there was no attempt to make a fundamental analysis of the system created by Stalin. All emphasis was on the mass persecutions carried out by him, although this was perhaps not the primary feature of his rule. This is why many members of the party and government apparatus who appeared on the political scene only after the war and who were not affected by the mass purges of the 1930's easily came to think that the Stalin system was not all that bad and that a return to it would be a good way of overcoming present difficulties. It does not occur to them that they themselves are largely responsible for these difficulties and for the slow and perfunctory progress of the reform."

4. In the same article N. says that reactionary and conservative-dogmatic views are comparatively more widespread among "party officials between forty-five and fifty-five. This generation did not experience the mass terror of the 1930's which affected a huge number of communists and particularly party officials, and it is therefore less opposed to Stalinism than the older generations. Furthermore their political education took place when the cult of personality was at its height in the postwar years, which distinguishes them from the younger generations, whose views were formed under the influence of the Twentieth Congress. This is, of course, only on a statistical average and does not necessarily apply to any particular individual."

5. Here one might mention the particular impact inside the party of the many speeches made at conferences on ideological matters by such officials of the party and government *apparat* as Trapeznikov, Stepakov, Sturua, Yegorychev, Yepishev, Pospelov, Tolstikov, Mikhailov, Semichastny, and several others. It is pleasing to note that many of these active neo-Stalinists have recently lost their posts and that their personal position within the apparatus has obviously weakened. This does not mean to say, however, that neo-Stalinism as such has lost ground.

Of all the political articles in the periodicals listed, the one that had the greatest repercussions both inside and outside the party was published in *Kommunist* (No. 3, 1969) over the signatures of five people: V. Golikov, S. Murashov, I. Chkhikvishvili, N. Shatagin, and S. Shamuyan. It was later disavowed by the Politburo as being contrary to the party line, but the vast majority of party members and party propagandists were not informed of this.

6. A most detailed political discussion of Kochetov's novel with its right-wing aspersions on the present party leadership can be found in Raissa Lert's article entitled "He Wants to Go Back" and in another one circulated anonymously called "What Does Kochetov Want?"

Lert writes: "In the whole of Soviet literature there is no other book that could more justifiably be called defamatory. And this is not only because of the proportion of positive characters to negative ones (in Kochetov's novel the former are no better than the latter), but rather by virtue of his complete certainty that every person without exception is by nature a villain, and that if he is not kept under strict control, treated as a mere cog in a machine and subjected to draconian laws and restrictions, then he will immediately go to pieces, begin to steal, indulge in high living and betray his motherland. . . . It would be a great mistake to say, as some people do, that Kochetov's novel, though artistically weak, contains some truthful ideas. In fact it is his ideas that are despicable, false, and immoral—he deliberately misrepresents the realities of our life, holding up its worst aspects as the best ones, trying to rehabilitate things that are beyond rehabilitation and substituting the ideals of Stalinism for those of communism."

The author of the article "What Does Kochetov Want?" concludes by saying: "There is no need to refute all of Kochetov's libelous statements since the reason for his attacks on the present course of the party is quite clear; he and his friends want the party to go back on the line proclaimed at the Twentieth Congress and confirmed at all subsequent congresses and plenums of the Central Committee. They want a return to the old administrative methods now condemned by the party. It is no accident that the publication of Kochetov's novel was timed to coincide with the ninetieth anniversary of Stalin's birth."

7. The following story about the ninetieth anniversary of Stalin's birth illustrates the position of the "moderates." Under pressure from neo-Stalinists, it was at first decided to celebrate the day (December 21, 1969) in various ways. In particular a large article spread over two pages was prepared; it was to have appeared in Soviet newspapers and in those of certain other socialist countries, accompanied by a portrait of Stalin. Although containing certain reservations, it would have been taken as a definite act of rehabilitation. During discussion about the article, however, there was considerable disagreement and apparently even some foreign communist leaders protested. As a result the article was rejected by a majority of votes in the Politburo, and a totally different one was published in Pravda, which was greeted with some satisfaction by a majority of the intelligentsia. Other papers failed to mention the anniversary at all. Only the Mongolian paper Unen published the article in its original form, quoting Pravda as its source. Evidently some official had not found the time to call Ulan-Bator or had forgotten to do so.

8. On this subject the author of "Words Are Also Deeds" has the following to say: "The new age is infiltrating the apparat and creating a party intelligentsia within it. True, this is only a thin, unevenly distributed layer and is constantly being eroded through the corruption

of some and the promotion of others up the bureaucratic ladder, not to mention the fact that they are heavily outnumbered by sycophants, fools, martinets, degenerates, scandalmongers, Jesuits, Babbitts, cowards, and other such types spawned by the process of bureaucratic selection. Yet even so, in certain favorable circumstances, this new layer within the *apparat* might well be able to join forces with the intelligentsia in our society at large for which it already serves as a kind of 'lobby' inside the machinery of government. This 'lobby' will inevitably grow and in the process will become an invisible opposition without organization or even awareness of its own existence, but nonetheless very real and deeply entrenched throughout the various arms of the administration. Everything depends on whether or not it will be possible for the *internal* forces of renewal, i.e., those within the bureaucracy, to make common cause with the *external* ones, i.e., those outside it, whether or not the intelligentsia will be able to join up with its 'bureaucratic branch.' "

9. If only for the benefit of some of our dogmatists, it is worth noting that in the mid-1920's even Stalin was not so primitive in his treatment of this question of party unity as some of the people who write about it at the present time. In those days Stalin acknowledged that inner-party struggle was not only permissible but even right and proper. At the seventh, enlarged plenary session of the Comintern in 1926, he said: "Looking at the history of our party . . . it can be stated without exaggeration that the history of our party is the history of struggle between contradictions within this party—the history of the overcoming of these contradictions and the gradual strengthening of our party by means of overcoming these contradictions. . . . It is possible and necessary to compromise with people inside the party who think differently about questions of current policy, about questions of a purely practical nature. But if these questions involve differences of principle, no compromise or 'middle line' can save the situation. There is not and cannot be any 'middle line' in questions of principle. The work of the party must be based either on one set of principles or on another set of principles. A 'middle line' on questions of principle is a line that clutters up people's minds, a line that smooths over differences, a line that leads to the ideological degeneration of the party, a line that leads to the ideological death of the party. What is the present course of development in the West European social democratic parties? Are there contradictions inside their parties, differences of principle? Of course there are. Do they reveal these contradictions and try to overcome them honestly and openly in full view of the masses or the rank and file? Of course not! The practice of social-democrats is to turn their conferences and congresses into an empty masquerade, shop windows designed to make believe that all is well, while they carefully cover up and smooth over their internal differences. But nothing can come of this except the cluttering up of people's minds and the ideological impoverishment of the party. This is one of the reasons for the decline of West European social democracy which was once revolutionary and is now reformist. But we cannot follow such a course of development, comrades. A policy of following a 'middle line' on matters of principle is the policy of

parties which are in the process of withering away and such a policy is bound to lead to the transformation of the party into an empty bureaucratic apparatus which operates in a vacuum and is divorced from the working masses. This way is not our way" (*Sochinenia*, Vol. 9, pp. 4–5). Unfortunately here too there is a distinct discrepancy between Stalin's words and his deeds.

10. Lenin, *PSS*, IX, p. 19. Not only the Rules of the CPSU but evidently those of most of the other communist parties also fail to incorporate this very wise proposal of Lenin's. In the summer of 1968 possible changes in their party rules were being discussed in the Czech press. At this time a number of communists (for example, see the proposals by R. Parolek in *Rude Pravo*, June 26, 1968) suggested that the rights of the party minority should be safeguarded by a provision in the rules. Parolek wrote that it was necessary "to ensure the following rights for the party minority while still preserving in full the principle of democratic centralism: representation on governing and controlling bodies of the party; the right to defend one's position and to publicize it in the party press; after a specific period of time has elapsed, the right to put forward one's position for discussion in district, regional, and national forums." A reply to this was published in *Pravda* in the form of a long article by S. Selyuk entitled "The Strength of the Party Is in Its Leninist Unity" (July 25, 1968). Selyuk denounced Parolek's proposals, arguing that they were "directed in effect against democratic centralism," "against those organizational measures which guarantee unity of will and action in party ranks," etc. To buttress his arguments Selyuk quoted Lenin: ". . . unless the will of the majority is implemented there can be no question of party solidarity or even of any organized political action in general" (*PSS*, XXV p. 409). This is blatant and deliberate juggling with the facts. Selyuk's interpretation of democratic centralism belongs not to Lenin but to Stalin and his henchmen. Nor should it be forgotten that Lenin always insisted that the minority opposition be represented in the governing bodies of the party. After the group of Left Communists had been broken up at the Seventh Party Congress, Lenin proposed that many of the supporters of the group still be elected to the Central Committee, although its leaders continued to defend their point of view and for the time being had no intention of disbanding their faction. Once Lenin's line had triumphed at the Tenth Congress, Lenin himself proposed the election to the Central Committee of a number of Trotsky's supporters, as well as members of the Democratic Centralists and certain other groups.

11. Lenin, *PSS*, IX, p. 10.

12. *Voprosy istorii KPSS*, 1965, No. 2, p. 34.

13. Lenin, *PSS*, XIII, p. 129.

14. Lenin, *PSS*, XIV, p. 125.

15. *Ibid.*, p. 126.

16. In his interesting reminiscences about the Tenth Congress, Mikoyan describes how Lenin, at the time of the congress, organized a strictly conspiratorial meeting of his faction for which invitation tickets were privately printed. Even Stalin voiced the fear that this meeting could be used by the Trotskyites to accuse Lenin's supporters of factionalism. Lenin smiled good-naturedly and replied with a joke: "What's this I hear from an old dyed-in-the-wool factionalist?" (A. Mikoyan, *Mysli i vospominaniya o Lenine* [*Thoughts and Memories About Lenin*] 1970, pp. 136–39).

17. *X syezd RKP(b)*. *Stenograficheski otchet*, Moscow, 1963, p. 521 (italics added).

18. *X syezd RKP(b)*, p. 540 (italics added).

19. Lenin, *PSS*, XLIII, p. 108.

20. *X syezd RKP(b)*, p. 523.

IV. *Political Trends Outside the Party.*
Nationalist Trends and Groups

1. It is appropriate here to quote Dr. Valentin Turchin, a physicist who is very familiar with the present mood among young people and the scientific intelligentsia. In *The Inertia of Fear,* we read: "The discrepancy between word and deed in our country has reached catastrophic proportions and as a result ideological work is in a very sorry state. In order to prove the unprovable we resort to evasion, juggle the facts, or even simply lie. We insist that our ideology is scientific, and we train people to think scientifically and critically and then confront them with rigid dogma, every line of which is deemed to be a priori truth not subject to discussion or modification. . . . Adults whose thought patterns and habits are already set often hold on to certain basic attitudes out of inertia—new, invalidating factors are simply ignored. In this way they can preserve traditions that give shape to their lives, and they continue to function according to habitual criteria. But these attitudes cannot be transferred to the younger generation. A monstrous void is formed in the minds of the young who have ceased to believe in anything. . . . But in view of the growing role and influence of the intelligentsia, this is quite clearly an intolerable state of affairs" (pp. 56, 59).

2. The authors of this document entitled "Survey of the World Situation" (*Obzor mirovogo polozhenie*) do not conceal their extreme hostility toward the Soviet Communist Party, the October Revolution, and the system it created. They reject the teaching of Marx and assert that Marx and Engels observed capitalist society in its infancy and therefore came to incorrect conclusions. The democrats insist that the social evils of capitalism are not organic, but an unhealthy aspect of its growth, and it is already in the process of curing itself. They attempt to prove that

in recent decades capitalism is managing to overcome various ailments such as overproduction crises, unemployment, crime, racism, etc. There is not a word about the struggle of the working class to achieve its rights and freedoms, certainly the source of many reforms enacted by capitalist governments. The authors of the "Survey" even justify colonial expansion. They argue that "the capitalist countries have carried out a great cultural and civilizing mission in the colonies and have also made the previously untapped resources of the colonies available to all mankind." They declare themselves to be adherents of nonviolent action, because violence "is always evil and nullifies any objective"; but surely capitalist colonial expansion was responsible for an unprecedented unleashing of violence and was the major cause of two world wars. The socialist countries are referred to as species of "Eastern socialism" and all achievements are discounted. But is not socialism also only in its infancy when seen in a historical perspective? And therefore here too is it not easy to reach incorrect conclusions?

Another programmatic document of the extreme westernizers is the voluminous manuscript entitled *Our New World. Theory. Experiment. Result (Nash novy mir. Teoriya, Eksperiment, Rezultat,* 1969) signed by the pen name V. Bogdan. The author produces an extensive but extremely biased selection of statistical material to prove that Western countries are not only still outdistancing the Soviet Union in terms of various technical and economic indicators but also that capitalism offers better opportunities for development in all respects. Bogdan deliberately identifies socialism with Stalinism. He maintains that "there has been no watershed, there is no basic difference between the present and the past just as there is little to choose between the views of Lenin, Stalin, and those in power today." Bogdan places the blame for Stalin's crimes on Marxist-Leninist theory. He believes, as do many Western anticommunists, that Stalin was the embodiment of the socialist system and "socialism can take no other form apart from its present one . . . it is a dead end" from which there is no way out other than collapse or a return to capitalism. On the other hand, Bogdan ignores the shortcomings of contemporary capitalism. He even justifies American aggression in Vietnam as an attempt to stop the spread of communism and Maoism in Asia.

Obviously this kind of extremism serves only to compromise genuinely democratic trends in the USSR. Such programmes benefit the Stalinists. But as it is entirely a question of views and convictions, there is absolutely no excuse for the criminal prosecution of westernizers and democrats, some of whom were arrested in 1969 and 1970.

3. The homilies of our extreme westernizers must seem very strange to radical intellectuals and workers in the West. However, members of the progressive Soviet intelligentsia are equally puzzled by the articles of certain Western writers such as James Aldridge and Dean Reed, published in the Soviet press, which endeavor to prove that there are no violations of freedom of the press or other democratic freedoms in the Soviet Union.

4. Available in English translation in *Sakharov Speaks,* New York and London, 1974.—Trans.

5. A film about Lenin that appeared on our screens several years ago included the following obviously fictitious episode. Lenin, seriously ill, wants to hear news of the party and Soviet life but the doctors have forbidden him to read newspapers or magazines and his visitors are enjoined to avoid political conversations. However a certain worker, a jack of all trades, manages to get through to Lenin, who asks him to construct a small radio. Lenin conceals it from his doctors and relatives and listens to it at night. From a foreign broadcast he learns about the bitter struggle going on within the party, that Trotsky has challenged the party leadership and is striving for power. Lenin is extremely disturbed. With his last ounce of strength he unexpectedly travels to Moscow and makes a speech at a workers' meeting attacking Trotsky and the Trotskyites. It is all, of course, pure fabrication. But the film clearly illustrates the principle that a man starved of information will inevitably turn to any source to satisfy his own craving.

6. The writers of the letter argue as follows: "We have witnessed the appearance in our society of the morally split personality. On the one hand there is the ceremonial moral code just for show, with all its sham pretensions to collectivism, while on the other there is the hidden, private moral code which is extremely primitive, egotistical, and predatory. And so in spite of a mechanical appearance of unity, society is in fact composed of estranged individuals afraid of each other, who experience themselves as insignificant and alone vis-à-vis an enormous state machine. . . . It is relevant here to stress the following question: Do we not lay too much blame on the demonic personality of Stalin and his trusted 'cadres' for many of the things that happened? Surely society as a whole bears a direct responsibility. Its inertia, indifference, servility, ignorance, and finally its all-pervasive cruelty helped to allow the excesses of the personality cult. There can be no idol without worshipers. And if a new 'Stalin' were to appear, it could happen all over again from the beginning, because the moral, psychological, and social prerequisites are still present. The danger of a bloody orgy can be effectively resisted only if there is a rise in moral standards, if there is active participation in civic affairs and an awakening of the sense of personal responsibility."

7. Lev Ventsov sees a way out for the intelligentsia through the fulfillment of its basic task—the creation of new cultural values that will perhaps in the course of time transform the "spiritually dead, ignorant, stupefied masses" that we now see on all sides. He writes: "Until there is full recognition of culture as an end in itself and not just a means, until there is absolute acceptance of the inherent value of the life of the spirit, until we realize that social conditions change while the achievements of free creativity endure, that it is senseless to use crude physical force against truth, justice and beauty—we will continue to live in conditions that, far from being ideal, are not even normal. . . . Cultural creativity must become a positive means of struggle. We need the sort of comprehensive and reliable knowledge that can be obtained only through the efforts of many people; there must be painstaking economic and sociological research of the highest contemporary sci-

entific standards. We need our own philosophy, which at present does not exist. We need to assimilate the riches of world culture. I shall probably be told that my proposals are rather utopian—there is only an unbelievably narrow circle of truly cultured individuals in our country, whose aspirations are alien to the people, and by remaining in the world of culture they will find no common language with society at large; they will not be able to exert an influence or withstand the burdens of censorship and other persecution. But all these objections and warnings only support the basic premise of my analysis. Yes, I agree. But, if this is the situation, does it mean we must do nothing?"

Ventsov continues, "Those who persecute culture do know what they are about. They feel that culture has a restricting effect, it compels them at least to be more vigilant and deprives them of the confidence that allows them to behave as if truth and peace were amorphous lumps of clay. There is no need for culture to constitute itself as a political party, putting forward a programme of social transformation in the name of which the masses could be led to the barricades. This is not the way that culture functions, and we have seen the unfortunate results in our country when it was tried. . . . Let ten, twenty or one hundred understanding readers absorb the works of literature and scholarship now in the process of creation; they would then ultimately prove to be a vital contribution to the spiritual development of the country and of enormous historical importance. Rarely in history have even the most prominent writers or philosophers been able to exert direct influence on the course of events. . . . Thomas More, for example, had his head chopped off. But who would dare to suggest that culture, in its essence, has had no influence on the fate of mankind? And why should we suppose that our own activity must have an immediate social effect and otherwise refuse to take any action whatsoever? . . . Our options are very limited—we can either put up a fight or wait for better days. But our struggle must be creative and not simply a negative marking of time. The better days are inside us, if they are destined to appear at all. But this is exactly why we must not allow ourselves to become accustomed to poverty of the spirit. Even if better times do not arrive . . . we shall still fulfill our task and leave our mark on our own culture and also that of the whole world."

Clearly Ventsov is essentially concerned with the development of some kind of elitist culture based on a very small section of the intelligentsia, cut off from the mass of the people. He is reckoning on change in the very distant future and believes that the personal cultural development of a few hundred individuals is more important than the promotion of a single programme of social transformation. Rejecting Marxism, Ventsov and those who signed the letter from the "representatives of the Estonian intelligentsia" admit that as yet they have no philosophy of their own but that one must be created. Yet how many decades will this take? It is an untenable position. Genuine Marxism (as opposed to the vulgarized form) gives ample scope for a plan of democratic reforms acceptable to the majority of the people. There would not only be material improvement but also a raising of moral standards, and culture would flourish. Of course it is necessary to create works of literature and scholarship that will live for centuries and that are not just of ephemeral interest. But we also need to develop movements that will have a more "immediate social effect."

8. With his novel *August 1914*, Solzhenitsyn departs even from the ideas of ethical socialism. In the description of prerevolutionary Russia, his main sympathies lie with characters who are in favor of a "healthy" and free capitalist development but who are obstructed on the one hand by the totally corrupt autocratic system and on the other by all the revolutionary parties without exception. These views are basically in line with the ideology of the Kadets, who during the First World War were instrumental in forming the Progressive Bloc in the Duma. The leaders of this party occupied major posts in the Provisional Government as it was first constituted in 1917. However, this evolution of Solzhenitsyn's thought is not just a result of inner causes—it also reflects the external conditions in which he is now forced to live.

9. See *Neopublikovannoe* (Unpublished Works), Frankfurt, 1972.—Trans.

10. There are evidently specific epistemological reasons for the revival of religious sentiments among the intelligentsia, including scientists. The tremendous scientific gains of the last twenty or thirty years have not only vastly extended our knowledge of the world, they have also made us aware of our infinite ignorance. There has in fact been only a very small advance in the endless process of understanding the essence of nature and of man. Almost all scientists today are proud of what has been achieved, but at the same time it is easy to see how little we have managed to discover about the origins of the world or the nature of the human mind. The fact that so much remains unknown (being perhaps by its very nature unknowable, given the limitations of human consciousness) provides fertile ground not only for scientific speculation (not to mention the products of science fiction) but also for belief in the idea that in its primordial origins nature consists of both matter and spirit.

11. The first programmatic statement of the Committee declared: "Proceeding from the conviction that the problem of safeguarding human rights is important for the creation of favorable conditions of human life, for the strengthening of peace, and for the development of mutual understanding, and is an integral part of contemporary culture; striving to encourage international efforts to publicize human rights and to seek effective means to safeguard these rights; noting the growing interest in recent years among Soviet citizens in this area of culture; expressing satisfaction with the achievements of the USSR in this field of law since 1953 and hoping to assist by means of our advice the further efforts of the state to establish guarantees for the protection of rights while taking into account the special problems arising under a socialist system as well as the specific nature of Soviet traditions in this field, A. Sakharov, A. Tverdokhlebov and V. Chalidze have jointly resolved to continue their activity directed toward constructive study

of this problem by forming a Human Rights Committee. . . . The purposes of the Committee's activities are:

"advisory assistance to state agencies in creating and applying safeguards for human rights, such assistance to be initiated either by the Committee or by interested governmental authorities;

"creative help for persons occupied with constructive investigations of the theoretical aspects of human rights and the study of the specific character of this problem in a socialist society;

"the furtherance of legal education and, in particular, the dissemination of documents of international and Soviet law concerning human rights." (See *Dokumenty Komiteta prav cheloveka* [Documents of the Human Rights Committee], New York, 1972.—Trans.)

12. For example, in his letter to the Consultative Conference of Communist and Workers Parties in February 1968, Grigorenko wrote that in the Soviet Union, democracy had been liquidated "utterly and without trace" although Marxism-Leninism supposedly called for the "unlimited expansion of democracy." Quoting Engels, Grigorenko urges the immediate "withering away of the state," which has become a "gigantic bureaucratic octopus, strangling the whole of society and crushing all its vitality." Grigorenko rejects many of the values created by the Soviet people in the course of the last fifty years and now an important part of the general human heritage. He maintains that in the USSR we have witnessed "the total failure of man's first attempt to create a more just social order beyond capitalism. . . . No sane person, knowing the whole truth, would agree to exchange even the most backward form of capitalism for this kind of 'socialism.' " In this typically extremist statement, Grigorenko calls on the European communist parties to disassociate themselves absolutely from "socialist" practice within the Soviet Union. He claims that the "faint glimmer of democratization within the party" which appeared after the Twentieth and Twenty-second Party congresses "has long since been extinguished," that "the organs of state security have been restored to their former position," and that the people are being deceived to a far greater extent than in Stalin's time. As for the leaders of communist parties meeting in Budapest, Grigorenko protests against the very idea of such gatherings and advances the demagogic and anarchist notion: "Talks on unity must be left to rank-and-file communists." He goes on to say: "Only by putting forward this principle can your meeting justify the hopes that have been placed in it. It is astonishing that no one has ever suggested this before." (See *Mysli sumasshedshevo* [Thoughts of a Madman], Amsterdam, 1973, pp. 103–26.—Trans.)

In another document, "A Letter to Academician Sakharov," Grigorenko states his views on international problems and advocates the abolition of secret agreements. He demands that the UN be given the right to replace any government whose policies do not aim toward détente. Sakharov had written that in Stalin's time the peasantry were "almost in a state of serfdom," but Grigorenko corrects him: in fact the situation in the countryside was far worse in the 1930's and '40's than under serfdom. Grigorenko suggests that scientists and workers be put in charge of the economic life of the country, thus eliminating the need for professional administrators. Most sectors of the national economy should not be planned. "In their present form branches of industry should produce in response to demand and their products should be sold through a free market system. Scientific statistics should be the only central 'planner' . . ." He proposes that the whole state apparatus be disbanded at once since its officials have "always belonged to the exploiting class." He believes that the role of the Soviet state is purely that of a parasite, basically no different from a capitalist state. All these typically anarchist sentiments are very far removed from Marxism, although Grigorenko still calls himself a Marxist.

But while criticizing his views, one can only respect Grigorenko's personal courage and honesty. His letters and articles, with all their mistakes and exaggeration, express a definite position shared by others. His confinement in a psychiatric hospital was an illegal and arbitrary act.

13. It is important to be aware of the difference between the terms "national" and "nationalist" (movement, demand, consciousness, etc.). A national movement usually arises as a justified protest against the violation of the natural and legal rights of a particular nation. It is thus a question of progressive and democratic aspirations which do not contradict those of the communist movement. However, national movements often become entangled with *nationalist* ones. As a rule, nationalist movements are associated with ideas of national exclusiveness, a condescending or hostile attitude toward other national groups, and a striving in the direction of national separateness. The national question is given first priority and all other economic and cultural problems are viewed as secondary. There is often an attempt to preserve outmoded aspects of national life while natural and progressive forms of integration and cooperation between nations are opposed. Thus we are confronting conservative or even reactionary demands which contradict the aims and objectives of the communist movement. In the USSR today there is often an extraordinary blending of national and nationalist ideas in people's consciousness—which is why we are in need of a judicious and extremely subtle nationalities policy.

14. A letter was brought to Moscow in 1966 demanding that the Crimean Tatars be allowed to return to the Crimea with the full restoration of their national autonomy. It had more than 130,000 signatures, i.e., the greater part of the adult Crimean Tatar population.

15. Certain Ukrainians, Georgians, Estonians, Latvians, and Lithuanians have tried to demonstrate that their republics contribute far more to the central budget than they get back. But this is perfectly normal in a multinational state and is probably true for all the republics without exception, since a considerable proportion of our material resources is absorbed by military and defense requirements, foreign aid, the maintenance of the central government apparatus, etc. Also certain northern and eastern areas of the country could not be developed without the help of the older industrial regions. At specific stages of their history, various republics did receive far more from the center than they paid in, and this was quite proper.

16. In 1959, when Khrushchev intended to visit Sweden and other Scandinavian countries, it was decided not to observe the 250th anniversary of the Battle of Poltava. No one seemed to mind; in fact, very few people even noticed that the press made no reference to Peter the Great's famous victory over the Swedish army.

In 1966, in order to avoid casting a shadow over a proposed visit by the Turkish head of government, the central press ignored the fiftieth anniversary of a terrible Armenian national tragedy—the destruction of the Ottoman Empire's Armenian population (more than 800,000 Armenians were killed by rabid Turkish nationalists and some 700,000 others were dispersed around the globe). There were even attempts to ban commemoration of this date in Armenia itself, which caused a great deal of displeasure and resentment.

In the same year a new movement appeared in Abkhazia, protesting against the contemptuous approach of various Georgian government bodies toward the legal interests and historical legacy of the Abkhaz people.

17. The rapid plowing up of millions of hectares of virgin land in Kazakhstan upset local cattle breeders, who had been using the land as pasture. Furthermore, the whole scheme was planned rather carelessly. A considerable part of the newly plowed territory soon fell easy prey to wind erosion and was lost to agriculture altogether. The soil was rendered useless not only for growing crops but also for raising cattle.

18. Obviously demands for the preservation of national identity must not become an obstacle to the economic development of a particular republic. After spending some time in the Baltic states, however, I became convinced that certain large industrial enterprises were being built where there was no sufficient economic rationale for them. On the whole they use raw materials brought from other regions and are situated in areas where there is no labor surplus, and so their workforce must be recruited from other republics. This often means that office and factory workers leave areas such as Siberia, where there is an acute labor shortage, to come and live in the Baltic states. At the same time other parts of the country suffer from a surplus of labor. The national intelligentsia quite naturally objects to the whole policy and justifiably so—the majority of those now living in Tallinn and Riga are neither Estonian nor Latvian.

I heard the following brief but typical story in Lithuania; it serves to illustrate how there is sometimes a lack of respect for national traditions that really should be preserved and developed. In a small Lithuanian town there is a monument to a semilegendary Lithuanian queen (probably Biruta). In Lithuanian folklore she is the personification of female love and fidelity, as she waited long and faithfully for Vitautas, the king who loved her. She is considered to be the protectress of lovers and, according to ancient custom, young lovers and engaged couples place flowers at her monument. However one fine day the local militia suddenly forbade this. Some official had interpreted it as a manifestation of nationalism. They began to bring flowers at night. And early in the morning the militia came and removed them. One can easily imagine what young and also not so young Lithuanians thought of this behavior by the authorities.

19. The majority of Tatar children in the Tatar Autonomous Republic are taught in Russian schools. Many of them have refused to attend Tatar language instruction available in the senior classes because their parents feel it would mean too much work, causing them to neglect other subjects and thus decreasing their chances of access to higher education. In an attempt to overcome this tendency, the Tatar regional party committee passed a special resolution on May 21, 1968 making it obligatory for Tatar children in Russian schools to study their native language and literature. This resolution remained in force even after a law was passed in December 1968—"On strengthening links between school and life and the further development of education in the USSR"—which gave parents the right to decide whether or not their children should study Russian in a native school or their native language in a Russian school. Yet one leading representative of Ukrainian culture persistently demands that Ukrainian children be forbidden to attend Russian schools in the Ukraine and that it be made mandatory for Ukrainian children to be taught in Ukrainian if they have gone with their parents to live outside the Ukraine.

Taking a different point of view, the Council of Ministers of the Chuvash Autonomous Republic passed a resolution in 1962 instructing Chuvash schools to teach all subjects in Russian with the exception of the native language and literature. This decision was a response to persistent demands by a majority of parents. When the measure was being discussed, it was pointed out that textbooks in the Chuvash language were of very poor quality, including those that had been specially translated. This meant that the standard of teaching in Chuvash schools was lower than in Russian ones.

20. In republics such as Georgia, Armenia, the Ukraine, and Estonia, much original scientific research, including highly specialized work, is published in the native languages. This hardly seems to be very practical. And sometimes local authors who have written in Russian are required to translate their work into their native tongue before it can be published. Many of these studies thus become virtually inaccessible to scientists outside the republic. Editions are usually very small, but more important, once a book appears in a republican language, there is normally a long delay before translation and publication in Russian. And often this never happens at all. There is also the problem of scientific journals in local languages—subscriptions are almost entirely within the republic. The whole situation is rather ludicrous, given the assumption that any original scientific study is presumably meant for all Soviet scientists (and ultimately those abroad as well) working in the same field. Of course we must approach this question with extreme circumspection. It is perfectly understandable that every nation would like to have not only literary but also original scientific works in its

own language. Yet surely an author should have the right to choose the language he prefers to work in. If more scientific research were published in Russian, this would in no way deprive scientists in the republics, since much of what they have to read is in Russian anyway. Almost all scientific and technical terminology has become part of an international idiom. Therefore the whole question of national character, so important in creative literature and art, is not very relevant when it comes to scientific research and publication.

21. In 1971 a rather novel manifesto, entitled "The Word of the Nation" (*Slovo natsii*) and signed by anonymous "Russian patriots," was put into circulation. It was a declaration of blatant chauvinism preaching racism and state supremacy. The authors of the manifesto attack Soviet "liberals" for holding views that would allegedly bring disaster on the Russian people. These "patriots" champion the purity of the white race threatened by "uncontrolled hybridization" and call for a rebirth of the "great, united and indivisible" Russia and also the restoration of the Russian Orthodox Church. Certain other groups of extreme Russian nationalists advocate the separation of the RSFSR from the other Soviet republics in order to avoid the "intermingling" of the Russian nation with other peoples.

Since 1971 a typed journal called *Veche* has been passing from hand to hand in Moscow, "published" by a different, more "moderate" group of Russian nationalists. They urge us to "turn back to Russia, to restore and cherish our national culture and the moral and intellectual resources of our forefathers." The journal calls on people to "continue along the path of the Slavophiles and Dostoevsky." Its editors state that *Veche* is a "journal of Russian patriots," whose objective, however is not "to belittle the other nations of our country."

22. *Molodaya gvardia*, No. 9, 1968.

23. *Molodaya gvardia*, No. 6, 1969.

24. *Molodaya gvardia*, No. 8, 1970, p. 316.

25. S. Semanov has this to say about Stalin and the Stalinist era: "Today it is quite apparent that the mid-thirties were a crisis point in the struggle against destructive elements and nihilists. How much abuse has been poured on this period retrospectively! There are those who love to sigh nostalgically for the 'golden age,' the literary and artistic salons of the twenties, seeing nothing else of value in our culture and national life. But they would do well to remember that it was only after the adoption of our Constitution (giving legal recognition to the existence of social change on a vast scale) that Soviet citizens became completely equal before the law. This was a momentous achievement. . . . From that moment all honest workers of our country became as one, a united monolithic whole. It seems to me that we have not yet fully realized the significance of the colossal transformation which took place at that time" (ibid., p. 319).

In his poem, "By the Right of Memory," the great Soviet poet

Alexander Tvardovsky, a communist, wrote about the "full equality" of 1937 rather differently:

> *Outside the limits of the law*
> *Fate leveled all men now:*
> *The sons of kulaks, commissars,*
> *Red Commandants and priests.*
> *But class distinction was no more—*
> *All men were brothers in the camps,*
> *Branded as traitors, every one.*
> *The Motherland had never dreamed*
> *That under the skies of Magadan*
> *Such a host of "enemies" would gather;*
> *Nor could she tell*
> *How it had all begun,*
> *How she'd contrived to rear*
> *Such a host of sons now held*
> *Behind wire in that far-off zone.*

(translated by Max Hayward)

There is a penetrating critique of Semanov's piece in Raissa Lert's brilliant essay "Treatise on the Charms of the Knout." She writes: "It is quite clear how such an apologia for 1937 crops up in an article with philosophical pretensions. We can see the place Stalinist repressions occupy in the scale of 'eternal values.' After all, it was only when Stalin utterly destroyed Soviet historical scholarship in the thirties that it became possible to falsify history and to rehabilitate Russian tsarism. For many years on Stalin's orders disciplined 'ideologists' engaged in the task of redeeming the Russian autocracy, ostensibly with the aim of glorifying the Russian people. Semanov, Chalmaev and other 'neo-Slavophiles' have good reason to feel gratitude toward Stalin. Of course the war made it much easier to graft alien ideas of national exclusiveness and privileged status onto communism. The fascist aggressors were real enough and chauvinism lives off genuine feelings of national pride (people certainly did have reason to be proud). By taking advantage of this mood, it was easy to rewrite history. Alexander Nevsky, Yuri Dolgoruky, Ivan the Terrible, and Ivan Kalita were all sanctified on the grounds that 'taken in historical context their lives had been progressive.' At the same time various movements for national independence were vilified (Shamil and others). There were virtually no acts perpetrated by the tsarist army, administration, or diplomatic corps which the obedient hacks could not portray favorably in a clever amalgamation of Marxist language and chauvinist ideas. Tsarist Russia disappeared; in historical studies, novels, and textbooks there was absolutely no trace of the 'prison of nations,' the 'gendarme of Europe' crushing revolution, or the empire oppressing its colonies yet at the same time dependent on foreign capital. Historical facts were glossed over in an intolerably specious manner. It became a criminal offense to extol the local rulers in Central Asia who restricted the Russian advance, but khans who did obeisance to the tsar were graciously endowed with the epithet 'progressive' (as if they had foreseen the October Revolution and the Union of Soviet Socialist Republics! . . .).

Stalin then declared that great-power chauvinism was the only true communist ideology and that anyone who disagreed was anticommunist and anti-Soviet. Internationálism was retained as window dressing 'for special occasions.' . . . The doctrine that Stalin imposed on Soviet historiography, now being successfully developed by people like Semanov, is the most common kind of great-power chauvinist idea, which would have been approved of by Arakcheev, Pobedonostsev, or Stolypin. The contribution of certain contemporary historians is twofold: either there is a clumsy attempt to camouflage it with phrases about communism and revolution, or they exploit the urgent moral problems that young people are concerned about today—the search for moral ideals, the re-examination of good and evil—questions which each generation must decide anew. The younger generation today have also become keenly interested in ancient Russian art, culture, and music, in itself a very worthy pursuit but one that produces fertile soil for chauvinist ideology. . . . Chauvinist methods must be clarified, made known, and discredited, because naïve young people are capable of accepting Semanov's writing as patriotic. They would be quite mistaken, for it is very much the opposite. Like all manifestations of great-power chauvinism, it provokes reaction, aggravating the nationalist sentiments of smaller nations. Naturally they can only be suspicious and distrustful of the nation held up by Semanov and his friends (with no authority whatsoever) as a dominant superior race whose whole history is sacred. This kind of approach hardly promotes the ideas of internationalism nor does it strengthen the state."

26. See *Kommunist*, No. 17, 1970, pp. 97–99.

V. *One-party and Multiparty Systems under Socialism*

1. Marx-Engels, *Sochinenia*, XXII, p. 237.

2. Lenin, *PSS*, XXXIV, p. 237.

3. Lenin, *PSS*, XXXV, p. 36.

4. *Protokoly TsK RSDRP(b)*, Moscow, 1958, p. 122.

5. Lenin, *PSS*, XXXV, p. 76.

6. *Syezd sovetov v dokumentakh*, vol. I, Moscow, 1959, p. 7.

7. There are dogmatists who even today continue to insist that any political alliance between communists and social-democrats can come about only if the other parties accept the leading role of the communists (e.g., see *Kommunist*, 1969, No. 5, p. 77). But this is a strange and absurd claim. It is not just that communist parties still, unfortunately, do not have adequate mass support or very much influence in many capitalist countries. The communist party has no automatic right to the leading role, it cannot unilaterally assume this position—rather it must

be arrived at historically, only after many years, often decades of struggle in the *vanguard* of the progressive forces of society. There is no need to discuss here the distinction between "leader" and "vanguard."

8. *Voprosy istorii,* 1971, No. 3, p. 204.

9. S. Carillo, *Problems of Socialism Today,* London, 1970.

10. *Kommunist,* 1969, No. 14, p. 45.

11. *Ideologia sovremennogo reformizma,* Moscow, 1970.

12. Ibid., p. 441.

13. The program of the Communist Party of Japan declares:
"1. The Communist Party of Japan is the only party in the country whose program states its goal to be the ending of organized and systematic violence, along with all other kinds of violence against man. For the last fifty years only the communists have opposed wars of aggression as the consummate manifestation of violence and have consistently struggled for the independence of the people.
"2. The Communist Party advocates the transformation of the administration of the country by peaceful and legal means through the creation of government supported by a united front of the national-democratic forces which constitute a majority in parliament. It would be quite natural for this government, in defense of national sovereignty and parliamentary democracy, together with the people, to apply necessary measures for the maintainance of order if the forces of external or internal reaction attempt to overthrow the state or resort to other illegal or violent measures.
"3. When Japan has become an independent and socialist country, the basic political system . . . will be a democratic people's state, in which parliament will be the highest organ of state power both *de jure* and *de facto.* All political parties, including those critical of the government or in opposition, will enjoy full freedom of action as long as they make no attempt to destroy the democratic system by force" (*Problemy mira i sotsialisma,* 1971, No. 10, pp. 38, 39).

14. The "leading role" of the communist party in a socialist society is often interpreted in an extremely one-sided and superficial way. It is wrong to view the Communist Party as the *source of power* in a socialist country. Surely the source of power is the whole people, all those who work. The party took power in their name and continues to act on their behalf. Its governing role is based on the mandate it received from the people which should periodically be renewed at election time; but given our present electoral system, the whole exercise is largely an empty formality.
What is true for the party as a whole is also true for its leading organs, and particularly applies to the leaders of party and state.
It is also quite wrong to think that because of its dominant role,

the party must necessarily guide and direct not only all state bodies
but even workers' organizations. For if this is the case, there can be
no place for political groups or organizations critical of party policies,
and the people—or a part of the people—are deprived of the opportunity to compare and choose. In other words, they cease to be a real
source of power and their "approval" of party policies becomes automatic and devoid of meaning.

The emergence of even small opposition groups should be welcomed as a means of exercising control over the activities of the organs
of power. Of course, even without an opposition, it is possible to create
a great number of structures for the purpose of exerting control from
below. In 1970 a Polish sociologist published a whole study of the
subject under the title *Control Without Opposition*. But in December of
that same year, dramatic events in the Polish Baltic ports forced the
removal of the party leadership, thus demonstrating that in fact there
had been very little popular influence on those in power. There can be
no doubt that the existence of a legal opposition would have improved
the functioning of all organs of party and state in Gomulka's Poland.
An opposition does not and cannot replace other forms of popular control in socialist countries. But nevertheless there can be no *effective*
control without the right of opposition.

15. Quoted in E. D. Mordzhinskaya, *Leninizm i sovremennaya ideologicheskaya borba* (Leninism and the Contemporary Ideological
Struggle), Moscow, 1970, p. 99.

VI. *Inner-party Democracy*

1. The right to express and defend an opinion *even after* a decision
has been reached does not conflict with the principles of democratic
centralism. It all depends on how it is done. In September 1920 the
Ninth All-Russian Conference of the Russian Communist Party approved a resolution "On the immediate tasks of party organization"
which stated: "The party will not tolerate repressive measures to be
taken against comrades who disagree with its decisions on particular
questions" (*RKP*[b] *v rezolyutsiakh* . . . , Moscow, 1936, Vol. 1. p.
360). The Tenth Party Congress declared that all decisions taken by
the party were "binding and must be implemented with maximum
speed and precision" (ibid., p. 368). But far from revoking the resolution of the Ninth Conference, the Congress even reaffirmed it in
Paragraph 24 of a new resolution on party organization. The Tenth
Congress prohibited the propagation of views that contradicted decisions already taken by the party. However, it preserved the right of a
minority to formulate and defend its opinions in special collections of
documents for restricted circulation and in scholarly publications. The
Tenth Congress resolution "On syndicalist and anarchist deviations in
our party" is of particular interest in this connection. Paragraph 6
states:

The Congress categorically rejects the ideas put forward by the
syndicalist and anarchist deviations and resolves that:

1. there must be an undeviating, systematic struggle against these ideas;

2. the propagation of such ideas is incompatible with membership in the Russian Communist Party.

At this point, however, there is the stipulation that "while instructing the Central Committee strictly to implement these decisions, the Congress is at the same time in favor of the most thorough exchange of ideas among party members on these questions in special collections and publications" (ibid., pp. 367–77).

2. On the eve of the Third Comintern Congress in 1921, the journal *Komintern* published an article by Otto Kuusinen devoted to the problem of bureaucracy in workers' organizations. He wrote: "It is an over-simplification to regard bureaucracy as a disease of petty bourgeois circles which has managed to infiltrate worker, proletarian and intelligentsia organizations. . . . In the prerevolutionary legal workers' movement, it was common enough to see a worker leave the factory bench for the role of professional representative (whether as a deputy, journalist, etc.) and undergo a rapid transformation, very quickly mastering all the worst aspects of bureaucratic methods."

He also pointed out that in many workers' organizations "the most deplorable forms of bureaucracy were described as democratic centralism" and that bureaucracy in proletarian organizations "invariably led to a sectarianism which was very closely related to bureaucracy, in fact its younger brother." Not only did Lenin express complete agreement with Kuusinen's views, he insisted that the article be read out at the Congress (*Leninski sbornik* XXXVI, pp. 257, 260). Lenin helped to draft proposals laid before the Congress on "The Formation of Communist Party Organizations," in which bureaucracy and rigid centralization were condemned in no uncertain terms (*Komintern v dokumentakh* [The Comintern in Documents], 1933, p. 203).

3. Lenin, *PSS*, XXIV, p. 144.

4. Lenin, *PSS*, XXXVI, p. 500.

5. At the end of 1923 and the beginning of 1924 there was a lively discussion in the press and within the party about the need for urgent measures to make party life more democratic. One is sometimes astonished by the amount of criticism published fifty years ago—the views of men who died soon after or were killed during the purges. Here are just a few samples:

"At meetings of party cells, endless reports are read out on already decided questions . . . this inevitably leads to a certain apathy. The alleged ignorance of the rank and file is really in fact passivity very much encouraged of late by the leading party organs. Members of the Central Committee and the Moscow Committee are for the most part strangers to ordinary communists; they never address party meetings, rather as if there were nothing to talk about" (G.Ya., *Pravda*, November 16, 1923).

"Party meetings are either boring or full of endless harangues—

'like a church service,' some comrades have been heard to say. The party masses . . . must be given the opportunity not just to listen and vote but to put forward their own ideas" (K. Ksenofontov, *Pravda*, November 17, 1923).

"During the war communists were taught to submit to discipline like soldiers. Therefore many party members still feel that 'the generals know best.' But any communist should be able to understand the issues and judge for himself" (F. Klimov, *Pravda*, November 18, 1923).

"We may find all kinds of deviation undesirable and dangerous, but a total lack of it—party members without their own opinions . . . is in fact a hundred times more dangerous" (M. Charny, *Pravda*, September 22, 1923).

6. A few years ago two communists from Georgia protested to the Central Committee about the fact that luxurious *private* houses were being built for the local leadership at public expense, some of them on land that had been part of the Tbilisi botanical gardens. One of the complainants was an architect who had helped to build the houses and could therefore speak with authority. When Mdzhavanadze was informed about the letter, its authors were whisked off to a psychiatric hospital. Although they were soon released after intervention by the Party Control Commission and the Procurator General, no proceedings were taken against Mdzhavanadze or the many owners of the houses in question. This kind of return to Stalinism, the equation of any criticism of party and state leaders with political crime, is today the exception rather than the rule. What usually happens is that criticism from below comes up against blank indifference.

7. A mathematician has calculated the average age of the 195 members of the Central Committee to be sixty-one, while that of the 24 members and candidate members of the Politburo and the secretaries of the Central Committee is approximately sixty. "What conclusions can we draw from this?" he asks. "As a rule elderly people find it difficult to change their style of work . . . their outlook is bound to be conservative. There is an old saying that a man lives his life as he crosses the street—first he looks to the left and then to the right. Yet to govern a country as large and centralized as the USSR in such a complex international situation demands excellent health, endurance, strength of will, the ability to make quick decisions, etc.—all qualities that deteriorate with age. . . . Just why is the average age of the party leadership so high? It is largely because the road to the top is usually through the bureaucratic hierarchy. Rapid promotion is seldom possible, primarily because there are no clear-cut criteria for judging the quality of party work, while the bureaucratic organization tends to reject lively, daring individuals who would be capable of shaking the whole system."

8. One of my correspondents has observed rather harshly but quite legitimately: "It must be said without mincing words: Cadres policy, i.e., the method of selecting and placing personnel in the power struc-

ture, is essentially the same as in Stalin's time. The system he created has hardly been touched and continues to be a destructive obstacle in the way of building communism. The main shortcoming of such a system, or rather its intrinsic vice, is that capability and talent have no chance to compete in the open. Promotions are decided behind closed doors where the decisive consideration is usually the candidate's behavior toward superiors—his dealings with subordinates are totally ignored. Nobody asks the rank and file; they only have one 'right,' to accept the person who has been appointed or to vote for the one who has been recommended."

9. Apart from the original *apparat*, a huge new one was created specially for the Central Committee's RSFSR Bureaus. After the abolition of industrial ministries, the Central Committee's single department was replaced by more than ten specialized departments for various branches of industry (and the same thing happened in the RSFSR Bureau!). But this was not all and before long parallel *apparats* of Party-State Control were set up in the Central Committee and the RSFSR Bureau. Since the chief function of the central party apparatus had always been not only to prepare instructions and decrees but also to supervise their implementation, the creation of yet another parallel inspection agency (though not empowered to check on the work of the highest party bodies, something Lenin had believed essential to any system of party control) was an extremely dubious move indeed. In practice these new party-state inspection agencies became just one more auxiliary *apparat* grafted on to party committees at various levels—their subsidiary role was underlined by the fact that they were always headed by a secretary of the party committee in question.

10. Lenin, *PSS*, XLV, p. 61.

11. R———v, a party member since 1920, criticizes the overextension of party leadership: "The government and its ministers, chosen by the Supreme Soviet and invested with its confidence, find themselves subordinate to the heads of Central Committee departments whom nobody elected and who are often far removed from the realities of daily life. Newspaper and magazine editors submit practically every more or less important article to officials in the propaganda department of the Central Committee for approval. The appropriate official in the Central Committee *apparat* 'clarifies' the essential nature of socialist realism and all writers and painters must make their work conform. In the past we have even seen the Central Committee give 'directives' on linguistics, on Hegelian theory, on the classification of classical Russian literature, etc. . . . I can recall a most extraordinary directive on the 'expulsion' of foreign words from the Russian language. A commission was set up in the Academy of Sciences headed by Academician Skachinsky which developed new Russian terminology for the mining industry . . . eliminating all words of foreign origin.* The whole 'reform'

---

* Many common words in Russian mining terminology are of German origin. The campaign against foreign influences, "cosmopolitanism," etc., was characteristic of the late forties.—Trans.

never got anywhere in the end but succeeded in leaving a trail of
irritation and bitterness. . . ."

12. The procedure for election to party organs introduced at the
Twenty-second Party Congress has proved highly dubious in practice:
a candidate who has received more than fifty per cent of the votes is
deemed elected without regard to the number of places on the committee previously laid down. All that happens under this new rule is
that those responsible for drawing up the lists either see to it that the
number of candidates is the same as the number of places on the committee or after the elections agree to an increase in its size. Since the
previous electoral procedure was also hardly ideal and was the object
of well-founded criticism, it would have been better, in my view, to
adopt an electoral practice whereby if there are more candidates than
places, anyone who receives no less than two-thirds of the votes would
be elected. Thus where there are to be seven members on a committee
and eight candidates are nominated, then all eight would be elected if
they all received more than two-thirds of the votes; if one of the eight
receives less than two-thirds, then he would not be elected; if two
candidates receive more than fifty per cent but less than two-thirds of
the votes, then the person who received more votes would be elected.
This procedure would increase the element of *choice*.

13. In a resolution of 1922, "On consolidation of the party and its new
tasks," the Eleventh Congress urged that there be a reduction in the
size of the central *apparat:* "During the present transitional period,
with the party guiding the political and economic life of the whole
country, each party organization has to play some kind of active role
in all aspects of life, in economic, cultural, and political affairs as
well as administration. But in order to do this, party organizations have
had to methodically build up large *apparats* which have been gradually
expanding. They in turn have taken on a bureaucratic complexion and
are absorbing an excessive amount of the party's strength. One of the
party's most important tasks is to curtail this bureaucratic aspect of its
functioning, a process already under way in the Central Committee and
local organizations" (*VKP[b] v rezolyutsiakh* . . . , part 1, 1935,
p. 439).

14. Some Secretaries of the Central Committee forbid their apparatus
officials to write articles for publication or at least to do so under their
own names. This is because an official must not be publicly linked
with a specific point of view—he must always be ready to take a different line in accordance with the desires of his superior. When one
of the Central Committee section heads began to display excessive independence and insisted on expressing his own point of view, he was
dismissed from the apparatus with the characteristic explanation: "not
apparat material."

15. In an article called "Certain Problems Related to the Development
of Democracy in the USSR," written not by a philosopher but by a
physicist, there are interesting reflections about the influence of the

system and its institutions on the behavior of its officials: "It would be a very grave mistake indeed to attribute too much significance to the personal qualities of a particular individual in our system of leadership. From the point of view of social psychology, a man's actions are determined by his social role within the group. It follows that a man must act in accordance with group norms or be expelled. As an official advances up the ladder, his peer group becomes increasingly rigid and his range of choice reduced—members of the group are more and more bound by their colleagues' expectations. For this reason the secretary of a remote rural district committee has more independence than a Secretary of the Central Committee. In periods of intense social change, however, the individual does have the chance to play a much greater role. At such moments personal qualities do in fact become very relevant indeed. . . . Of course it is true that the bureaucratic system does not favor bold or independent personalities, but on the other hand, it is also the case that versatile, highly intelligent people make no effort to arrive at positions of leadership in view of the way that top leaders become victims of their social role. They are forced to work long hours, far beyond the legal requirement, which leaves them little leisure time for cultural pursuits. They are weighed down by responsibility for the fate of millions and are burdened with secret information. Often they are obliged to do things they disapprove of. They are restricted in their public utterances and in their choice of friends. Clearly, in order to attract highly cultured, well-educated people to leadership positions, there must be a change in the structure of power, a loosening of bureaucratic fetters on personal freedom."

16. *VKP(b) v rezolyutsiakh,* 1935, vol. I, p. 360. (*Izvestia* [News] was the former organ of party committees, not to be confused with the newspaper *Izvestia,* which still exists and is the official organ of the Supreme Soviet.—Trans.)

17. *Ibid.,* p. 374.

18. *XXII Syezd KPSS. Stenograficheski otchet,* Moscow, 1962, vol. 3, p. 344.

19. There are various ways of dealing with this problem in bourgeois democracies, and we certainly should study them. For example, the United States Constitution provides that a man may not be elected President for more than two consecutive terms. In Sweden, however, the Prime Minister and leader of the Social-Democratic Party, Erlander, remained in office for twenty-three years and then retired voluntarily. Even the most eminent of leaders should never forget one of Parkinson's laws—that if a boss stays at his post too long, his closest assistants and possible successors gradually lose their ability to take charge.

20. Some people think that it was Article 25 that created an insurmountable breach between Khrushchev and many Central Committee members on the one hand, and senior officials of the regional party committees on the other. A powerful clandestine opposition to Khru-

shchev developed inside the party *apparat* because of this article, and a few years later he was replaced.

21. A pre-Congress letter to the Central Committee proposed that the whole system of professional party workers be abolished: "Positions of leadership, particularly in the party, should be filled by the best communists in industry, agriculture, science, and culture for periods of two to four years, who would then return to their original occupations. This would bring about a restoration of Leninist principles: leading party posts must be elective with provision for regular replacement. The same practice should apply in the case of state officials."

This proposal is too radical and hardly acceptable. Politics must be regarded as a science that requires serious professional preparation. Leaders cannot be changed every two to four years because in many positions it takes at least two years to become familiar with all the details, people, and problems involved. In my view officials should remain in most senior party and state posts for a minimum period of four to five years, for a maximum of ten or twelve.

The letter also suggested that more ordinary workers, collective farmers, and members of the intelligentsia should be represented on the Central Committee. Its author calculates that at present, out of 195 members of the Central Committee, only three are workers—the rest are leading officials, who occupy the highest positions of party and state. Lenin, in a "Letter to the Party Congress," long ago also urged that the Central Committee should include more workers straight from the shop floor. This suggestion should be taken seriously and put into practice.

22. A. Bebel, *Budushchee obshchestvo*, Moscow, 1959, p. 23.

VII. *The Soviets*

1. See, e.g., *Literaturnaya gazeta*, December 2, 1970.

2. Lenin, *PSS*, XXXIV, p. 304.

3. *Ibid.*, p. 305.

4. *Problemy mira i sotsializma*, 1963, No. 5, p. 60.

5. When a minister, a commander of a military district, or a Secretary of the Central Committee is registered as a candidate for deputy, the election in that constituency inevitably takes on the character of a vote of confidence in the individual concerned as well as the institution he represents. This makes it rather difficult to have two or more competing candidates.

6. Writing about Soviet electoral practice, Professor A. Denisov states without the slightest trace of embarrassment: "Under Soviet law there is no limit to the number of candidates who may be put forward for

election to the Soviets in a particular constituency. And this is indeed how it works in practice. As a rule, several candidates are carefully scrutinized in each constituency. Each citizen has the right to support, criticize, or propose the rejection of any candidate. And any candidate may withdraw in favor of someone else. In the course of this free discussion, the will of the workers is made known both in general terms (their approval of the party election programme and evaluation of the activities of the preceding Soviet) and also in a concrete way through their approval of the candidate to be elected as deputy" (*Demokratiya i sotsialism* [*Democracy and Socialism*] Moscow, 1967, p. 12).

7. A more accurate picture of Soviet electoral practice is given by V. Savin in *Novy mir*. It is true that two or three candidates are usually put forward in each constituency. For example, in 1966 in the Bryansk region, five electoral districts were formed for elections to the Supreme Soviet. "However," he writes, "although each district was to choose only one deputy, three candidates were nominated in each of the five constituencies. In the Bryansk municipal district the three were Brezhnev, Voronov [a member of the Politburo and Chairman of the RSFSR Council of Ministers], and N. Zlobin, a metal worker from a Bryansk engineering plant; in the rural district they were Suslov [Politburo member and a secretary of the Central Committee], Polyansky [Politburo member and First Deputy Chairman of the Council of Ministers], and the chairman of the Bryansk district party executive committee, D. P. Komarov; in the Klintsovsk district they were Kosygin, Kirilenko [Politburo member], and a loom operator from a local textile factory, N. G. Kuzmina.

"However, the Politburo members had been nominated in other constituencies as well. On the recommendation of the Central Committee, they therefore withdrew their candidacy in the above and other districts and agreed to stand only in the Bauman district of Moscow (Brezhnev), the Oktyabr district of Novosibirsk (Voronov) and the Chkalov district of Sverdlovsk (Kirilenko). Comrades Zlobin, Komarov, and Kuzmina were duly elected deputies for the Bryansk constituencies" (*Novy mir*, 1968 No. 5, p. 192).

But what would have happened if Brezhnev suddenly agreed to stand in the Bryansk municipal district? Or Polyansky in the rural constituency? Savin does not raise this question, since he is perfectly well aware of the fact that the nomination of Politburo members in various constituencies is purely a formality. If they did suddenly decide to stand in Bryansk rather than in their traditional constituencies, it would be necessary for Zlobin and Komarov to withdraw. But so far this problem has never arisen.

8. A few years ago *Komsomolskaya Pravda* (April 27, 1967) published two letters from young voters. "I am eighteen," wrote a member of the *Komsomol* from Kiev, Oleg Dovgai, "and I would like to know, Can I consider myself to be a full Soviet citizen? I ask this question because on March 12 I was deprived of the right to vote. . . . I arrived at the polling place at about one o'clock and was told: 'Your vote has been cast already, you can go.' I know quite well that voting continues from

six in the morning to ten at night. But the adults responsible for the conduct of the election had evidently decided that I was too young, would probably not arrive, and so they had my ballot dropped in the box by someone else."

A student from a Kiev technical college, V. Pikus, also wrote to the paper: "On the 12th of March, 1967, I arrived at the polls at one o'clock in order to vote. But I was told that my vote had already been cast. A woman standing nearby was holding a list of technical college students who were still to vote written in red pencil. She asked my name and told me that my ballot had not yet been put in the box. One of our students, Vechkanov, was standing next to her holding a packet of ballots. The woman took mine, gave them to me, and I was able to vote."

The newspaper presented these experiences as if they were extraordinary. However the only unusual thing was the very crude and incompetent behavior of the electoral officials. In other polling places members of the commission wait until much later in the day before voting in the name of people who have not turned up. And if one of them does finally arrive, he is not dismissed in an offhand way. He is simply given one of the left-over ballots.

9. *Novoe vremya*, 1968, No. 29, p. 5.

10. *Problemy mira i sotsializma*, 1971, No. 7, p. 23.

11. An Old Bolshevik, P. Shabalkin, says in an article written in 1964: "Moralizing lectures are useless. Only a change in the electoral system that incorporates an element of competition will rouse all deputies without exception from their usual state of lethargy and force them to concentrate on the needs of the electorate. This means nominating two, three, or more candidates, both party and nonparty, for every seat. And then let them vie with each other to convince the people, let them explain how they see their function and what they propose to do for the voters. Let them earn the people's trust.

"Obviously we could not allow the contemptuous abuse, the squabbles and mud-slinging typical of elections in capitalist countries. But this would not happen with every candidate coming from a bloc of communist and nonparty candidates. Yet all candidates would have to meet the test of public approval. . . . But how will this test the people's faith in the party? If a voter has crossed out all the candidates' names, he has voted against the party. If he has left one, as he is supposed to do, it means he has voted for the party."

Shabalkin's suggestions should be tried out, particularly in elections for local Soviets.

12. *Problemy sotsialisticheskoi demokratii v period stroitelstva kommunizma*, Minsk, 1969, pp. 144–45.

13. An interesting experiment was carried out in Tartu during the 1967 elections to the Supreme Soviet of the Estonian SSR. The right to nominate a candidate for deputy from the town of Tartu traditionally

belonged to Tartu University. However, in fact, the candidate was usually selected in advance by the republican Central Committee and only then formally nominated at student and staff meetings. But in 1967 things happened differently. As soon as nominations were called for, elections meetings were held in all faculties and each one selected its candidate for deputy (or rather its own nominee for candidate). After this there was a meeting of the university party activists, who carefully discussed the seven nominees and finally selected one to be candidate. Although in the end this meant that the nomination fell to someone other than the person selected beforehand by the authorities in Tallinn, the Central Electoral Commission of the republic nonetheless confirmed as candidate the university teacher whose nomination had been arrived at collectively.

14. Yu. Shabanov also draws attention to the anomalies of our electoral practice. He writes: "Take the very act of voting—we are guaranteed the right of secrecy, and every polling place is equipped with booths for this purpose where a voter can examine his ballot in private. Most voters, however, drop their ballots straight into the box without entering a booth. It is as if the voters themselves 'violate' their right to a secret vote in spite of legislative and practical measures to protect it. Can this be avoided? Is there a way to give the will of the individual more weight at election time? Surely both questions can be answered affirmatively. There must be a technical reorganization of the voting process, whereby each voter, on receiving his ballot, is unable to approach the ballot box without first passing through a booth. The individual would also have a better chance to make his will felt if, for example, each person was asked to vote 'yes' or 'no' on various questions, with the requirement that the ballot be marked in the booth" (*Problemy sotsialisticheskoi demokratii v period stroitelstva kommunizma* [Problems of Socialist Democracy in the Period of Building Communism], Minsk, 1968, pp. 163–64).

15. Referendums have been widely employed in many countries of Western Europe. Several referendums have been carried out in France in the postwar period, and there have been more than 120 in Switzerland during the last eighty years.

16. V. Kotok, *Referendum v sisteme sotsialisticheskoi demokratii*, Moscow, 1964.

17. *Problemy mira i sotsializma*, 1971, No. 8, p. 16.

VIII. *The Judicial System and the Security Forces*

1. *Kommunist*, 1971, No. 9, p. 8.

2. *Pravda*, February 31, 1971.

3. Lenin, *PSS*, VII, p. 168.

4. For example, in a letter to the Central Committee by a group of Soviet philosophers on the lessons of the Sinyavsky-Daniel affair, we read: "In the history of the Soviet state there has never been a single case of a writer's being arrested and openly tried for anti-Soviet or anti-state activity as expressed in a work of literature, whether written and published in the Soviet Union or abroad. . . . Furthermore, so far as we know this never happened in tsarist Russia nor has it happened in Europe, America, Asia, or Africa in modern times.

"This, then, is an event without precedent. How thoroughly the trial must have been prepared—it all had to be weighed up and carefully thought out. And how was it conducted? Not one foreign correspondent was admitted to the courtroom. Not even the foreign communist press. . . . Anti-Soviet critics were thus given the chance to remind us of the presence of foreign correspondents during the political trials of 1936–38, and to ask, 'Why not now? Surely foreign communist journalists would not slander the Soviet Union. . . . If the trial was held strictly according to legal procedure, if the nature of the crime was clear and the evidence incontrovertible, and if the prosecution was confident of proving its case, why should foreign correspondents have been prevented from witnessing the triumph of Soviet justice . . . ?'

"Furthermore, there was no stenographic report of this unusual trial in our press or even a detailed account of the proceedings, making it impossible to counter reports in bourgeois newspapers. And so the bourgeois propaganda machine was able to do its work. But even without its influence, unbiased people were entirely bewildered. Unfortunately the statements published in our press in no way dispelled these feelings but on the contrary, made things worse. And so it turned out that the Sinyavsky-Daniel affair in the way that it was organized and handled and officially reported has done even more damage to our society, our state, our ideology and to the world communist movement than any anti-Soviet work by any single writer—since writing is only writing (there's no end to the nonsense you can put in a book), but facts are facts."

5. The trial of Alexander Ginzburg, Yuri Galanskov, and others provoked a large number of individual and collective protests. Here is a letter written by forty-six residents of Novosibirsk (mainly scientists) in February 1968 and sent to all the highest Soviet and party bodies, the Supreme Court of the RSFSR, and the editorial boards of the Moscow newspapers:

"The absence in our press of any coherent or complete information on the substance and course of the trial of A. Ginzburg, Yu. Galanskov, A. Dobrovolsky, and V. Lashkova, convicted under Article 70 of the RSFSR Criminal Code, has disturbed us and led us to seek information from other sources—namely, foreign communist newspapers. What we have been able to find out has caused us to doubt that this political trial was conducted with due regard for legal norms, such as the principle of open trial. This is a cause for alarm. Our sense of civic responsibility prompts us to declare most emphatically that we consider the holding of what in effect have been closed political trials to be impermissible.

We are alarmed at the fact that behind the virtually closed doors of the courtroom, illegal proceedings have taken place and unfounded sentences based on illegal accusations have been handed down. We cannot permit the judicial machinery of our state to slip from the control of the general public and thus once again plunge our country into an atmosphere of judicial tyranny and lawlessness. We therefore demand that the verdict of the Moscow Municipal Court in the case of Ginzburg, Galanskov, Dobrovolsky, and Lashkova be annulled, that the case be retried in fully public hearings with scrupulous observation of all legal norms, and that the evidence be publicized in the press without fail. We also demand that those guilty of having infringed the public nature of court proceedings and the judicial norms guaranteed by law be legally called to account."

Another letter sent by 150 members of the Ukrainian intelligentsia to Brezhnev, Kosygin, and Podgorny in April 1968 deals with the same subject: "In the course of the last years there has been a series of political trials involving young people from the creative and scientific intelligentsia. We are disturbed by these trials for a number of reasons. In the first place we cannot fail to be alarmed by the fact that they were not conducted in accordance with Soviet law. For example, all the trials held in Lvov, Kiev and Ivano-Frankovsk in 1965–66, in which more than twenty people were convicted, were closed, despite the absolutely unequivocal guarantees of the Soviet Constitution, the republican constitutions, and their criminal codes. Furthermore, because the trials were closed, it was possible for other laws to be violated as well. We believe that infringement of the principle of open trial is in direct contravention of the decisions of the Twentieth and Twenty-second Party congresses on the restoration of socialist legality, is contrary to the interests of Soviet society, and shows contempt for the highest law of the land—the Constitution. There can be no possible justification for it. The principle of the public's right to know is not only a question of open court hearings but also assumes comprehensive and accurate coverage in the press. As we all know, Lenin demanded that the broad masses should know everything, see everything, and be able to judge for themselves; particularly where the punitive organs were concerned, 'the masses should have the right to be informed about and to check on their activities down to the most insignificant detail' (4th edition, XXVII, p. 186). Our press, however, made no reference whatsoever to the political trials held in the Ukraine. As for those in Moscow, the brief accounts that did appear contained little real information about the rumored trials; they could only have caused greater bewilderment and were an insult to the intelligence of Soviet citizens.

"And this lack of information and the absence of any kind of public control made it possible to disregard constitutional guarantees and legal procedures. It has almost become normal at such political trials for the court to hear witnesses for the prosecution but not for the defense. A widely circulated open letter written by Pavel Litvinov and Larissa Bogaraz bore eloquent witness to the flagrant violations of law during the trial of Ginzburg, Galanskov, Dobrovolsky, and Lashkova. It is evident that in many cases people have been charged for advocating opinions and making statements that were in no way anti-Soviet but

merely critical of specific features of our social life, of blatant deviations from socialist ideals, or of nonobservance of officially proclaimed
standards. For example, the journalist Vyacheslav Chornovil was convicted by the Lvov district court on November 15, 1967, simply for
having collected evidence (which he sent to official bodies) exposing
the illegality and juridical incompetence characteristic of the 1965–66
political trials in the Ukraine. . . . These incidents and many others
show that the political trials of recent years have become part of an
attempt to suppress dissent, civic action, and social criticism, all of
which are vital for the health of any society. . . . We consider it to be
our duty to express profound alarm at what is happening. We call on
you to use your authority and the powers invested in you to ensure that
the courts and the procurator's office behave strictly in accordance with
the law . . ."

6. See, for example, M. Mikhailov and V. Nazarov, *Ideologicheskaya
diversia—oruzhie imperializma* (Ideological Sabotage: A Weapon of
Imperialism), Moscow, 1969, pp. 45, 47.

7. Ibid., p. 57.

8. *Zakonodatelstvo po zdravookhraneniyu* (Legislation on Public
Health), 1963, vol. 6, pp. 323–32.

9. One of the peculiarities of our life is the fact that many important
aspects of it are regulated by secret instructions about which the
population is almost totally ignorant. The instructions on compulsory
committal to psychiatric hospitals is just one example. Another is the
statute concerning passports,* concealed from the public even though
it concerns the vast majority of citizens (only a few provisions are
known—those printed on the last page of each passport). We are un-
informed about various important regulations dealing with residence
permits, particularly in relation to towns subject to stringent controls.
The whole penal system (prisons, camps, etc.) was until recently regulated by a multitude of semisecret or totally secret instructions.

10. The practice of committing people for political reasons is not only
a violation of fundamental democratic principles but also of elementary
medical ethics. In an attempt to prevent abuse arising from the fact
that there are no clear diagnostic criteria in psychiatry or generally
recognized guidelines on the clinical definition of mental illness, the
World Health Organization has recommended acceptance of the following definition of mental illness: "A *pronounced* breakdown of
mental activity, *sufficiently specific* in character to be always rec-
ognizable and corresponding to typical syndromes; *sufficiently serious*
to result in loss of working capacity or to such a degree of disability
as to necessitate prolonged absence from work or where there is need
to take specific legal or other action by the community." The most
difficult area of psychiatry is the diagnosis of schizophrenia (the con-

---

* Internal identity card; the term "passport" is always used in this sense
   unless there is specific reference to foreign travel. In 1974 the Soviet
   government did in fact publish new passport regulations.—Trans.

dition usually "identified" in political cases). The First International Seminar on Diagnostics, which took place in London in 1965, recommended that the following be accepted as the standard pathological symptoms: 1) unmistakable change of personality; 2) autism, i.e., withdrawal or isolation from the outside world, self-absorption in private experience; 3) emotional disturbance so severe as to lead to disruption of relations with other people; 4) disturbed perception; 5) behavioral disorders.

However, in Soviet psychiatric institutions, particularly when it is a question of obviously political cases, it is the practice to diagnose "schizophrenia" or "incipient schizophrenia" even when none of the above symptoms or indeed any symptoms of mental illness are present. In order to extricate themselves from this situation, certain psychiatrists employ pseudoscientific terminology in an attempt to make normal signs of human inadequacy or even positive traits qualify as symptoms of "mental illness." For example, if a scientist in addition to his professional work engages in publicist or public activity, he is diagnosed as a "split personality." A critical attitude toward social conditions is called "poor adaptation to the social environment." Persistence in the defense of one's views is defined by some psychiatrists as an "uncritical attitude." In the reports of some "special psychiatric examinations" one can find references to such symptoms of mental illness as "obsessional delusions of truth seeking," "obsession with detail," "wears a beard," "inability to judge circumstances," "considered the entry of Warsaw Pact troops into Czechoslovakia to have been an act of aggression," "pathological development of the personality with a strong tendency toward reformist ideas," "has dictatorial tendencies," "the patient has no clear symptoms but there is a breakdown in the emotional-volitional sphere combined with an inadequately critical perception of his condition despite retention of memory, acquired skills, and knowledge," "has an exaggerated opinion of himself," "his later work is inferior to what came before," "pretentious and inclined toward graphomania," etc.

Giving evidence at a political trial at the end of 1970 a psychiatrist from the Serbsky Institute stated that "the presence of incipient schizophrenia does not necessarily lead to overtly noticeable changes of personality." Another prominent Soviet psychiatrist, in answer to a question on the symptoms of schizophrenia at a diagnostics seminar, said: "It is no secret that schizophrenia can be present without any symptoms at all." It is obvious even to the uninitiated that this kind of approach to diagnosis is totally arbitrary and unscientific.

11. Western espionage services now acquire their basic information about our military objectives through analysis of intercepted radio messages, the press, the use of spy satellites, etc., and not from the reports of agents.

12. For many it has already become quite obvious that trials and psychiatric hospitals have both failed as a means of combating "dissenters"; they have even turned out to be counterproductive. However, there are signs that certain influential people in government circles are experimenting with "new" means of dealing with dissenters, such as

exile from the Soviet Union, instead of turning to more normal methods, which rely on propaganda and ideological struggle. It is hardly necessary to point out how unfortunate this is for the development of socialist democracy, whether the exile be compulsory or even semivoluntary.

13. See M. Lebedev's article in *Politicheskaya organizatsia sovetskovo obshchestva* (The Political Organization of Soviet Society), Moscow, 1967.

14. See V. Chkhikvadze, *Gosudarstvo, demokratia, zakonnost* (The State, Democracy, Legality), Moscow, 1967.

IX. *Freedom of Speech and the Press*

1. Marx-Engels, *Sochinenia*, I, p. 83.

2. A. Bebel, *Budushchee obshchestvo*, Moscow, 1959, p. 115.

3. *Literaturnaya gazeta*, March 6, 1958.

4. This was very well understood by the first leaders of the Soviet state who introduced censorship immediately after the Revolution. One need only recall the 1921 article "Freedom of Books and the State," by Lunacharsky, People's Commissar for Education. He wrote: "Censorship! What a terrible word! But the words cannon, bayonet, prison, and even state are no less appalling . . . yet we consider all these to be sacred weapons in the struggle that will eventually make it possible to do away with them altogether. Censorship is in the same category. It is necessary in order to stop the publication of even great works of art if they harbor blatantly counterrevolutionary sentiments; and we must be able to choose, to give priority to the most vitally needed books. Others, however worthwhile, will have to wait.

"Some may say, 'Away with all these prejudices about freedom of speech—in our communist society the state should have control over literature. In a period of change there is nothing terrible in censorship; on the contrary, it is essential for an orderly transition to socialism.' But he who then comes to the conclusion that there can be no criticism other than denunciation, or that works of art must be adapted to fit a primitive revolutionary framework—such a person may pretend to be a communist but underneath, if you scratch the surface, there lurks a policeman. And acquiring power he would above all take pleasure in being a bully and petty tyrant and would enormously enjoy pushing his weight around. Of course we do already have examples of such behavior—as a people we are far too uneducated, and there is a danger that proletarian power can turn into the rule of petty minions, police tyranny, and Arakcheevism.* This must be avoided at all cost" (*Pechat i revoliutsia* [The Press and Revolution], 1921, No. 1, p. 7).

* Count Alexis Arakcheev became particularly influential during the last years of Alexander I's reign—his name has become a symbol of despotism because of his reactionary policies.—Trans.

5. Marx-Engels, *Sochinenia*, I, p. 64.

6. Ibid., p. 69.

7. "Struggle is not eliminated by censorship," wrote Marx, "it becomes one-sided and is transformed from an open into a secret conflict; disagreement over theory is turned into a contest between powerless principle and unprincipled force. The only true censorship rooted in the very essence of freedom of the press is *criticism*. This is the tribunal generated by freedom of the press. Censorship is criticism exercised as a government monopoly. But does not criticism lose its rational character when it is not open but secret, not theoretical but practical, when it is not higher than party but is inseparably identified with the party . . . ?" Ibid., I, pp. 59, 60.)

8. On October 28, 1917, Lenin signed the *Decree on the Press,* which stated: "As everyone knows, the bourgeois press is one of the most powerful weapons of the bourgeoisie. Particularly at such a critical moment, when the new power of the workers and peasants is only being consolidated, it is impossible to leave this weapon entirely in the hands of the enemy, since in the present situation it is no less dangerous than bombs and machine guns. This is why *temporary* emergency measures have been taken to suppress the flow of mud and slander which the yellow press would gladly use to crush the recent victory of the people. *As soon as the new order is firmly established, any administrative interference with the press will be prohibited: absolute freedom of the press will prevail subject only to accountability before the courts and conformity to the law which will be unequivocally liberal and progressive.* However, in view of the fact that even at critical moments any constraint on the press is permissible only within the limits of what is absolutely necessary, the Council of People's Commissars resolves that:

    1. Only those organs of the press will be closed down that
        a. call for open disobedience or resistance to the workers' and peasants' government
        b. sow discord by means of overtly slanderous distortion of the facts
        c. call for manifestly criminal actions, i.e., such as are punishable under the law
    2. Organs of the press will be banned, temporarily or permanently, only by resolution of the Council of People's Commissars
    3. The present regulations are temporary in character and will be repealed by special decree when normal conditions begin to prevail in public life" (*Dekrety sovetskoi vlasti* [Decrees of Soviet Power], Moscow, 1957, vol. I, p. 24).

9. Marx-Engels, *Sochinenia*, I, pp. 62, 63, 67.

10. A. M. Nekrich's book *22 June, 1941* was published by the Academy of Sciences of the USSR. Before publication it passed through the hands of four censorship departments: the general censorship and then the military, the Ministry of Foreign Affairs and the Ministry of State

Security censors. The prescribed cuts amounted only to the equivalent of about one printer's sheet. The book was a well-documented, straight-forward account of Stalin's strategic errors before the war (and in fact assembled only a small part of the available evidence). However, two years after publication it was withdrawn from all libraries and the author was expelled from the party—hardly an inspiring example for other historians.

11. In a 1960 essay entitled "Science and Contemporary Society," the distinguished Soviet scientist P. Kapitsa wrote that our social sciences are overwhelmingly behind the needs of the time and cannot even re-motely be thought of as "advanced": "We transform Marxist science into a Procrustean bed which is at variance with both the meaning and spirit of Marxism. We should be carrying out a searching inquiry into the problems of transition from socialism to communism. We must examine the process by which the state withers away and also the question of relationship between man and society under communism." Kapitsa justly points out that there can be no further development of Marxism unless mistaken views as well as true ones can be expressed, since time must always elapse before the value of a theory can be tested. Truth can be established only by means of argument. "Dis-cussion and polemics are necessary elements in scientific creativity. We must therefore open the shutters in order to develop the social sciences. There is no real threat of a return to capitalism and there is absolutely no reason to fear free discussion. What is enormously dangerous for our society and for our future is a halt to the develop-ment of social science. Therefore we must refrain from pinning labels on things and allow freedom of research, encouraging scholars not to be afraid of being wrong. The sciences must be emancipated from the conservative state *apparat,* with greater participation by the community in scientific affairs."

It is worth quoting another important idea in the essay: "At present even in a capitalist society it is possible to achieve a level of labor productivity capable of completely satisfying the material needs of the entire population of the country. Therefore it becomes much more important (and is much more difficult) to provide for man's spiritual needs, to encourage the development of his individual quali-ties which will not only ensure a happier and more interesting life but also make it possible for each person to make the fullest use of his abilities for the benefit of society. A basic difference between man's material and spiritual needs is that material needs can be satisfied, whereas his spiritual capacities are limitless. Unfortunately much of the contribution made by Soviet writers, artists, scholars, and scientists in the last decades remains completely hidden from the Soviet people because of arbitrary preliminary censorship, although some of it is known and appreciated abroad. Similarly, certain major Soviet inven-tions have been put to practical use only outside the Soviet Union."

12. *O partinoi i sovetskoi pechati. Sbornik dokumentov* (The Party and the Soviet Press. A Collection of Documents), Moscow, 1954, pp. 346–47.

13. *Pravda,* October 5, 1966. The concept "socialist art" naturally presupposes that a work is in some way socialist in content. Therefore the term can hardly embrace the whole spectrum of Soviet art. For example, many of the poems and stories of Kornei Chukovsky or such classics as "Little Red Riding Hood" are concerned with universal problems of good and evil and do not attempt to convey ideas of socialism to our children. The same thing can be said about many other works of Soviet literature dealing with general human themes—love and suffering or stories about nature which usually have no "ideological content."

14. M. Lifshits, "Pochemu ya ne modernist?" (Why I Am Not a Modernist), *Literaturnaya gazeta,* October 8, 1966.

15. Abalkin's sectarian stand, along with others like his, is not confined to a wholesale rejection of modernism. We all know that many progressive intellectuals in the West, firmly opposed to monopoly capitalism, materialism, and fascism, are at the same time critical of certain aspects of Soviet domestic and foreign policy as "totalitarian." It would be natural for communists to regard such people as possible allies, to take them seriously and try to win them over.

But for Abalkin, this is completely out of the question. His logic is extremely primitive—any criticism of the Soviet Union is branded as "anti-Soviet" and therefore can have nothing in common with an antifascist position. This approach is quite unrealistic. In the first place, not all criticism of the USSR indicates an anti-Soviet attitude (similarly one can be critical of the communist movement without being anticommunist); many of our critics would simply like the first socialist country to become *better* than it is at the moment. Secondly, it is absurd to deny that many real opponents of communism can also be at the same time opponents of fascism and monopoly capitalism—to this extent they certainly can become our allies, at least temporarily.

16. One must note that in his later publications even Mikhail Lifshits has "softened" to some extent in regard to modernism. "It is necessary to separate the question of civil rights," he wrote in *Voprosy filosofii,* "or to be more precise, the rights of the artist, from aesthetic considerations. . . . For as one French writer rightly put it, ideas are like nails: the harder you strike them, the deeper they go. This is why, in order for realism in art to have genuine, permanent success, it must be voluntary; it is necessary to grant the artist the right to see the world in his own way—it will then be up to his audience and critics to judge, needless to say without recourse to 'obsolete' methods. Only on this basis can we overcome the trend toward barbarism that now threatens the art of the world. . . . It is necessary to allow the person who likes cubism, abstract art, pop art, and all the rest his right to enjoy them. There should be restrictions only on counterrevolutionary material, and here it is necessary to be very cautious in arriving at an ultimate judgment. But why should we not open to public view all the paintings by Malevich and Kandinsky now kept hidden away? They could be exhibited in special premises. Inevitably, the excitement over this for-

bidden fruit would disappear after six months, if not sooner; people would no longer see the miraculous where it does not exist. At the same time, one of the reasons for the transformation of realism into 'official baggage,' to use Pushkin's phrase, would be eliminated. And if these wise democratic measures were carried with sufficient boldness and confidence, combined with a sincere and systematic struggle to educate public taste in the spirit of realism, then not only would the Marxist world view attract new friends, it would even impress its enemies. For enemies are at the same time human beings who understand with whom they are dealing" (*Voprosy filosofii*, 1968, No. 1, pp. 107, 109–10).

Unfortunately there seems to be no sign of eagerness to display Malevich or Kandinsky even in "special premises," not to mention our famous art galleries. Lifshits is willing to allow enjoyment of cubism and abstract art. However, when it comes to criticism, he proposes to leave the realists in a monopoly position; his only stipulation is that former crude and obsolete methods must be discarded. But why such one-sidedness? Why should not the adherents and admirers of cubism and abstract painting be able to explain and analyze works of a given trend in accordance with their own aesthetic principles?

At the beginning of the sixties, how much irate abuse was poured on the work of such a talented sculptor as Neizvestny. How Khrushchev sneered even at his surname. Yet the use of abstract form is now becoming the prevailing trend in sculpture throughout the world, and even in the Soviet Union. Neizvestny himself has won several most prestigious international competitions. And recently there was a rumor in Moscow intelligentsia circles that Khrushchev's family had asked Neizvestny to construct a monument for Khrushchev's grave.*

17. Marx-Engels, *Sochinenia*, XXXVII, p. 374.

18. Marx-Engels, *Sochinenia*, XXXVIII, pp. 441–42.

19. Lenin, *PSS*, XXXII, p. 480.

20. Lenin, *Sochinenia*, 2d ed., XXI, p. 152.

21. Lenin, *PSS*, XXXIV, p. 212.

22. Lenin, *PSS*, XXXVII, pp. 495–96.

23. The episode of *Novaya Rossia* (*New Russia*), which began to appear in Petrograd in 1922, is worth describing in more detail. In content the journal represented the "change of landmarks" (*smenovekhovski*) trend, i.e., those Nepmen, émigrés, and bourgeois specialists who declared their support for Soviet power within the framework of NEP while frankly calculating on its eventual peaceful transformation. After two issues of the journal had come out, the Executive Committee

* In Russian, the name Neizvestny means "unknown," which provided an opportunity for Khrushchev's pun. The statue was in fact unveiled in 1974.—Trans.

of the Petrograd Soviet, convinced that the journal was neither Bolshevik nor Marxist, passed a resolution banning further publication. A propos of this, Lenin sent a letter to Dzerzhinsky in which he said: "My opinions about the two Petrograd publications: *Novaya Rossia* No. 2 was closed down by our Petrograd comrades. Was this not rather premature? It should have been distributed to members of the Politburo and discussed more carefully. . . . And then there is the other question of the Petrograd journal *Ekonomist*. That, in my view, was an obvious White Guardist vehicle" (*PSS*, LIV, p. 266).

Novaya Rossia was in fact circulated among members of the Politburo, who, on May 26, 1922, after discussing the whole issue, ordered *Glavlit*, "in its capacity as a more authoritative body, to allow the further publication" of the journal, thus reversing the original decree. However, the Executive Committee of the Petrograd Soviet objected and turned to the party Central Committee, requesting it to rescind the Politburo decision of May 26. The whole question was examined once again by the Politburo. Because of the inflexible attitude of the Petrograd comrades, a compromise decision was made to move the editorial board of the journal to Moscow and publish it there under the title *Rossia*. It continued to appear in Moscow until 1926.

24. S. Sheshukov, *Neistovie reviteli* (Frenzied Zealots), 1970, p. 82.

25. V. I. *Lenin o literature i iskusstve* (Lenin on Literature and Art), Moscow, 1969, pp. 662–63.

26. *Novy mir*, 1966, No. 9, p. 234.

27. In his "Speech Not Delivered at the Fourth Writers' Congress," the well-known Soviet author Venyamin Kaverin wrote: "But what about our other literature, a unique phenomenon both from a historical and literary point of view, made up of typed manuscripts passed from hand to hand and increasing every year despite attempts to stop it . . . ? An angry censorship and frightened editors prohibit first-class works which no doubt would have been the pride not only of our own but of world literature as well. Such works continue to multiply because our country has entered a new period, a time of intense examination of itself and its recent past. What has become known as *samizdat*, persecuted and forbidden, is a response to and a reflection of this self-scrutiny. Writers began to understand that there was no other way to make use of their own immensely rich experience of life. They saw that it was necessary to renounce all worldly ambitions and think only of truth, regardless of whether or not publication would follow. . . .

"This, then, is one of the important reasons for the appearance and growth of typescript literature. Of course among such materials one can find a great deal of sensational rubbish. But genuine literature, remaining for the time being in manuscript form, is by no means directed against those revolutionary ideas in whose name our country grows and develops, at times under agonizing strain. It does, however, absolutely condemn Stalin's arbitrary rule and all its fatal survivals. Contemporary shortcomings are revealed in a manner that is always sincere and well intended.

"And so what is to be done with this new literature, unwilling to lie or dissemble? Or with writers who refuse to acknowledge mistakes they have not made? What is to be done with writers no longer afraid, who as human beings and as artists have taken a moral stand felt to be more important than life itself? In fact nothing can be done about them. They work and will continue to work—unknown, isolated, deprived of support, and inspired only by the sympathy of an intelligentsia audience which is growing all the time. . . . Almost the entire edition of Radishchev's *Journey from Petersburg to Moscow** was destroyed—altogether only eighteen copies remained—but this did not prevent the book from becoming a powerful weapon in the development of Russian social thought. In any area of a country's cultural life, broad use is made of what came before. Yet why did we not learn from our experience with *Doctor Zhivago* or Evgenia Ginzburg's *Into the Whirlwind*? Why prohibit first-class works at home in the almost certain knowledge that they will find their way abroad to be used as indisputable evidence of the persecution of Soviet literature? These examples are very well-known ones. They multiply and will continue to do so if the responsible authorities do not at last come to their senses."

28. Marx-Engels, *Sochinenia*, I, p. 65.

29. A first step was taken in this direction in 1956, when, on the initiative of its party group, the Moscow section of the Union of Writers began to publish the anthology *Literary Moscow* under an editorial board of writers themselves (on a voluntary and unpaid basis). It contained a number of interesting works and had great success among writers and the intelligentsia, but at the same time attracted sharp criticism from the most dogmatic elements of the Writers' Union *apparat,* who convinced the leadership of the Moscow City Committee to close it down.

30. *Voprosy literatury,* 1966, No. 2, p. 4.

31. *Novy mir,* 1966, No. 8, p. 240.

32. It is instructive to see how differently our critics reacted to *Farewell, Gulsary* by Chingiz Aitmatov and to Boris Mozhayev's *From the Life of Fedor Kuzkin,* both of which were first published in *Novy mir.* Aitmatov is more successful than Mozhayev in demonstrating through his account of certain details in the life of one man many of the typical features of our contradictory reality during the last decades. But even so, Aitmatov has by no means shown us every aspect of the period. With all its virtues, so warmly and unanimously acclaimed by the critics, his story is in many respects one-sided. Mozhayev was less ambitious, taking an even smaller segment of life; but his story is nonetheless of great value for the light it throws on a side of village life that has been largely neglected in Soviet literature of recent years.

* Alexander Radishchev, 1749–1802, poet and philosopher, one of the first to advocate the abolition of serfdom.—Trans.

This did not prevent Mozhayev's talented work from being subjected to very biased criticism, and it was not allowed to be reprinted. The remarkable stage version prepared by Yury Lyubimov at the Taganka Theater was also banned. And all this on the pretext that the events described by Mozhayev were one-sided and atypical.

33. In his remarkable piece "Answer to Moskvityanin," Belinsky* wrote that "the gravest accusation against Gogol by the writers of the rhetorical school, hoping to demolish him, was that as a rule his characters were an insult to society. Above all, an attack of this kind reveals the immaturity of our social education. In countries whole centuries ahead of ours in their development, such an accusation is unthinkable. No one can maintain that Englishmen are not jealous of their national honor; on the contrary, there is hardly any other people whose national egoism has reached such extremes. Yet they love their Hogarth, who depicted *only* the vices, depravity, abuses, and vulgarity of the society of his time. And no Englishman would say that Hogarth slandered England, that he failed to see or recognize all that was human, noble, lofty, or beautiful. The English understand that talent has the absolute right to be one-sided, that it can be supreme by the very fact of its one-sidedness. On the other hand, because they so profoundly feel and recognize their national greatness, they are not in the least afraid that the divulgence of shortcomings or the exposure of the seamy sides of English social life could possibly have any negative effect.

"But we only have cause to regret our immaturity. . . . There is no lack of a feeling of national worth. The stronger a man is, morally as well as physically, the more courageously he can face his own weaknesses. This is even more applicable to nations existing for whole centuries, far beyond the human life span. A people that is weak, insignificant, grown old never having been able to move ahead, loves only to praise itself and above all is afraid to glance at its wounds, knowing them to be fatal; reality is no comfort and only self-deception can provide false consolation. . . . But a great people full of life and vigor should not behave in this way; consciousness of shortcomings, instead of causing doubt and despair, should provide strength and inspire new activity."

34. Lenin, *PSS*, XXXV, p. 21.

35. As the Old Bolshevik S. N. Smirnov has written, "Stalin put Soviet statistics under lock and key. There was a certain rationale for this in the past. But the present situation is entirely different. There are no longer any forces in the world who could risk a military campaign against our country. There is nobody to be feared and no reason to hide our shortcomings or our statistics. But the lock is still there. And apparently the reason for this is no longer a fear of external enemies but misgivings that our own people, once they become familiar with

* Vissarion Belinsky, 1811–1848, literary and social critic extremely influential among the radically minded youth of his own and subsequent generations.—Trans.

certain statistical data, will begin to have doubts about the wisdom of
certain past and present leaders of our country."

36. Obviously an author has the absolute right to circulate even his
unpublished works, to show them to his friends, to seek their comments
and reactions, to read them to colleagues, etc. This right is guaranteed
in Soviet legislation. Thus, for example, Article 479 of the Civil Code
of the RSFSR guarantees the right of the author to the "publication,
reproduction, and distribution of his work by all legal means."

37. *SShA* (USA), 1971, No. 3, p. 47.

38. *Kommunist*, 1971, No. 10, p. 53.

X. *Freedom of Movement and Other Problems*

1. Lenin, *PSS*, VII, pp. 133, 169.

2. *VKP(b) v resolyutsiakh*, 1935, vol. I, p. 22.

3. I have talked to certain officials who persistently deny the existence
of any kind of postal censorship and reject all assertions to the contrary as slander. But the reader may refer to *The Medvedev Papers*.
Zhores Medvedev made a careful study of the mysteries of the Moscow
International Post Office and by means of various experiments not only
absolutely proved the existence of a contemporary "black office" but
also described in detail the nature and extent of its activities.*

4. Holbach, *Sistema prirody* (The System of Nature), p. 442.

5. Marx-Engels, *Sochinenia*, XIX, p. 19.

6. Marx-Engels, *Sochinenia*, XX, p. 207.

7. See Lenin, *PSS*, XXXIII, pp. 42–44, 50, 78, 115.

8. M. Krivitsky, ed., *Ekonomika truda* (The Economics of Labor), 2d
ed., 1934, p. 179.

9. *Izvestia VTsIK*, September 17, 1921.

10. Z. A. Astanovich, *Pervie meropriatia sovetskoi vlasti v oblasti
truda* (The First Measures Taken by the Soviet Government on Labor)
Moscow, 1958, p. 45.

11. Lenin, *PSS*, XXXV, pp. 105, 459.

* A reference to the special section of the French post created by Louis XIII
   and Cardinal Richelieu in the seventeenth century for opening and
   checking correspondence.—Trans.

12. Lenin, *PSS*, XLIV, pp. 198–99.

13. Ibid., p. 351.

14. Andrei Sakharov, *Sakharov Speaks*, New York, 1974, pp. 102–3.—
Trans.

15. The poet Sergei Mikhalkov created a scandal when he published a
fable in *Krokodil*, No. 4, 1969, called "Hard-earned Bread," which
provided a rather original view of the right of ordinary workers to know
about and pass judgment on all the privileges enjoyed by leading
officials. The poem deserves to be quoted in full:

> At a certain stud farm a worthy dobbin
> trudged in harness before his wagon,
> bringing sacks of oats to the stables
> and carting loads of dung away.
> He knew what thoroughbreds got to eat
> according to their rightful due
> and envied them their stalls and shoes,
> their well-groomed tails and manes.
> But he'd never been to the race track
> and seen how a pedigreed three-year-old
> runs the last lap bathed in lather,
> gasping: "Shall I make it?"
> Exactly so some citizens see fit
> to stand in judgment on those above them,
> carping at the way they live.

(translated by Max Hayward)

16. At the end of the 1950's China attempted to solve the problem of
bureaucracy and contact between the leadership and ordinary workers
by a very simple method. If only for one day a week, each general
served as a private soldier, the Minister of Trade worked in a shop,
and the secretary of a district party committee joined the peasants
laboring in the fields. Of course this is hardly the best way to maintain
contact between government officials and the people. However, those
who govern a socialist state must always be in regular contact with
representatives from different sections of the population in order to
learn about the needs of ordinary citizens. There must not be total
reliance on written reports.

The leader of a socialist country should be able to invite any
foreign statesman to his office or home. Obviously the furniture and
decorations would have to be appropriate for this purpose but never so
lavish that delegations of workers or collective farmers could not also
be comfortably received. As in all things, there is a golden mean.

An acquaintance described his visit to Kosygin's dacha outside
Moscow. He had been invited together with a group of eminent colleagues in the arts. As might be expected, the guests of the Chairman
of the Council of Ministers were served by a waiter. Some time later
the same man found himself at the dacha of a deputy chairman of the
Council of Ministers. Here each guest was looked after individually by

his own waiter.—Afterward it was generally agreed that this was rather excessive.

XI. *Socialist Democracy and Socialist Economics*

1. Lenin, *PSS*, XXXIII, p. 79.

2. Lenin, *PSS*, XLII, pp. 210, 276.

3. The eminent Soviet economist A. Birman has also stressed the relationship between democracy and economics. He wrote: "In certain socialist countries, people refer to 'administrative enterprises,' by which they mean structures that are the result of official whim rather than economic need. In the following passage, Immanuel Kant may well have been describing the process by which planning can give rise to "voluntarism": 'Drawing plans is an easy and vainglorious affair—one can acquire the mantle of creative genius by making demands beyond one's own capacities, by condemning what one cannot rectify, and by proposing things that may be found one knows not where.' But the planned socialist economy possesses a powerful antidote against "voluntarism"—it is democracy, a quality basic to both socialism and science. "Voluntarism" can be radically cured by wide discussion of all projects, representative scientific conferences, debates and competitions, and many other ways of drawing a wide section of the public into economic affairs. Unfortunately, however, the return to Leninist norms is progressing very slowly indeed. Gosplan and other economic organs are simply unable to rid themselves of unnecessary secretiveness. Very little documentation on the changeover to new forms of economic management, new wholesale prices, and other important measures has become available. But there can be no scientific approach to economic problems where rigidity and bureaucratic dogmatism prevail, particularly in a country the size of the Soviet Union. It is common knowledge that serious damage was done to the economy by the hasty abolition of many tax exemptions in certain parts of the country, by the reluctance to take actual working conditions into consideration when regulating wage levels and other similar actions. Inflexible procedure exerts enormous influence on the setting of guidelines for labor, finance, and credit. One can say without exaggeration that in scientific research institutes, where regimentation can do greater damage than anywhere, it is still enemy number one. But other branches of the economy fare no better. I will restrict myself to two anecdotes as examples. The first concerns geology. The plan for geological research is confirmed in monetary form, that is to say in rubles. But if it turns out to take only thirty-five bore holes to achieve the desired result instead of the hundred that were planned and only part of the allocated funds are spent, the plan is considered to be unfulfilled. There have been cases where bores have been sunk without any need, simply in order to 'fulfill the plan.' The second example is that of state and collective farms that economized on fuel but until recently had to pay a fine for 'failing to utilize funds' " (*Novy mir*, 1967, No. 1, p. 185).

4. Marx-Engels, *Sochinenia*, XVIII, pp. 303–4.

5. Lenin, *PSS*, XXIV, p. 144.

6. According to the economist P. Petrakov: "The main defect of the system of administration before the reforms was not the total absence of material incentives. They did exist, but applied only to the lowest layer of the economic machine. The further away management stood from the worker or the collective farmer, the less it experienced the pressure of economic incentives and the more it depended on instructions from above. In the final analysis, planners and managers at intermediate levels lost all interest (and above all, economic incentive) in protecting subordinate production units when they came into conflict with higher bodies. As a result, pressure from the top down constantly increased, while signals moving in the opposite direction—from those who took orders to those who gave them—remained almost totally ineffective. . . . How many irate lampoons have been written about bureaucrats who are only concerned about 'the honor of the uniform' and are totally uninterested in the job itself! But where do these bureaucrats come from? Why are they obsessed with harvest or profit *statistics,* but not with the actual results? Why are they interested in ton-kilometers rather than in ensuring delivery to the customer on time? The reason is that incentives for these people have often been geared not to getting in the harvest or making a profit, but to quite other considerations" (*Novy mir,* 1970, No. 7, pp. 176–77).

7. In the course of discussions about the reforms, some economists wrongly suggested that there is a basic incompatibility between plan and market and proposed that we virtually abandon centralized planning and rely largely on market forces. Yet in the Soviet Union and in certain other European socialist countries, various types of "market" or "cooperative" socialism have begun to appear. The most common model is the Yugoslav system. It is interesting that during the sixties some of the most far-sighted bourgeois economists (for example, John Galbraith in his book *The New Industrial Society*) began to call for more planning and regulation under capitalism. They demonstrated the objective need of modern heavy industry for long-term planning on a nationwide scale. At the same time economists in socialist countries have proposed the replacement of planning by a system of forecasting, with state interference in the economy restricted to the absolute minimum. Of course the Yugoslav venture needs careful and unbiased study. However, fifty-five years of accumulated experience in the Soviet Union indicates that both planning and the market are tremendously important. It is absurd to construct an artificial opposition between the two. Any rational plan should be based on careful study of the market, although the state plan should not simply be geared to consumer satisfaction; it should also influence the market and to some extent regulate consumption and demand. There is no place in a socialist society for a cult of the consumer or the acquisition of expensive luxuries as status symbols. Everyone knows it is the case that in capitalist countries a large part of demand is created artificially with little attention paid to

the public interest—men often become slaves to their possessions. And even though there are still many underprivileged citizens in the richest capitalist countries, manufacturers pour onto the market large quantities of goods that are hardly necessary for the welfare of society.

A. Rumyantsev correctly describes the relationship between the plan and the market under socialism: "There are economists who continue to view the law of value as something alien to a socialist economy; they treat the money-commodity relations that exist in real life only as a convenient way to calculate the circulation of the products of labor. Others, on the contrary, exaggerate the role of the law of value and even oppose it to the law of the planned development of a socialist economy. These economists demand that market relations be given 'full scope' and that the role of the state be restricted to influencing the economy by means of commodity-monetary levers (such as credit, taxes, etc.). They maintain that in this way market relations would automatically ensure control by consumers over manufacturers, there would be improved product quality, more initiative, technological progress, etc., while the balanced development of the economy is guaranteed by direct links between enterprises and by the fact that enterprise production plans would be directly based on customer orders. People with such ideas ignore the fact that centralized direction of the economy based on a single national economic plan is an objective requirement of a modern industrial society. Optimum development of the national economy cannot be achieved by using the market as regulator. This has been proved by the experience of capitalist countries. . . . It is possible to add that today this is also borne out by rigorous mathematical analysis" (*Problemy sovremennoi nauki ob obshchestve* [Problems of contemporary sociology], Moscow, 1969, p. 190).

8. Lenin, *PSS*, XXXVI, pp. 392, 408.

9. *Voprosy filosofii*, 1971, No. 5, pp. 36–38.

10. During 1970 alone some 80 independent enterprises in nonferrous metallurgy were abolished, together with 104 other organizations, 12 trusts and bureaus, 1,300 workshops, sections, and other factory subsections. The subsequent amalgamation made it possible to reduce management staff by 14,000, which meant a saving of 32.5 million rubles. According to the minister for nonferrous metallurgy, P. Lomako, management efficiency will be further increased as a result of the formation of enormous combines and production associations out of economically linked and related enterprises, regardless of administrative or territorial boundaries, in the course of which superfluous elements in the administrative structure will be removed (*Kommunist*, 1971, No. 1, p. 93).

11. *Kommunist*, 1971, No. 17, p. 51.

12. *Problemy sovremennoi nauki ob obshchestve* (Problems of Contemporary Sociology), Moscow, 1969, p. 286.

13. Andrei Sakharov has written: "The wide use of various kinds of self-programming automated machines will make them the most influential factor in the management of industry, transport, and the economy, in the improvement of living and working conditions for millions of people, and in the progress of scientific research. At present automated systems perform 0.1 per cent of man's work. An increase of 20 per cent per year will mean that in twenty-five years most work will be done by machines. The pace will inevitably be even more rapid in science, since in all five basic sciences, and in most of the applied sciences, research has become meaningless without the extensive application of cybernetics. Progress in cybernetics will lead to profound transformations in ideology and philosophy and will have considerable social consequences. It is possible that the development of cybernetics in technological and social fields, together with advances made by biologists, physicists, astrophysicists, and social scientists specializing in political organization, will prove to be the most important and unexpected corrective to present-day forecasts about the political and social structure of the society of the future" (*Sbornik Nauka budushchevo* [from the collection *Science of the Future*] *Gos. Komitet SM SSSR po nauke i tekhnike*, 1966, p. 47).

14. *Kommunist*, 1966, No. 1, p. 43.

15. Two social scientists from Lvov recently proposed a system for recruiting senior administrative personnel in the economy which they provisionally called "Pulsar" (see *Literaturnaya gazeta*, September 2, 1970, p. 11). Explaining their suggestion, they argue that: "The whole apparatus of administration can be seen as a pyramid of ascending steps with each one corresponding to a specific level of management. Our idea is to make this pyramid 'pulsate' at regular intervals, say, for argument's sake, once every two years. It would be 'compressed' and 'expanded.' At every level some 10 per cent—the most incompetent— would go down a step (compression) while another 10 per cent—the best—would move up (expansion). Thus the essence of the system is that there would periodically be a compulsory transfer of some management cadres at every level. This is the crucial point. Each official would know that if he is in the lowest 10 per cent he will inevitably be demoted, whereas new horizons open up for those who are most effective in their work. The 'pulsar' system must not, however, be seen as one of administrative sanctions. If a man is unable to handle his work, it does not mean that he is guilty of something and deserves to be punished. 'Pulsar' is designed to allow people to find their right place and fulfill a role in keeping with their abilities, knowledge, qualifications, and interests; it is a system in which they can be of the greatest service to society."

This is of course a most interesting suggestion and it is not surprising that many highly placed officials have advocated its introduction on an experimental basis. On May 26, 1971, *Literaturnaya gazeta* reported the first results of such an experiment carried out at the Electron Combine in Lvov. The outcome was basically favorable. As was to be expected, however, the main difficulty lay in determining the criteria for selection and, in the final analysis, *who* was to evaluate the evidence and make the choice. Obviously, the collective should have the final say and not some higher official.

16. Lenin, *PSS*, XXXVI, p. 369.

17. Ibid., pp. 155–56.

18. *VKP(b) v rezolyutsiakh*, 1936, vol. I, pp. 383–84.

19. See *Izvestia*, September 28, 1971.

20. *Gosudarstvo, demokratia, zakonnost*, Moscow, 1967, p. 282.

21. *Rabota na sebya*, Moscow, 1970, pp. 17, 19.

22. A. Volkov, *Problemy izmenenia sotsialnoi struktury sovietskogo obshchestva* (Problems of Change in the Social Structure of Soviet Society), Moscow, 1968, p. 237.

23. Lenin, *PSS*, XXXVI, p. 481.

24. According to traditional Marxist views at the beginning of the twentieth century, the formation of capitalist monopolies would reduce the drive for technological advance; this was shown to be true by the growing tendency toward decline and parasitism in capitalist society. Lenin wrote: "It is inevitable that a capitalist monopoly . . . like any monopoly . . . will engender stagnation and decay. Once monopolistic prices are established, even only temporarily, incentives for technological progress and therefore progress in general largely disappear. It also becomes much easier to hold up technological progress artificially. . . . Of course monopoly capitalism can never completely or for very long eliminate competition from the world market. . . . And the possibility of reducing costs and increasing profits by means of technological improvements is an important factor in support of change. But the tendency toward stagnation and decay characteristic of monopoly also continues to have an effect, sometimes an overriding one, for long periods of time within some branches of industry in certain countries" (*PSS*, XXVII, pp. 396, 397).

It is almost sixty years since Lenin wrote these words. There has been an enormous growth of monopoly within the capitalist system. But this process has hardly produced the state of technological stagnation that Lenin predicted. On the contrary, in the last ten years we have seen the capitalist world increase its efforts to apply scientific and technological advances to industry and agriculture. There are isolated instances of a particular monopoly buying up a patent in order to suppress it, but this does not happen very often. Of course it is by using the tools of Marxist analysis that we can most accurately explain why capitalism has not only been able to survive and utilize technological progress but has also to a very large extent been responsible for the very development of the recent scientific-technological revolution. Certainly a relevant factor here must be the intensifying struggle between gigantic monopolies of different capitalist countries. It is also the case that monopolies are in a much better position to spend incredible amounts on scientific research. Another stimulus has been the growing competition between capitalist and socialist systems. Nor should we neglect the fact that the standard of living has risen in capitalist countries as a result of the struggle of the working class, and this in turn has led to the growth of the internal market. But another, probably even more surprising development is that very important aspects of economic life in socialist countries, far from facilitating technological progress, even work to inhibit it.

On September 6, 1967, an article was published in *Literaturnaya gazeta* by R. Bakhtamov and P. Volin entitled "Where do the conservatives come from?" After acknowledging that better use was being made of inventions in the Soviet Union in recent years, the authors went on to protest that ". . . the situation is far from ideal. Only 30 per cent of new inventions are taken up by industry. In view of the fact that sixteen thousand inventions are registered annually and each one used in a small enterprise would mean an average saving of 50,000 rubles (of course the vast majority could be used in more than one place), it is quite easy to imagine the extent of the waste involved."

Bakhtamov and Volin go on to explain the reasons behind the quite astonishing degree of inertia typical of Soviet planners and economic organs. They cite the fear of taking a risk, as well as defects in the patent system. Also Soviet enterprises often lack the necessary incentives to improve the quality of many commodities, particularly if improvement does not lead to reduction in cost price. Many enterprises are in no hurry to introduce new ideas—by waiting for others to do so first, they have less trouble and less expense. Even though most inventions usually involve direct benefits (e.g., savings in raw materials and labor), the enterprise itself is often not aware of the potential advantages. As a result, many inventions have to be introduced by essentially administrative methods. The authors quote examples of Soviet ministries patenting inventions abroad and selling licenses for their manufacture, and some years later it transpires that these Soviet inventions are being widely used in other countries without ever having been taken up in the USSR. (On many occasions Soviet inventions have been used abroad without licenses, while at home, for years, they remain under discussion.) "How can one ensure," write Bakhtamov and Volin, "that work of real value (discoveries, inventions, and research) will be eagerly seized upon. . . . There is only one possible way, and that is to extend the economic reforms to cover inventions. The speedy introduction of technological innovation must bring an enterprise direct and tangible rewards, whereas refusal to do so or procrastination should be penalized."

25. *Pravda*, June 12, 1971.

26. Various kinds of small privately owned factories and service facilities are *supported* by the state in Yugoslavia and also in Poland,

Hungary, and even in highly industrialized East Germany. This experience of state and private production should be studied; but even more
important, various features of the system should be reproduced in the
Soviet Union. It is surely indicative that even in many of the most
developed capitalist countries, while huge monopolies and trusts grow
ever more powerful, the number of extremely diverse small businesses
is not simply static but rising (as can be seen in the economic literature). In Japan between 1951 and 1966, the number of small and
medium-sized enterprises rose from 3.2 million to 4.3 million. The
major increase was in firms employing from one to four people, most
of them in the service sector (see *Mirovaya ekonomika i mezhdunarodnie otnoshenia*, 1971, No. 2, p. 88). In spite of constant bankruptcies,
the number of small and very small firms in the United States is also
growing. Summing up this data, the Soviet economist G. Rudenko
wrote: "Thus the prevailing trend in capitalist states is for very large-
scale business undertakings. They are the arteries of the economic
organism. But there are also very many firms in industry and the service sector—one can regard them as the organism's capillary system"
(ibid., p. 96).

Everyone knows that communism has never advocated the total
abolition of small-scale private ownership. Nor do the programmes of
Western communist parties make such a demand. On the contrary,
they invariably refer to the encouragement and support that the future
socialist government will give to small private businesses. Thus the
new programme of the United States Communist Party states: "The
several million small businessmen engaged in trade, service, and manu-
facturing help to make life easier and contribute to the maintenance
of industrial production in the United States. Many of them could
continue to serve a useful role under socialism. At the same time, the
conditions under which they work would be substantially improved.
For example, the owners of small filling stations and stores would no
longer be subject to pressure from large oil companies or wholesale
food monopolies. But many would undoubtedly prefer to turn their
businesses over to public ownership, receive just compensation, and
become salaried managers with fixed daily working hours. Alternatively, the owners of small businesses might choose to form cooperatives. As a form of socialist economic activity, cooperatives would be
given financial and technical aid" (*SShA*, 1971, No. 1, p. 95).

Economic policies within the Soviet Union are keenly observed
by workers throughout the world, and they must not give grounds for
doubt about the sincerity of programmatic statements by Western
communist parties.

XII. *The National Question*

1. I recently made a particularly detailed study of certain aspects of the
"Jewish problem" in the USSR. Interested readers may consult my
article "The Middle East Conflict and the Jewish Question in the

Soviet Union."* Two interesting *samizdat* manuscripts expressing views similar to my own are "The Near and the Far" (signed "A Russian Jew"), which is a historical study of the problem, and V. Kapshitser's "Critical Study of the Nature, Ideology, and Practice of Contemporary Anti-Semitism." Although his approach is basically valid, I cannot agree with some of his rather oversimplified conclusions about the causes of anti-Semitism in the USSR today. All three manuscripts first made their appearance in 1970.

2. Lenin wrote: "Self-determination signifies a nation's absolute right to political independence and to secession from an oppressor state. Specifically this means that in a political democracy there must be *total freedom to agitate for secession* with the question decided by a referendum held in the nation seeking independence. In making this demand, I am certainly not calling for secession, fragmentation, and the formation of splinter states. It is a question of supporting a means of expressing the struggle against any form of national oppression. However, the closer a democratic state comes to obtaining full freedom to secede, the less likely that it will take advantage of this right since larger states are unquestionably at an advantage from the point of view of economic progress and the best interests of the masses, and these advantages grow as capitalism develops" (*Sochinenie*, 4th ed., XXII, p. 135; italics added).

Lenin wrote this in 1916, having in mind the future democratic revolution. But he continued to insist on the right of self-determination even after the victory of socialism, including absolute freedom to agitate for secession.

In his last letter on the nationalities question to the Central Committee and to the party congress dictated on December 30 and 31, 1922 ("Autonomy and the Nationalities Question"), Lenin recognizes the possibility that great-power chauvinism might arise in a socialist state, with a larger nation adopting an "imperialist attitude" toward smaller ones. In Lenin's view this would undermine our support of the struggle against imperialism (*PSS*, XLV, p. 362).

XIII. Foreign Policy

1. In his essay "The Crowded World," containing certain debatable points as well as a good deal of wisdom, one of the greatest natural scientists of the twentieth century, Julian Huxley, writes:

> There are many urgent special problems which the population explosion is raising—how to provide the increasing numbers of human beings with their basic quotas of food and shelter, raw materials and energy, health and education, with opportunities for adventure, meditation and fruitful leisure; how to prevent frustration exploding into violence or subsiding into apathy; how

* See *Survey*, Spring, 1971, vol. 17, No. 2(79).—Trans.

to avoid unplanned chaos on the one hand and over-organized authoritarianism on the other.

Behind them all, the long-term general problem remains. Before the human species can settle down to any constructive planning of his future on earth (which, let us remember, is likely to be many times longer than his past, to be reckoned in hundreds of millions of years instead of the hundreds of thousands of his prehistory or the mere millennia of History), it must clear the world's decks for action. If man is not to become the planet's cancer instead of its partner and guide, the threatening plethora of the unborn must be forever banished from the scene.

Above all we need a world population policy—not at some unspecified date in the future, but now. The time has now come to think seriously about population policy. We want every country to have a population policy, just as it has an economic policy or a foreign policy. We want the United Nations to have a population policy. We want all the international agencies of the UN to have a population policy.

Its first aim must be to cut down the present excessive rate of increase to manageable proportions: once this is done we can think about planning for an optimum size of world population—which will almost certainly prove to be less than its present total. Meanwhile we, the people of all nations, through the UN and its agencies, through our own national policies and institutions, and through private foundations, can help those courageous countries which have already launched a population policy of their own or want to do so. . . .

We do indeed need a World Population Policy. We have learnt how to control the forces of outer nature. If we fail to control the forces of our own reproduction, the human race will be sunk in a flood of struggling people, and we, its present representatives, will be conniving at its future disaster (from *Essays of a Humanist*, Chatto & Windus, London, 1964, Harper and Row, New York, 1964, pp. 249–50.—Trans.).

2. *Mezhdunarodnoe soveshchanie kommunisticheskikh i rabochikh partii. Moskva, 1969* (Moscow International Conference of Communist and Workers Parties), Prague, 1969, p. 25.

3. *Literaturnaya gazeta,* July 15, 1970.

4. V. Zagladin, ed., *Mezhdunarodnoe kommunisticheskoe dvizhenie* (The International Communist Movement), Moscow, 1970, p. 91.

5. E.g., speeches by V. Kreisky and Willy Brandt. See *Mirovaya ekonomika i mezhdunarodnie otnoshenia,* 1971, No. 2, p. 49.

6. *Voprosy filosofii,* 1971, No. 4, p. 58.

7. A. Rumyantsev, *Problemy sovremennoi nauki ob obshchestve*, Moscow, 1969, p. 286.

8. Herbert Aptheker refers to the strong anti-Soviet mood of the new left in an article published in the American Communist Party journal *Political Affairs* (Nos. 3 & 4, 1969). For example, the manifesto of the Students for a Democratic Society (SDS) states that "the SDS rejects totalitarian movements whether communist or on the extreme right." Analyzing the reasons for the new left's hostility to the Soviet Union, Aptheker suggests that it is not only because the young generation grew up in the midst of the cold war but is also a reaction to the deformation of socialism under Stalin. He writes: "We must not underestimate the extent to which the crimes of the Stalin period have influenced the new generation."

In an interesting essay by a Soviet scholar entitled "Disarmament and Democracy," we read: "It must be pointed out that the many organizations linked with the new left tend to display varying degrees of anticommunism. . . . Different groups attack communism from different positions. I have already argued that monopoly capitalism in the United States characteristically strives to enslave the personality, to transform it into a cog in the enormous bureaucratic machine, and that this process of depersonalization embraces all spheres of social life. Traditional bourgeois liberalism comes into conflict with it, and as a result the individualist begins to feel a strong antipathy toward any kind of collectivism or organization. His way of life compels him to submit to the laws of the system, he is persuaded to comply. But certain less conformist elements, such as the intellectuals, struggle to retain their individuality. And since Americans think of communism as, above all, linked with collectivism and the subordination of the personality to society, it is assumed that under communism (or socialism) the individual will suffer an even greater degree of depersonalization than under monopoly capitalism, and it is therefore quite natural that many intellectuals are hostile toward communism. It would astonish them to hear that the object of communism is the all-round development of the individual, that a collective is composed of clearly defined individuals and not cogs.

"There are objective reasons to explain the distorted American view. In the first place, the classical works of Marxism are very poorly distributed in the United States. Secondly, ideas of socialism and communism were discredited because of the way in which Marxist theories were put into practice in the USSR, not to mention the deformations of Stalinism. Events in China over recent years have had a similar influence. It must be stressed that bourgeois propaganda does not present the abuses of the Stalin period or the cultural revolution in China as distortions of Marxism-Leninism but rather as an entirely logical development. The result of all this is what at first appears to be a rather puzzling political type—activists who bitterly criticize their government's aggressive behavior in foreign affairs and its reactionary policies at home, but who at the same time are anti-Soviet and anti-communist. Their attitude is rather in the spirit of Shakespeare—'A plague on both your houses.' "

9. The essay "Disarmament and Democracy," quoted in the previous note, deals at great length with the way in which democratization would have a positive effect on the prospects for disarmament.

XIV. Bureaucracy under Socialism

1. The Procurator of the Holy Synod, Konstantin Pobedonostsev, an archreactionary but not without intelligence or powers of observation, wrote to the future tsar Alexander III in 1877 describing bureaucracy as it prevailed in the higher echelons of the Russian Empire: "Two evils took root in our administration long ago—irresponsibility and bureaucratic indifference. All began to work in a spirit of careless unconcern, as if any matter would ultimately take care of itself. And as those in charge became increasingly undisciplined, self-indulgent, and obsessed with the comforts of life and all kinds of emoluments, they connived at the same condition among their subordinates. It would seem that however stupid or inept, there is no person unable to prosper in his post for years in a state of total inactivity without taking any responsibility or running the slightest risk of losing his position. They have all become so used to this state of affairs that any serious attempt to interfere with their lethargy is viewed as a violation of rights" (*Pisma Pobedonostseva Aleksandru III* [*The Letters of Pobedonostsev to Alexander III*], vol. 1, pp. 91, 92).

2. Klara Zetkin, *Vospominania o Lenine* (Memories of Lenin), Moscow, 1955, p. 12. (She was a German social democrat.—Trans.)

3. Lenin, *PSS*, XLV, p. 397.

4. In a *samizdat* manuscript signed A. Mikhailov, "Reflections on the Liberal Campaign of 1968," we read: "Stalinist administrative methods that prevailed until the 1950's did achieve practical results, however cruel, inhumane, and primitive they may have been, and therefore *by and large were justified*. The Stalin epoch was a time of undivided rule by an entire stratum of administrators who autocratically determined all aspects of social and industrial life. If this stratum had been a little more experienced and enlightened, if those in charge had been clever enough to avoid all those imbecile savage extremes, there might have been even greater achievement at much less cost. But the underlying principles of Stalinism were *appropriate and progressive* at the time and were fully in accordance with the demands of industrialization and war. And even allowing for the terrible cost, the country achieved a great deal very quickly." (Italics added.)

I, of course, absolutely reject this argument. It is quite wrong to equate "administrative methods" with "Stalinist administrative methods." Strict centralization and certain other elements of "tough" leadership were indeed necessary in the twenties and thirties. They were not introduced by Stalin, however, but had begun to be practiced in Lenin's time. The *essence* of Stalinism was those very "imbecile savage extremes" that Mikhailov regards as a minor detail. Stalin's terrorist dictatorship was a parasitical growth on the body of society and the centralized Soviet state. And if the Soviet social and economic organism continued to progress during this period, it was not thanks to Stalin's leadership, as Mikhailov argues, but in spite of it.

5. In a *samizdat* article called "Time Does Not Wait," signed by Zorin and Alekseev, the authors relegate all *nomenklatura* officials to the "new ruling class" in the USSR. They go on to argue that, "just as in a bourgeois society capital is inalienable, so it is with *nomenklatura* in the Soviet Union. It lies at the very basis of our system much in the same way as the right to private property does under capitalism. What we have in fact is our own peculiar variety of ruling class. . . . The *nomenklatura* functions as a form of property. It is a unique state-monopoly corporation in which a position is much the same as a block of shares." Further on, they say that our state is a "collective capitalist which exploits the workers," arbitrarily fixing wages and prices.

All these arguments are not only wrong but also unoriginal. They merely repeat Djilas and various Western sovietologists. It is not difficult to show that *nomenklatura* is in fact alienable and always has been. Under Stalin, tens of thousands of *nomenklatura* personnel not only very suddenly lost their power and privileges, they were also physically destroyed. Tens of thousands were expelled from the *apparat* under Khrushchev. Since 1925 there has been almost a complete turnover of the basic roster of *nomenklatura* officials not less than five or six times. The *nomenklatura* in our society is not comparable to the principle of nobility under feudalism or private property under capitalism. *Nomenklatura* officials do not own the means of production and have no permanent claim to their own positions. Therefore they do not make up a special class in the specific Marxist understanding of this term. It is wrong to exaggerate the power of functionaries in the *apparat*. Their position is nowhere near as secure as that of lord or clergy in feudal society or the bourgeoisie in capitalist society. Our upper echelon bureaucrats (this does not include all the highest leadership) are much more vulnerable, less sure of themselves and their right to govern, than ruling groups in presocialist societies. This is the source of their inclination toward repression, their rejection of democracy and the public's right to know. But when repression becomes impossible or more difficult, those at the top may well display a greater capacity for yielding to pressure from below than the leadership of capitalist countries. It is simply that our ruling elite have never yet been compelled to face such pressure—this experience still lies ahead. Bureaucracy in our country is hardly as strong and omnipotent as Alekseev and Zorin make out.

6. This question comes up in "Words Are Also Deeds": "We must to some extent revise our view of the peculiarities of our bureaucracy as a class (or stratum, estate, caste—I do not want to argue about terminology for the moment, keeping in mind Bukharin's apt remark that 'in an age of social upheaval on such an enormous scale, classes are to some extent losing their contours; it is in principle possible for certain

sections to become totally distorted and out of them new classes will take shape.'). . . . In its present aspect, the bureaucratic corporation as a whole, including the party and state *apparat* and also administrative structures in public organizations, has undoubtedly become established as the exclusive owner of the means of controlling people and material processes, i.e., in effect, the means of production. The essential point, however, is not that it controls but that it assumes the managerial function as a form of *private privilege* and therefore is unable to perform it well. But the internal hierarchy of relations in the corporation places its personnel in an objectively ambiguous position: they are participants in the monopolistic phalanx, in a sense co-owners and proprietors, but they are at the same time *servants* of management and are therefore bound to be collectivists at heart. An individual official is always a *small* proprietor, a miniature 'boss' hemmed in on all sides by general corporation regulations. The internal struggle has until now invariably favored the proprietor over the servant, the bureaucratic element over the personal qualities of the individual; for more than half a century this has been the dominating undercurrent of Soviet political history. Nevertheless one cannot rule out the possibility that in accordance with the Leninist formula, the servant can become disassociated from the proprietor and, realizing that he cannot get anywhere as an insignificant individual, he will come to support socialist, nonbureaucratic, cooperative control, i.e., democracy."

This quotation contains some profound insights into the nature of our officialdom. I cannot agree, however, that a bureaucratic corporation (but not a class, as the author writes in a number of other places) is now the exclusive proprietor of the means of production. This is as yet only a tendency, a possibility that conforms to the wishes of the bureaucracy but fortunately has not yet come about, or at least only partly so. The process that can be viewed as the formation of a new class continues, but very slowly, and it is still entirely reversible.

Another writer comes much closer to the truth about the character of the Soviet bureaucracy: "It is necessary to look at the problem of bureaucratic degeneration as Lenin did: it is a question of contradictions arising out of the contrast between the socialist character of industrial relations and the bureaucratic form of management. . . . During the Stalin and post-Stalin periods, the bureaucracy took shape as a special social group, a special stratum, and it is urgent for us to understand its peculiar social characteristics better. Of course it is not a new exploiting class representing state capitalism, but apparently we need a more precise intermediate category which does not correspond exactly to the social and economic structure (although, parenthetically, there can be no doubt about the fact of appropriation of part of the surplus product). It is no longer good enough to refer to 'elements of a caste system' if power is in the hands of a self-appointed and self-perpetuating social group, standing above society. Any 'fresh blood' comes from the ranks of the trusted, who are able to satisfy the social requirements of the bureaucracy. It is possible to point to a number of other features that are turning the bureaucratic *apparat* into a social group not only 'in itself' but also 'for itself.' The whole point of 1937 was to create a social stratum to act as a support for the dictatorship of one man, for which even the highly bureaucratized cadres of the past were no longer sufficiently reliable. A new party was needed, and for this purpose there was a revolution from above."

7. The instability of our bureaucratic caste leads it to cling to power as long as possible, since power is its primary asset. A bureaucrat also tries to use his power to assure a place for his children among this same elite.

XV. *The Intelligentsia*

1. One often comes across definitions of the term "intelligentsia" that include not only the more or less obvious features such as a professional occupation requiring complicated mental work, etc., but also various moral or psychological qualities, particular virtues of character, progressive social activism, etc. And there are those who insist that it is necessary to distinguish the purely Russian "intelligentsia" from the "intellectuals" of the West. There is also a confusion between the terms *intelligentsia* and *intelligentnost* (i.e., the educated): thus some people argue that while Tvardovsky and Rostropovich are typical members of the intelligentsia, Kochetov and Sofronov are not, inasmuch as their views are blatantly reactionary. The reasoning behind this point of view is unscientific and difficult to accept. Berdiaev, whose works were often full of arbitrary and unreal constructions, wrote: "It would be wrong for people in the West to identify the Russian intelligentsia with what they call intellectuals. Intellectuals are those who do intellectual or creative work, particularly scientists, writers, artists, professors, teachers, etc. The Russian intelligentsia is an entirely different group—people may belong to it who do no intellectual work and who are on the whole not particularly intellectual. Many Russian scholars and writers certainly cannot be considered to be members of the intelligentsia in the strict sense of the word. The intelligentsia is more reminiscent of a monastic order or sect, with its own very intolerant ethics, its own obligatory outlook on life, and with its own manners and customs, and even its own particular physical appearance, by which it is always possible to recognize a member of the intelligentsia and distinguish him from other social groups. Our intelligentsia was a group formed out of various social classes held together by ideas rather than a common profession or economic status. At first it derived largely from the more cultured section of the nobility, later from the sons of the clergy, minor government officials, and the lower-middle classes, and after the Emancipation, from the peasants. . . . A lack of roots in the soil and a break with all class life and traditions are characteristic of the intelligentsia, but these qualities took a particularly Russian form. The intelligentsia was always carried away by some idea or other, for the most part social ones, and devoted itself to them absolutely and selflessly, acquiring the ability to live by ideas alone. . . . It began to emerge as a peculiarly Russian phenomenon in the eighteenth century. Radishchev, author of *A Journey from Petersburg to Moscow,* was the first. His words, 'My soul was

wounded by the suffering of humanity' set the tone for succeeding generations of the intelligentsia" (from Nicolas Berdiaev, *The Origin of
Russian Communism*).

Unfortunately some articles by the highly original contemporary
thinker Grigori Pomerants suffer from a degree of pseudoscientific
rhetoric in the manner of Berdiaev. Writing about the intelligentsia, he
says: "It is part of the educated stratum of society where spiritual
development is taking place, where old values are being replaced by
new ones, and where a further step is being taken in the progression
from beast to god; this class is the moving force of history. Good individuals can be found anywhere. . . . But nowhere is there such a
progressive social group as the intelligentsia. From the beginning of
its existence the intelligentsia has acted as a gauge by which both
progressives and reactionaries could be measured. When contrasted to
the intelligentsia, all other classes and the whole people merge together
into one reactionary mass. . . . The intelligentsia is unable to ignore
political events which arouse its moral feelings. But once it plunges
into politics and begins to thirst for political victories, to seek allies
among the people and wage a systematic struggle against whatever
happens to be the enemy (tribalism, feudalism, or the bourgeois), it
rapidly loses identity in the struggle and becomes a counterelite, a
bureaucracy in reverse. After its victory, it carries on the traditions
of the old bureaucracy, only with even greater thoroughness. . . .
Membership in the intelligentsia is perhaps a modern form of righteousness. But righteousness developed by education, an equilibrium
between spiritual wealth and spiritual poverty. . . . It is possible to
define the intelligentsia as a part of educated society which recognizes
its own imperfection and the remoteness of its goal. . . . In the final
analysis, all ideological rivers flow into the swamps of philistinism:
some directly and simply, others via rapids, waterfalls, heroic or
quixotic feats. But no man, once he has identified himself with an idea,
has ever raised himself above the dust. It is the inevitable fate of the
intelligentsia to be rootless and cut off from the traditions of the
people. The intelligentsia as a particular social stratum, a small intellectual nucleus, always appears in a society in which popular values
have been lost. The chief feature of this new God-bearing stratum is
its lack of firm links with any particular milieu or class and a certain
statistical connection with what I have rather vaguely referred to as
middle and higher education. The second feature is an escape from the
restrictions of national barriers, a consciousness of unity across con-
tinents . . . and a feeling of openness toward other great cultures."

We find analogous and equally misleading arguments in the works
of certain Western authors. For example, the Austrian Marxist Ernst
Fischer writes: "The general task of all those who have the courage
and the right to call themselves representatives of the intelligentsia is
to unite not only their own people but the whole of mankind" (*Iskus-
stvo i sosushchestvovanie* [Art and Coexistence]).

2. E. Arab-Ogli, *Nauchno-tekhnicheskaya revoliutsia i obshchestvenny
progress* (The Scientific-Technological Revolution and Social Progress), Moscow, 1969, p. 8.

3. A special intermediate group has now arisen that can provisionally be called worker-intelligentsia. For example, at the Likhachev factory in Moscow, 11.2 per cent of the technicians were still employed as ordinary workers in 1965. At the Kalibr plant, the figure was 14.2 per cent. Out of 2,311 engineers employed in the Chelyabinsk metallurgical factory, 925 were workers—40 per cent of the total. (Yu. Novgorodski, *Tekhnicheski progress i rabochie kadry* [Technical Progress and the Workers], Moscow, 1967, p. 13.) The worker-intelligentsia deal not with people but with machines, and their function has a great deal in common with that of skilled workers. It involves both physical and to an even greater extent mental labor. Not only are the two combined, there is at the same time a blurring of social distinctions.

4. In the manifesto "For progressive democracy: for a socialist France" adopted by the Central Committee of the French Communist Party in December 1968, it is stressed that "the number of engineers, technicians, scientists, and teachers is constantly increasing. In all spheres of activity today, representatives of the intelligentsia number millions. Despite great differences in their various positions, the overwhelming majority of them are experiencing the intensifying oppression of capitalist exploitation. The monopolistic regime denies them any kind of creative participation in deciding economic and political issues or in developing the cultural life of the nation. Their role in the class struggle is growing. Of course their education and social origins do not make it easy for them to accept a decisive role for the working class. But the struggle in the spring of 1968 showed that some of the intellectuals, and indeed a much more substantial number than ever before, were capable of active cooperation with factory and office workers. The French Communist Party is devoting a great deal of attention to this indispensable alliance between the working class and the intelligentsia, in the belief that it is now a crucial question."

5. E.g. see *Ot sotsializma k kommunizmu* (From Socialism to Communism), Moscow, 1962, p. 324.

6. Often this refers only to engineers and technicians. In *Problems of Change in the Social Structure of Soviet Society* (*Problemy izmenenia sotsialnoi struktury sovetskogo obshchestva*, Moscow, 1968, p. 133), we read: "The contemporary industrial intelligentsia possesses all the features of the working class, particularly the part that applies its high level of specialized and general knowledge to the productive process. The interests, aspirations, and daily life of engineering and technical staff to a large extent coincide with those of the workers, and they are more closely tied to the workers than to other groups doing mental work. Therefore the intelligentsia-workers are no different from the worker-intelligentsia and by rights must be included in the working class."

7. *Voprosy filosofii*, 1971, No. 5, p. 23.

8. Marx-Engels, *Sochinenia*, XXIII, p. 431.

9. *Pravda*, May 25, 1968.

10. *Kommunist*, 1972, No. 6, p. 85.

11. J. K. Galbraith, *The New Industrial State*, Boston, 1971, pp. 382–83. Medvedev's reference is *Novoe industrialnoe obshchestvo*, Moscow, 1969, p. 442, published by the Progress Publishing House, best known for its translation and publication of Soviet works in foreign languages to be distributed abroad. But it also publishes foreign works in Russian for *restricted* distribution at home.—Trans.

XVI. *The Methods of Struggle for Socialist Democracy*

1. G. Boffa, *Posle Khrushcheva* (After Khrushchev), Progress Publishing House (see note 11, chapter 15), Moscow, 1965.

2. My view that democratization must be a gradual process is very different from that of V. Molokhov, who writes that in the course of thirteen centuries there was no democracy in Russia, that on the whole the peoples of our country are not prepared for democracy, and for this reason rapid democratization would lead to the growth of extreme right-wing movements and pogroms. Thus he concludes that we need *several generations* to change the moral climate in a way that reaches the very depths of the people, and he proposes that this be done by means of Christian ideology and Russian classical literature.

3. That pressure from below can to some extent influence the policy of the leadership is illustrated by the Twenty-fourth Party Congress. Many of the important social programmes and plans for a more rapid increase in the workers' standard of living proclaimed in two congress reports had already been approved in advance. But the first drafts of the Directive and Summary Report, formulated before December 1970, looked entirely different. Undoubtedly the changes were influenced by events in Poland as well as various spontaneous demonstrations by workers in our country protesting against the unavailability of meat and dairy products (in Ivanovo, Sverdlovsk, Gorky and several other cities).

4. I use the term "constitutional" in the first instance because certain of our laws and instructions conflict with the Constitution of the USSR. This was discussed in Chapter VIII. Thus someone using "illegal" methods is not necessarily acting unconstitutionally.

5. Further on in his article Antipov puts forward the following argument: ". . . the world of ideas in our society must of course to a large extent function outside the sphere controlled by the censor. In recent years we have begun to witness a mass circulation of various manuscripts, stenographic reports, records of proceedings, letters, memoirs, sociological and historical studies, and also novels. The quantity of material grows from year to year. . . . An important

quality of literature of this kind, whatever the genre, is that the texts intended for circulation in manuscript are prepared without any concern for the official point of view, i.e., without interference by the internal censor which inevitably watches over the author of any work meant for normal publication. For those accustomed to publishing in the ordinary way, whether scholarship or fiction, it certainly is not easy to write without inhibitions, but the process of learning how brings enormous compensations—new and higher pleasures to be experienced and enjoyed. Another important consideration is that uncensored literature will also create a new type of reader. A written critical response is apparently becoming the most usual and natural reaction to reading such material. Thus we have a kind of symposium without a chairman—each person who has something to say uses his own rostrum from which he calmly, without interruptions from others, expresses his point of view. Pen, paper, courage, prudence—nothing else is needed. Important works will thus provoke a lavalike flow of criticism, criticism of the criticism, comments on the comments. One pragmatic point: for ease of reference, each text should be signed (obviously, often by a pseudonym) and divided into small sections with subheadings. It is wrong to think that the circulation of literature in manuscript form substantially limits the audience. Plato, Euclid, and Plutarch enlightened their contemporaries and continue to enlighten us in spite of the fact that their works were written long before the invention of the printing press. The book is older than book publishing. We should clearly understand that the invention of printing is not comparable with the creation of the alphabet. The first is an important technical advance, the second—a great achievement of the human mind. In present conditions another clever device, invented even still later, acquires particular significance: in our situation the typewriter can do what Gutenberg's printing press cannot. It is important to note that works "published" in manuscript form, as experience has shown, have a tendency to autoreproduction; soon after the manuscript's appearance, without participation by the author or any special organization, the optimum number of copies are produced, on the basis of the active demand. Therefore the size of the 'edition' turns out to be approximately commensurate with the social value of the work."

6. Lenin, *PSS*, IV, p. 184.

7. Lenin, *PSS*, XXXVI, pp. 301–2.

Index

RUSSIAN HISTORY IN NORTON PAPERBACK EDITIONS